To Janet Walton
who embodies the
best of Union Seminary
and the Gospel!

Don Saliers
3/29/'05

Honest Patriots

Honest Patriots

*Loving a Country Enough to
Remember Its Misdeeds*

DONALD W. SHRIVER, JR.

UNIVERSITY PRESS

2005

OXFORD
UNIVERSITY PRESS

Oxford University Press, Inc., publishes works that further
Oxford University's objective of excellence
in research, scholarship, and education.

Oxford   New York
Auckland   Cape Town   Dar es Salaam   Hong Kong   Karachi
Kuala Lumpur   Madrid   Melbourne   Mexico City   Nairobi
New Delhi   Shanghai   Taipei   Toronto

With offices in
Argentina   Austria   Brazil   Chile   Czech Republic   France   Greece
Guatemala   Hungary   Italy   Japan   Poland   Portugal   Singapore
South Korea   Switzerland   Thailand   Turkey   Ukraine   Vietnam

Copyright © 2005 by Oxford University Press, Inc.

Published by Oxford University Press, Inc.
198 Madison Avenue, New York, New York 10016

www.oup.com

Oxford is a registered trademark of Oxford University Press

Library of Congress Cataloging-in-Publication Data
Shriver, Donald W.
   Honest patriots : loving a country enough to remember its misdeeds /
Donald W. Shriver, Jr.
      p.   cm.
   Includes bibliographical references and index.
   ISBN-13 978-0-19-515153-4
   ISBN 0-19-515153-4
1. Repentance—Christianity.   2. Restorative justice—Religious aspects—Christianity.
3. Social ethics—United States.   4. United States—Moral conditions—20th century.
5. Reparation—United States.   6. Restitution—United States.   7. Reconciliation.
8. Victims of crime—United States.   9. United States—Politics and government—
Moral States—History—20th century.   I. Title.
   BT800.S54 2005
   320'.01'1—dc22   2004021769

9 8 7 6 5 4 3 2 1

Printed in the United States of America
on acid-free paper

Dedicated to
Honest Patriots Everywhere

Acknowledgments

Honest Patriots is a sequel to my 1995 book, *An Ethic for Enemies: Forgiveness in Politics*. There, I maintained that the longtime association of forgiveness with personal ethics and religion is overdue for an interpretation in a political, collective context. There, too, with historical illustrations, I argued that repentance is indispensable to a genuine forgiveness-transaction between human beings.

The present volume explores the concept of social-political repentance in the recent histories of three countries: Germany, South Africa, and the United States. Helps from colleagues in all three countries are too numerous to mention *in toto*, but some deserve special gratitude.

Chapter 1, on Germany, has its origin in the luxury of four months given me by the new American Academy in Berlin, founded by the generosity of the late Stephen M. Kellen, his wife, Anna-Maria Kellen, and the family of Hans and Ludmilla Arnhold. Academy president Everett Dennis, director Gary Smith, and staff member Marie Unger helped me at many stages of these months in Berlin. They secured for me introductions to officials, scholars, and religious leaders whose interpretations of current German work to acknowledge the painful history of Nazism were unfailingly instructive. Among others were Dr. Annegret Ehmann of the Wannsee Conference Center, Dr. Eugene DuBow of the American Jewish Committee in Berlin, Dr. Hans Dieter Holzmann of the Academy of Social Sciences, Bishop Wolfgang Huber of the Evangelical Church in Germany, Dr. Geiko and Helga Müller-Fahrenholz, University President Gesine Schwan, Dr. Ralf Wüstenberg, Dr. Heinrich Bedford-

Strohm, Paul and Adelheid Stoop, and Bundespräsident Richard von Weiz-säcker. To this list of distinguished Germans I must add four special friends: Renate Bethge and the late Dr. Eberhard Bethge, custodians-extraordinaire of the legacy of Dietrich Bonhoeffer; and Drs. Helmut and Erika Reihlen. Beyond all calls of duty, the latter have devoted much time and energy to locating historical sources, memorial locations, and translations vital to my attempts to understand the three-generation struggle of Germans to "master the past."

My debts to South Africans are similarly numerous, especially to the staff of Cape Town's Institute for Justice and Reconciliation, outgrowth of the work of its director, Charles Villa-Vicencio, who headed the research arm of the Truth and Reconciliation Commission, 1996–1998. Staff members Fanie DuToit, Tyrone Savage, Nyameka Goniwe, Deborah Gordon and Carol Esau were un-failingly helpful in facilitating my two months in the spring of 2002 in South Africa. In all, since 1986, I have visited South Africa four times and have been privileged to observe the vast changes in that country's recent tortured history. Among the leaders there who have spent precious time with me interpreting this history have been Archbishop Desmond Tutu, Dr. Alex Boraine (Deputy Chair of the TRC), Bishop Peter J. Storey, Stanley Abrahams of District Six, former President F. W. De Klerk, Dr. Kader Asmal (in 1992) and his associate Dr. June Bam in the new Ministry of Education (in 2002), Dr. John de Gruchy of the University of Cape Town, and a dozen other scholars of that university whose works are quoted in chapter 2. Stellenbosch University faculty were similarly generous in time spent with me, among them constitutional scholar Lourens du Plessis, political philosopher Johan Dagenaar, and theologians Rus-sel Botman, Dirke Smit, and Denise Ackermann. Among other friends who have shared with me their own distresses under the apartheid regime have been Ginn Fourie, Patricia Gorvalla, Joseph Seramane, Beyers Naudé, Glenda Wildschut, Michael Lapsley, and Richard Goldstone. Though I have never met Nelson Mandela, his presence pervades the new South Africa, personifying its turn from racism to democracy and, most of all, personifying the struggle of thousands of his colleagues over many decades. Were I to dedicate the South African chapter to any group of people, it would be to those millions of black, colored, and Indian people, plus a select band of whites, who endured the apartheid era in cities, towns, and farms in stubborn hope that a new South Africa could come to be without a tragic descent into war.

In turning to the United States in chapters 3 and 4, I mean to suggest that Germany and South Africa have some lessons to teach us in how and why my country needs to work harder on acknowledging pasts of which we have no reason to be proud. Without long association with certain African American colleagues I would never have learned to follow closely our own current Amer-ican attempts to "master" our own negative past. Among those scholars and church leaders who have extended their knowledge and patience to me have been Union Theological Seminary faculty James H. Cone, Delores Williams, Cornel West, the late James Washington, the late Annie Powell, and my pastor–friend–mentor James Forbes, preacher without peer. As I suggest at the beginning of chapter 3, it might well be dedicated to the late Lucius H. Pitts, who first awoke me, at age twenty, to the tragedy and triumph of the African American presence from the beginning of this country's history.

Native Americans are the more ancient presence, and only with the writing of this book have I begun to study that presence carefully. I owe some of my belated focus on them to Dr. JoAllen Archambault, longtime scholar at the Smithsonian Institution and fellow with me in 1999 at the American Academy in Berlin. More recently, I have been enormously aided by the work and friendship of my upstate New York neighbors Shirley Dunn and Steve Comer. The former is the region's premier student of the history of the Mohican Nation in what is now Columbia County. The latter is the one lineal survivor of the Mohicans still living in this Hudson Valley area. Richard Powell, professor of history in Columbia-Greene Community College, has provided similar assistance. All three are leaders in the recent founding of the Native American Institute of the Hudson River Valley.

In chapters 3 and 4, for my analyses of American high school history books in the period from 1960 to 2000, I am much indebted to my New York neighbor, Carolyn Jackson, whose experience in the baffling world of school text writing, adoption, and teaching has been invaluable. Much travel has fed these pages. My companion in that travel—geographic, intellectual, and spiritual—has been Peggy Leu Shriver, who across fifty years has made all thirteen of my books better by far than they would have been without her. She has written five books of her own. As in our life together, in poetry and prose, she has often tapped at the door of Wordsworth's "thoughts that lie too deep for words."

I claim the profession of Christian social ethicist, and in the writing of this book it has become clearer than ever to me that my chief scholarly companions are the historians, especially those who agree with Professor Gordon Craig that their essential work is to "restore to the past the options it once had." For some of my partners in the field of Christian ethics, the following pages may not dwell consistently enough on the Christian roots of my interest in history, which began to flourish in my academic major at Davidson College. My chief aim in writing has been to demonstrate that it is both possible and necessary for societies to face and to repent of certain evils in their past. The evils identified here are rugged. They need little extended theological or philosophical investigation before being tagged as evil indeed. The important thing is for a society to learn to acknowledge and turn away from those evils in firm, institutionalized forms of the collective commitment, "Never again." How to do that is the theme of these pages. Underneath it all is my conviction as a Christian that the human capacity for repentance, like that of forgiveness, in either religious or secular forms, is our hope for a future less evil than our pasts. Whether defined as a "turning" (*shuv*) with the Hebrew Bible or with the Christian New Testament as "a mind change" (*metanoia*), repentance is an act of hope. That hope has nourished these pages.

Contents

A photo gallery appears after page 206.

Honest Patriots

Introduction

There are three kinds of patriots, two bad, one good. The bad are the uncritical lovers and the loveless critics. Good patriots carry on a lover's quarrel with their country, a reflection of God's lover's quarrel with all the world.

—William Sloane Coffin[1]

At 10:00 A.M. on September 11, 2001, this author had just written the twenty-fifth manuscript page of this book. At that moment, millions of American lives were interrupted by an awful event that focused our collective minds on a new fact, which Samantha Power put in context when she wrote: "To earn a death sentence, it was enough in the twentieth century to be an Armenian, a Jew, or a Tutsi. On September 11, it was enough to be an American."[2] On that day, our fingers left the keyboards, the telephones, the other tools of our trades while our eyes stared at the televised image of two large New York buildings crumbling into rubble along with the bodies of almost three thousand of our fellow human beings.

From that moment until the last day of 2001, writing the twenty-sixth page of a book concerned with moral assessments of the German, South African, and American past seemed almost impossible. On that day, December 31, 9/11 + 111, my fingers returned to the keyboard with a new understanding of how difficult this book is to write.

In the wake of September 11, 2001, a great flood of agreement seemed to sweep across the United States under the summation "everything has changed." In that exaggeration hid a grain of truth:

all of our past is subject to reunderstanding in light of our present and the tasks imposed on us for our future. Suddenly, with an attack by foreigners on two cities of this country, we glimpsed a future more dangerous than we had ever imagined. Our minds retreated from past history into present history and grim overtures to future history.

A December 31, 2001, editorial of the *New York Times* put the matter crisply: "The effect of September 11 was to make many of our old concerns look puny."[3] As for making money, going out to restaurants, looking forward to the World Series, and even an author's commitment to write a thirteenth book, the remark was psychologically accurate and morally pertinent. Many persons who worked in the World Trade Center and who survived to remember the horror testified that their priorities really had changed. Concerning the death of one young fellow worker in his investment company, a colleague said, "Now we care for each other more, we care for life. Making money is still important but secondary."

With equal pertinence in that same issue of the *Times,* novelist Joyce Carol Oates reflected that even the most terrible of public events fade in personal and public memory: "Amnesia seeps into the crevices of our brains and amnesia heals." Ingrained American optimism concurs: For us, "the future is ever-young, ever forgetting the gravest truths of the past."

But forgetting those truths is fraught with danger and delusion, as survivors of death camps in Nazi Germany and prisons in apartheid South Africa will testify in the first half of this book. In the latter half, I center on certain "grave truths of the past" which, from the standpoints of our moral, psychological, and political health, Americans need to remember more accurately and more publicly than has been the habit of our culture to date. On the face of it and for the moment, such a project encounters, in 9/11, a great upsurge of resistance from Americans high and low. On the day after, two popular evangelical church leaders, Pat Robertson and Jerry Falwell, experienced that encounter when they broadcast a version of the surmise, "Americans deserved it." No less than a president of the United States rebuked these two theologians, and most of their supporters shook their heads in disagreement, too. America has its faults, most said in response to this moralism, but the first real moral truth has to be that the murder of three thousand civilians is wrong, that this is no way to correct the possible errors of Americans' relation with global humanity, and that instant condemnation of an assaulted people insults the moral priority of compassion. Furthermore, as many an American pondered the question, "Why do they—terrorists and others—hate us?" we were driven to the defensiveness that cries, "There are things about this country that we are proud of! There are values that others may attack, but we are not about to deny them! We will defend them militarily, too."

Sober academic critics—such as this author has often tried to be—came in for their share of popular and political scorn in the fall of 2001. Politicians and citizenry said to us, "This is no time for USA-bashing. We must come together as a people. We must defend America and what it stands for." To this, many of my colleagues, including numerous journalists, have replied, "One value that America stands for is the value of self-criticism. Bury that in a blizzard of unalloyed patriotism, and you kill democracy in America."

The latter phrase resonates with the very title of a great book on the peculiar nature of this country. In that book, *Democracy in America*, Alexis de Tocqueville reported that, everywhere he went in the young United States of the 1830s, he met citizens who proudly celebrated the individual freedoms of their new country. But, observed this shrewd French aristocrat, these individualistic Americans bristled when one raised some criticism of their country. Their pride in its freedom did not seem to evoke any use of that freedom to identify the flaws in their still-evolving republic. Often they said to him: Has not America escaped the corruptions of Europe? Who are Europeans to detect anything wrong with us?

> The American, taking part in everything that is done in his country, feels a duty to defend anything criticized there, for it is not only his country that is being attacked, but himself. . . . Nothing is more annoying in the ordinary intercourse of life than the irritable patriotism of the Americans. A foreigner will gladly agree to praise much in their country, but he would like to be allowed to criticize something, and that he is absolutely denied.[4]

Academics and theologians who have dared to criticize aspects of American domestic and foreign relations in the post 9/11 atmosphere were often accused of being foreigners. We are told: "A nation at war needs unity and support by all its citizens. Under attack, no nation can afford to give much leeway to those who question its official and widely affirmed virtues. It is time to rally around the flag."

This book means to reply to this view in a way that combines criticism with celebration. In her op-ed of December 31, Ms. Oates also remarked that "the future doesn't belong to those who only mourn, but to those who celebrate." In that remark she distinguished what I mean to connect. What *is* celebratable about democracy in America? One answer is: *Those public moments and events when we mourn some features of our national past with new present awareness that we must never repeat such events in our future.*

This is a book about citizens in three countries who have revisited pasts of which their moral and historical sense makes them ashamed but who have done so, not in a spirit of moralism but with explicit intention to confront a past for the sake of ridding the present and future of its lingering effects. I will call that citizen spirit and intention honest patriotism.

De Tocqueville himself distinguished between "instinctive patriotism" and "well-considered patriotism."[5] My hope is that the patriotism exhibited in this book is well considered in light of historical accuracy, political practicality, and moral clarity. Most of all, however, the book concentrates on actions of citizens who, in recent years, have sought to demonstrate that there are forms of public action that constitute public repentance for flaws in how we have remembered the past. Shared memories are no small part of public culture. The latter will never be truly reformed, I argue, unless the past we ought to mourn is mourned in fact, in public, and in a context of concrete gestures and measures that put the past behind us in our very act of confronting it. For such a difficult project, we all need the encouragement of those who have pioneered in the effort. Among them are citizens and institutions of countries outside the United States. Two such countries are the focus of the first two chapters here: Germany and South Africa. The rest concerns the United States. In short, this is more a "how to" book than an "ought to." How do a public and its leaders go about the task of repenting of a historical past and building barriers against its repetition? The heroes and heroines of these narratives are people who have answered this question in public deeds and demonstrations.

Becoming an Honest Patriot: An Autobiographical Note

The origins of these pages are deep in my life story, at least as deep as that fall day in 1952 when I embarked on my first trip outside the United States. For two days prior to climbing aboard the S.S. *Queen Elizabeth*—not long before a troopship in World War Two—I roomed overnight with a friend in the dormitory of Union Theological Seminary in New York. We were both second-year theology students. Knowing my interest in issues of social justice, he took the occasion to arrange for me a brief interview with Professor Reinhold Niebuhr. Token of that meeting was a parting gift to me presented by my friend at pierside as the ship was about to sail: Niebuhr's 1952 book, *The Irony of American History.* On the flyleaf Niebuhr had written: "To Donald Schriver with good wishes for the great journey."

The slight misspelling of my name in this inscription resonated with a difference in our respective family histories. "Shriver" is an anglicized version of the common German name "Schreiber." Niebuhr was the American-born son of a German-speaking household in St. Louis. So far as the genealogists of my own family have determined, the first of our American lineal family members arrived in Philadelphia from Germany in 1688. Not long after, some of their descendants changed the spelling of the family name to conform more nearly to the habits of English pronunciation. My family has probably not spoken German for 150 years. Indeed, it has never occurred to me to call myself a "German American," particularly in light of the fact that I grew up in a pervasively anti–German American century. My uncle was wounded on the

Western Front in 1918. With most of my cousins I was drafted into the U.S. Army of World War Two.

Niebuhr, on the other hand, along with the German-language congregation in Detroit of which he was pastor in 1917, had to go to great pains to make clear his loyalty to the United States in that year. His congregation began to conduct its worship in English, and it took up a collection of ten dollars to purchase an American flag.

In an uncanny way, my "great journey" outside the United States would bring to consciousness a question that seems never quite settled in the minds of many of us in this immigrant nation: *What does it mean to be an American?* I was about to have that question surface in many a conversation over the next five months in visits to some dozen countries. I was on my way to India to attend the Third World Conference of Christian Youth, sponsored by five world organizations including the World Council of Churches. Successor to a conference in Amsterdam in 1939 and another in Oslo in 1947, it was the first such ecumenical youth conference in Asia, a continent that Niebuhr never visited. In one sense, however, he was on his way to India with me as I sat on the deck of the *Queen Elizabeth* reading *The Irony of American History.*

The book is a sustained critique of the virtues and vices of American political culture. As a fledgling theologian, I found it a bracing intellectual and spiritual tonic. Here was an eloquent demonstration that one could be both appreciative and critical of a country that had recently fought the most destructive war in human history and emerged as an undoubted world power. The book is full of deft Niebuhr aphorisms that summarize his take on what it means to be an American:

> Next to the Russian pretensions we are . . . the most innocent nation on earth. We find it almost as difficult as the communists to believe that anyone could think ill of us.

> We are . . . more virtuous than our detractors, whether foes or allies, admit, because we know ourselves to be less innocent than our theories assume.

> [H]ow much more plausible and dangerous the corruption of the good can be in human history than explicit evil.

> "American power in the service of American idealism [said one European statesman] could create a situation in which we [Europeans] would be too impotent to correct you when you are wrong and you would be too idealistic to correct yourself."

> There is a hidden kinship between the vices of the most vicious and the virtues of even the most upright.[6]

The pertinence of all this to someone on his way to Europe and Asia for the first time is clear. On those two continents, over the next five months, I would confront many a critic of my newly powerful home country. I would have my first conversation ever with a member of a communist party. I would meet young people from Japan, the Philippines, Korea, Kenya, West Germany, and the Soviet Union, all of whose lives had been touched, for better and worse, by the power of the United States. In the midst of these new experiences of a wide world, however, one sharply clear sense of identity dawned on me: I really am an American! My language, habits of communication, political assumptions, and character already carried marks of my local cultural upbringing. Whether I celebrate or despise that upbringing, I am as unlikely to shed that cultural skin as my physical skin. Niebuhr's analysis of "virtue and vice" in this identity lifted the curtain on a lifelong project of intellectual exploration of "Americanness," but in the first twenty-four years of my upbringing I had already absorbed American culture in my childhood in Norfolk, Virginia. The mix of acceptance and discomfort in this fact puzzled some of my new friends in these other countries: Some asked, "Why do Americans so often ask others what they think of America?"

The answer for persons of my upbringing was complex. The conflict between certain American ideals and the facts of American society were easy to read in 1952, especially in the matter of relations beween white and black Americans. Strangely enough, this matter does not often enter the text of this 1952 Niebuhr book. Occasionally in other writings he does comment on the hypocrisy of a country that affirms the "inalienable rights" of all humans whatsoever and denies many of those rights to some of its citizens. As moralist and theologian, however, he relentlessly pursued the question: What about the defects of these very ideals? For example, what about famous American praise of individualistic "freedom" with its vocal neglect of the social roots of selfhood and the social responsibilities of selves to each other? Or the classic American belief that we are a beacon of enlightenment to the other nations of the world alongside the belief that they have little to tell us about how to organize a just society? What justifies a certain pride in one's Americanness, and what (if anything) prevents that pride from turning into arrogance?

In everything he wrote, Niebuhr turned up tensions and ironies in mixes of power, interest, and cultural ideals in American and world history. The ultimate source of his talent for irony was Christian theology and ethics. If explanation is where the mind is at rest, he was always explicit about resting finally in a Christian view of the world, which summoned in him a restlessness about reigning dogmas in economics, politics, and culture. His "Christian realism" gave him some leverage on his own American upbringing, some norms by which to identify the mix of virtue and vice in American history. This leverage enabled him to engage in the "difficult but not impossible task of re-

maining loyal and responsible towards the moral treasures of a free civilization
. . . while yet having some religious vantage point over the struggle."[7]

Among other precipitates of theology in his political outlook was an ethic
of respect for all human beings in their cultural differences as well as in their
cultural kinship. The "otherness" of many humans in our domestic and world
neighborhood, he said, are signs of finitude in everything we may bring to
relations with each other. "The other," he writes late in *Irony*, "is the limit
beyond which our ambitions must not run and the boundary beyond which
our life must not expand."[8] It was his principled rebuke to traces of American
imperialism in the twentieth century.

That rebuke had great pertinence to my Asian journey. Here was my opportunity to explore experientially the proposition: "Loyalty to the community
is . . . morally tolerable only if it includes values wider than those of the community." And the thesis: "A democratic society requires some capacity of the
individual both to defy social authority on occasion when its standards violate
his conscience and to relate himself to larger and larger communities than the
primary family group."[9] Reflecting that official American ideology owed much
to the eighteenth-century Enlightenment as mediated through Thomas Jefferson, Niebuhr appreciated the irony that this Jefferson could advocate the "rights
of man" with no explicit regard for the rights of women or humans who happened to be slaves on his own plantation. With one exception, glaring contradictions between American ideals and American fact constitute the major
themes of all eight chapters of *The Irony of American History*.

The exception was the continuing *legacies* of slavery in the United States
of 1952. References to those legacies are almost totally absent from the 1952
book in spite of the fact, as we now know, a prominent historian asked Niebuhr
in 1951 about just this omission.[10] In my case, there was a kindred irony also
not explicit in this book. As a college graduate, with a major in history, and as
a second-year theology student, I already possessed some capacity to critique
versions of Christian faith offered to me in my Methodist and Presbyterian
upbringing in Virginia. Hardly any of my immediate family or local neighbors
took pains to dilute their pride in being Virginian with the sobriety of this
Niebuhrian critique. In fact, the writings of Reinhold Niebuhr, up to 1950,
trickled very little into the college bibliographies and other educational reading
lists in the American South. However famous and listened to avidly in the halls
of Union Seminary in New York and among a growing number of political
leaders and social scientists, Niebuhr was not yet a vivid literary presence in
the seminary that, in 1952, was my own: the "other" Union Seminary, in the
former capital of the Confederacy—Richmond, Virginia.

Tell most northerners that you were a Virginian studying theology in Richmond, and most would assume that you had to be a "provincial." Escaping the
truth that every human life begins in some province, such comments by north-

erners about southerners are an old story in American cultural history. In fact, the American South in 1950 could still lay claim, with a certain pride, to being the most distinctive cultural province of the United States, an area whose people sensed themselves shaped by a history different from that of much of the rest of the nation. When they become world travelers, southerners take with them an identity shaped around a certain dualism: I am an American, but I am an American with a certain difference.

In 1952, what might have been that difference?

The Hurt and Healing of Human Provinces

In 1953, C. Vann Woodward, an eminent southern historian, had an answer to the question which, in one place, was explicitly shaped by his reading of *The Irony of American History*. The final chapter in his book of essays *The Burden of Southern History* was titled "The Irony of Southern History." Parts of this essay could have been written by Niebuhr. For example, writing at the beginning of the Cold War, the rise of McCarthyism, and unprecedented flexing of American economic muscle on a world scale, Woodward cocked a critical eye at capitalism:

> We [Americans] have showed a tendency to allow our whole cause, our traditional values, and our way of life to be identified with one economic institution. Some of us have also tended to identify the security of the country with the security of that institution. We have swiftly turned from a mood of criticism [in the 1930s] to one of glorifying the institution as the secret of our superiority. We have showed a strong disposition to suppress criticism and repel outside ideas. We have been tempted to define loyalty as conformity of thought, and to run grave risk of moral and intellectual stultification.[11]

This is faithful replication of the Niebuhrian critique of American triumphalism. But Woodward adds another dimension of irony in recording the fact that not only did many southerners of Jefferson's generation express a painful awareness of the contradiction between their revolutionary ideals and the slavery that supported their way of life, but that this awareness flourished more in the Upper South in the 1820s than anywhere in the North. In that decade there were more antislavery societies in the Upper South than in the North. About these few years,

> [it] is not too much to say that this was a society unafraid of facing its own evils. The movement reached a brilliant climax in the free and full debates over emancipation in the Virginia legislature during the session of 1831–32. . . . [But then] it withered away to almost

nothing in a very brief period during the middle thirties. By 1837
there was not one antislavery society remaining in the whole south.
. . . Opponents changed their opinions or held their tongues.[12]

Americans have often spoken superficially of their society as one "unafraid
of facing its own evils." That pride is compatible with an ideology of perpetual
improvement, a liberal dream of progress, and ever expanding success. Lacking
in that ideology is any ambiguous but instructive respect for *failure*. On this
point the South really is different. Against the will of any of its leaders, said
Woodward, the American South is the one region of the country that remembers failure as the deepest, unforgettable fact of its history. Two decades before
the end of the Vietnam War, Woodward put his historian's finger on a dimension of American history concerning which southerners had special acquaintance and stubbornly persistent memories:

> For from a broader point of view it is not the South but America
> that is unique among the peoples of the world. This peculiarity
> arises out of the American legend of success and victory, a legend
> that is not shared by any other people in the civilized world. The col-
> lective will of this country has simply never known what it means to
> be confronted by complete frustration. . . . Whether by luck, by
> abundant resources, by ingenuity, by technology, by organized clev-
> erness, or by sheer force of arms America has been able to over-
> come every major historic crisis—economic, political, or foreign—
> with which it has had to cope. This remarkable record has naturally
> left a deep imprint on the American mind. It explains in large part
> the national faith in unlimited progress, in the efficacy of material
> means, in the importance of mass and speed, the worship of suc-
> cess, and the belief in the invincibility of American arms.[13]

What Woodward wrote about American political culture in 1953 could well
have been written about a people, two generations later, who watched with
horror as the two tallest buildings in Manhattan and a section of the headquarters of the world's mightiest military force crumpled at the onslaught of
American planes hijacked by foreign terrorists. As Woodward said, for the
southerners who lost the Civil War it would be forever impossible to pretend
that "history is something unpleasant that happens to other people." However
obscured to their successors' modern memory may be the "late unpleasantness" of 1860–1865, whatever the growing number of young southerners who
in recent years have finally joined the ranks of the prosperous, there remains
in the history of their region a potential resource for credible identification
with the failures that have haunted the majority of humankind:

> For the inescapable facts of history were that the South had repeat-
> edly met with frustration and failure. It has learned what it was to

be faced with economic, social, and political problems that refused to yield to all the ingenuity, patience, and intelligence that a people could bring to bear upon them. . . . It has learned to live for long decades in quite un-American poverty, and it has learned the equally un-American lesson of submission. For the South had undergone an experience that it could share with no other part of America—though it is shared by nearly all the peoples of Europe and Asia—the experience of military defeat, occupation, and reconstruction. Nothing in this history was conducive to the theory that the South was the darling of divine providence.[14]

There is one flaw in this Woodward description, however, one omission that is both historical and moral. When it came to experience of "poverty" and involuntary "submission" no segment of the South could rival that fourth of its population who were slaves. In his cultural generalizations, Niebuhr never much distinguished regionally different experiences of "America." Even Woodward, when he spoke here of southern defeat, concentrated on the war and its cost to southern economics, political power, and pride. But there were always two "Souths" with two different perspectives on southern and American history. This was the point of a remarkable 1964 book by a southern writer named James McBride Dabbs. In the title of his book he posed the question, *Who Speaks for the South?* Dabbs, unimpeachably a southerner, heir to a plantation deep in low country South Carolina, rendered an answer that his neighbors undoubtedly found radical and disturbing: *African American southerners*— they speak most authentically for the South. They are the ones who, most of all, learned the un-American lessons of poverty, submission, defeat, and centuries-long humiliation at the hands of the powerful who used them to sustain their power, their wealth, and their belief in their white superiority. Having thus endured the worst crime in American history, the slaves and their descendants have had the most right to speak credibly about living in and struggling against the injustices of a society that believed only selectively in "liberty and justice for all." But more: In their combination of endurance of suffering at the hands of American white-dominated institutions with determination to become full members of American society, the descendants of American slavery and segregation have offered to their very oppressors a unique lesson in what it means to be human: to endure defeat, "the great equalizer," without capitulating to it. In this, African Americans' only major domestic rival are Native Americans, who were being forcefully exported from the South as slaves were being imported. Dabbs's acquaintance with descendants of the latter led him to write:

> In the experience of defeat, Negroes are our equals, perhaps our superiors; certainly they have been able to make better use of defeat than we [whites] have. If the whites of the South could realize and accept their defeat as a mark of their humanity, an indication of

their participation in the common human doom, they would see all about them the faces of Negroes who had also participated, even more deeply, in that doom, and they would turn to them, as men in distress always turn to their fellows, seeking the outstretched hand, the encouraging word.[15]

To have encouragement offered in the neighbors whom one's society has done so much to discourage is a difficult thought. It is a strange form of justice that goes beyond ordinary justice, involving victims in ministry to the health of victimizers.

It would be some years before this young white southerner, on his way to India, would come to acknowledge that two or three African Americans among his shipmates, bound for the same ecumenical conference in South India, embodied this perspective more authentically than could he. Born in the South, acquainted with all the dimensions of racial discrimination except the experience of being its object, I was at most a spokesman for the South at one remove from those who could claim some special authority as representatives of my region. What they brought in their consciousness to India was what a great majority of its population knew at first hand during most of their lives: privation, injustice, suffering.

The duty of citizens to pay attention to the unjust, yet-to-be acknowledged historical suffering of some of their fellow citizens is the principal subject of the following book. In particular, I mean to explore how some Germans, South Africans, and Americans, tempted to amnesia toward that suffering, have learned to resist that temptation in new public acts that do justice by remembering injustice. I will call this subject: repentance in politics. And I will dare to assert that even from the hurts and losses to Americans in the event of September 11, 2001, we may find anew reasons for both pride and repentance in the history of our country.

The Germans and South Africans soon to be quoted are of like mind. No one has expressed it better than Dietrich Bonhoeffer, who loved his country enough to go to prison on behalf of its best in opposition to its Nazi worst. There in his cell, in 1943, he wrote:

> Gratitude gives me a proper relation to my past; gratitude makes my past fertile for my future. Without gratitude my past sinks into darkness, mystery, nothingness. And yet, in order not to lose my past, which God has given me, but to regain it, gratitude must be complemented by contrition. In gratitude and contrition my present life and my past are united.[16]

I

Germany Remembers

Only thank God men have done learned how to forget quick what
they ain't brave enough to try to cure.

—William Faulkner[1]

Forgetting is the shears with which you cut away what you cannot
use, doing it under the supreme direction of memory. Forgetting
and remembering are thus identical arts. . . . When we say that we
consign something to oblivion, we suggest simultaneously that it is
to be forgotten and yet also remembered.

—Søren Kierkegaard[2]

We who were drafted into the armies of World War Two are glad to
remember it as "the Good War." Whether any war is good, we may
doubt; but we remember the Nazism defeated in that war. Sometimes we wonder if the Germans remember, too.

Not to worry. A single day of touring modern Berlin will dispel
any American's suspicion that Germans in general have forgotten all
about the Nazis once headquartered in their capital city. A good vehicle for a first survey of Berlin's "memorial landscape"[3] is Bus 100,
which stops at a shelter on the fashionable West Berlin Kurfursten-
damm. Not advertisements but history blinks out from the glass:
This was the 1940s street address of Adolf Eichmann. From a war-
destroyed building once here, he administered plans for transporting
Jews from all over Europe to death camps. If you had forgotten what he
looked like, a big portrait is there to remind you, along with data on
the trains, the bureaucrats, and the victims involved in his operation.[4]

Virtually all the buildings in this center of Berlin were devastated by the bombs of 1944–1945. So it took determined effort for Hanna Renate Laurien to insist on this public-transport memorial to a man who perfected a very different purpose for public transport. Get on Bus 100, and it takes you past many a former location of Nazi terror. Left and right are the new museum of modern art, the new national library, and the curving heights of modernistic Philharmonic Hall. Near the latter is a curving steel wall sculpture which marks the place where the organization and technology were planned for the gassing of the mentally ill and others judged by the Nazis as *Leben unwertes leben*— "life unworthy of life." By the time one has rounded the great central park of Berlin, the Tiergarten, one may have postponed a plan to visit the statue of Goethe there. Goethe-Eichmann dualism may already have begun to infect the mind with a certain cognitive dissonance.

One is about to encounter complex layers of history at the entrance to Unter den Linden, the most famous boulevard in Berlin. To the left is the restored gray eminence of the Reichstag, built as a gesture to republican government by Kaiser Wilhelm II and Bismarck, inhabited by the legislators of Weimar, burned by an arsonist probably hired by the Nazis, left empty by Hitler, and reduced to semiruin by Soviet shells in 1945. Get off Bus 100, stand in the spacious Platz where huge crowds used to gather for purposes of pleasure and politics, and you are likely to stumble over a tribute of modern German democracy to a failed earlier one: a row of some forty slate slabs, two feet high, arranged on the sidewalk like an uptilted deck of thick cards. On the edges are engraved the names of Weimar legislators murdered by the Nazis in their effort to obliterate every remnant of the Republic in 1933. Beside the slate memorials to the Weimar murders, along a fence, are white crosses with names of East Berliners shot as they attempted to cross the Wall at various times between 1960 and 1989.

Step through the columned Brandenburg Gate, and these histories begin to collide with each other. Here on the Parisier Platz clustered embassies, offices, and businesses in the 1930s. The new American embassy will be built on an acreage to the right, especially if the diplomats can settle on the claim of a terror-conscious American government that all of its embassies must be surrounded by a fifty-foot security rim. The problem is possible incursion into five empty acres across the street, set aside for the new, great central Mahnmal to the Holocaust. A few buildings farther on is the former Soviet embassy, new hotels, and Friedrichstrasse, whose well-guarded S-bahn station was the transfer point between East and West Berlin. The linden trees "under" which generations of Berliners walked, of course, are all gone. Hardly a tree survived the bombing, the artillery, and the fuel shortages of 1945–1946. Reminders of the classic architectural glory of eighteenth-century Berlin do survive just ahead, restored by East German Communists with a pride first engraved in stone by emperors: the Opera, Humbolt University, and Museum Island with its art treasures from all over the world. In these buildings worked artists, scholars, composers, scientists, and theologians who helped shape two centuries of western cultural life. At this university, founded in 1810, lectured men with names precious in the physical science, social science, and theological curricula of the whole western world: Von Humbolt, Planck, Einstein, Wellhausen, Harnack, Tillich, Bonhoeffer. But directly across the street, in a cobblestone pavement beside the opera house, is a square-meter put-down of academic glory: Here, says the plaque, took place the burning of "un-German" books by faculty and students of this university on May 10, 1933—books yanked out of a great library, branded as degenerate by Nazi criteria, and reduced to ash as an act of intellectual purification. Through a square-meter glass pane set in the cobblestones appears an underground bookshelf, painted white, empty of books. Above, on the plaque, is a quotation from the philosopher Heinrich Heine: "Wherever they burn books they will also, in the end, burn human beings."

A few steps further is a classic, low, columned stone building, the Neue Wach—the "New Guardhouse." Soldiers of King Friedrich Wilhelm III used it to guard him in 1818. Architect Karl Friedrich Schinkel designed it, and architects still celebrate it as one of his numerous gems on this street. In succession, the Weimar, Nazi, East German, and Federal Republic governments designated the Neue Wach as a general memorial to war dead. Its latest inscription dedicates the place to the memory of "all victims of war and tyranny." Take the "all" literally, and one might remember that wars which Germany instigated in the twentieth century killed over 50 million people.

By now, lingering here and there, one has walked about a mile down Unter den Linden accompanied by a growing suspicion that this is only the beginning of memorials to the Nazi past around this one street in central Berlin. Just a few blocks away is the excavated site of the former headquarters and prison block of the Gestapo, now named the Topography of Terror. Further south by a kilometer is the new Jewish Museum, whose jagged, off-kilter design by Daniel Liebeskind ushers the visitor into visual and kinetic experience of disorienting Nazi slashes in the fabric of German culture. Objects reminiscent of the Jewish contribution to that culture now fill these slanted halls, but the building itself is likely to become the reason why visitors will leave with chills and shivers. Nothing is "straight" in this building. One climbs and descends on slanted hallways. The high walls of one oppressive, claustrophobic room recall Auschwitz and the lie that "Work Makes Free."

So, hardly halfway down Unter Den Linden, one may have had enough history for one day. On another day, perhaps, a stroll up to Hackescher Markt and Oranienburger Strasse, the former neighborhood where thousands of Berlin Jews built one of the great Jewish communities in the world. On the wall of the partially restored New Synagogue there is a plaque calling to memory the Berlin policeman who prevented a Nazi crowd from burning it down on November 9, 1938—*Pogromnacht*, Germans now call it, in Nazi nomenclature,

Kristallnacht. In the neighborhood are remnants of the former Jewish cemetery where Moses Mendelssohn was buried. Across the street, the walls of several apartment buildings bear signs that name predeportation occupants. With guidebook help and another bus ride, one can locate the two rail depots where these residents left Berlin never to return.

So to walk through central Berlin is to meet the grandeur and the misery of its history. The tilt of recent monuments is toward the misery. Berlin's modern leaders are determined that it will never forget 1933–1945. Without doubt, Berlin is a city that remembers.[5]

Outsiders' Stakes in Germans' Capacity to Remember

Any non-German, born in the twentieth century and surviving to the twenty-first, has reason to feel implicated in the question: Can present-day Germans be counted on to so remember the Nazi past that they are solidly committed to resisting any repetition of that past? Those of us alive during World War Two ask the question more intensely, perhaps, than do our children and grand-children. We are the ones nagged by the suspicion that Germans, like Americans, like to forget the past amid urgencies of getting on with the future. When asked about it, contemporary Germans are likely to reply with weary patience, "Our reality is complicated. Our third postwar generation is saturated with calls to remember. Young people want to know how to recover *some* pride in being German. We of the older generation know that we have to install in upcoming generations a *permanent* awareness of our Nazi past, else our security as a democracy may be threatened. Neither wallowing in guilt nor luxuriating in amnesia can be a key to the German future. We have to help each other to resist being time-prisoners of one or the other side of the bridge between past and future. That is not easy for our fourth postwar generation. We remind them so often of the Holocaust that we can hardly blame those who say, 'We have had it up to here.' "[6]

The 1999 American director of the new Jewish Museum in Berlin, Michael Blumenthal, was astutely aware of the balance that Germans must achieve between the rememberers and the forgetters in their modern civic conversa-tion. Blumenthal was born in Germany in 1929. His father was briefly im-prisoned in Buchenwald in 1939; his family then left Berlin in the nick of time. Jewish and non-Jewish Germans, he says, share an analogous problem:

> If Jews at times seem frozen in their role as victims, many non-
> Jews are similarly imprisoned by a self-image of shame as citizens
> of a nation of perpetrators. A clear split on the German side also
> exists between this group which cannot free themselves from a
> sense of national guilt and the urge to bear constant witness to re-

morse and readiness to do penance, and a growing number of others who are tired of it all, and look for reasons to justify that it is time to be done with it.

Blumenthal goes on to describe the democratic relevance of struggles to relate negative national memory to positive national change:

> What matters is that Germans find ways to remember with a purpose and for the right reasons—remembrance, not as a form of breast-beating or routine remorse and not merely through stones and rituals, but for lessons to be learned about the rights of minorities, about fairness and civic courage in a democratic society.[7]

Blumenthal implies two principles that ought to guide all efforts (like this book) to justify citizen-visits to negative pasts in their own society. If "it" happened once, it can happen again. Secondly, something like it may be happening still in new guises. Potentials for hate sleep everywhere. The stranger may still feel threatened in the midst of longtime natives. If and when post-9/11 Americans ponder these unpleasant truths, we might well think first of people in our midst who look Middle Eastern.

Foreigners may now trust Germans not to forget, but in fact some Germans do not yet trust each other to remember. They may even welcome help from outsiders in fortifying their national memory, while being well aware that citizens in other countries are adept at hiding their own negative history. They can quietly ask what Americans are doing these days to address, for example, the history of Native Americans since 1492. Abroad and at home, many younger Germans readily identify themselves as "European" in their awareness that "German" is sometimes a conversation-stopper. They may wish that others would more often acknowledge the genuine democratic changes in modern Germany, but they know that what others think of them remains important for their own sense of freedom from the Nazi shadow.

As this is written in 2004, American public interest in books, drama, and film coming out of World War Two remains surprisingly strong. Before all of its veterans die, stories of their part in this "good war" command large audiences. Some say that every American war since has lacked justification as clear-cut as that of 1941–1945. As one who lived through those years, this writer remembers most the images that came to us in the spring of 1945: the camps, the piles of dead bodies, the crowds of starving and diseased survivors. Well informed as many were, our government leaders never told us the truth about the camps until Allies opened the gates and let the photographers in. Then we had indelible ideas of the evil called Nazism. If any of us had any reservations about the importance of defeating that evil militarily, the camp pictures put reservations to rest. This really was a good-against-evil war. The big question was whether we had really killed the evil or would have to fear its ugly head rising again. We looked at the pictures of local German citizens compelled by Eisenhower to view the death pits and the emaciated half-alive bodies in Dachau. We wondered if Germans were being honest when they said, "We didn't know." It would be years before we learned that our own leaders did know.[8] Meantime we wondered if Germans and their children were capable of joining yet another intoxicated crowd cheering yet another Adolf Hitler.

For the next twenty years, some of that worry receded as a new democratic political order emerged in the western side of a divided Germany, as a swiftly knit NATO rose to oppose an aggressive Soviet Union and as America went to war in Korea and Vietnam. Even when we became vocal critics of the American involvement in Vietnam, none of us from the generation of the 1940s were likely to change our minds about the absolute evil of Nazism. Even if we were so inclined, our movie and television industries were sure to refresh our convictions in the matter. Among the political symbols we wanted our children and grandchildren to recognize as signs of evil, the primary one was the Nazi swastika.

A Three-Generation Struggle to "Master the Past"

As late as the 1990s, young Germans coming to visit America could be assaulted by fellow high school students with the question, "Do you know what a Swastika is?" The question could only have been posed by a non-German profoundly out of touch with what German governments, teachers, authors, artists, and public media had been doing especially in the past twenty years to make sure that no student in any cranny of the German educational system had any doubt about what a swastika was and what it symbolized. A survey of the means by which this education has transpired is worth considerable world effort. Nothing is more instructive in such a survey than the story of how three generations of Germans successively assumed responsibility for educating the next generation not to forget the years 1933–1945.

The awareness "we were wrong" is likely to overtake the citizens of any country decisively defeated in war. *Something*, at least, went wrong, else our sufferings would not be so great nor our defeat so total. Many Germans at the end of World War One were far from certain that they had been defeated, and Hitler took shrewd advantage of this uncertainty. May 8, 1945, was radically different: No doubt about Germany's utter defeat at terrible cost or that Hitler's Third Reich was a disaster. For years the burdens of that disaster would shadow every German household: grief, poverty, collapse of life support. Well into the 1950s only a few had much energy for speaking about the evils which the Nazis had perpetrated on vast numbers of Jews and non-Germans. One's own suffering can impose hard strictures on one's ability to think about the suffering of others. In addition, for ordinary West Germans of the 1940s and 1950s there were some convenient escape hatches from having to think about their own roles in the Nazi era: the imposition of a new liberal democratic govern-ment by the victorious Allies; the Nuremberg trials of leading Nazi war crim-inals as scapegoats for the disaster; the eventual domestic trials of some five thousand other Nazis, also candidates for signifying to "ordinary" Germans that they were victims, not agents, of the debacle; plus the prompt collaboration of the "new" Germany with NATO against the threat of the USSR, a made-to-order excuse for many a private German reflection that, after all, Hitler knew who was Germany's biggest enemy.

So German adults of the war generation had many a public inducement to avoid talk about their own possible culpability for the Nazi disaster. Numer-ous indeed were the psychological reasons for repressing the question: "What did we do or not do in the 1930s and 1940s that permitted the triumph of Nazism?" Furthermore, during twenty postwar years German survivors of the war were busy founding businesses, getting married, having children, seeing them grow up, and sending them off to universities. Then, especially in the universities in the mid-1960s, public and private avoidance of the great buried questions got rudely challenged. Children plied parents and grandparents with the questions. "Did you vote for Hitler? What did you know about the fate of your Jewish classmates or of our Jewish neighbors? Did you, as a German soldier in the Soviet Union, witness the mass executions of civilians or see Russian POWs dying of starvation and disease?" As one member of the second generation remembered.

> I was born in 1934. When I was around seventeen years old, I asked my parents questions like these. They answered, reluctantly at first, but they answered. There ensued a painful process of discus-sion between the generations. The younger generation: search for their lost fatherland, reproachful, unjust to their elders, and, deep down, uncertain of how they would have behaved under the chal-lenge of a popular and determined dictatorship. The older genera-tion: bitter, betrayed in their exploited idealism, relieved and forget-ful after surviving the catastrophe, frightened by the demanding questions of their disrespectful children. Post-war Germany was a divided nation.[9]

By 1968, German university students were joining many of their contem-poraries in Europe and America in protesting the Vietnam War and the nuclear bomb threat; but youthful German protest drew particular power and passion from an undertow of resentment at the silence of elders in their own house-holds. From the silences and evasions as well as from the honest answers they extracted from the older generation, they began to piece together a commit-ment to study the Nazi period and to ensure that Germans of the future would remember its evils—in detail, in the eyes of neighbors who suffered most from it, and for the sake of building public barriers against any renewal of the Nazi horror in any future generation.

To those second-generation postwar sons and daughters we now owe a range of public phenomena which qualify Germany as the country whose various authorities have worked hardest to merit an award as "A Country That Wants Never to Forget." Prior to 1970, one might have been skeptical of any such assessment of public culture in Germany—what one German historian calls "the morals of millions." But by the end of the 1970s there began to accumulate in public times and places so many visible reminders of *die Nazizeit* that not even small children in Germany were likely to be innocent of some factual answers to the question, "Who were the Nazis?"

Why So Belatedly?

Before venturing a survey of these reminders, one might readily ask: Why did it take three and four decades for the politicians, the educators, and other public leaders of this society to launch a vast series of public rehearsals of the history of the 1933–1945 era?

Contemporary Germans who were in high school history classes in the 1950s and 1960s say that those classes often ended with the 1920s, with the Weimar Republic, and with teacher excuse of "too little time" for getting into the 1930s. Historians like to say that they cannot write serious history about events less than twenty-five years in the past, but this assumption hardly explains why history books and history teachers in Germany of the 1950s avoided 1933–1945. An amalgam of pain, guilt, and repression must have haunted those classrooms. While a world reading public was beginning to image the Holocaust through the eyes of Elie Wiesel, Primo Levi, and Anne Frank, students in the thirteen-year curriculum of the German territorial educational systems were not required to read much of this literature. Few citizens of the town of Dachau, forced to visit the neighboring camp in 1945, visited it again, nor did they advise their children and visitors to do so.[10]

Such a psychology of avoidance in history teaching has parallels all over the world. Stalin did not plan to make one of the gulag camps into a memorial of the cruelty practiced there, nor did tour guides, until recently, point visitors to Mount Vernon and Monticello to the sites where the slaves on those plantations used to live. Most official, government-sponsored educational systems celebrate collective pasts. Few are the politicians who expect the young to learn how to mourn the guilt of the ancestors.

But first-generation amnesia among postwar Germans disguised slumbering private and public memory. Psychiatrists take great interest in such resistance. What we hide we have not really forgotten. What we have apparently forgotten we can recover. We may want to forget a painful event and go on living as if it had never happened, but as Søren Kierkegaard suggested, effective forgetting requires genuine remembering. Really to put something in the past, one must consciously *put* it there. To do so may require an access of strength for coping with weakness.

From Private Memory to Public Memorial

Exactly forty years after the end of the war in Germany, a former lieutenant in the *Wehrmacht,* now President of the Federal Republic, delivered a memorial address to its Bundestag in words that achieved immediate worldwide acclaim. In great detail the President, Richard Freiherr von Weizsäcker, catalogued the evils that the Nazis and their German collaborators inflicted upon millions of human beings in a dozen European countries. It was, as a columnist of the *New York Times* remarked, "one of the great speeches of our time." It was certainly one of the speeches that few political leaders dare to deliver to their own constituencies: a sustained litany of the evils done by recent predecessors.[11]

Fourteen years later, in the spring of 1999, I asked the author of that speech, "Why did it take forty years before a political leader of your generation—and your political party—felt that he or she could speak as you spoke on May 8, 1985?" (Von Wiezsäcker wrote most of the speech himself.) He answered: "Because we Germans needed time to recover a certain inner and outer security. We had to have enough confidence about our ability not to repeat those evils. We had to feel secure enough to talk openly about it."

The crucial security was not so much in the NATO alliance against the threats of the Soviet Union as in the thirty-five-year experience of Germans in building democratic institutions. That, says one American historian, was an achievement of the first prewar-born generation of leaders. Without it, without the coming of unprecedented limits on government power, freedom of speech, minority rights, and other entrenchments of human rights in their public institutions, Germans in the 1970–1990 era would not have been liberated into a culture of spreading *public talk* about the Nazi past. University students who scorned the silences and defenses of their parents played an important role in this development; but, like some Americans on college campuses of the 1960s, they did not succeed in shuffling off the "unresolved psychological baggage" of their elders, nor did they acknowledge what they owed to those elders in their very freedom to criticize them. As A. D. Moses says in his study of the two generations, changes that come in the later often are rooted in leadership already present in the earlier. "Generations are complex," he notes. They are often composed of minority voices which one day will achieve majority support. Early leaders of Germany's postwar democracy such as Gustav Heineman and Kurt Schumacher might have been muffled by the pragmatic leadership of

Konrad Adenauer, but they were forerunners of the historical honesty demanded by the students of 1968, just as those students taking up positions of
responsibility in the 1980s began to unveil *die Nazizeit* and thus prepared the
way for their children to deal with that challenge in less strident, more matter-
of-fact ways.[12]

The denazification coercions of postwar Allied occupation of Germany
played a vital part in this chain of fifty-year change, but as Moses makes clear,
the Allied insistence on democratic freedom could only become a power for
change as young Germans began to use it for asking their own questions and
pursuing their own answers. In their occupation sector of Lower Saxony, for
example, the British invited young people to form discussion groups but practiced a hands-off policy of leaving the groups free to talk about anything. "These
often informal groups were of enormous importance in providing time and
space for reorientation after the war years, and about 40 percent of young
Germans were members of one. 'In probably no other period of German history did such discussion-circles and solidarity-communities play such a great
role as in the postwar years.' " In addition, in the late 1940s over a million
young Germans participated in church youth groups, and a growing number
were able to attend international conferences.[13] Forced into freedom of opinion
and expression, so to speak, postwar Germans began to experience "a long-
term learning process." In each other they could perceive varieties of being
human. Such freedom was most experienced, Moses concludes, in the new
public structures of German life. It was most muffled in families, where the
pain of the war generation persisted into silence around many a dinner table.
The ironic psychological effect upon some sons and daughters was a super-
sensed burden of responsibility for countering parental silences. From the early
1980s on, they began to produce a mass of public declarations, books, monuments, and study projects in all regions of Germany. Rather than asserting a
clean break with the feelings and ambiguities of the domestic culture in which
the second generation had been raised, Moses concludes, this perspective "re-
places the asperity of censure with the emollient historicizing insight that the
generations are related to one another by intricate webs of psychological interdependence."[14] Germans are not alone illustrations of that facet of the human
story. The American campus revolt of the 1960s owed some of its passion to
ideas learned in some classrooms and around some family dinner tables.

One of the notable beginnings of widespread public dialogue about Nazism in Germany was the American television series, *Holocaust,* first viewed
there in 1979. Americans raised on the death camp photographs of the 1940s,
tutored by the books of Elie Wiesel, and touched early by *The Diary of Anne
Frank* had difficulty understanding the impact of this series on Germans. The
scenes of the drama fell far short of many previous historical and fictional film
portrayals of the roundups and executions of Jews in the 1930s and 1940s.
Like the writing of Anne Frank, *Holocaust* reduced massive human evil to

small-scale, individualized experience. It made politically engineered evil accessible to personal understanding and imagination. The result in Germany was the recruitment of hundreds of thousands into discussion groups, family talk, and media-analyses that catalyzed, for a while, a national preoccupation.

With such breadth of public deliberation, a cross section of West German leaders from the second generation took up the multifaceted task of translating private, sequestered memory into public acknowledgment and public institutional expression. They planted seeds in the 1980s that were to flower everywhere in the 1990s in an array of studies, monuments, anniversaries, unearthed sites of Nazi terror, museums, and study centers. Slight though such an American's survey of this array has to be, I have tried below to describe something of the educational impact of these developments on Germans—but most of all on the education of the American I know best: myself.

1. Marks in Time: Anniversaries

In the late 1990s, the Bundestag of the Federal Republic, still meeting in Bonn, debated the question: If Germany is to observe an annual official "Day of Remembrance," what should be the date? Among the candidate days were May 8, the day the war in Europe ended, and November 9, *Pogromnacht*. The latter would have been a tempting choice, for by coincidence it could also mark the founding of the Weimar Constitution in 1918 and the day in 1989 when the Berlin Wall fell. Pride in either day to the contrary, the final two candidates in Bundestag debate were January 20 and January 27.

The former was the day of the 1942 meeting of some fifteen upper-level Nazi bureaucrats in a villa on the shore of Berlin's largest lake, the Wannsee. In scarcely two hours, under the leadership of SS Commander Reinhard Heydrich, these men quickly agreed on the procedures for arresting, transporting, and killing of all the Jews of Europe. Secretary of the gathering was Adolf Eichmann. As described below, the Wannsee Conference Center would become, in the mid-1990s, its own remarkable *Denkmal* for contemporary education on the history of Nazism. But January 27 won the Bundestag vote. It was the day in 1945 when Soviet armies broke into Auschwitz and liberated what remained of its haggard prisoners.

It seems likely that one stable feature of this annual commemoration will be a speech to the Bundestag by the Bundespräsident, who in 1999 was Roman Herzog. He was eleven years old in 1945. Like his predecessor Von Weizsäcker, Herzog was active in church as well as civil affairs over several decades. His position in the parliamentary system was largely symbolic, but as representative of the nation (rather than the government) a German president has a "bully pulpit" less compromised by immediate political interests than is usually the case with an American president or a German chancellor.

Herzog's 1999 speech was a worthy successor to that of Von Weizsäcker in 1985.[15] Auschwitz, he began, must become permanent in the national memory, for "if a people seek to live in and with their history, it is good advice that they live in their whole history and not only with its good and pleasant parts." But he added: "If I attempt to place myself in our history, I attempt it not in shame but in dignity."

That there is moral dignity in facing the sins of the past enters only occasionally into the rhetoric of political leaders, and the concept itself escapes most definitions of patriotism. By reminding Germans of the moral dignity of uncovering past evils, Herzog was not far from the word of Saint Augustine: "There is something in humility that lifts up the head."

Herzog soon turned to the audience he wanted most to reach: young people. Some may say that the Nazi era was no business of theirs, that facing it is a task of the elders. That may be the view of perhaps one fourth of German youth, but surely three fourths of them "know what's what" regarding: *Die Nazizeit*. They study that shadow side of our history because they are oriented to the future of our people, not just to debates about the past. "How they think about the future of Germany is incomparably more important than all the debates and conceptual clarifications" of the older generations.

But, Herzog warned, members of no German generation should assume the pose of moral superiority over a previous generation, as though in hindsight fantasizing they think that *they* would have stood on the side of the victims or would have joined the resisters. "Nazism is our common, frightful inheritance." None of us has the right to forget it or to assume that we are utterly immune to the temptations of our ancestors.

How should young people go about their education concerning this negative past? Herzog offers a catalogue of concrete suggestions that many youth are already undertaking. They have read *The Diary of Anne Frank*, a book about Hitler by Sebastian Haffner, and the diary of Victor Klemperer. They have seen the television series *Holocaust* and the film *Schindler's List*. They travel to the sites of terror, they care for monuments and graves, they work on documentation projects with their schools, they see historical broadcasts. Among themes for high school essay competitions none is more likely than "Daily Life Under National Socialism." "No question about it: Our young people discuss and research, they ask and inquire." And they often inquire in their own unique ways, however different these may be from those of us elders.

Turning to the wider German public, Herzog notes that there is much left for securing the Nazi horror in the national memory. There is the great Mahnmal to the Holocaust to be built in the center of Berlin, not for the sake of Germany's image in the eyes of foreigners and not with cheap identification with victims, but above all in memory of the victims and their suffering "and a warning to the living." But one big monument in the national capital is not enough. We must spread these memory joggers all over Germany.

Everywhere were the scenes of horror. Everywhere were the schools from which Jewish children were taken. Everywhere, the shops whose owners were taken off. Everywhere, the SA's torture-cellars. Everywhere the collection places for the transports. . . . People should know this: All of these things took place, not in some remote place and in remote antiquity, but here, in Germany, in my city, in a time in which there were already automobiles, telephones, and radios, between humans who lived not very differently than do we. The topography of terror could be found in the daily life of our world. . . .

This is no ordinary academic piece of objective study, Herzog warned.

Whoever stands in this history will be placed in it as a moral subject. He must simply ask himself: How did the perpetrators go about their business? How, the collaborators? How could they not empathize with their victims? How did seduction and mass-suggestion function? And he will not avoid the question: Am I certain that I would not have collaborated? Would I not have been only an onlooker? Would I not have had such fearful anxiety that I would not have resisted?

Herzog goes on to call Germans, especially the young, to undertake "practice in empathy and mistrust of all simplifiers." It is no simple thing, he implies, to understand both the perpetrators and their victims. We must distinguish between the two and deepen our understanding "in the head and in the heart."

And what about modern German responsibility? "The great majority of Germans living today are not guilty of Auschwitz. But surely: They are also in special measure responsible that never again will something like Holocaust and Auschwitz be repeated." Let no one make excuse for 1933 by saying that "everyone had to follow" Hitler, nor let anyone indulge in the surmise, in 1999, that "we are immune" to the same dangers. "The one is an historical mistake, the other a pious illusion."

In a powerful paragraph near the end of the speech, Herzog turned to moral-historical anthropology, striking the same note as did Weizsäcker in 1985:

One thing is clear: Auschwitz has darkened our image of the human. What once was historical reality belongs forever to the fearful possibilities of humans, whose repetition, in whatever form, cannot be ruled out. The dam and safeguards must therefore ever again be built up anew.

In the very years of the Herzog presidency, such "fearful possibilities" had already come to pass in Rwanda and Bosnia. Americans would soon add September 11, 2001. The speech ends with an allusion to Bosnia in a quotation from the novel *Bridge Over the Drina* by Nobel prize winner Ivo Andric. Herzog recollects that, beginning in Sarajevo in 1914, Europe suffered a catastrophe rooted in service to alleged "higher interests." As Europe went to war that August, "whoever then lived with a pure soul and open eyes could see how an entire society changed in a day."

All in all, this address breathes accumulations of German "memory culture" in the years 1980–2000. In these years leaders high and low were recovering images of the Nazi era in increasing depth, detail, and public candor. Especially remarkable about this address is its appeals to youth and to their obligation to deal with the scars of history in the *localities* of the land. For calling attention to sites, sources, and events still to be publicly recognized, the speech was an apt reminder of the diverse forms of a growing, honest German "mastery of the past."

2. Locations of Concentrated Evil: The Camp Museums

The fall of the Berlin Wall in 1989 opened up a huge acreage between the two halves of a politically divided city. For almost thirty years, across this no-man's land, one hundred to two hundred yards wide, Berliners East and West had stared at each other. To clear out this area in the early 1960s, the DDR government demolished buildings and fortified the space with dense arrays of barbed wire, mines, automatically activated machine guns, and a paved road for military vehicles. In twenty-eight years at least seventy-eight people lost their lives in attempting to escape from East to West across this zone. The century-old Protestant Church of the Resurrection was caught between the two walls and was finally dynamited by the DDR in 1985. After the Wall came down, a new church by that name rose on the same site.

As we have seen, central Berlin (Die Mitte) was already thick with history: imperial museums, a gilded opera house, palaces, and classic Schinkel-designed facades galore. To this neighborhood the Nazis added their own layers of sleek, angular office buildings. Here Adolf Hitler built the bunker in which he would die. Comparable only to the no-man's land dividing the two Koreas, the weedy emptiness of this space epitomized the Cold War as few other places on earth. Over the next three decades grafitti on the western side of the Wall advertised the scorn and frustration of the "Wessies" for this violent slash through their city.

With November 9, 1989, and the reunification of the two Germanies a year later, the space suddenly opened up to an urban planner's dream: the roomy heart of a capital city, ready for filling with new structures for a new era. The government of the Federal Republic could now move from modest quarters in Bonn. It could build new transparent-looking offices symbolizing a nation shorn of nationalism. Here, where Hitler and Albert Speer wanted to establish a victorious Nazi government in architectural grandeur, democracy would build its home.

A year before the Wall fell, well-known television talk-show hostess Lea Rosh had proposed a large, ambitious memorial to the Holocaust for West Berlin. With the fall, as space for the memorial, she nominated the newly open five acres to the south of the Reichstag. Then began a decade-long debate in Berlin and throughout Germany around the question: "How could an artist's design give form to Germany's need to remember the Holocaust?" What memorial to that horror, if any, would be appropriate in the heart of the new capital city, many of whose leaders wanted to signal publicly that the new Germany would not forget the evils of the old?

The debate was complicated with another key question: how to remind an upcoming generation of events that they could not have directly experienced? Survivors of the death camps often said to others, "You cannot really know what it was like." Non-Jewish Germans living through the Nazi tyranny could say much the same: How can outsiders understand the price of survival in a police state? War veterans of every country know about a kindred despair that anyone else can rightly comprehend the horrors of a battlefield.

In the immediate post-1945 years, suffering and hating the devastations of defeat, many Germans declared that their history now had to begin all over again—with *null stunde*, zero hour. Twenty years later, an aroused second generation exploded in furious disagreement. It was high time now for all Germans to deliver the Nazi past from public amnesia.

Many of those who urged a return to the past under the cry "Never again!" knew that foreigners would be viewing their project with skeptical scrutiny. Perhaps the most skeptical of all would be Jews throughout the world, many of whom had vowed never to trust Germans again or even to visit the country. At the same time, especially in the early writings of Primo Levi and Elie Wiesel, the evils of Nazism acquired fearful importance as *worldwide* warning. "This is where hate leads," said Wiesel in an interview in 1992.[16] Worldwide fascination with Nazism continued to grow. But underneath the interest hid anxiety that what "those people" did we people might be capable of doing. Therefore, in a troubling way, Germany became a test case of whether one nation, coping with painful memories of its past, can do memory work on behalf of outsiders.

Though it shrinks the focus of my inquiry, I want to begin, precisely as an outsider, with further accounts of my own experience of this German project. What do Americans have to learn from contemporary German efforts to master their past? Readers can answer for themselves. It is important for this

American, born five years before Hitler came to power, to begin by trying to answer the question for himself.

No American student of this same project offers more insightful justification of this method than James E. Young. In his now classic study, *The Texture of Memory: Holocaust Memorials and Meaning*, he underscores "the essentially participatory nature of all memorials," including those whose shape and location have vivid historical connections. Memorial stone tablets on battlefields and museums in the former sites of concentration camps, he observes, have in common the reminder, "Precisely *here* humans suffered and died at the hands of other humans." By itself, Young reminds us, a "site" cannot remember. Rather,

> it is the projection of memory by visitors into a space that makes it a
> memorial. The site catches visitors unaware but is no longer passive:
> it intrudes itself into the pedestrians' thoughts. Of course, such
> memory can also be avoided by simply crossing the street. . . . But
> even this would be a memorial act of sorts, if only in opposition. For
> to avoid the memorial here, we would first have to conjure the
> memory to be avoided: that is, we would have to remember what it
> is we want to forget.[17]

Germans who want to avoid seeing memorials of the Nazi era will have to emigrate. There are thousands scattered across the country.[18] For even an introduction to this array, some order of contemplation seems necessary. One way to organize a survey is to travel back from the notorious hearts of the Nazi evil (the camps) to the technical support of the camps (railroads and bureaucratic structures) to the civil society that passively or actively supported these systems (local citizens) to the promulgation of *ideas* that defined the Nazi vision of a "Thousand-Year Reich" (educational systems). Below is a backtracking into this typography of German memory: from some camps, to a railroad line, to a meeting of Nazi bureaucrats, to some Berlin neighborhoods, and finally to a school.

DACHAU. Memorials are only doorways to history. They invite further investigation. They alert visitors to what they already know but may be in danger of forgetting. They are also invitations to learn what visitors do not yet know.

Having met Dachau's most famous prisoner, Martin Niemoeller, in 1952 and remembering the 1945 photos, I did not want a first trip to Munich to lack a visit to the place. For most American tourists in 1966, however, finding Dachau was not easy. We found it by following a railroad track. Once inside the gate, we experienced the cognitive dissonance of remembering the photos from 1945 while looking at a wheat field dotted with white crosses, a Star of David, and a small Catholic chapel. Only later would we learn that in 1960 fifty thousand Germans had gathered at Dachau at the behest of Munich Catholic bishop Johann Neuhaeusler to make of Dachau the last Station of the Cross, a "Monument of Atonement." The chapel monument was completed in 1964, when "two model barracks were reconstructed, symbolic concrete foundations laid to recall those destroyed, and the grounds were covered with white gravel."[19]

Whatever the historical detail this American brought with him to Dachau, however, my most abiding memory was the absence of any local public acknowledgment of the site's existence. One speculated that the citizens of Dachau might be glad to change the town's name. But that very gesture toward future public amnesia would have required current citizens to articulate a negative memory. A short visit to Dachau thus turned out to be for two Americans an accurate, experiential introduction to the challenges facing public efforts among younger Germans to "master the past" in the mid-1960s. German art historian Detlef Hoffmann, James Young reports, visited Dachau in 1961 and "had to blaze his way through brush so high that it concealed the fences and outer moat. Twelve years of concentration camp history, he felt, had gone to ruin after the war." That weedy help to amnesia was a paradoxical symbol, contrasting ironically with the weeds that in 1961 began to divide Berlin. Thousands of Bavarians knew enough of Dachau to want to forget it. In 1933, "every citizen of Dachau watched the camp being constructed, as well as many Müncheners, who traditionally took Sunday excursions to Dachau and its castle." By 1966 Dachau was getting sanitized to yield a landscape neat, clean, and even beautiful. Hoffmann described it as a "sparkling renovation," Young as "antiseptic." Now with the weeds and brush cleaned up, "the town's former repression had itself been lost to memory," making it easy to forget the years of forgetting.[20]

SACHSENHAUSEN. As the Nazi system for total control of Germany developed in the mid-1930s, the Nazis established Sachsenhausen, some twenty-five miles north of central Berlin, as a special model and organizational center of the camp system. No town in Nazi Germany was far from one of several thousand camps and other prisons in the network of terror. Diverse purposes marked the system and yielded a sliding scale from the relative amenities of Dachau to the industrialization of mass murder in Auschwitz. But thousands died at Dachau, which still has its remnant crematory oven. It is impossible to believe that villagers never glimpsed the smoke from the ovens or the increasing trainloads of prisoners transported past the town to the camp. To be sure, Nazi designs for the specialized death camps called for locating them outside of Germany proper, in conquered territory to the east, under the surmise that this massive dirty work might disturb the feelings of many ordinary German citizens. Specialized murder required specialized murderers. Heinrich Himmler, whose SS troops managed the camp system, put the psychology of this strategy into words that became famous after the war. Speaking to a group of his lieutenants in Posen, Himmler paid tribute to their ability to become murderers without ceasing to be "decent" human beings:

> Most of you will know what it means when a hundred corpses are lying side by side, or five hundred or a thousand are lying there. To have stuck it out and—apart from a few exceptions due to human weakness—to have remained decent, that is what has made us tough. This is a glorious page in our history, and one that has never been written and can never be written.[21]

In Sachsenhausen, a crematorium, a whipping post, and an execution ditch are surviving reminders of daily life and death in the camps. But the survival of Himmler's words constitutes a memorial of a special fundamental terror: Here was the rhetoric of systematic, racism-inspired murder on the lips of a human agent who, with his obedient collaborators, was putting the concept into action throughout Poland, the Ukraine, and all of Nazi-occupied Europe.

A picture of Himmler and this text sit in one corner of a museum which the Soviets established in their 1945 takeover of Sachsenhausen. Like the Nazis, they used it for confinement of political enemies, including Nazi officials and German POWs. The museum displays many tangible tools of oppression—chains, whips, tin plates, work tools, striped uniforms. Just outside the gate the post-1989 local territorial government has vividly signaled the technical and social refinements of the place in a diagram of the *Idealplan* for the camp as conceived for its 1936–1937 construction. The design called for an inner triangular fence around whose base are arrayed, like a fan, dozens of prisoner barracks. This symmetry served surveillance and composed "a stark architectural expression of control and terror."[22] Around the inner camp, in close proximity to the residents of the neighboring village of Oranienburg, the SS built a large complex of slave-labor factories plus barracks, homes, and offices for its own personnel. Sachsenhausen served as the model, staff training ground, and organizational heart of the developing camp system in Germany and beyond. Some two hundred thousand prisoners from forty countries eventually were confined here: political dissidents, Jews, gypsies, homosexuals, and other "lawbreakers," most of whom would be dispatched to Auschwitz. A wide ditch near the crematorium served as execution ground. By disease, overwork, hanging, and firing squad, at least ten thousand died here. Model crematorium technology met some of its first technical tests in Sachsenhausen. Inmates helped build the Berlin autobahn and worked for numerous adjacent war factories of corporations whose names would survive the war and achieve worldwide renown.[23]

In 1961 the East German government designated Sachsenhausen, along with Ravensbruck[24] and Buchenwald, as one of a trio of major national memorials of the Nazi era. To one of these camps schoolchildren, citizen groups, and officials made annual pilgrimages in celebration of the Communist resis-

tance to Nazism and of the Soviet liberation of the camps. One historic photograph shows a crowd of thousands of East Germans behind the DDR president, all emerging from Sachsenhausen with smiles of liberation joy on all
faces. In every sense the evils of the place lie behind them, and Communism
takes the credit.

When, after the fall of the Wall, the Brandenburg territorial government
assumed responsibility for the camp, a new emotion afflicted every aspect of
the site. No celebration now—mourning rather—and no disavowal of ancestral
responsibility for the terror. The section of the camp built by the Soviets for
their prisoners has been reidentified as integral to camp history. Outside the
gate now, along with the schematic of camp design, is a poster display of the
original eighteen Nazi categories of prisoners, all marked by their own triangular badges. As one enters the gate, with its famous mocking wrought-iron
motto, *Arbeit macht frei,* one sees at the far end of the camp a tall chimney-
shaped pillar with a high-up replication those eighteen triangles. From the
Soviet era, however, all the triangles were colored with the red that the Nazis
reserved for designating Communist prisoners. Soviet ideology required that
the victims of the camp be selectively remembered. Notoriously, as in other
Soviet-zone camps, the deaths of Jews, homosexuals, Sinti, Roma, and other
non-Communists had little recognition of their places in the Nazi catalogue of
the biologically unfit—*lebensunwertes Leben.*

The technology of murder partly survived the Soviet takeover in remnants
of crematorium ovens on one edge of the camp, in easy sight of the town of
Oranienburg. In an odd, coincidental experience of this particular visitor on a
spring day in 1999, a plume of black smoke was ascending from the village.
It was easily visible from the crematorium site. Later we learned that a local
town business was burning a large pile of rubber tires.

Feelings, and most of all fantasies, have small ordinary place in guidebook
writing, not to speak of history writing. What can one make of a nearby fire
that attended that day's visit to Sachsenhausen? The smoke assaulted this visitor with a sudden sense of how human bodies were burned here more me-
thodically than were those old tires. Yet smoke, even crematorium smoke, is
only an abstract remnant of human lives and those who murdered them on
this very ground. During visits to Auschwitz, as one gazes at bins piled with
shoes, toothbrushes, luggage, or eyeglasses, the English guide is likely to say,
"Try to remember that behind every pair of these eyeglasses was once a real
human person." She is seeking to furnish and discipline the visitor's imagination and feeling. Were one to visit any of these camps and to carry out in
memory only a bundle of objective images and "the facts" of the place, shorn
of shadows and weights of feeling, one might say that one has not really visited
this place. Black smoke over Sachsnsenhausen has an indelible place in our
memory of going there.

Remnants of methods by which some humans have perpetrated evil on others are only "metonymies"—parts that signify a whole. Yet they can speak with eloquence and realism that overcome a viewer's emotions. If they did not, would one really be "seeing" what is here before one's eyes? For many visitors to the Nazi (and other) sites of terror in recent history, notably those with well-developed imaginations, the visit can be devastating. Even for those with learned capacity for keeping their distance emotionally from typographies of terror, there is a limit to what they can absorb about the human suffering here so partially symbolized.

Stories of humanly enacted evil should include not only the victims but also the perpetrators. In remembering twentieth-century terror we are likely to pay first attention to the victims and to dismiss the perpetrators as hardly worth remembering. This is a moral mistake. For the sake of putting teeth into the commitment "Never again!" we must try to understand the perpetrators—a task more difficult than understanding the victims. Only in later years have the museum makers of Sachsenhausen begun to ask, "What should we do with the barracks in which the SS lived around the camp, the residences of the officers, and the other buildings in which rules were devised for administration of the death camps in Poland?" Doubtless the ordinary citizens of nearby Oranienburg, in the 1990s, are sorry to hear that question raised. Second- and third-generation families now live in some of the former SS residences. Nearby slave labor factory sites have long ago been adapted to new productive uses. What if the village itself became part of the Sachsenhausen memorial? Discussion of this possibility—and the prospect of foreign visitors like me trooping down these village streets—disturbed many a local resident in the late 1990s. Outside one home in 1997 hung a poster in German: "Former SS houses, now a memorial?"

That day in Sachsenhausen, some in our party declined to visit one of the last little structures in the camp. They already knew what was inside: the laboratory where camp doctors dissected bodies on way to the crematorium for "scientific" and other purposes. Says a German inscription beside one of the display cases: "Skins with tattoo marks were tanned and fashioned into objects (book covers, handbags, cases). Skulls with a perfect set of teeth were special 'souvenirs' for the brutal SS-Leader. A special skeleton-collection was done for the Institute of the Central Office for Race-Settlements." One remembers that the SS insignia included a human skull. At such moments of memorial viewing, one is likely to come up against a wall in the self that prompts the confession: "No feeling of mine is adequate to this horror, nor will I ever conceptualize it in language or art adequate to it." Such awareness has long-since dimmed the enthusiasm of many German artists, including writers, for expressing the truth about the Nazi terror and most of all the Holocaust. Their anxiety about doing justice to the object has an analogy in the anxiety of mystical theologians about trying to describe God. Demonry prompts the same anxiety. For the less mystical, the compromise of St. Augustine prevails: "We speak in order not to be silent." Not to speak of Sachsenhausen, once visited, is inexcusable, as would be the removal of the place from sight and memory. One remembers that the Nazis expected to plow under all the death camps once their work was done. But to speak and memorialize as though speech and memorials match the reality of what transpired here, is to deny human expressive finitude and the self-effacing function of symbols. In short, one passes back under those iron-wrought words, "Work makes free," newly aware of the limits of one's awareness *and* willingness to become aware. It is as though, on a descent into Dante's Inferno, one caught a glimpse of its lower, lowest depths and asked the guide to take you back to Purgatory.

BUCHENWALD. Located like Sachsenhausen in the formerly Soviet-dominated zone of East Germany, Buchenwald is also a site of contested history. The Nazis collected political enemies there plus growing numbers of Jews en route to Auschwitz, in a total of at least 239,000 people, some 56,000 of whom died.

Patton's Third Army overran the camp in April 1945, on the heels of a prisoner revolt which the East German government was to make into an icon of the Communist role in the liberation of Germany from the Nazis. For the next forty years, in ceremony, history books, and mandatory citizen visits, Buchenwald would be understood as a place where Communists finally won the battle against the capitalists. By 1958 the eastern government completed a monument to the heroes of the revolt: eleven giant figures lifting fists and guns in the hours preceding the arrival of the Americans, representative of the struggle and victory of the working class inmates over their tormentors. The architects of 1958 set this monument on the far slope of the mostly empty spaces of the camp as the climax of a trail that led past "eighteen pylons with bowls flanking the 'Street of Nations,' seven granite cubes emblazoned with reliefs telling the camp's story" in its Communist version. In the pre-1989 era Buchenwald became the central monument of the DDR regime, "the most gargantuan complex of memorial sculpture and edifices located in any of the German camps." Over the years since 1958, millions of east Germans, young and old, gathered around this monument to applaud this version of history, to celebrate the heroic Communist resisters, but not to mourn the vast range of fellow sufferers alive or dead. No visitor to Buchenwald up to 1989 would experience it as a place of sorrow, contrition, or humility before the evil uses of political power. Like pre-1989 Sachsenhausen, only small scattered stones served as reminders that Jews, gypsies, homosexuals, POWs, and other non-Communist enemies of Nazism all died here, including eight to thirteen thousand anti-Communist Germans killed in the post-1948 years.[25]

A visitor to Buchenwald in 1999 walks on another layer of history laid down by new local and national governments. James Young relates the visit of a Western reporter soon after the 1990 reunification of the two Germanies. He found the Buchenwald museum closed for renovations and a sign reading,

"Dear Visitor: Be patient. Changes are being made." Among the changes would be new museum tokens of the Germans who died here under Soviet command.[26] Now, when pan-German chancellor Helmut Kohl came for memorializing a new version of post-1945 German history, he could place a wreath in memory of those Germans.

For this 1999 visitor, the most imposing feature of the new installations of the 1990s is a multistoried major research center whose documents, books, artifacts, and biographies of victims and perpetrators offer scholars depths of detail on the operation of the camp and its place in the Nazi system. Here is a workshop for historians dedicated to the axiom that some facts, buried in the past, must be unearthed before ideology gets its chance to shape their meaning. Just to visit the rooms of this center is to touch the contemporary German commitment to get as near to the bottom of *Die Nazizeit* as such remnants of the evil permit. But again, this research, as many a modern scholar is bound to testify, never reaches bottom. Where *is* the "bottom" of the evils of 1933–1945? 1966–1976—China? 1992–1995—Bosnia? 1994—Rwanda? 2003—Abu Graib prison? Those who have excavated the typographies of these terrors are likely to confess that no one can really get to the bottom of it all. A "mystery of iniquity" haunts Buchenwald.[27]

It certainly haunts Germans who live in Weimar. No sign evokes this fact so vividly as one that stands directly in front of the Weimar train station. In the spring of 1999 it read:

WEIMAR LIEGT BEI BUCHENWALD

("Weimar Is Neighbor to Buchenwald")

In 1937 the National Socialists built Buchenwald concentration camp on a slope of the Ettersberg—near Schloss Ettersburg, the setting from 1776 to 1780 for Anna Amelia's Court of Muses. The camp served to remove political opponents, known as "criminal and antisocial" elements, from the "national German community." From 1938, inmates were also sent here on racial grounds. They were brought to the camp from the railway station in Weimar. Other trains, carrying deportees to the death camps, passed through. During the final months, the camp had a larger population than the town. Although Buchenwald was not specifically intended to play a role in systematic genocide, of its 250,000 or more prisoners, from about 40 nations, over 56,000 died. On 11 April 1945, the camp was liberated by the Third U.S. Army. On 16 April General Patton ordered a thousand residents of Weimar to visit the camp. From August 1945 until January 1950, the Soviet intelligence service ran the site as an internment camp: Special Camp No. 2 Buchenwald. Of altogether 28,500 detainees, 7,100 died from disease and neglect.

The year 1999 was special for this special German city. The European Union had designated it as the year's "Cultural City" of Europe. Weimar had long signified to the world both political failure and artistic eminence. The 1919 constitution was written here. Goethe and Schiller called Weimar home. For a time so did Richard Wagner. The Bauhaus Movement museum is one of the town's gems. Spruced up in the post-Communist era, with its repaired houses, streets, statues, shops and hotels, Weimar in early 1999 looked prepared for an influx of tourists. The double statue of Goethe and Schiller stood proudly in the platz before the opera house, whose banner announced "The Marriage of Figaro." Nearby is Goethe's carefully preserved house, replete with the art and the lifestyle of early nineteenth-century romanticism.

But there is another remnant of Goethe's life and work in the region that amounts to an ominous, fearsome historic scar. It is the stump of an oak tree. It remains there in an open space on the grounds of Buchenwald. Here, in the former eighteenth-century forest, the great German poet wrote and meditated on the beauties of the Ettersberg Valley. Himmler had the tree cut down to make way for the camp and a new, corrupt version of romanticism.

Blaise Pascal remarked that humans are creatures of "grandeur and misery." If there is anywhere in Germany associated with the grandeur of its classic culture, it is Weimar. If there is anywhere in contemporary Germany where government has decided to assert public clarity about a misery-laden chapter in its history, it also is Weimar. In the 1930s Hitler mouthed the name "Weimar" to remind Germans that in 1918 their politicians betrayed a scarcely defeated country and wrote a failed democratic constitution here. Now the name stands for a more awful betrayal, three miles away: Buchenwald.

The dualism must have afflicted many a visitor to Weimar in its cultural year of 1999. The sign in front of the Bahnhof provides a rare bit of tourist orientation: "Yes, this is the city where so much great art was created. It is also the city next to Buchenwald. Weimar is both, and we want you to be aware of this awful contradiction while you are here."

The contradictions are so many that a plunge into memories of ideological conflicts that have swirled in and around this city can pull the feelings of a visitor into depression and vertigo. James Young captures the irony, tragedy, and fearfulness of this history in an eloquent paragraph:

> When Himmler cynically designated Goethe's oak as the center of the camp he would begin in July 1937, he hoped to neutralize the memory of Goethe even as he invoked the philosopher's cultural authority. What better way to commemorate the obliteration of Weimar culture than to seal it in barbed wire, to turn it into its own prison?

Indeed, Buchenwald was chosen as the center of the GDR's commemorative activity for some of the same reasons the Nazis chose to
build a camp there in the first place: this stunningly beautiful region
seemed in both cases to exemplify the cultural heart of Germany. As
the nearby Ettersberg mountain range and city of Weimar would
suggest the majesty of German culture, the charred and withered remains of Goethe's oak would symbolize the depths to which the culture had sunk.[28]

Among the people visiting Buchenwald on that spring day were two groups
of Germans: high school students and new army recruits. For over thirty years
such groups came, at the behest of the DDR government, for instruction in its
version of modern history. Now, along with us foreigners, they visit under the
canopy of a different orientation: "See how low a high culture can stoop. Visitor,
be warned." In sum, the camps are all public warnings, rooted in a characteristic German high respect for history.

The German language has several words for site-witnesses to history:
Denkstätte, Denkmal and *Mahnmal*. The first and second suggest a place for
meditation, reflection, thinking. They designate monuments or memorials that
celebrate events and persons occasioning pride and celebration. *Mahnmal,* on
the other hand, is a place for grief, warning, and mourning over negative
history. From about 1980, Germany began to have more such places in its
towns and cities than does any other country in the world.

Brian Ladd remarked of this movement, "They use the power of place to
make the past vivid."[29] The most powerful, least subtle places are the camps.
Hardly any foreign visitors can go there without murmuring to themselves the
unanswerable question, "How *could* they?" In the "they" is some provisional
protection against an anxiety that German visitors find not so available. They
are more likely to ask, "How could *we?*"

Perhaps nowhere in Germany does that latter question resound with such
pain as Weimar-Buchenwald. The change in pronoun carries tremendous
political-philosophical freight, for it assumes a real connection between Germans past and Germans present. Americans separate themselves from their
ancestors more blithely than do Germans, whose country has long counted as
citizens only those who can demonstrate lineal German family connections.
Foreigners with no such connections still face obstacles to full citizenship under German law. Hitler radicalized this tradition, by using the notion of
"German blood" to exclude Jews, Slavs, Gypsies, Poles, and many others from
any share in the biological good fortune of Aryans.

The notion of "Germanness" is not dead among modern Germans, and
an event like September 11, 2001, gives many Americans a sense that we too
share a national bond. But the German bond is different. Long before the

unification of the German state under Bismarck in 1870, Germans participated in a community of language and culture. They had Bach, Beethoven, Schiller, and Goethe whether or not they had a unifying government. The very strength of this bond exacerbates the pain in the question, "How could we?" No wonder that young Germans these days often call themselves "Europeans," even as they express yearnings to become citizens of a "normal country." How can they be normal when in many an international encounter they meet neighbors who are still anxious to know if Germany really has put its Nazi past into the past?

Fortifying this sense of connection to ancestors is a strain of German culture not much shared by Americans: knowledge of history. Someone has observed, "Americans begin speeches with the statement of a problem to be solved, Germans with a rehearsal of a history to be acknowledged." It is no mere academic habit. For most Germans the past is somehow more real than it is to many an American.

Given that predisposition, survivors of the Nazi era had to *work* at resisting notions of their own participation in the evils of that era. Resistance required ignoring a knock on the door by someone you did not want to meet. When, in the 1960s, children began to ask parents, "What did you do?," both were beginning to ask, "What have we now to do?" In that question hid a positive corollary to the dawning shame of the young at being legatees of the Nazi horror: We are not personally guilty of that past, but we are all responsible for doing what we can (a) to remember it, and (b) to continue building barriers against its repetition.

If the first postwar generation of Germans (1945–1970) deserves world-wide credit for constructing Germany's first genuine political democracy, the second (1970–1995) deserves credit for a gathering crescendo of public witness to an evil past which future generations are thereby warned not to repeat. In their demand for public acknowledgment of the Holocaust, in particular, leaders of the second generation engaged in some furious interpersonal and public battles. Remarkably, many of their own children, the third postwar generation, now see themselves as inheriting additional shares of the same task. They seem to approach that task with composure grounded in the certainty that guilt for the past is one thing, ongoing responsibility for the future another. The third generation has many members who understand that they are responsible for educating the fourth, which is a way of saying that they expect awareness of *die Nazizeit* to remain permanent in German public consciousness.

This intergenerational commitment to ongoing public affirmation, "Never again!" has two dimensions that will impress any visitor to contemporary Germany: One is the growing spatial *localization* of lament for the past; the other is the honest detailing of that lament in formal and informal systems of *education*.

3. Localizations of Negative History

The camp sites are vivid places indeed. Here the murders actually took place. But the eventual fates of victims in these places required social-political inventions: laws, police, bureaucratic organization, active and passive citizen collaboration. *Who* were responsible for the debacle of Nazism? In the 1980s and 1990s growing numbers of Germans shook their heads and confessed, "A lot of people like us."

Local memorials with that message were slow to come to many urban neighborhoods. Berlin is a prime example. Soon after the war, church and city leaders opted to leave the broken tower of the Kaiser Wilhelm Memorial Church as ambiguous reminder of the devastations of 1945. In upper-class Zehlendorf, a modest four-foot slab of stone in a park, erected in 1960, reads simply, "To the victims, 1933–45." Established in 1952, Berlin's first official *Gedenkstätte* was the Plötzensee prison, where the Nazis executed some 3,000 people including members of the failed conspiracy of July 20, 1944, against Hitler. A few sites of destroyed synagogues acquired markers in the early decades, but on the whole, memories of Berlin's former Jewish population of 50,000 had few public images into the 1970s. For Germans with eyes to detect a vast absence, the invisibility of Jews in Berlin—once home of a great community of Jewish intellectuals and business leaders—is haunting. By the 1970s a few began to ask each other and a growing number of their neighbors: How can the once-upon-a-time existence of Jews and other Nazi victims become real to ongoing generations of Germans in the ordinary intercourse of their daily life? Especially, the victims who once lived right down the street?

Among ongoing individual efforts to help neighbors answer that question was that of a sculptor, Gunter Demnig, who in 2003 was pursuing his project of hammering brass plates—*Stolpersteine*, "Stumbling Blocks"—into sidewalks in Cologne, Hamburg, Berlin, and other cities. Each plate he placed before a house from which a Jew or a Gypsy or other victim had been deported. Each bore an inscription such as:

> Here Lived
> Hermine Baron
> Born Löw
> J8 1866
> Deported 1942
> Theresienstadt
> Murdered
> 22.1.1943

Said Demnig of the 3,200 Stumbling Blocks so far pounded into German sidewalks, "It goes beyond our comprehension to understand the killing of six million Jews. But if you read the name of one person, calculate his age, look at his old home and wonder behind which window he used to live, then the horror has a face on it."[30]

A multitude of such local answers began to emerge in the 1980s and into the 1990s in cities over most of Germany.[31] Taken as a whole, they are the most amazing collection of local testimonies of civic *shame* in any country on earth. Berlin, again, is the outstanding example.

TRACK 17 (THE GRUNEWALD RAMP). From the far southeast corner of Berlin one takes its S-Bahn toward the city center, passing through a forest-park, Grunewald ("Green Wood"). Berliners have great affection for it. They can spend many leisure hours here. S-Bahn tracks pass the park, parallel to those of the major rail line. Sometime in the late 1980s railroad managers planned a track renovation which would have eliminated a freight-loading platform on the southeastern side of the rails. A handful of Jewish leaders had long known that this was the place where thousands of Berlin Jews were gathered in the 1940s for transport to the death camps. With that knowledge publicized in the early 1990s, a movement gathered for permanent marks on the platform detailing the times, the numbers, and the destinations of the Berlin Jews who left Grunewald station never to return. An inscription reads: "To the memory of ten thousand Jewish citizens of Berlin, who from October 1941 until February 1945 were deported from here by the Nazi executioners and murdered in the death camps."

The markings of this history look permanent. Along the full length of the restored platform runs a line of heavy steel plates on which raised letters say: "4/13/1943—56 Jews—Auschwitz . . . 12/10/1944—31 Jews—Auschwitz" on and on down some seventy-five yards of platform. Below on street level rests a memorial sculpture set in a jagged wall. Indented are silhouetted human figures, tilted and off-center. The figures are akin to the crevices and slashes that many recent German architects have used as symbols of irrational, un-centered, wild incursions of evil into "normal" human life. The Nazis dug a deep *ditch* across Europe, these slashes seem to say, a ditch filled with death.[32]

Strollers in Grunewald can easily avoid Track 17 on the park perimeter. As the current catalogue of memorials remarks, the site "is not easy to find." Out of S-Bahn car windows passengers cannot easily identify those steel plates on a far side of the tracks. But the plates are there for any residents of this suburban neighborhood who have learned what the name "Track 17" means in the history of their city. To this track, for example, came some two thousand Jews from the nearby upper-class southeastern borough of Steglitz. In 1993, an association of Steglitzers proposed that the whole community create a local reminder of this fact.

THE STEGLITZ MIRROR WALL. Steglitz is a southwestern Berlin suburb incorporated into the metropolitan government in the 1920s.[33] In the 1930s a large number of upper-level Nazi officials lived here, as well as many other professionals in industry and education. Its S-Bahn stop hosted prosperous shops, theaters, apartments, government offices, churches, and a busy market square. The SS located an office here for arranging contracts with various industries for their use of slave labor from the camps and satellites.

In the 1930s some 3,000 Jews, out of 200,000 other residents, lived in Steglitz. By 1939 emigration reduced the Jewish population to 2,000. Back in 1873 a textile dealer name Moses Wolfenstein had built a small synagogue, not far from the square, with seventy seats for use by the "Religious Association of Comrades in the Jewish Faith in Steglitz." A Nazi gang looted the synagogue on *Pogromnacht*, November 9, 1938. In view of the danger of fire to nearby residences, they decided not to burn it. A bombing raid in 1943 destroyed the Wolfenstein structure as, meantime, the Steglitz Jewish population was sinking from the 2000 of 1939 to the 145 of 1945. Visible reminders of the synagogue sank from public memory as well. The 1980s saw the erection of an apartment building on the site, all but hiding a small remnant of Wolfenstein's "prayer house," now turned into an office.

By 1991, with second-generation leaders now in charge of most local institutions, an association of citizens petitioned the borough council to develop a memorial to the Jews who once lived in Steglitz and to locate it in the marketplace. After a year-long design competition, a jury voted for a *Spiegelwand*, a "mirror wall," eleven meters long and three meters tall, constructed of reflecting black stainless steel, on which would be engraved the name, date of birth, and deportee-destination of every former Jewish residents of the community. Local Gestapo records had survived the bombs, and the final memorial arranges the names of the deported by the page numbers of these records.

In 1993 local residents gathered to view the proposed design, and there followed eighteen months of public quarrel, inside the borough council and outside in Berlin and nationwide. It was, said two residents, Erika and Helmut Reihlen, "a great political consciousness campaign." On the one side were objectors who demonstrated how mixed was general German willingness, forty-five years after 1945, to join in public displays of shame for the Holocaust, the deepest evil in all the evils that Nazism perpetrated in its twelve years of terror: "It doesn't fit our urban environment. . . . The majority doesn't want it. . . . We are no longer anti-semitic, and this wall doesn't bring anyone back to life. . . . This terrible story is now 50 years old. . . . Won't it just attract graffiti? . . . It will just lead to depression and hysteria, destroying optimism. . . . We should honor all victims of the war, such as my relatives. . . . Steglitz was not a site of terror. Fine people have always lived here."

In reply to these claims, supporters of the Mirror Wall stressed that without memory of the Steglitz Jews, reconciliation with any of their few surviving descendants in the community would be forever impossible; that freedom from moral tragedy requires the freedom to remember it; and that this memory was important to transmit to children and grandchildren. The advocates agreed to another round of public discussion of the submitted memorial designs. When a poll was finally taken, a majority of participants voted for the Mirror Wall, but leaders perceived that, among Steglitz residents as a whole, "there was a silent majority against it." That likelihood persuaded the borough council to change the size and central marketplace location of the wall and certain accusing inscriptions. When advocates refused this compromise, the project was stymied. In February 1994 the council voted to abandon it. Particularly embarrassing in this meeting was the loudest objector to the memorial, a neo-Nazi councilman elected by the required 5 percent of the voters. At the testimony of a Jewish guest, a former resident of Steglitz, the deputy walked out slamming the door.

That meeting and abandonment of the project made local, national, and international news headlines, much to the embarrassment of the Berlin city government, especially to members of its elected Senate. A seldom-invoked provision in the city constitution permits the Senate to override decisions of borough councils. A long debate now ensued on the wisdom of invoking this right. The Senate first asked the borough council to reconsider the project. In May 1994 the latter refused, and the Senate promptly voted to override the borough council on the ground that "the mirror wall project was an important cultural event for the whole of Berlin, located as it was at a main crossroads of the city"—located, also, as all Berlin was, in the focus of world concern for Germany's relation to its past. Berlin had a world reputation to build, and its local communities could either fortify or spoil that reputation. It was an unusual override, touching the postwar political sensitivities of the architects of the 1950 Federal Republic: Its constitution had embodied a principled revolt against centralized power.[34]

In September 1994 the foundations of the Mirror Wall were laid, and on June 7, 1995, borough residents and guests gathered in the marketplace to honor its completion. Among the guests were representatives of the Jewish community of Berlin and of Steglitz's sister-community in Israel, Kiriat Bialik. Those present said that they would not soon forget the powerful voice of a Jewish cantor, Estrongo Nachama.

Nine years old in 2004, the Steglitz Mirror Wall stands there, reminding living residents of the murdered dead. It is also there for visitors like myself, who need to be reminded that these 1,723 inscriptions on twelve yards of black steel, to a height of seven feet, are the names of humans once as real as any one of us who stand before the wall. To look at the wall is to see, scattered across some eight or nine names, a reflection of one's own face. You can take photographs of this wall, but you can hardly do so without clicking on that reflection of the photographer.

The two longtime Steglitz residents on whose report this narrative is mostly based summarized the meaning of the memorial and the debate that raged over its construction in these words:

> In what language can we speak about the Holocaust? It is relatively easy to condemn genocide and racism as an anonymous, abstract crime. But with these names, dates of birth, and addresses of homes near *my* home, the murdered neighbor moves up unpleasantly close to me and my family. This hurts. But repression of an evil past hurts more.

> Now the Mirror Wall is the place of two annual memorial assemblies of Steglitz citizens—November 9 and January 27, the one for *Pogromnacht,* the other for Steglitz participation in Germany's national Remembrance Day, the anniversary of the liberation of Auschwitz. Young people come as well as adults. They are the successors of the young who, ten years ago, lifted posters and distributed flyers on behalf of the wall project.

> So now the wall stands there, in the middle of pulsating commerce and social life. These years after its inauguration it is an accepted part of Steglitz. Market merchants protect it. Not a single bit of graffiti has besmirched the wall to date. Often people put flowers there. Our grandchildren ask us what it is all about; and we may find ways of telling them how the Lord finally, in spite of our sins, brought us out of Egypt. Our grandchildren listen. They look into the mirror and make faces. And they go on sucking on their ice cream cones.

THE SCHÖNEBERG LAMPPOSTS: "MULTILAYERED TYPOGRAPHY OF REMEMBRANCE." The Steglitz memorial embodies the next-to-last stage of the road to Auschwitz. A contemporary memorial in nearby Schöneberg informs passersby how it all started. Steglitz citizens are informed, "This is how it ended." But how did it begin? That question invited a more subtle memorial which might steal up on pedestrians as they go about their ordinary daily business, much as did the vast majority of Germans as the lethal tide of the Final Solution began to seep into their society in the early 1930s.

In 1993 the Berlin Senate held a competition entitled, "Art in City Space." Already in Schöneberg, neighbor of Steglitz, a company of several researchers had plowed into local borough records and discovered abundant evidence of how Jews were gradually excluded from meaningful participation in that local community. Organized by architect Florian von Buttlar, an elaborate contest attracted ninety-six designs for a Schöneberg memorial. A jury of thirty diverse professionals pared the candidate designs down to eight, and a small jury of nine chose the winners—Renata Stih and Frieder Schnock, the one an artist and the other an architect specializing in uses of public space. Their proposal: Around one of Schöneberg's beautiful central squares, the Bavarian Quarter, let us put up eighty lamppost "signs of the times," that is from the 1930s, bearing on their one side symbols of everyday life in this upper-class Berlin borough and, on the other, quotations from the 1934 Nuremberg and subsequent laws that gradually severed all civil connection between Jews and their neighbors. Stih and Schnock, says James Young, perceived their upper-class neighborhood as "haunted by its own lying beauty, its most placid and charming neighborhoods seemingly oblivious to the all-too-orderly destruction of its Jewish community during the war."[35]

In the early 1930s some sixteen thousand Jews lived in Schöneberg, which Berliners liked to call "Jewish Switzerland." Physicians, business leaders, public officials, artists, academics, and scientists in great numbers lived here, especially around the graciously upscale Bavarian Quarter. Among them, in 1933, were Albert Einstein, Karl Kautsky, Nelly Sachs, and the three Jewish members of "The Comic Harmonists." In short, if any Berliners had doubt that Jews were thoroughly assimilated to modern Germany, they had only to look to Schöneberg. As one catalogue observes, Jews' banishment from this community was "in a special way inconceivable."[36]

The Nazis had proclaimed the concepts behind the anti-Semitic laws early in their drive to power. In the Schöneberg signs, quotations from the deceptively mild Nuremberg laws ("Jews cannot become actors") give way to a stream of harsher laws over the next ten years ("Jews are not permitted to own radios"). The signs resurrect the steady stream of official laws that would finally take Jews to Auschwitz, offering current residents daily reminders of the insidious "legal" progression toward the genocide of their former Jewish neighbors.

The eighty signs made their first appearance around the square with no public announcement of their significance. Having won the Senate-sponsored contest, Stih and Schnock simply began affixing the signs, provoking protests to the police that neo-Nazis had invaded the neighborhood! The two artists countered with the observation that, when these laws were first introduced to Schönebergers in the 1930s, no citizen called the police or otherwise publicly protested. Well that most Germans are now on their guard against anti-Semitism. How then had they once fallen prey to this virus?

Silent, passive consent was the most pervasive reason. As law tightened its noose around Jewish neighbors, non-Jews stood by in silence. The *dating* of every one of the eighty signs reminds the modern pedestrian of the progressive nature of the disease. (Biological metaphors dominated Nazi ideology, but Nazism itself could as well be subject to the metaphor.) The earliest laws must have seemed almost innocent: Jews forbidden to become actors in 1934— was it not a minor restriction? Or, in 1935, to forbid more than twenty Jewish youths to travel together? Young people like to form gangs, do they not, and gangs can be disturbing, can they not? Swimming pools in the summer, who needs them? But by 1939, the heart of essential community services came under the ban and the jobs of thousands of Schönebergers: "Dentists, dental technicians, druggists, doctors and nurses," forbidden to practice.

In three places adjacent to the square, visitors can find a complete catalogue of the eighty signs. A foreigner needs knowledge of German to comprehend the evil bite in these bits of "art" decorated on reverse sides with innocent pictures of bread, cameras, telephones, radios, bathing trunks, a sidewalk hopscotch drawing, and a shaving razor. The signs clearly and painfully address ordinary local social life. One imagines that a parent, strolling in this attractive square with young children, is likely to be asked, "Why is that picture of a loaf of bread up there?" The answer has to come from the other side of the sign: "Jews in Berlin must buy groceries only during the afternoon hours of four to five." When the inevitable next "why?" comes from a child, adults have some painful explaining to do.

Merely a sample of these signs, with their "nostalgic"[37] little domestic pictures on one side and the sinister genocidal terror inscribed on the other, suggests how subtle, educative, and powerful is this array of historical-artistic public "notices." Here are fourteen others:

> Jews must bear the names "Israel" and "Sara" as additional forenames.
>   (1938)
> Jews are not to go into Berlin bath facilities and swimming pools. (1938)
> Aryan and non-Aryan children are forbidden to play together. (1938)
> Jews must keep their wireless sets off. (1939)
> Jews cannot be members of the German Red Cross. (1938)
> Jews on the Bavarian square must use only the yellow-marked benches.
>   (1939)
> Houses of Jews can be sold without observance of leases and they will be
>   shown so-called Jew houses. (1939)
> Jews must no more leave their homes after 8 P.M. or 9 P.M. in summer.
>   (1939)
> [Jews are] forbidden use of public telephones. (1941)
> Jews will no more get soap and shaving cream. (1941)
> Jews can have no more cigarettes and cigars. (1942)
> During rush hour, Jews must not use public transport. They may sit on
>   seats only if other passengers are not standing. (1941)
> All Jews older than 6 years must wear the yellow star with the label
>   "Jew." (1941)
> Jews must no more buy newspapers and magazines. (1942)

All of these signs belong to the legal clamps of state terror, but there is one late-dated sign that tells of the coming military defeat of the state and the surmise of its leaders that the victors would make vengeful use of proofs that genocide was official Nazi policy: "Documents about anti-Jewish activity are to be destroyed (1945)." Not conscience, but fear of vengeful victors wrote this sign.

There is one lamppost picture not dated and with no written text: three cannisters of Zyklon-B, the poison used to kill in the death camps. Of all the symbols on the eighty signs, this one may be the hardest for parents and grandparents to "explain" to the children. Q: "What happened to the Jews?" A: "They were arrested and deported from Schöneberg, about six thousand." Q: "What were the cans for?" A: "It's the gas used to kill them in Poland."

We hear frequently that "the devil is in the details." This conventional wisdom turns into real history in the demonic details of the Final Solution arrayed across public space in this upper-class Berlin community. Evil can creeps up slowly on the nerve endings of a body politic. It can turn to routine what once was unimaginable. Like the proverbial frog who dies in water gradually heated to boiling, a public can get used to systematic official murder, especially if the final actual murders occur mostly in a far-off Polish place.

Florian von Buttlar, the professional architect who managed much of the process that led to the selection of the Stih-Schnock proposal, has described this work as "art, memorial, and a tool for learning all in one." At the beginning of the selection process, he says, older citizens stated their preference for a memorial resembling that of Steglitz—a public display of the names of all six thousand Jewish residents deported after more than half had emigrated. But young people, in particular, raised deeper questions. "They wondered how all this could have developed in this wealthy quarter of Berlin." Eighty quiet little signs are one answer. Von Buttlar accounts for the widespread admiration of the project along three lines: (1) "It makes sense because it is specific to particular people, places, and events. It addresses a local audience that accepts this art as part of their urban space and daily experience. (2) It shows that the public process of bringing about such a memorial is crucial to its success and acceptance. (3) It shows that the claim that the medium of art cannot deal with this subject is over-generalized. This case is related to many of the concepts of modern art: it refrains from generalized symbols, does not appeal only to emotions but also to discovery, understanding and learning without being purely didactic."[38]

The Schöneberg memorial has prompted large international attention and appreciation. Perhaps no foreigner has written so appreciatively and soberly as has James E. Young. Of artists like Stih and Schnock, who have tried with utmost ingenuity and historical specificity to remind a twenty-first-century German public of the crimes of its twentieth-century predecessors, he writes:

> Where past citizens once navigated their lives according to these
> laws, present citizens would now navigate their lives according to
> the memory of such laws. . . .

The most important "space of memory" for these artists has not been the space in the ground or above it but the space between the memorial and the viewer, between the viewer and his or her own memory: the place of the memorial in the viewer's mind, heart, and conscience. To this end, they . . . return the burden of memory to those who come looking for it. Rather than creating self-contained sites of memory, detached from our daily lives, these artists would force both visitors and local citizens to look within themselves for memory, at their actions and motives for memory within these spaces. . . . [T]hey have attempted to build into these spaces the capacity for changing memory, places where every new generation will find its own significance in this past.[39]

Education of the Young: The Teaching of History

What to remember and what to forget is an important issue for personal mental health, for the writing of history and for the formation of public culture. As two scholars of memory have commented: "An unedited memory is like an unedited book: sprawling and awkward, and having no *sense* against which completeness, interestingness . . . might be measured. As Kierkegaard observed in *Either/Or*, 'If a man cannot forget, he will never amount to much.' "[40] Nor if he or she cannot remember. Utter amnesia and utter photographic memory are heavy personal burdens and, without a mix of remembering and forgetting, history writing, culture, and society itself would be impossible. "A society can be constrained or enabled, disgraced or ennobled, by its own history, depending on how or how much it remembers or forgets."[41]

As we have seen, contemporary Germans have debated, pressured, and fought each other over this "how and how much." What one generation would have preferred to edit out of public memory a second rose up to edit in. A third has now agreed with the second: We must edit our 1933–1945 history by moral measures, they say, no matter how unpleasant it is for most of us.

Psychiatrists are modest about patient control of memory and forgetting. But the architects of Germany's memorials, illustrated here, have had to assume that degrees of *public awareness* of their nation's negative past are subject to citizen deliberation, decision, and political construction. Institutions, leadership, and events internal and external to a society can invite or smother public attention to a morally painful past. As we have seen, sheer pain can be so harrowing to remember that generations as well as individuals can sink into denial. We know from study of victims, perpetrators, and passive viewers of gross human suffering that each is likely to mix memory and forgetting in their own way. The SS murderer seeks comfort in convenient amnesia or in the one or two kindnesses that he did to camp inmates. The camp survivors may try to forget the torture but are not likely to be as successful. Their wounds keep opening. Too horrible to forget, too horrible to remember—that is the mental dilemma of victims worldwide. A third group—the "bystanders" (Mit-läufers or "fellow travelers") has the easiest escape. By extension, the next generation has it easier yet: "Who are we to feel either guilty for what the ancestors did or responsible for paying the cost of remedy to the survivors?"

German Mahnmal makers take up the task of persuading a later generation to assume that responsibility They have learned that intergenerational memory and response have to be skillfully cultivated. One may have to acknowledge the sins of the fathers and mothers rather gradually, step by step, persistently, that is, *educationally*.

I conclude this chapter with two illustrations of ongoing institutional educational work around Germany's negative memory. Those who do this work know the power of public memorial sites of terror, but their devotion to learning, especially in the lives of the young, is more focused on the slow processes of reading books and initiating discussion in school classrooms.

Wannsee

Sometime in the late 1980s there appeared on American Public Television a German-produced documentary film, "The Wannsee Conference." Dubbed in English, the film portrayed, almost to the minute, the two-hour meeting of January 20, 1942, when high Nazi officials perfected plans for the Final Solution. The film introduced me to this bit of history. I remember the genial spirit shared by all fifteen of civilian and military leaders around the table, and the commanding role of the convener of the meeting, Chief of Security Police and the SS Security Service, Reinhard Heydrich.

Built in 1914 for a wealthy Berlin merchant, the Wannsee mansion fell into SS hands for recreational use by its functionaries and their families. Heydrich foresaw the time when the villa would become his own office and home— a dream soon cut short by his assassination by partisans in Moravia. After the war, the villa was successively used for Soviet and American military officers, as a college, and for thirty-six years prior to 1988 as a vacation home for Berlin children. By then very few Wannsee boaters or residents could have identified the villa as a place where the fate of six million Jews was finally sealed.

Young reminds us that the best memorials to negative history "return the burden of memory to those who come looking for it." During my first visit to Berlin in the spring of 1991, I asked my hostess if she would take me to the site of the Wannsee conference. She took me via the road that winds around one of Europe's largest, loveliest lakes, neighbor to the Grunewald, suburban residence of families who can afford it. We reached the gate of the villa only to find it locked. On the pillar to one side of the gate, however, was a plate with an inscription which made the trip worthwhile:

In this house took place in January 1942 the infamous Wannsee Conference.
In memory of our Jewish fellow human beings [*Mitmenschen*]
who perished from the Nazi despotism.

For the moment, the plaque informed me that some Germans, determined to
unearth a buried past, had identified this beautiful place as a sluice-gate to evil.
It would soon become a permanent place of political education, especially for
youth.

Unknown to me in 1991 was the work of historian and Auschwitz survivor
Joseph Wulf, who proposed locating in the villa an "International Documentation Center for Researching National Socialism and Its Consequences." By
1972 political and financial support had failed to materialize, and in 1974 Wulf
took his own life. In 1982 an array of second-generation institutional leaders
would take up his cause. In 1986 they acquired the political and financial
support of the Berlin Senate and then organized an association, "Remembering
for the Future," which brought together government, church, Jewish, museum
and human rights leaders for the purpose of turning the villa into an educational center. In 1989 renovation began, and in 1992, on the fiftieth anniversary of the "notorious conference," Joseph's Wulf's dream of a research center
on "National Socialism and Its Consequences" officially opened under the direction of Gerhard Schönberner.[42]

So, in the winter of 1995, this American walked into the Wannsee Conference Memorial and Place for Learning. Here, if anywhere in Germany,
Mahnmal designers had "used the power of place to make the past vivid." But
it is different from almost all the other places. Its location is far from the center
of Berlin and from well-traveled tourist walkways. You must want to come here.
For four decades the villa was subject of the "displacement process" which
enabled Berliners and others to ignore the disconnect between mass murder
and the bureaucratic planning that produced it. Here in Wannsee, behind doors
decorated with classical motifs, in rooms graced with mirrors and expensive
rugs on spacious grounds that speak of leisure, reflection, and good taste, was
the terror-behind-the-terror, prior to the prison bars, the execution pits, and
the ovens.

The ground floor of the villa spreads out into a dozen rooms to the right
and left of the central "Hall of Nations" which suffered Nazi terror. Across the
walls of all these rooms spread photographs of the roundups, the deportations,
the resistance, and the deaths of Jews from the early to the last years of the
regime. Many of these pictures are familiar worldwide to people of my wartime
generation, but not to all the young people for whom the Wannsee center is
specifically designed. Any day one is likely to find groups of high school students touring these rooms under the guidance of a staff member.

The large room to the right, labeled "The Conference," most visitors are urged to see first. Its beautiful appointments breathe luxury in every detail: floor-length windows for sunniness, space for flowers and garden views, and a long polished table in the middle. On the wall opposite the lake view are photographs of the fifteen participants in the conference of January 20, 1942. Here is Heydrich, who controlled the meeting and turned it from a "conference" into an announcement of plans the SS had already devised for dealing with "the Jewish question." Here is Eichmann, secretary to the meeting, already at work on the transportation system for getting Jews from all over occupied Europe to death camps in "the East." And here were the assorted other military and civilian bureau chiefs, some super-ready for the solution that Heydrich brought with him, some queasy about its absolute violence.[43]

No visitor with imagination will absorb the quiet beauty of this room without an inward gasp, especially if he or she turns an eye to a one-page document that the Center has put under glass on the table. It is an original typescript. On one side of the page is a list of some thirteen countries—"Germany, Poland, France, Ukraine. . . ." On the other is a column of numbers—"200,000; 3,000,000; 100,000; 1,000,000. . . ." And at the bottom a total: "11,000,000." That was the agendum of the two-hour meeting. Eleven million European Jews.

The purpose of the Wannsee Center is not to impose paralysis on any visitor, but this one American must admit that a single sheet of paper, in this setting, exerts paralyzing effects. As in the camps, one keeps asking: How could they? For a while one asks without expecting any answer.

This center does not mean to leave that question unanswered. It invites visits to the second floor, locus of its research library and educational department. There in shelves and files are specialized records of educational projects from throughout Germany for acquainting a coming generation with the origins, the processes, and the results of the murders of 1933–1945. To plow through a few of these documents is to glimpse the determination of thousands of German school teachers and their students, post-1945, to get as close as possible to comprehending the incomprehensible. One file, for example, records the work of a local high-school teacher in Kassel, where in 1982 the 1932-Berlin-born sculptress E. R. Nele designed and built a memorial to a military prison camp once located in Kassel. The artwork is a railroad boxcar from which people seem to be exiting. Looking closely, one sees only shells of empty clothes. The human wearers have disappeared. In 1985 this memorial went up in flames set by a local gang of protesters, whereupon a Kassel high-school teacher asked her students to undertake a restoration. They did so along with study of the history of the Nazi time in Kassel.

The file on E. R. Nele contains a late entry from 1997, a poem by her friend Erich Fried. It could stand as succinct expression of the duality of remembering-and-forgetting that will haunt any careful student of this fearsome subject.

> Remembering,
> That is perhaps
> The most agonizing way
> Of forgetting
> And perhaps
> The kindest way
> Of relieving
> This agony.[44]

As this example suggests, the materials of this library cross many disciplinary boundaries. Poetry, fiction, autobiographies, photographs, film, tapes, newspapers, microfiche, and government reports on neo-Nazism abound, all open for use by scholars and other visitors. But to this passive resource the staff of the Center adds an active educational program which draws participants from adult education groups, professional training schools, local high schools, and student groups from Germany and European countries.

The Center's most striking educational specialty focuses on trainees in the professions. Whether for the trades or the so-called learned professions, the licensing and accreditation process in Germany is rigorous. One unique requirement among some current official regulations is that candidates must have at least minimal acquaintance with recent German history, the Nazi era in particular. So young trainees for careers in medicine, the military, business, education, public safety, transportation, religion, or the skilled trades are apt to be sent by their schools for a day at the Wannsee center. The staff aims at helping students to imagine their way into the circumstances of their peers in the Nazi era. How were railroad employees persuaded to pull out of Track 17 with boxcars full of Jews? How was it that police and firemen stood by while the hooligans burned synagogues on *Nazikristallnacht*?[45] Why did young Wehrmacht lieutenants stand by as Jews and Russian prisoners of war were done to death? Why do the rules governing the conduct of even privates in the modern German army *require* that they disobey immoral orders and know what constitutes such orders? After 1933, if you were a schoolteacher, would you have reported on parents whose children showed signs of disagreeing with the Nazis? As a nurse, would you have secretly given scarce medical treatment to Jewish patients? As a factory manager, what were your inducements for accepting slave labor? How might the government have persuaded you to manufacture Zyklon-B? As a rental agent, would you have taken a commission for hastening the evacuation of a "Jew House" for reoccupancy by a local Aryan family? Had you been a hair-dresser in the 1930s, would you have obeyed the government preference for uniform female hair styles that signified ideal German womanhood?

For the teaching of interwoven history, empathy for the dilemmas of everyday life among one's peers of the past, and the meaning of professional-civic responsibility, this philosophy of youth and adult education is powerful. It seeks to add to sober appreciation of a past society an equally sober imperative of personal integrity in the present.

Two pages of catalogue note that this *Bildungsstätte* teaches young Germans to envision the "bureaucratic, everyday side of Nazi crime," against the camps and the former Gestapo prisons which embody the raw, brutal side. Both were servants of one "social process of repression" requiring the collaboration, in some dimension, of millions of citizens. One leaves this beautiful lakeside mansion less able than before to project full blame for the evils of one's own society onto someone else.

Public Education: History Classes and History Books

The two-hour Wannsee conference was a fearsome demonstration of the power of a coordinated set of bureaucratic systems. Under the Nazis, preparing the minds of young Germans in the 1930s for collaboration with those systems was a prime task of public schools. They, too, were subject to "coordination" (*Gleichschaltung*).

How that coordination took place in one local Berlin community has been remarkably documented in a book researched and published in the same years of the movement for the erection of the Steglitz *Spiegelwand*. Under the leadership of historian Dr. Doris Fürstenberg, a teacher and staff member of the Steglitz office of public education, a cross section of twenty citizens undertook study of the records of the 1933–1945 era documenting how the new government molded every sector of the local community to conform to Nazi aims for the whole country.[46] The book could never have been written apart from the official German habit, assumed under the Nazis as well as among the perpetrators of other genocides, of keeping careful official records of virtually every contact between the agents and the victims of state-sponsored terror, as, for example, Cambodia in the mid 1970s.

The step-by-step processes for expanding the ideological reach of the central government into the schools included measures like these:

- The "freeing" of library collections from "alien writings" and documents, such as books by and about Jews, including music manuscripts of Felix Mendelssohn, all allocated to a special "Poison Bookshelf" not open for general use.
- With the collaboration of local physicians, an elaborate system of classifying the fits and the misfits of German society, ranging all the way from Jews to children of racially mixed marriages, the incurably diseased, mental defectives, epileptics, cripples, and other hereditary defectives—some to be designated as candidates for sterilization, others to be killed. In reverse, the racist scale went up to young couples

deemed fit for marriage to the yet more fit for becoming godparents (e.g., to Heydrich Himmler's daughter) to the highest class of all, local Steglitzers thought to be fit for SS membership.[47]

- The split in local churches between "German Christians" and "The Confessing Church," which in Steglitz yielded public debates, disputed elections of officers, mutual rejections of leadership, demonstrations of opposition and of loyalty to the "German way" of Christianity, competition for use of church spaces and schedules, and standoffs that endured all through the war.
- The collaboration of some church leaders in official persecution of Jews, in contrast with a few "people of good will who did what they could" to protect Jews, to no avail against "the murder of unnumbered human beings" that was to come.[48]
- A sketch of the rising bureaucratic career of Steglitzer Martin Wülfing who "through his unspectacular exercise of power" became one of the numerous bureaucrats who were "indispensable for a consolidation of the National Socialist regime."[49]

In view of the anger and shame which the twenty authors undoubtely felt as they researched this local history, the entire volume is another Steglitz Mahnmal. Because most in the 1990s worked in some quarter of educational institutions, the final hundred pages of this research on the Nazi Steglitz school system must have struck home to them with great mixtures of feeling. Here they record how Nazism infiltrated public education to effect:

- The measures taken to set up "schools for backward children," with orders to top officials to assign some to sterilization, others to execution.
- Official versions of German history set down for history teachers in middle, vocational, and high schools, accenting Nazi theories of race, the historical formation of a "pure" German people and national "character," and the climax of German development on January 30, 1933.
- Regular monthly meetings of teachers in every school, to strengthen their work "from the standpoint of national uplift. . . . [W]e seek above all in the monthly conferences to build up trust in the good concepts of National Socialism." In particular, an official protocol mandated in 1938,

> (1) The most important political events of the day must be continuously mentioned, not so much as to what happened as how it happened. This is not only a matter of explanation to children but also so that through them the parents may also be influenced. . . . (3) It is established that the Leader of our people pulls us not to war but to peace and pursues no

agitation for war. (4) All of our discussions must be aligned
with the thought: "Führer command! We follow thee!"[50]

Along with flag-raising at the opening of the semester, mutual Nazi salutes
between teachers and students, plus singing of the German national anthem
and the Horst Wessel song, ceremonial obeisance to the State here completed
the conceptual. But as they conclude their chapters on the schools, these authors of the 1990s are most explicit about depths of collaboration to which
their predecessors of the 1930s descended as their daily work in and outside
the classroom led inexorably to the elimination of the Steglitz Jews and their
children from local society. Theories of race and ridicule of Jewish students
before their peers were standard classroom procedure, and then, after November 9, 1938, the very study of Judaism fell under comprehensive *Verbot*. As of
November 10 no classes for Jewish children in their religion would "any longer
be tolerated." It was a moment in which "the politics of 'Race-separation' between 'Germans' and 'Jews' turned out finally to be a stage on the way to racist
mass-murder in all Europe."[51]

The book that traces this embarrassing history, authored by contemporary
educators in Steglitz, constitutes an act of professional repentance for the fall
of a whole generation of public school teachers into the clutches of Nazi ideology. Postwar West Germany saw a massive revulsion against it all in the
organization and philosophy of education throughout the country. Teacher
training and selection, curriculum planning, and textbook choice became decentralized to the twelve states (*Länder*). While teachers in East Germany found
themselves bound to official central control of the details of classroom process
and content, West German schoolteachers had to make decisions about how
to approach their subjects. Students were to be trained in the arts of independent, critical thinking. By about 1970, gone were the days when a teacher could
avoid controversy over the Nazi era by ending the study of history with the
Weimar Republic. Now students expected to hear all about the horrors with
which their grandparents were active or passive collaborators. The second postwar generation of teachers was determined, like the authors of the Steglitz
studies, not to protect a future generation of German young people from memory of that dark past. They were so thorough in serving that determination that
some of their students, in the 1990s, raised a question: "Are you trying to
crush us with knowledge of that past? Isn't it a bit much?"

That was one of the issues in a class discussion which this author joined
in the spring of 1999. A high school (*Gymnasium*) teacher in the upper class
borough of Zehlendorf—neighbor to Steglitz—invited us to visit a history class
composed of level thirteen students. The "academic" curriculum of the
German public school system extends over thirteen years. At three different
points—level 4, level 8, and level 12 or 13—teachers expect to introduce materials about the Nazi era and the Holocaust. By the time students come to this

formal study, they have already seen television, film, memorials, and public events that furnish many images of this history. They may not have visited a concentration camp site, but before they graduate they are likely to do so. Average age in this class was seventeen.

Soon after introductions of the two American visitors, it became clear that these students had an intense interest in their American peers. Several class members had spent summers in the United States, and they reported with amusement how little American high school students seemed to know about contemporary young Germans. "They would ask us if we knew what a *swastika* was. It took a while for us to understand that it was their word for the Nazi symbol we call *Hakenkreuz*. Know what it is? We have known for years and years! We get the impression that Americans don't study history as much as we do."

The discussion then turned to the experience of these several students in observing how Americans celebrate national holidays, especially the Fourth of July. "All those flags, all those bands and fireworks, and the big patriotic speeches—they're frightening if you are a German." The minds of these young people were replete with images of Nazi banners, torch parades, military bands, and mass marches. They had been raised to reject it all, and they were not very patient with their peers in America entranced by Fourth of July flags, parades, and picnics. Among all young generations on earth, Germans are suspicious of any public event that smacks of "nationalism." At the same time they are frank to say that they wish they could be counted as citizens of a "normal" nation, one not perpetually freighted in the eyes of others with the burden of the Holocaust.

They are so well acquainted with the gross facts of the Holocaust that the eyes of many will glaze over when you ask, "Do you know all about Auschwitz?" More than one member of this class allowed that they knew only too much about it. "By this time we have studied it three times over, and frankly one gets 'up to here' with it." Touched here is an educational issue that ought to concern every educator convinced that a younger generation should be informed of the dark side of their national history as well as the bright. Can the study of past horror become so routinized that it is no longer felt as horrible? Confronted too often, do histories of genocide become subject to the "psychic numbing" to which *genocidaires* themselves are vulnerable?[52] The question troubled one of the young women in this class. She came up to us at the end of the hour and said, "It is true that you will find a lot of people my age saying they have 'had it up to here' with the Holocaust. But I believe that this was an evil that we must study and study again. It is too important for us ever to stop studying it."

Those who plan the modern German public school curriculum obviously agree. They intend to keep teaching the facts and the moral corruptions of the Nazi era, and they adopt history textbooks that portray it all in blunt, vivid terms. Decentralized as public education became in West Germany after the war, there is undoubtedly a great variety of approaches to the study of this negative history, all influenced by the choices of individual teachers. By the late 1960s West German teachers were stoutly resisting ideological curriculum control. They were trained to raise questions about the past, to encourage class discussion, and to equip students to undertake individual projects of historical investigation, as the Kassel story illustrates. To be sure, adults who had graduated from West German high schools in the 1950s and early 1960s testify that their history teachers often ended the semester with the Weimar Republic. To do so must have been very tempting for any teacher who feared the question from students, "What did you do in the Nazi-time?"

A small sample of high school history books from the 1990s will strike any foreigner with a certain astonishment at the candor, realism, and comprehensiveness of accounts meant for reading by German youth. With no standard text mandated by government, German history teachers have more choice in textbooks than do teachers in Texas and California. In a country whose laws forbid the display of a swastika and a revival of the Nazi party, a national supervisory board does ensure that there is no blinking at the evils of 1933–1945 in high school history classes.

For example, a top-listed text from one publisher is *Geschichte und Geschehen*, a three hundred-page survey of twentieth century history, published in 1997, slated to be used with students of about age fifteen. Eight university-based historians author the book, all, probably, scholars of the second postwar generation.

At first blush, an American who remembers high school history courses will blink at the intellectual maturity assumed here for ninth-and tenth-grade students. They are clearly assumed to have graduated from "elementary" history. Not only does the prose not speak down to them but the scope of its content assumes minds engaged with the widening world of nations in the twentieth century, beginning with the Soviet revolution of 1917 and ending with "the many worlds in the one world" of Germany, Europe, the Americas, Asia, Africa, and the intercontinental poor. Black-and-white and color photographs, maps, graphs, time lines, political cartoons and posters, paintings, drawings, survey data, and original period documents enliven the prose on almost every page, like many modern school texts in American schools whose systems can afford such richly appointed volumes.

As an aid to the grappling of young minds with the shadows of the Nazi era, this history text has four striking features: (1) In text and in pictures, it spares few details of the persecution of peoples by the Nazi regime. (2) It probes this and other periods of German history in chapter-ending *Fragen und Anregungen* (questions and discussion suggestions) that call for students to identify the contradictions, the unresolved issues, and the mix of decision and external influence in the actions of a former generation. (3) At the end of the volume it invites readers, to formulate their own philosophic positions on the key ethical issue of the place of war and violence in human society—is peace possible between human beings? (4) Finally, in a striking invitation to think about the complexities of history writing, it asks how "history" gets constructed, who makes it, what "good" its study serves, how limited it is as a guide to contemporary action, yet how utterly indispensable it is for a truly human life.

In a last word to readers, the text quotes Erich Kaestner, author of many books for young people, who states the German predilection for historical grounding of human consciousness. History may be either curse or blessing to remember, but remember it we must if we are to retain our humanity:

> Whoever begins to tell about himself must begin with his forebears. For without the forebears one would be like someone shipwrecked in the ocean of time on an uninhabited desert island, all alone. Utterly alone, without mother, grandmother, or great grandmother. Through our forebears we are joined with the past and from centuries back closely related and married to them. And one day we ourselves will have become forebears. For human beings, those who today are not yet born are nonetheless already connected with us.[53]

This is weighty philosophic stuff for fifteen-year-olds, born after 1980 but informed from childhood of grandparents whose generation bequeathed to their grandchildren convincing evidence that philosophies can yield human benefits and harms on a vast scale.

The Nazi-era pages of this text begin with a collage of pictures of a torch parade through the Brandenburg Gate, Russian civilians fleeing from the burning of their villages in 1942, the court trial of leaders of the failed plot against Hitler in July 1944, the ruins of Dresden in early 1945, and the scarcely alive survivors of a liberated concentration camp. The ensuing fifty pages ask students to understand and critique: Nazi posters, propaganda concepts from the mouth of Joseph Goebbels, the mass rallies, the "coordination" of primary and high schools for training in National Socialist ideology, the Hitler youth organizations, the book burnings of 1933, the controversies of the Protestant and Catholic churches over obedience to the new government, anti-Semitic caricatures and slogans in school texts, Anne Frank, the "Judenpass" system, Jews in transport to Auschwitz, children there, the crematoria ovens there, the "selection" process there, camp survivor writings on life and death in the camps, the Himmler Posen speech to the SS, accounts of resistance movements, the German invention of air bombing of civilians in Guernica, Rotterdam, and London, the countervengeance of the Allied air war, statistical totals on the deaths of Jews in the Final Solution, and the final catastrophe of 1945 that left the women of Berlin to pick up bricks for the building a new Germany.

To compile a summary list like this may be to image this or any history book as a catalogue of dates and events which render the study of history (famously in the United States) as the most boring subject in the curriculum. Through over-repetition it may be so for many contemporary German high school youth, but the authors of this text punctuate and tie together these narratives with questions for class discussion of how the debacle of Nazism could have occurred, how the history might have turned out differently, and what connection it all has with questions facing German society today. A skilled and committed teacher will use this book to engage students with active back-and-forth analysis of past and present. Here is a sample of the questions that dot the *Nazizeit* section of the text:

> Put yourself in the place of a concentration camp prisoner. How would you respond to the poster that tells you to practice "obedience, honesty, cleanliness, truthfulness, sacrifice and love for Fatherland"?
>
> How do you understand the weak resistance of the churches?
>
> You see in this chapter evidences of Nazi "art." What must art be if it is not to be assessed as "degenerate"?
>
> How do you understand hate and the repression of minorities?
>
> Look at the picture of the crowd of SA troopers and their banner slogan, "The Jew is no citizen (*Bürger*) but a murderer (*Würger*). How do you interpret their gestures and mimicking?
>
> The order to German armies in the USSR in 1941 calls for "merciless extermination of the alien malice and cruelty," i.e. the Soviet troops. What is the meaning of saying that the German soldiers now have a "duty to surpass the weak, one-sided military tradition" of the past?
>
> In response to the 1985 statement of Günter Grass that after Auschwitz "a millstone hangs over us Germans," how should one deal with the memory of Auschwitz?
>
> Explain why the women of Rosenstrasse[54] were successful. Can one learn from them?
>
> Why did so many early opponents of the Nazis come to support them?
>
> What is the right word for May 8, 1945? "Defeat, capitulation, catastrophe, Day of Liberation"? Was it the result of "fate" or "capitalism" or "guilt"? Were our contemporaries of the postwar years over-occupied with this question? What about us? What answers would you give today to the questions of that time?
>
> "This past should forever engage us." Justify your agreement or disagreement with this statement.

Modern historians have often debated whether or not history writing should be "value-free." Whatever else can be said about the history that

German high school students are now asked to read, it is far from value-free. Doubtless some students and teachers bristle at some of these pages—"We are tired of being preached to about that Nazi past!" Ethical preaching of a sort does indeed shout in the above section of *Geschichte und Geschehen*. Not only do the authors say loudly and clearly, "Nazism was a horrible moral error," but they challenge young readers to assume a burden, not of collective German guilt, but collective German shame:

> It was easy to say "the circumstances" or "capitalism" or "fate" were to blame. We rightly assign shares of guilt to the leadership of the economy, bureaucracy, aristocracy, and military. But: greater civil courage belonged then and belongs now to those who are responsible for their own guilt, their own omissions, their own neglects, their own cowardice and to learn from it. . . .
>
> Margaret and Alexander Mitscherlich called their own unreadiness to come to terms with their own past, and to be responsible for their own guilt, the "Inability to mourn." Most Germans made Hitler responsible, him alone. Or they shoved the guilt off on the National Socialists—them alone. It was controversial whether there was a general German guilt, a "collective guilt." Little disputed was the claim that there should be a common German shame, over what Germans had done in crime against humanity: a "collective shame."[55]

This is history speaking about the past for moral instruction to a young generation. It speaks to the present in tones not far from those of Thomas Mann, in exile in America during the Nazi era. On the last page of this high school text is an article by Mann, written only four days after May 8, 1945, for a Ruhr newspaper. He sought to speak pointedly to every surviving German. One would like to have been in more than one high-school classroom in 1999 to hear the discussion of whether contemporary students accept or resist so blunt a moral sermon from an eminent German of the past:

> The thick-walled torture cellar which Hitlerism has made Germany is broken up, and our shame lies open before the eyes of the world, to the foreign commissions, to whom these unbelievable images now will be shown and reported at home, surpassing everything in hideousness, what humans can conceive.
>
> "Our shame," German reader. For everyone who speaks German, writes German, has lived in Germany, is hit with this disgraceful naked exposure. It was not a few criminals, it was hundreds of thousands of so-called German elite, men, young people, and inhuman women, who under the influence of insane doctrine have been led by the nose into the sick joy of these crimes . . . Humanity

shudders. In the presence of Germany? Yes, in the presence of Germany.[56]

For fifty years many young Germans have echoed that shudder. Out of thrice-over study of the Nazi era in classrooms and regular reminders of television, film, public gatherings, and the presence of a Mahnmal down almost every street, they have been schooled in every sense to experience the difficulties of ever experiencing unambiguous pride in being Germans. "You Americans seem to think that patriotism is a good thing. We Germans had too much partiotism. We wonder if it is possible in today's world to be patriotic."

Is patriotism possible? Is there a formula for combining civic shame with civic pride to yield an honest patriotism? The rest of this book explores the question. Germans have memorably posed it.

2

South Africa

In the Wake of Remembered Evil

During my lifetime I have dedicated myself to this struggle of the African people. I have fought against white domination, and I have fought against black domination. I have cherished the ideal of a democratic and free society in which all persons live together in harmony and with equal opportunities. It is an ideal which I hope to live for, and to achieve. But if needs be, it is an ideal for which I am prepared to die.

—Nelson Mandela[1]

I could walk the length of my cell in three paces. When I lay down, I could feel the wall with my feet and my head grazed the concrete at the other side. The width was about six feet, and the walls were at least two feet thick. Each cell had a white card posted outside it with our name and our prison service number. Mine read, 'N. Mandela 466/64,' which meant I was the 466th prisoner admitted to the island in 1964. I was forty-six years old, a political prisoner with a life sentence, and that small cramped space was to be my home for I knew not how long.

—Nelson Mandela[2]

Both warders expressed affection for Mandela and the clear recognition, even then, that he would some day be the President of South Africa.

—Walter Sisulu[3]

Mandela would be eighteen years there plus nine more in mainland prisons.

The place is seven and a half miles offshore from beautiful Cape Town. For millennia its semitropical shores have been host to forest, penguins, springbok, whales, and fish innumerable. From the seventeenth century it served governments of South Africa as sea defense outpost, asylum for lepers and the insane, and prison for aggressive political opponents. After the last rebellious tribal chiefs died or left in the nineteenth century, it remained rather deserted. Then, in 1961, the apartheid government decided to turn it into its version of Alcatraz: maximum security for dangerous criminals and political radicals.

From 1964 to 1982, this place, Robben Island, would be his "home." When at last the government let him out of prison he was already a world-class hero. He remained in 2004 a living memorial to the tragedies and triumphs of political struggle in his remarkable country. No museum, statue, library, or study center will ever personify twentieth-century South African history as forcefully as will the career of Nelson Rolihlahla Mandela.

But heroes and their biographies suffer diminishing images in the minds of their young successors. The new leaders of the new South Africa have a profound stake in being sure that a younger generation does not take the collapse of the racist apartheid order for granted. Teachers in the country's professional schools in 2002 testified that their young students, white and black, are eager to "get on" with tools for taking advantage of new economic opportunities. They know that honor belongs to a son of a Xhosa chief who became their first black president, but his inauguration was eight years ago, and his successor, Thabo Mbeki, is also eager to get on with the future. Nowadays young South Africans take the new nonracial political order so much for granted that they pay only episodic attention to the struggles of those who resisted the old order.

Lourens du Plessis, for example, a distinguished professor of constitutional law at South Africa's Stellenbosch University, the academic crown of Afrikaner higher education, participated in the extensive national debates, 1993–1996, on the country's new constitution. In a March 2002 interview he said of his law students: "Yes, they look chiefly towards their own future. But I tell them: 'You had better pay attention to the recent history of this country. One of these days your children and your grandchildren will ask you if it is true that once the country was organized around blatant racism. They will want to know how that was possible and how it stopped. You will need an answer.' "

Racism has a thousand faces the world over, but its South African version has long exerted a powerful pull on the imagination of Americans, especially those of us whose lifetimes have encompassed struggles against the racist legacies of our own national history. In turn, South Africans, especially black South Africans, followed the course of the American civil rights movement in the 1950s, and 1960s, just as the clamps of apartheid pressed tighter around the whole of that society. Analogies between the struggles in the two countries have been unavoidable as well as inexact. The legalized racism of modern South Africa was so blatant that the somewhat less radical version in the United States comforted some Americans, especially whites, that "at least we are not as bad as South Africa." The more sober observation would have been: "Thanks to the civil rights movement, our battle against this democracy-corrupting virus was one generation in advance of the South African." From that fact some South Africans drew their diverse lessons. Whites there could say, "But South Africa's problems are different." Blacks could say: "If Martin Luther King and company could do it, so can we."

Ironically, in 2003, African American leaders of the civil rights movement of 1955–1970, also express anxiety about the historical consciousness of their younger constituents. "They take for granted that they have all the rights of anyone else. They are shocked and puzzled that any of their parents and grandparents could ever have put up with segregated water fountains, restaurants, and universities. They don't understand what their elders had to go through to reach the current level of opportunity in American society."[4]

Like their German counterparts, modern South Africa has leaders determined that the young of their country will not forget the costs of the changes they have enjoyed for a scant decade. As in Germany, these leaders are at work to preserve certain remnants of an awful past for the sake of training upcoming generations in the moral and political tasks of a democratic order. For this task foreigners have reason to visit South Africa, if only for reassurance that a world struggle against racism is not hopeless. Surely, if any country on earth represents both the making and unmaking of racist society, it is South Africa. The skeptics watch South Africa to see if it can really be the place where a Nelson Mandela and a Desmond Tutu will have a steady stream of successors. Racism is a mutable virus.

That is reason enough for recommending to foreign visitors to South Africa that they begin their travel in the country with a visit to Robben Island. No place is a better start if one wants to touch the stubborn threads of evil woven through the fabric of this country's remarkable modern history.

The Island

A ferry will take you there now, every hour through the day, for one hundred rand.[5] The island's bean-shaped perimeter measures eight miles. Around it laps "a bitterly cold sea that snaps at the hulls of ships. Thick islands of kelp bob in the waters close to the shale beaches, and crayfish, lobster and perlemoen drift in its small inlets." Its geological history remains uncertain, but its human history over the past four centuries makes it "a small heart cut from the mainland bosom that for years monitored and regulated the pulse of a nation." Only a tiny handful of prisoners have ever escaped, by rowboat or swimming, through these rolling ocean waves to the mainland.[6]

On a clear day, one can just glimpse it from atop Table Mountain, the massive escarpment that frames the beauty of Cape Town. From the dockside of the island, a glance back at the city clustered under the shadow of that flat peak persuades most visitors to nominate Cape Town as the world's most beautiful city.

But history afflicts that beauty with slashes of memory that bring tears. One thinks of Weimar and the Liebeskind museum in Berlin.

The ferry pulls into the island harbor, and on the wharf passengers see first signs of what the place used to be: photographs of prisoners who arrived on ferries, chained together and manacled, the last accrual of the "Lawbreakers, Lunatics, and Lepers"[7] who have been exiled here for three centuries. The crowd of forty visitors, mostly white and foreign, climb aboard a bus for the first of two stages of tour. On this day in 2002, our first tour guide is a young man whose images of the island history are secondhand. The second will be an older man who spent seven years here, 1983–1990. His crime was protest against the Bantu Education Act of 1983, whereby black children were to be taught reading, writing, and arithmetic through only seven grades. Someone in our group, asks him, "How do you feel about the time you spent here?" He replies: "I'm angry, but I am not sorry. I am angry at the loss of seven years of my youth from sixteen to twenty-three. My generation of protesters were *hauled* up to maturity, we didn't grow up. While my peers were pursuing marriage and careers, I was in this place. But I'm not sorry as I look back. *Somebody* had to pay a pound of flesh to get rid of apartheid. I had to be one of them."

Our other, younger guide has appropriated his own mixture of anger and pride at the men imprisoned here, not for murder but for politics. He uses humor to interpret history. We draw up to a razor-wired fence that encloses a dozen watchdog pens and a lone six-by-eight-foot bungalow. "How many of you know the name of Robert Sobukwe?" he asks. Two or three hands go up. "How many, Steve Biko?" A dozen hands. "How many, Nelson Mandela?" All hands go up. They are all heroes for him. But finally he asks, "How many, Lukas Mothale?" Questioning looks, tentative memories, several hesitant hands. He smiles mischievously. "That's my name."

One passenger alights from the bus and shakes his hand. "I have just shaken the hand of another great man!" she testifies. "Yes!" he exclaims. "Each of us!" He knows that apartheid was the denial of that proposition.

By our long stop and long explanation at the site of the Sobukwe "home," Lucas Mothale wants to rectify the ignorance of most white visitors concerning this man, as fully a hero in his estimate as Mandela. In the 1950s Sobukwe was the president of the Pan-African Congress, an anti-apartheid movement, rival to the ANC and loosely affiliated with Poqo, an organization which was openly committed to violence against white and black supporters of the government. He was a powerful orator; so powerful that, under Prime Minister Vorster in 1963, he acquired the distinction of having an annual parliament law passed against him personally, a law that sent him, after his 1960–1963 years in mainland prison, to Robben Island for the next six years. His "private home" there marked him as a leader whom the government both feared to kill and feared to give the chance to influence fellow prisoners. Instead it killed him by degrees. He lived in this little house under absolute solitary confinement, forbidden reading material, outside exercise, and the right to speak with anyone, including the guard. Prisoners like Mandela, "walking to and from the quarries would risk punishment by waving to him or singing to boost the spirits of the lone figure standing at a window."[8] But in his utter isolation Sobukwe's mind, body, and spirits began to collapse. The government finally removed him to house arrest on the mainland in Kimberly, where he lingered until death in 1975.

For Lucas Mothale, the Sobukwe house is a memorial to one of new South Africa's founding fathers. He regrets that the name Sobukwe receives little mention in the West, and he educates visitors accordingly. He does not say so, but the suggestion is there: Had Nelson Mandela been subjected to the same extreme cruelty of isolation during his eighteen years in this place, he too might have gone mad.[9]

The moral madness of the apartheid system gets token expression in our older guide's tour of the former cell blocks. In the 1960s prisoners slept here on sisal mats spread on the concrete floors. By the late 1970s bunk beds arrived. Along the rims of a courtyard lie the individual cells of political prisoners. One cell was Mandela's for eighteen years. Late in his time here bookshelves graced this cell, but the museum makers in 2002 chose to display only the necessities of the early years: latrine bucket, mat, blanket, and tin cup. The prisoners on this hall all belonged to a band of heroes, so both of our guides want us to know. They continued the revolution under these new conditions, and Mandela himself would later say that their captors' big mistake was letting them remain in communication with each other.[10]

In the dormitory side of the prison we are introduced to more of the absurd, vicious refinements of the apartheid system as it governed men confined here. Rules required every prisoner to have a pass card, parallel to the infamous passes which every mainland black person had to carry since 1960.[11] As on the mainland, different prison privileges adhered to different races. (The greatest privilege belonged to white criminals, exempted altogether from being sent to The Island.) Inside these walls, an Asian or a "colored" inmate had a richer diet than blacks. The latter got less meat, no bread, tea or coffee once rather than twice a day, and in general fewer calories. A poster advertises the discriminatory diet system: If one is not fully human, one needs less nourishment. Our guide is especially furious as he tells it.

After two hours on Robben, our ferry pulls away from the dock and heads back across the seven and a half miles of ocean to Cape Town. A crew member solicits passengers for a donation to the Mandela Museum, the displays on his career at the Cape Town dock. Artifacts related to the island museum are still being collected under the direction of scholars at the University of Cape Town. A year or so from now, visitors will have yet more vivid images of what went on in a place that was "without question the harshest, most iron-fisted outpost in the South African penal system."[12]

One hardly has to ask why there are so few black visitors in this company of tourists. The hundred-rand ferry fee is intimidation enough, but one suspects that some are not ready for the pain of visiting here. Besides, plenty of information about the apartheid system lodges in the memory of everyone more than fifteen years old in South Africa. What may need explaining is why white Europeans, Americans, and (one hopes) white South Africans currently flock to this memorial every day of the week. What about this horrible remnant of oppression attracts them—attracts *us*?

For American visitors the answer depends very much on whether you are white or black. In 2003 Congressman John Lewis of Atlanta joined a group of colleagues in visiting the Island. After seeing the cells, Lewis broke down in tears, shaken by the contrast between the oppression and the new liberation represented in the emptiness of these cells, shaken, too, by the analogy to his own history as a leader of the civil rights movement. No white American can miss the justice in that analogy.

On the trip around the island the guides take you to the limestone quarry where prisoners of the 1960s worked day after day in hot summer sun and cold winter winds. The glare from the white stone injured the eyes of many prisoners, including Mandela. For three years they tried to persuade a prison physician to recommend to the chief warden that dark glasses be permitted, else prisoners would go blind.[13] In the quarry and elsewhere the best educated prisoners carried on their covert "university" for teaching their fellows to read, write, and grasp principles of law and politics. Now, at the entrance to the quarry, there rests a rounded pyramid of stones, about three feet high, placed there, we learn, by former political prisoners who in 1996 undertook a reunion on the island. Nelson Mandela, by now President Mandela, put down the first stone. The others followed. They decided to have this reunion every five years. So there it is—a heap of rocks whose meaning has to be perceived through the viewer's knowledge of the history of this place. Like the first ripples of stones thrown into a pond, these stones radiate history. Robben Island is no incidental link in the chains of injustice that have infested this vast continent over many a century. Its temporal ripples touch large histories of slavery, colonialism, racism, and struggles for power between peoples near and far. Nazi racism had its agents and allies on this tip of the continent. Here, as in the United States, a post-1945 fight against robust racism erupted around the burning question: Are white people justified in classifying the rest of humanity as "nonwhite"?

An angry, sad, repentant "no" brings me to Robben Island. I find myself hoping that, in one form or another, my fellow white visitors have come here for the same reason. Among us were two over-sixty white men posing for a snapshot beside a photo from the 1960s, now posted in the yard of Section D. In that decade a group of British journalists visited, and for them the warders put a reassuring face on the treatment of prisoners. Some photography was allowed. My white companions want to be snapped alongside the picture of Mandela and Walter Sisulu. They are proud to be associated, I assume, with men whose years here did not destroy their hope for the coming of a new South Africa. Most of us like to be associated with winners. We are not sure that we are up to paying the cost of winning, but we know enough of the best in our own humanness to salute those who do pay the cost. Here lived victims of systemic racism who saw their guards and other white oppressors as their future fellow citizens. In ministry to that future, they taught young, illiterate Afrikaner guards to read, counseled them in their family troubles, and refused to shore up plans for eventual revenge. They responded to inhumanity with humanity. Faced with that example, from somewhere deep in our own auto-biographies, one touches a contradiction to the racism in our American up-bringing, and we manage to say: Thank you, Lucas Mothale. You are right. You too are great.

District Six

Three-centuries-old scars of colonialism and apartheid will litter South African landscape and memory for a long time to come. Democracy, economic justice, health, education and their requisite institutional helps are now growing on every hand, though too slowly for rescuing many from the burdens of past oppression before they die. To visit South Africa in 2002, however, was to encounter a country of hope whose roots extend far back into the past, espe-cially in the visions of a nonracial society which the founders of the African National Congress publicized in 1912. How they managed to sustain that hope for the next eighty years composes one of the great chapters of modern human history. As a not very patient people, we Americans expect our hopes to be fulfilled in short order. Short-term hope did not work in South Africa.

In a moving passage of his autobiography, Nelson Mandela illustrates the stubborn persistence of his long-range hope after fourteen of his eighteen years on the island. His daughter Zeni marries a Swaziland prince. He has not seen her since she was a very young child. By 1979, the authorities had loosened some of their restrictions on family visits; so Zeni, her husband, and their new baby come to Robben Island.

It was a truly wondrous moment when they came into the room. I stood up, and when Zeni saw me, she practically tossed her tiny daughter to her husband and ran across the room to embrace me. I had not held my now grown-up daughter since she was about her own daughter's age. It was a dizzying experience, as though time had sped forward in a science fiction novel, suddenly to hug one's fully grown child. I then embraced my new son and he handed me my tiny granddaughter, whom I did not let go of for the entire visit. To hold a newborn baby, so vulnerable and soft in my rough hands that for too long had held only picks and shovels, was a profound joy. I don't think a man was ever happier to hold a baby than I was that day.

The visit had a more official purpose and that was for me to choose a name for the child. It is the custom for the grandfather to select a name, and the one I had chosen was Zaziwe—which means "Hope." The name had a special meaning for me, for during all my years in prison hope never left me—and now it never would. I was convinced that this child would be a part of a new generation of South Africans for whom apartheid would be a distant memory— that was my dream.[14]

The more distant in daily experience the old dark days of apartheid, the better, say the great majority of South Africans. But the dreams of many include the hope that the nation will find ways of remembering those days for the sake of honoring those who had to live in that darkness. Africans may not "worship" their ancestors, but they have strong convictions about the abiding presence of the dead in the lives of the living. In this tradition, honor to the living requires honor to the dead, the more so if the latter were once dishonored through no fault of their own. If this conviction survives in African culture in the future, it will be an ally to the determination of westerners, like the Germans, not to sweep the human past, positive and negative, under the rug of cultural amnesia.

One Capetonian who embodies just this version of hope is Stanley Abrahams. His personal story roots in the local neighborhood of his birth, "District Six." Standing in the vacant fields that composed this site in 2002, he looks down the slope to the office buildings of downtown, the docks and warehouses of the port, the curving beaches to the west, and out toward the Atlantic and Robben Island. Behind is Table Mountain. It is so stunning a view that one wonders why it took so long for Cape Town whites to discover that this was a choice residential location.[15] On that discovery hangs the story of District Six.

Stan Abrahams was born there in 1928, one of nine children in a family that the apartheid system classified as "colored."[16] The original settlers here were descendants of Malay slaves, other Asians, and immigrant Africans who labored first in docks and then in factories down the hill. The district could lay claim to being one of the oldest Cape Town neighborhoods and to having served the city's prosperity for at least two centuries. By 1950 some sixty-six thousand people lived on this hillside.

The Abrahams family attended nearby Methodist Central Mission on Buitenkant Street on the eastern edge of the district. In the early nineteenth century the building was a wine store. Methodist missionaries bought it in 1873, renovated it, and built a church above it.

Stan has many pleasant memories of his childhood here: In my interview with him in March 2002, he described District Six in glowing terms:

> People got to know each other in this neighborhood. We were not only a mixture of ethnic and cultural background but a mixture of religions, too. We mingled freely, respecting each other's religious observances and sharing in holidays and celebrations. As children we played games in the evening in the streets until, around 8:30, our parents would call us in. We were within walking distance of shops, docks, and factories where most of them worked. We had a wonderful view of the harbor and ocean, and we could go swimming at the Woodstock Beach, which was destroyed with the building of highways and new port facilities. In the other direction was the glory of Table Mountain with its changing colors at sunset and the trails we could explore up the mountain anytime we wished.
>
> As I grew up, of course, I knew that the apartheid regime's "reserved jobs" were not for me. I wanted to be an engineer, and in fact, when I went to work in a nearby fabric factory, I learned all the engineering skills but was repeatedly told, "You cannot be an engineer. A carpenter, painter, bricklayer, yes. But engineering is not for you."
>
> Then in the early 1960s came the amendments to the Group Areas Act of 1950, and the government began to tell us that we had to move. Already the city government was neglecting to repair our streets, buildings, and sanitary services. They wanted to make it a real slum, to prepare us to move out, all 66,000 of us, to new townships in the Cape Flats, fifteen or more miles from this center of the city. No longer would we walk to work. We would have to come by train or bus. So, in 1966, the bulldozers arrived. Our houses, businesses, and churches came down. By 1980 it was all vacant land with the exception of a mosque, a church or two, and a few good Victorian-style houses that whites soon occupied. They took down our street signs and scraped away the sidewalks. They loaded our possessions and ourselves in trucks and took us to the Flats.
>
> But in the process we raised public protests that got into the pa-

pers, and we got the attention of friends in other parts of the world. Even after the destruction of our houses, our protests kept the authorities from turning all the land into residential sites for whites. The new Technikon [Technical University] did take over one section, but they have recently apologized for doing so. If nothing else, we wanted the land to remain *vacant* as a sign of what apartheid had done to us. It has remained so.

Throughout the 1970s and 1980s I clipped news articles on the destruction, the protests, the forced removals. Along about 1985, when the violence of the regime was at its height, I had a vision of the importance of remembering the people who once lived on this ground. Gradually a few others joined me in that vision, and at a 1989 conference of anti-apartheid NGO's in Cape Town I raised the hope that we would have a museum for remembering District Six and the generations of people who had lived here. By then our former neighbors were scattered around Cape Town, dead, or emigrated. The conference endorsed the idea.

In the meantime in 1988, our Methodist congregation had shrunk. We used to have 600–700 members, as had the nearby "white" Methodist church up the street. Our church still had energy, vision, and spirit; but they had the money! So we decided to merge the two, to meet in the other church, and to consider turning the Buitenkant building into a museum. For several years into the 1990s, as apartheid fell apart, the church went unrepaired. But by 1995 we discovered support for the museum idea in a Quaker foundation, and soon after other foundations began to help us. When they came to visit Cape Town, world figures had heard of District Six, and they paid us visits. Eventually we raised four million rand, and we began to recruit artists, architects, museum specialists, and—especially—former residents to help us design the museum around the records and memories of what used to be here. We wanted children and grandchildren to catch glimpses of how we lived in this place as they come back with parents and grandparents to spend time in the museum. We have collected many remnants of our past here. On the floor of the former church sanctuary, we have painted a diagram of the streets of District Six, so that people can show each other exactly where their families used to live. We have a tower composed of original street signs at one end. That became possible when a white man who had supervised the bulldozing came forward with the confession that he had saved many street signs, probably hoping he could sell them. He accepted a token gift from us for turning them over to the museum.[17]

[So it all began with your dream of finding a way to keep District Six from vanishing from South African memory?]

"Yes. In all those years in which the system told us that we were second-class humans, my Christian faith kept me hoping for liberation from such a claim. And here we are!"

Stan Abrahams' vision now embraces new housing for the weed-overgrown acres. An artistic version of that hope, a collage of images of the former community, adorns the sixty-five-square-meter outer wall of a surviving church center on the lower edge of the area. Completed by artist and museum theorist Peggy Delport in 1982 just as the bulldozers were finishing, this mural has the title, *Res Clamant—the Earth Cries Out*. For those with memories, this earth continues to cry out.[18] But in 2004 some of the cries were changing to celebration as new homes were beginning to rise on land vacant for almost forty years. Already, Abrahams says, some 2,700 former residents have expressed interest in re-establishing residence here. But the heart of his own commitment is vivid memorialization of a former community whose pluralism and tolerance, in spite of poverty, he believes, offered a model for future South African urban society.

Not lost on any visitor to the museum is a brass plaque beside the church door directly across the street from the central Cape Town police headquarters. It reads:

ALL WHO PASS BY
REMEMBER WITH SHAME THE MANY THOUSANDS
OF PEOPLE WHO LIVED FOR GENERATIONS
IN DISTRICT SIX AND OTHER PARTS OF
THIS CITY, AND WERE FORCED BY LAW TO
LEAVE THEIR HOMES BECAUSE OF THE
COLOUR OF THEIR SKINS

FATHER FORGIVE US.

Church pastor (1967–1972) Peter J. Storey composed this text in 1971. At first he could find no local engraver willing to manufacture it. He finally found one who agreed to make it on the condition of anonymity. After attachment to the wall on Buitenkant Street, police from across the street removed it. Reattached, it had to be cleaned regularly from graffiti. Now it remains there, a moral-historical summary of what this urban space means in the memory of thousands of victims of apartheid's Group Areas Acts. It was the first public anti-apartheid monument anywhere in South Africa to survive into the present.[19]

No plaque or visitor's impressionistic summary can do justice to the profoundly human, concrete specificity of the memories housed in this museum. Specialists helped design the place, but "ordinary" people furnished it with detailed echoes of the former neighborhood. They describe it variously as "a vibrant, noisy, energetic place . . . Hanover Street . . . a river of people, cars, barrows, horses, horse-drawn carts and small boys racing down slopes in soap box carts: a bustling, laughing, hooting, whistling, shouting, chatting river of people" and as "at times . . . a place of violence. But mostly it was a place of love, tolerance and kindness, a place of poverty and often degradation, but a place where people had the intelligence to take what life gave them and give it meaning."

Often repeated in these testimonies is the word *meaning*: meaning lost in the forced removals and meaning found again in this museum: "The day I left our house in District Six, never to return, I knew my life had changed forever. . . . I thought my happiness had received a blow from which it would never recover. Who would have thought that, with the establishment of the District Six Museum, there would be a return of meaning into my life."[20]

This is high tribute to a mere museum and even higher tribute to an urban community which, by many objective measurements, had indeed become a slum and which from long ago had housed people in extreme poverty as well as prosperous shopkeepers and allegedly amiable criminals.[21] Former residents seldom speak of the negative sides of their life here; they accentuate the positive and avoid the word "slum." They know that to call any human settlement a slum is to tag it as a place unfit to live in. As historian Amos Oz remarked, "The defilement of language precedes and prepares the defilement of life and dignity"—a principle that the Nazis put to consistent political use.[22] But slums can be places where relatively poor people find ways to overcome the threats of their environment. Run-down or not, homes and streets can be objects of affection. They can also be vulnerable to collaboration with the injustices of the wider society:

> Crime and violence were part of everyday life and gangsters were
> not the harmless rogues portrayed in these recollections. Although
> black residents were the first group to be moved out under the Act,
> the community did not voice opposition to it. There is no doubt that
> poverty, overcrowding, competition for scarce resources and violence
> existed alongside neighborliness and community solidarity.[23]

By visiting the District Six Museum, a foreign visitor can ponder a cross section of possible answers to the puzzle of how a "mere" museum becomes a restoration of meaning to the lives of many former residents. It is one test of the visitor's capacity for empathy: What accounts for the passion for this memorial among its founders, former residents, and their descendants? I think of five answers:

- All told, the Removals Acts of 1950 and subsequent amendments transported at least 3.5 million South Africans out of their "black spot"

homes into newly devised townships on the fringes of cities. Aside
from prison and official murders, few other apartheid strategies inflicted more radical damage on the daily lives of so many families.
Once informed of their removal-future, some District Six residents realized for the first time the gross injustice of the society that already
surrounded them. It was one thing to know that you could never be an
engineer, another to know that a bulldozer was about to destroy every
bit of your homeplace. So radical a trauma might be repressed, but it
could not be really forgotten. Like aftermaths of terrorist trauma worldwide, to suggest to survivors that it be forgotten amounts to outrageous insult. Echoed in many narratives of unjust suffering, brought
to public attention, is the implicit relief, "At last! Someone has publicized what happened to us."

- The surviving empty hillside space that used to be District Six is part
of the Museum itself. The emptiness pays tribute to local and international protests. By 1980 white city planners had wanted to make it an
enclave of new, upscale white housing. But with their other problems
of law and order under a declared national emergency in the 1980s,
the plans never came to pass. Thus, many who viewed this vacancy in
the 1980s saw it as a promise of a restoration to come.

- Remarkable among museums is the development of this one in close
collaboration with hundreds of direct and indirect participants in the
history here remembered. In no small sense the concepts, contents,
and accents of the design reflect a process that has been (and still is)
"of the people and by the people" central to the history. Invited by museum leaders to do so, hundreds of former residents and their descendants have written their names and marked their previous residences
on a clear plastic cover over the floor map of the District. In addition,
thousands have registered their names and comments on a wide, con-
tinuous white cloth now measuring over a kilometer long, much of
which has been given more permanent form in threads of seam-
stresses who work regularly in the museum. Like the Holocaust Museum in Washington, this display seeks to overcome the psychic
numbing of statistics by breaking down "sixty-six thousand" into personal units—photographs, names, reconstructed rooms, tools, kitchen-
ware, clothes, signs, dolls, bits of crockery, and a growing collection of
audiorecordings of resident memories. All sixty-six thousand are not
likely to have tokens of their life in District Six registered, but this is a
work in progress. It invites former residents to offer tokens of personal
memory for public memory. It also invites visitors to interact, through
their own experience and imagination, with these inert tokens of once-
vibrant human lives. The result is an astonishing, intimate introduction to a history of massive human pain and promise. It is also a trib-

ute to the power of personal memory to defy official versions of
history.[24]

- All memorials speak of present human awareness as well as of the
  past. They speak of future hopes, too. If, in the minds of some elderly
  District Six survivors, a certain romance about the past veils the daily
  grimness of life then, enthusiasm for its pluralism, tolerance, and in-
  tercultural energy cannot be dismissed as fantasy. Present in these
  warm memories is a vision of what modern urban life has been and
  might yet be: a confluence of human diversity, a community of like-
  ness and unlikeness which can exist in spite of, and even because of,
  shared poverty. The profundity of loss was sadly expressed by "Mr.
  C. B." when he contrasted life in the artificial "community" of a township on the Flats to what he had once enjoyed:

> Here [in the township] it's everybody for themselves. They
> don't worry about nobody. It was a happy family that stayed
> in District Six. Everybody knew everybody. And then if
> there is any trouble, they come together quickly, not like
> here. They were all together, Muslim, Christian, Jewish and
> Indians.[25]

"Everybody for themselves" will resonate with many residents of an
American suburb, though few of us know what it is like to be thrown
out of a community of the inner-city poor into a "suburb" like Khayelitsha or Guguletu. At the founding of these townships, personal and
communal histories collided with such intensity that "community"
took a long time to develop anew. Not pluralism and not community,
the townships began in chaos, on the ashes of disintegrated communities.[26] Residents of both the townships and the affluent white suburbs
of Cape Town might both have reason to envy the version of *ubuntu*
which the District Six museum celebrates in testimonies like this:

> On Sunday afternoons people would sit outside their
> houses. . . . If you sit in one spot you can see others sitting
> up the hill. People would sit on the pavement outside
> having tea and whoever comes around sits and just enjoys
> themselves. . . . [People] were free and hospitable at that
> time. They would shout over there and have conversations
> with people about three or four houses away. Everyone
> would just chime in.[27]

The District Six Museum thus preserves the wisdom that selling human connection for a large disconnecting increase in wealth is a poor
bargain. Not romance, but the reality of humans' local need of each

other, is the wisdom memorialized here. Visitors domestic and foreign are likely to find themselves sobered and encouraged before the display of this wisdom on Buitenkant Street.

• Finally, like memorials to negative pasts the world over, the District Six Museum enshrines the determination, "Never again!" Long before the 1990s, as the bulldozers went about their iniquitous work, this plot of land was acquiring a certain fame worldwide as symbol and embodiment of the injustices of official racism. Local memory and local vision created this museum; its roots are deeply democratic. But if it is indeed "of" local people and "by" them, it is also a place "for" people more than local. The designers have purposefully adorned an outside wall of the building with flag-symbols of institutions inside and outside South Africa where struggles against forgetting and visions of repaired community are being nourished. They have consciously tried to fend off the localism that tempts survivors of disasters to say to the world, "Ours is the centerpiece of suffering. We endured the most!" To the contrary, the creators of the District Six Museum see themselves as part of a world project. They have officially joined their own effort to an "International Coalition of Historic Site Museums of Conscience", composed of institutions as diverse as the House of Slaves in Senegal, the Proyecto Recordar in Argentina, the Liberation War Museum in Bangladesh, the Terezin Camp Museum in the Czech Republic, the Gulag Museum in Siberia, the Workhouse in London, the Lower East Side Tenement Museum in New York City, and the National Park Service of the United States.[28] (The inclusion of the latter will surprise American visitors—until they remember that our NPS has charge of many sites that commemorate the post-1492 history of Native Americans, whose case will occupy Chapter 4 in this volume.)

As one of the places in South Africa where gross official injustice acquired worldwide acknowledgment years before 1990—along with Soweto, Sophiatown, and Sharpeville—District Six was one catalyst of the foreign attention which ultimately helped spell the demise of the apartheid regime. The curators of this museum proudly consider themselves as custodians of an important bit of hope for justice everywhere in the human world. But also hope for healing after intolerable injustice. As such, this museum is kin to a place of deeper evil called Vlakplaas, where Eugene de Kock and his police tortured and killed hundreds of apartheid enemies. In 2001, parliament was deciding how to make it a new "government-run museum and center for healing" as well as a "reminder that human beings have the potential for total degeneration."[29] Such memorials form a nexus of grief, repentance, and hope. The German Mahnmal is no more and no less so.

The Cape Town Holocaust Museum

Among the warnings of the twentieth century to the twenty-first, none has acquired more pervasive international memorialization than the Holocaust of six million European Jews. Yet many a western visitor is likely to be surprised that far-off Cape Town has a newly established Holocaust Museum as well as an adjacent Jewish Museum.

The latter grew naturally out of two centuries of Jewish immigration to South Africa, but the former has a special relation to that history which the founding director of the museum, Marlene Silbert, critically personifies. A longtime resident of Cape Town, she rues the fact that, under apartheid, many Jews rested comfortably in their official status as white. "I have always been pained by the pain of my own Jewish people, but I have been ashamed of being always classified as a white South African." She says this against the background of her own protests against apartheid as a young woman and as a longtime high school history teacher. Tellingly, in the late 1990s, when approached with the proposal that she become the lead designer and first director of the museum, she replied to the sponsors, "Unless you permit me to show the conceptual and political connections between the Holocaust and apartheid in South Africa, I cannot take the job."

On that condition, she did take the job, so that, upon entering the museum, one confronts anti-Jewish German newspapers and posters of the 1930s alongside contemporary versions of Nazi and anti-Semitic propaganda in South African media: caricatures of European Jews disembarking in South Africa in the previous century, prewar rallies of South African Nazis—"Gray Shirts"—and parallels between benches marked "Nur für Juden" in the German 1930s and "Blacks only" benches in the South African 1950s. Here, among the more intimate connections made between the German and South African versions of genocidal racism are pictures of persons of different races having their heads measured with calipers for differences of cranium and nose sizes. One German set of photographs contrasts six "Aryan" youths to six Jewish youths on the assumption that any viewer can see the racial differences. Other photos record the trek of Europe's Jews from home to ghetto to death camp—images of horror now familiar around the world, duplicated on the walls of the Wannsee and Washington museums. But for South Africans who come here, the context of apartheid casts a local shadow over the exhibits, making "Holocaust studies" anything but remote from the history of their own country.

Silbert's second condition for taking the job was that she be free to organize Holocaust studies in programs for high school students and other citizen groups. The first people needing education, she says, were staff of the new South African department of public education. "In 1997, 95 percent of them knew nothing about the Holocaust and hadn't thought of its connection with apartheid. Nor had it entered into high school history books." At her initiative much has changed. A film, a teacher's guide, and student books (that will eventually be translated into the country's eleven official languages) are now in place. She says with satisfaction, "Now the Holocaust is part of our national education curriculum."

As a teacher she takes more satisfaction yet from the direct educational work she and her associates undertake regularly with high school students and members of police forces. In its first two years, the museum has hosted fourteen thousand students—all over age fourteen[30]—some one thousand teachers, and three thousand police for seminars ranging from several hours to all day. Three thousand more police were registered for 2003.

> With the students I try to stress the human capacity for good and
> evil, the danger that it can happen again, the danger of individual
> silence, the necessity for resistance and individual citizen responsi-
> bility. With the police I ask them: "Have you ever witnessed an act
> of racism? Or participated in such an act? It's a battle we all have to
> wage, all of us, every day of our lives." The police talk readily about
> their memories of the apartheid era, but they hesitate to identify the
> racism that still survives in South African daily life, including them-
> selves.[31]

Photography, an art a century and a half old, aids modern perceptions of the human past in a concreteness that words and drawings of earlier eras never quite achieve. One wall of this Holocaust museum displays a collection of six hundred photos which the Nazis took of the Jews from the Austrian village of Bedzin before deporting them to Auschwitz. "On average in the camps," Silbert tells visitors, "the Nazis killed six times six hundred people every day for four years, simply because they were Jews. A Jewish man, a survivor from Bedzin, visits us from time to time. He has identified over a dozen of his relatives among these photos and many of his former neighbors, all of them murdered."

In an alcove at one turn of the hall, silhouetted in black, stands a quotation from Archbishop Desmond Tutu: "We learn about the Holocaust so that we can become more human, more gentle, more caring, more compassionate . . . and the world will become a more humane place."

"Will," "should," "must," "can," and "may" compete as verbs of choice for such inscriptions. Museum makers and teachers use the latter four in persistent hope for the first.

Contested Spaces

"We are a country of pockets."

On reflection, any visitor to South Africa recognizes the validity of that description by one of the country's leading Afrikaner novelists, Etienne van Heerden.[32] Varieties of immigrations, English and Afrikaner rivalries, and exclusionary colonialist discriminations against nonwhites are old in the history. Even if the apartheid system, from 1948 on, had not aimed at pocketing racial groups for "separate development," the cultural and political conflicts between Asian and black, English and Afrikaner, eleven language groups, and as many African ethnic groups, all told, would have guaranteed a South Africa riven with divisive loyalties far from composable into a national identity. As the great modern Xhosa novelist, Zakes Mda, puts it: "South Africa is still fumbling along, in search of an African identity." He registers the historical irony that when the early Dutch settlers coined the word "Afrikaner" for themselves, no other groups living in the southern part of the continent were calling themselves "African." In a double irony, "In the nomenclature of the [post-1948 government] . . . the indigenous people became Natives, Bantu, Plurals, and even a more respectable Black, but never Africans!"[33]

The new South African constitutions of 1993–1996 institutionalized both human rights and a political system legally embodying the concept "South African" for the first time. How long will it take for the majority of people in this diverse population to consider themselves members of a single nation? The question could be asked of almost any country in the modern world, even in the United States but notably now in western Europe, where old restricted definitions of "citizen" are under legal scrutiny. Every nation may now be more a work-in-progress than serene nationalists like to suppose.

Meantime great political and cultural tasks await those who mean to bring a tangible unity out of this diversity while protecting and even enhancing particular identities. This diversity infuses almost every public attempts to memorialize a collective past, as Professor Sean Field of the University of Cape Town testifies when he reports the decisions that yielded the current version of the District Six Museum:

> Every inch of the District Six Museum is contested space. For example, was it to be only for "colored" memories? "Nomvuyo's Room"—a one-room reconstructed home with a view to the sea—had to be negotiated as representative of black family life, and the same for Rob's Room upstairs as representative of a colored family. There is as yet no presence of gays in the exhibitions, and other groups are missing, too.
>
> And this is because the past is always about *contestation*. South

African museums in general do not yet represent our many different, contradictory voices. We should let these voices speak for themselves, expecting museum visitors to makeup their own minds. Not
yet here do you hear about colored residents who were anti-black.
Some have said that the museum "only represents happy coloreds,"
for whom there was no crime, no unhappiness, no conflict, and no
collaboration with apartheid. Such a memory, of course, is heavily
imbued with myths, the myths that people the world over use to
protect their nostalgia and to cover up painful facts.[34]

Nothing illustrates the truth of Field's observation more vividly than current controversies over abolishing, preserving, and reinterpreting old public
monuments and memorials to South Africa's past. Below are some examples
of how the country's history is getting revisited, revised, recovered, and repub-
lished in public times and spaces, often in ways that either cancel or reduce to
obscurity former official versions of that history.[35]

Public Monuments

At a major downtown intersection of the Cape Town suburb of Rondebosch, a
bronze plaque from the 1950s reads in Afrikaans and English:

> On or near this spot stood a clump of thorn trees named by Johan
> van Riebeeck, founder of our country, "T Ronde Doornbosjen," from
> which Rondebosch took its name in this vicinity on March 1, 1657.
> Nine free burghers took permanent title to land and became the first
> citizens of our country.[36]

A short trip up Table Mountain from this spot takes one to the huge marble
installation that celebrates the most famous of the subsequent "first citizens"
of South Africa—entrepreneur colonialist Cecil John Rhodes. The grandeur of
this statuary matches the scope of Rhodes's ambition to exploit the wealth of
southern Africa for his own and Great Britain's greater glory.

The power to name and rename public objects and public events is no
trivial power. Zekes Mda has a tongue-in-cheek description of the exercise of
this power by a famous nineteenth century British colonial governor of South
Africa, Sir George Grey:

> He had been a governor in Australia and New Zealand . . . where his
> civilising mission did many wonderful things for the natives of those
> countries. Of course he had to take their land in return for civilisa-
> tion. Civilisation is not cheap. He had written extensively about the
> native people of those countries, and about their plants. He had even
> given names to ten of their rivers, and to their mountain ranges. It
> did not matter that the forebears of those natives had named those

rivers and mountains from time immemorial. When Ned told them about the naming of the rivers, a derisive elder had called Grey The Man Who Named Ten Rivers. And that became his name.[37]

Along with that of Cecil Rhodes, a statue of George Grey occupies a prominent place in the Cape Town Gardens, a stone's throw from Parliament. Not yet has a statue of Nelson Mandela been erected there, but his image and name flood the landscape now as almost everyone's favorite emblem of the great recent transition. In Pretoria, in its new Freedom Park, four new busts were recently dedicated to heroes of the liberation struggle: Mandela, Oliver Tambo, Steve Biko, and Robert Sobukwe. Who were the "first citizens" of South Africa? For one leader of the ANC, the question has a simple moral-political answer: "For us history begins in 1994."

That view, of course, opens up to the further question of who belongs to the future of South Africa and how a future status of all its inhabitants as citizens can be assured unless the distinct histories of all are honored. Under this umbrella issue great "contestations" will take place for many years to come. Can diverse, much-neglected histories be honored without casting dishonor on some of the alleged heroes of the past?

The answer is "no." On one side of the Cape Town Gardens, before the rear gate to Parliament, rises the equestrian statue of Louis Botha, Afrikaner commander in the Boer War who, in 1910, eight years after he had formally surrendered to the British, became the first prime minister of the new British-dominated Union of South Africa. Beginning with the 1913 Land Act, over the next thirty-eight years this regime would tighten white controls of the majority black population and lay the groundwork for the yet tighter repressions of post-1948 Afrikaner apartheid. Is the statue of Louis Botha to remain at the gates of Parliament in Cape Town?

If public statuary can change, so can the names of public institutions. For years Pretoria had a D. L. Malan Boulevard, named after the founding president of the 1948 apartheid regime. Now it bears the name of another Afrikaner, theologian Beyers Naudé, a hero of the anti-apartheid struggle, who abandoned his privileged position in the Dutch Reformed Church in the early 1960s, suffered banning by the apartheid government, and spent the next thirty years protesting the theological and political heresies of the apartheid church and state.[38]

The status of old Afrikaner and British statues will be up for debate for quite a while to come. Around no particular icon will civic debate circle more fervently than the Voortrekker Monument in Pretoria. High on a hill near the city center, this structure salutes the "Great Trek" of the Boers in 1838, who fled from the oppressions of the British Cape Colony and Natal, fighting their way through Zulu country and across mountain ranges to found their own state in the Transvaal. Most of all, the monument celebrates the victory of the trekkers over the Zulus at Blood River by dint of firepower and "circled wagons." The wall enclosing this hilltop Pretoria monument consists of images of those wagons. To estimate how sacred this site is for many Afrikaners, Americans should think of the Tomb of the Unknown Soldier in Arlington and the Lincoln Memorial. Black South Africans were not permitted entry here. In every respect the monument excluded them from identification with the heroism here remembered. Erected during the regime that came to power in 1948 and dedicated in 1949, this white stone structure can only signify to blacks the major source of their oppression.

Easily imaginable, therefore, are reasons why, in the late 1980s, the generals of the armed wing of the ANC,[39] in their exile headquarters in Lusaka, Zambia, would approach ANC president Oliver Tambo with the proposal: Shall we dynamite the Voortrekker Monument in Pretoria? They had carefully calculated the technical requirements and the political impact of the operation, in accord with the usual MK strategy of attacking physical objects of symbolic significance without direct attacks on civilians. Tambo turned down the proposal for two reasons:

> First, the ANC was involved in a struggle against a state that had consistently and systematically destroyed the sanctity of the land, the lives, and the human rights of the people of South Africa. In opposing that desecrating state, the ANC had to maintain a moral position in which it would never descend to destroying something that anyone held to be sacred. Even the monumental shrine of a triumphalist Afrikaner nationalism, therefore, could not be a legitimate target because it would implicate the ANC in an act of desecration. Second . . . the ANC had to look forward to the possibility that in the future South Africans might be involved in a process of national reconciliation. In that event, reconciliation would only be made much more difficult if the ANC were to destroy a nationalist monument that was held sacred by a segment of the South African population.[40]

Of a piece with this remarkable story is a visit which former President Nelson Mandela paid to the Pretoria monument in March 2002. Some blacks criticized the visit as highly inappropriate: Why honor this place by the presence of a hero of the resistance? Moreover, Afrikaners had recently added another figure to the monument—a statue of Danie Theron, a Boer soldier famous as a skillful scout, killed in 1900 in the war against the British. Mandela saluted the new statue and hailed the scout as a fellow freedom fighter along with black allies of the Boer cause. He thus underscored South Africa's current struggle to substantiate the claim, "We are all South Africans." His gesture also expressed the relative ease with which many blacks now identify with the Afrikaners in contrast to the British. Not only is the Boer War of 1899–1902 perceived as a freedom fight, but the longtime intimate relation of black laborers and Boer farmers in the countryside has produced a sense of common cause that defies the usual outsider perception of the Afrikaner and the black as bitterest of enemies. For both, the British are sometimes perceived as having the latest, weakest, and most tentative presence in the country's history.[41]

As this is written in 2004, new names and new rosters of public heroes accumulate all over South Africa. A statue of Hendrik Verwoerd has been pulled down in Blomfontein, a statue of Steve Biko raised in Port Elizabeth, and the D. F. Malan airport in Johannesburg renamed for Mandela. The Jo'burg neighborhood named "Triomph" by whites has now reverted to its old name, Sophiatown, familiar to readers of Alan Paton's prophetic novel, Cry, the Beloved Country.

By 2006, South Africa's most extensive memorial to the anti-apartheid struggle will be the 130-acre Freedom Park on a Pretoria hill not far from the Voortrekker Monument. Boulders and soils from all eleven provinces have already been set here in a "Garden of Remembrance." Eventually, says Wally Serote, chief executive of the park, its various features will combine "history, spiritualism, conflict, resolution, evolution, and biodiversity. It is essentially a national memorial where we can commemorate pain and loss and celebrate our heroes and heroines. . . . The process [of planning] has humbled me. The initiative for the park came from ordinary people, and it has been an engrossing and challenging project.[42]

Will ordinary citizens of the new South Africa find it possible to honor both Freedom Park and the nearby Voortrekker Monument with a visit? Some, perhaps, cannot do so. Others will imitate Mandela by saluting the courage symbolized in both.

Blood River: No Bridge Yet

Perhaps the most ambiguous combination of monuments in contemporary South Africa rests on the site of a famous battle between the Voortrekkers and the Zulu on December 16, 1838. On their way north to the Transvaal, fighting thousands of Zulu behind their circle of wagons, three hundred Boers won the battle at a cost of three thousand Zulu lives. Tradition—perhaps myth— has it that they entered into a "covenant" with God to the effect that they would build a church to commemorate the victory and would always acknowledge the date in an annual celebration.

This they did. They built a church in Pietermaritzburg, and in the twentieth century December 16 became "The Day of the Covenant" (or "the Vow") in the public calendar. Dutch Reformed churches regularly celebrated the day, and in 1938 the hundredth anniversary of the battle, Boer leaders modeled wagons collected from all over South Africa and built at Blood River a bronze replica-circle of the original fortification. The monument became the site of an annual ceremony, which in 1938 drew several hundred Afrikaners.

But the site acquired a freight of ambiguity in the 1990s when ANC and

Zulu government leaders decided to counter historic Boer nationalism and denigration of "savage" society by building on the battle site, on the opposite side of the river, a monument to the courage of *their* ancestors. The structure currently consists of a long, curving wall of red tribal shields. Nearby is a museum devoted to the Zulu side of the story. For them and many Afrikaners December 16 is still "Dingane's Day," after the 1838 Zulu chief. In 2002, one kilometer downstream, a small bridge was begun, but by car the trip was still thirty miles over rough roads. It was as though, in this opposing statuary, the battle continues, as another battle continues for many American visitors when they visit Gettysburg.

But South Arica's leaders have an interest in promoting a new, synthetic interpretation of this ancient event. In 1998 officials of the new government, including President Mandela, Deputy President Thabo Mbeki, the Zulu King, and Inkatha Freedom Party leader Mangosuthu Gatsha Buthelezi, joined in the dedication of the Zulu memorial. For the occasion Buthelezi hailed a new meaning for the anniversary: "Let us consider this the day of a new covenant which binds us to the shared commitments of building a new country."[43] After their ceremony on the far riverbank, a small delegation of Afrikaners waded the river to join the three thousand Zulus in a gesture of post-apartheid reconciliation.

Meantime, on the national calendar, December 16 is no longer "Dingane's Day" or "The Day of the Covenant" but "The Day of Reconciliation." No doubt, if they ever do build that bridge on this very site, they will dedicate it on a December 16.[44]

Ambiguities of National Calendar: Calls for Inclusive Celebration

Changes in official times of celebration and memorialization are highly political transactions. The most radical is the abolition of one holiday and substitution of another. In contemporary America, the best illustration is the official annual celebration of the birthday of Martin Luther King, Jr.—January 15. A declining number of Americans are aware of how this birthday has overwhelmed another that school children of one section of the country invariably had called to their attention: January 17, birthday of Robert E. Lee. Not many died-in-the-wool southerners make much of this substitution, which for African Americans is a blessed exchange. Yet nostalgia for the "lost causes" of American history continues to infuse the civic holiday agenda of descendants of some events in that history. Like the celebration of Columbus's "discovery" of America, one citizen group's monument to courage is another's memorial to oppression. Conceiving a national holiday that invites celebration by all citizens is no simple political challenge.

In this dimension of its nation-building South Africa, too, is very much a work in progress. The new government's tactic of "Reconciliation Day" is politically imaginative, parallel to President Mandela's decision in 1994 to blend a new national anthem out of the anthems which Afrikaner and ANC leaders had once sung for their respective causes. Two historians have called this event "a crowning symbol of the Government's effort to deracialise public opinion."[45] The parliamentary collaboration between the old National Party and the ANC in 2002 was a like political parallel to this stunning musical conjunction.

The civic holiday schedule of the new South Africa is replete with such invitations to unity. We can be sure that not all citizens accept all the invitations. Some of these days face backward to atrocities—Human Rights Day (March 21, in memory of the Sharpeville Massacre of 1960) and Youth Day (June 16, in memory of the student protests and deaths in Soweto, 1976). Some enable celebrants to be selective in what they remember—January 1 reminds some Capetonians of the emancipation of their slave ancestors in 1834, as it also reminds some African Americans of January 1, 1863, when Lincoln's Emancipation Proclamation came in to effect. But for most, it is just New Year's.[46]

The day whose recent roots convey the least ambiguous hopes for South Africa's future is April 27, Freedom Day, anniversary of South Africa's first population-wide democratic election in 1994 and the climax of a revolution achieved through negotiation without war. December 16, Reconciliation Day, holds out the same hope. But Afrikaner and Zulu memories open few doors easily to the inclusion of English, Indian, Colored, and non-Zulu black identification with either of the enemies who fought at Blood River. South Africa's forty million citizens live still in "pockets" of memory as well as pockets of geography and social class. Melding them all into shared identification with each other as *South Africans* remains a huge political task. Memorials, monuments, and holidays can be helps to this effort; but they will never escape contestation, which no one in a democracy should want to escape.

Contested Monuments and Memorials: Cradock and Bloemfontain

Christian ethicist William Everett points to four options for monument memorial revisions: (1) Supplant (Naudé for Malan), (2) preserve and reintegrate (two national anthems into one), (3) add on (the Zulu Blood River memorial), and (4) transform (Reconciliation Day).[47] Mixtures of these intentions are likely, leaving behind continued political contestation over what monuments old and new mean. One example concerns "the Cradock Four." In 1984, as the Bantu Education act began to take effect and as state-sponsored violence intensified, student boycotts resumed in many communities. In the Eastern Cape town of Cradock, one of four leaders of the boycott was a teacher, Matthew Goniwe, who refused the transfer which the authorities imposed to remove his influence from the school. One year later, in July 1985, Goniwe and three colleagues were murdered by state assassins. The Cradock Four then entered the legacies of gross injustice that in the late 1990s would occupy many hours of hearings of the Truth and Reconciliation Commission. In the same years the Cradock community erected a modest public memorial to the atrocity, bearing the names of the four men. Present at both the TRC hearing and the memorial dedication were the four widows of the murdered men. In 2002, one of them, Nyameka Goniwe, recalled both events with a certain sadness:

> When one appeared before the TRC it was difficult to feel at ease in the presence of all those important people, and the time for telling one's story was quite limited. . . . Then there was the dedication of the memorial in Cradock. The four of us have supported each other in all the years since 1985, but our experience of the memorial design and dedication left us with a mixture of gratitude and resentment. Once the community political leaders got into the community discussion and into the dedication ceremony, *they* took center stage to advance their own interests. The four of us felt used and pushed aside by politics.[48]

Perhaps there is no more difficult, poignant question about public monuments than: Whom do the *designers* mean chiefly to remember, and in subsequent years whom will *viewers* decide to remember? All students of monuments/memorials observe that subsequent generations bring their own interpretations to their viewing of these supposedly inert objects. Monuments and memorials are not really inert. Their perceived meanings change with history.

A convincing illustration of this phenomenon is the Women's Monument in the former Afrikaner-settled city of Bloemfontein, erected in memory of the women and children who died in the British camps at the end of the 1899–1902 war. The statue consists of one woman standing behind a mother sitting with her dead child on her lap, in unmistakable analogy to Michaelangelo's *Pieta* in the Vatican.[49] In an extraordinary essay, Afrikaner scholar Johan Snyman traces the history of this memorial from its inspiration in the repentant ethical conscience of Englishwoman Emily Hobhouse to its ideological appropriation for the Afrikaner cause by leaders who came to power in 1948. From her biography, writings, and the speech Hobhouse delivered at the 1913 dedication of the memorial, Snyman concludes:

> What strikes one as remarkable is the elegant, unabashed feminism of Emily Hobhouse, and the consequent direction of her particularism and universalisation. . . . [She] elevates the Boer woman to the ranks of the Universal Woman's struggle for recognition. And the Boer woman forms part of a whole that transcends itself: she fights along with other women in that part of the world. The meaning of her struggle is not parochial, but universal. It is a contribution towards a greater solidarity of humankind. That is what makes her

struggle moral, and allows the Boer woman to teach others a lesson in history which speaks across the political divide between Boer and British, white and black.[50]

But that was not the interpretation which would be promoted by the architects and enforcers of the subsequent apartheid regime. In 1963 the government published a text of Hobhouse's address of 1913, minus passages in which she transcends the suffering of Boer women and children. Censored out were the paragraphs:

> We in England are ourselves still but dunces in the great world school, our leaders are still struggling with the unlearned lesson, that liberty is the equal right and heritage of every child of man, without distinction of race, colour or sex. . . .
>
> We, too, the great civilised nations of the world, are still but barbarians in our degree, so long as we continue to spend vast sums in killing or planning to kill each other for greed of land and gold. Does not justice bid us to remember today how many thousands of the dark race perished also in Concentration Camps in a quarrel which was not theirs. . . . ?[51]

No wonder the fathers of apartheid refused to publicize these heresies: Not only did Emily Hobhouse call for political "liberty" for all women, not only did she rebuke the "greed for land and gold" that was beginning to run rampant over the rights of non-Europeans in the South Africa of 1913, but she also imputed to the unveiled Women's Memorial repudiation of the racism at the base of the whole apartheid system. Unabashed, she had the historical wit to remember what the censors of 1963 wanted their public to forget: the 13,315 black Africans who died in those English concentration camps, a portion of an estimated 116,000 people whom the British confined there for their cooperation with the Boer cause, pursued, like the British side, interracially.[52] Adding insult to injury, this same apartheid government celebrated Emily Hobhouse, pacifist and moral universalist, by naming after her "a Daphne fighter class submarine of the South African Navy"![53] The transformation of the public face of the Bloemfontein statue, the ensuing fifty years, was therefore radical. It is time, Snyman says, to restore Hobhouse's memorial philosophy:

> To wrest the meaning of the concentration camp history from its nationalist mould may offer a way to the search for justice. Instead of fetishing a historical instance of suffering by elevating it to the ultimate instance of suffering in a limited universe of suffering and injustice, memorials should facilitate the ability to recognise suffering whenever and wherever it may occur. . . .
>
> It is for the sake of the search for justice that the true war memorial functions as Mahnmal. It speaks silently on behalf of a "we"

regardless of gender, class or race, and it seems to say that as a particular people we have come to know what suffering entails, and we shall never let it happen again, neither in ourselves not in any other human being. The future course of history has to be different from what is commemorated by this monument.[54]

As an Afrikaner teaching in an Afrikaner-founded university in 2002, Snyman illustrates in eloquent, honest ways the service of a historian to moral-intellectual critique of widely shared public political ideology. He achieves this as member of the very ethnic group whose power got served by a twisting of the history. For foreign eyes, long inclined to stereotype the Boers for their racist patriotism, Snyman is splendid antidote. He embodies the virtues of intellectual repentance for elements of the culture in which he was raised. And he illustrates the danger that historical honesty can pose to many a political establishment

New History Books for the Young

The history of South Africa did not really begin in 1994, as one ANC leader proudly claimed; but neither did it begin in 1652 when the first Dutch settlers arrived. With the 1994 political control of government shifted so decisively into nonwhite hands, the writing of history books for public schools was sure to shift as well. Whether or not historical narratives are invariably shaped to suit the needs of the people in power—as postmodernists claim—no one doubts that power does influence education. In this section I want only to offer a few illustrations of the current effort of South Africa's scholars, teachers, and educational administrators to furnish the minds of young citizens with versions of history in which the majority of their neighbors are no longer almost invisible.

THE SOUTH AFRICAN HISTORY PROJECT. From 1983 to 1995, Dr. June Bam taught history in a "historically coloured" secondary school in the Western Cape. In 1995 she undertook to teach classes of future history teachers in the newly integrated Teacher Training College in the Western Cape. There, she had reconfirmed her experience that "this is not an easy time to be a history teacher." In the book that she and fellow historian Pippa Visser wrote in 1996 charting new content and new methods for teaching history in anew South Africa, she documents her own attempts to write, teach, and introduce young students to "a history that involves us all."[55] She describes the first days of class in the training college:

> [T]he tension in the class was so high that the history class became
> a particularly uncomfortable place for both students and lecturer.

While students were reasonably comfortable with class discussion on non-threatening issues such as the integrated curriculum and the philosophy of history, tension grew once issues involving racism and prejudice in school textbooks were discussed. . . .

These were sons and daughters of parents from opposing economic and social positions coming face to face, confronted with the task of having to engage in discussion about events which they have not as yet come to terms with on a personal level. There are still many gaping wounds of this past, many painful memories as well as feeling of guilt and shame, or alternatively bitterness and resentment.[56]

New approaches to South African history teaching will demand new learning by the teachers themselves. Bam and her colleague Visser acknowledge the difficulty of equipping teachers to pursue four goals for students in their study of history: (1) student ability to identify *bias* in historical documents and narrative, (2) *empathy* for the variety of actors in a complex past, (3) skill in historical *argument*, its possible inconsistencies and contradictions, and (4) ability to mount *their own argument* or conclusions about what once happened and why. Successful achievement of these goals in any school class, they believe, will equip students to become contributors to the social, political, and interpersonal reconciliation that remains as one of the country's great unfinished tasks. "No other subject [than history] can play such a direct and healing role in the process of nation building. . . . Any notion of reconciliation that seeks to avoid this essential process is utterly inadequate, since it pretends that reconciliation can be achieved without engaging with the very real conflicts of the past, the consequences of which are still around us today."[57]

Of all four of these declared new goals, that of empathy for past actors is probably the most ambitious—as the teacher to be quoted below agrees. In her teacher training class, says Bam, "I had the impression that for some of the students it was the first time they had permitted themselves to imagine what racism feels like to its victims. This moment of empathy was a turning point in our discussions." It can be a turning point for students of any racial background.

It will not suffice simply to turn the old version of South African history on its head. . . . Teaching history for the future would defeat its purpose if, for example, both young Sarie van der Merwe and her classmate Geina Khumalo were left with the impression that *all* Afrikaans-speaking whites were racist oppressors, or led to believe that *all* blacks were heroic resisters. *All* students need to be able to find people and incidents in the history lessons with which they can identify. We therefore need to find a way for the history of the nation to present diverse perspectives and allow each student to find a place in that history[58]

—and to perceive the places of all of one's national neighbors.

Bam and Visser devote a chapter to close analysis of how school texts of the apartheid era fell woefully short of their four stated goals for a new history. They also raise the honest question of how it was possible for them, in their own education as budding historians in the 1970s and 1980s, to escape captivity to biases they are now committed to correcting. Indeed, they say, "The most interesting thing about South African history education is not that it produced so many people who believed the school version of our history, but rather that it produced so many people who arrived at a very different understanding of the past. For that we must often credit their teachers."[59]

The Bam-Visser book of 1996 is full of illustrations of how they themselves honor the innovative precedents of their own dissident teachers by building upon their work.[60] Rather than further summaries of this richly suggestive text, however, I want to introduce one of their contemporary white colleagues who teaches in an integrated private high school in Cape Town. Her work echoes the prescriptions and the difficulties of Bam's and Visser's hope for the future of history texts and teaching in the new South Africa.

One History Class

Jennifer Wallace graduated from the University of Cape Town in 1990. She took a position as history teacher in St. Cyprian's, the local Anglican preparatory school for young women. With official loosening of certain segregation policies in the late 1980s, the school had already begun to accept students of all races. Wallace began her career as member of a generation of white university graduates prepared to teach history from points of view quite absent from the books she studied in high school.

The walls of her classroom are now plastered with a hundred or so emblems of the new content and method that she has introduced to the teaching of history to students fourteen to eighteen years old. Posters from the struggle against apartheid include the Pass Laws; Bantu Education; Soweto; heroes of that struggle—Desmond Tutu, Oliver Tambo, Steve Biko, and Nelson Mandela; principals in the politics of the early nineties—P. W. Botha, F. W. De Klerk, Mangosuthu Buthelezi; and then the foreigners—Mother Theresa, Martin Luther King, Jr. All the posters are student creations from their study of eras, issues, and leaders in the history of the past twenty-five years. Ideologies and interests clash on these walls, but the majority of the posters and slogans recall people and causes that high school history books of Wallace's own youth treated with far different perspective and selectivity.

Early in her work at St. Cyprian's, Wallace virtually created her own texts, but in the 1990s she worked with others in the province and the national government (including June Bam) to advise on the writing of new texts for a new South Africa. Three books from a 1995–1999 series, *In Search of History*, she says, "have restored my faith in textbooks." Authored by university historians who played various roles in the student revolts against Bantu education, these volumes are studded with pictures, source documents, biographies, maps, charts, and narratives that contrast radically with both the content and style of the government-controlled school histories of the 1980s.

Any perusal of a text she studied as a high school student in the 1980s, for example, *History for Standard 10*, will prepare foreign visitors to comprehend the educational groundshift that her own work now represents.[61] Often reprinted in the years 1976–1981, the book was written by four Afrikaner scholars for "preparing pupils for the final public examination" in history, the matriculation exams that determine the student's graduation from secondary school and eligibility for university. For a country that had little or no television available before 1975, it is perhaps understandable that pictures are rare in this volume—a stylistic feature which the new books would alter on almost every page. But page after page of dense printed text are more than a question of style here. The post-1948 history comes across in factual, objective tones. The authors document the skein of legal discriminations against nonwhite people woven across these decades by the National Party, but there are few invitations to readers to evaluate these measures, which often get described in a pervasive passive voice. New townships "were planned," new segregated houses "were envisaged" for Indians, an advisory council "was decided," homeland development "was announced," the meeting "was broken up," Blacks "were allowed" to do semiskilled work, "non-Whites have been prepared to accept much lower wages than Whites," "a number of acts were passed," "many slum areas . . . have been cleared." Even when this verbal voice describes an event that might attract a certain initial moral applause (e.g., slum "clearance"), this style obscures the human *agency* that makes history. A student in the 1980s would have to have been a regular newspaper reader to view the statement, "many slums have been cleared" as a cover for forced removals and vast destructions of personal, family, and social lives in Sophiatown, District Six, and Crossroads.[62] This text does not invite critical discernment of either fact selectivity or implicit moral principle.

Protest movements against apartheid do get their mention throughout, and occasionally a murmur of author agreement with the protests peeps out in touches like the quotation marks in the sentence: "In 1924 came the government's decision to employ only 'civilised' labour in state departments, . . ." as well as in the clarity about little political power granted members of the Colored and Indian "Councils" of the 1960s in the italics *advises* and *recommendations*.[63] On the whole, however, this history of the apartheid era to 1976 is an implicit apologia for its political system and ideology of "separate development." Concerning the dormitories for immigrant black mine workers, we learn:

> Provision is made for hygienic sleeping accommodations, a balanced diet, and recreational facilities, such as cinema shows, sport and tribal dancing. The workers also receive medical attention.

And concerning the supply of infrastructure to the new homelands:

> In [homeland] territories whose people still lived from hand to mouth 50 years ago, now 5 000 dams; 40 000 km of roads; 132 000 km of fencing; agricultural and technical schools; tens of thousands of hectares under irrigation; etc.[64]

Like the "sleeping accommodations" in the first quotation, the "etc." in the latter homeland statistics covers a multitude of sins.

In addition to the passive voice the *absent* voices in this text begin to shout as one nears the end of the book. Were tenth-grade readers likely to intuit that black men in the dorms were there precisely because the economy of their "homelands" was so desperate? Or to glimpse how the migrant mine labor system was destroying many a family in those homelands? Or how cosmetic were many of the alleged improvements in homeland infrastructure, overlaying the fact that homeland soils were of such low quality that white farmers had long ago shown little interest in living there? No surveys of black opinion accompanies references to migrant labor, homeland "development," or the experience of nonwhite children in the schools available to them under Bantu Education. After all, only white eyes were supposed to read this tenth-grade book, only white minds wrote it, and a whites-only electorate stood behind the government that adopted this approach to history in public high schools. In a slip that a postapartheid perspective would find humorous, this text describes a referendum of 1960 as indicating that "a majority of the people wanted a republic. . . ."[65] The authors did not see fit to remind the student that "the people" meant 12 percent of the population.

The tone of objectivity that pervades *History Standard Ten* makes its apologia for apartheid mostly implicit. But the veil of value-free South Africa history writing vanishes in a final page of the volume, which observes that "*Western Powers* . . . do not appreciate the seriousness of the communist threat" in the 1970s, nor, a final paragraph implies, do they appreciate the fact that

> *South Africa* has committed herself to the task of leading the Black and Coloured peoples within her borders and in South West Africa [Namibia] along evolutionary lines toward self-reliance and independence. As regards the Black peoples, this is being done through the separate development of Black homelands. . . . Meanwhile the

Coloured and Indians are being given opportunities to gain experience in political self-government and engage in direct negotiations with the government of South Africa.[66]

This is an example of the high school history texts on which the Jennifer Wallaces of the 1980s were allegedly educated and which she learned in university classes and in personal observation to dismiss as history distorted by voices left out, criticism discouraged, and biases submerged in "fact."

The books which have restored her confidence in the uses of history texts for the young have different looks, authors, biases, and approaches to student participation. These days in South African university departments of history, academics debate conflicts between nationalist, colonialist, liberal, Marxist, and Africanist historiographies, but common to all is the admission that every narrative of the past has some debatable assumptions about the important, the trivial, and the uncertain "facts" of the past. Striking, in the new texts to be sampled below, is their request to students that they seek to uncover these assumptions, including those in these very books. Up front its authors say that they hope the book will help students to use their own personal, modern African world as a starting point for studying the past. The authors say they aim to describe how change happens over time, but they want the student to develop "an open-minded, questioning, critical attitude" toward the text itself. They invite readers to "challenge stereotypes, to evaluate sources, to apply tests to evidence, and to assess the historiographical differences over which professional historians argue." Students are thus invited to take intellectual initiative, to become actively involved in the search for historical knowledge, and to resist subservience to experts while learning how to respect the discipline that goes into the making of expertise.[67]

Most of all, these books declare their bias toward a history of South Africa that is maximally inclusive of all its people. The introductory pages of one Standard Eight text defines the subject of history as "ordinary people and how they lived." It warns the student to think critically about the concept of "race." "In this book the words 'black,' 'white,' 'coloured' and 'Indian' are used about different groups of people. But you should remember that although people have different skin colours and speak different languages, we all want the same things from life and we all have the same rights."[68]

The earliest inhabitants of southern Africa have their rights to history respected here in the fifty pages devoted to the San and Khoikhoi peoples. This beginning contradicts the later Afrikaner claim that they came to an "unpopulated" area of Africa, a view quite in sync with contemporary European visions of North America and Australia. After a survey of extant evidence of San religion, art, and social customs, an inserted study question asks: "Do you think it is correct to dismiss the San people as 'primitive' or backward?" And later comes the project: "With a partner, discuss why you think many whites before 1980 wanted to believe that Africans could not organize complex societies."[69]

Perhaps the most striking departure from the old "learn the facts" method of the pre-1990 history texts is this book's regular resort to assignments that ask the student to empathize with a great variety of people of the past. One elaborate exercise calls for groups of seven to discuss how the British governor of Natal should have distributed agricultural land among seven claimants—a British commercial farmer, a Hlubi refugee, a trekker farmer, a Zulu convert to Christianity, the Zulu king, and a Zulu farmer. The governor's actual decision came down to siding with the commercial farmers, thus adding another plank in the platform of segregationist systems to be perfected in the laws of 1913 and the 1948–1980 eras.[70] The exercise opens up questions of agency, conflicting interests, and diverse effects of governmental power among all the parties to complex historical events. The student is likely to conclude: "It could have been different, and for some people involved, it *should* have been different."

The classroom management of such approaches to history requires an alert, open-minded, flexible teacher, who knows some of the dangers of asking for degrees of empathy for which a student may be unprepared. Like asking a southern white teenager in the 1950s to imagine what it was like to live as a slave in the 1850s and asking a German in the 1960s to identify with an inmate of Auschwitz, these ventures into historical imagination can have deep emotional impacts. Modern educational psychologists are well aware of this fact. The education that most of us remember is the education that touched our intellects and our emotions. The writers of these new South African high school history texts are unapologetic converts to this truth as they ask the student to juxtapose alternative views of what "really" happened in the past, whose interests were really at stake, how the complex story might have been told differently, and how its agents might have made it different. The intellectual-emotional struggle to understand the past here must sometimes put strains upon students and teachers together. Not from every one of these exercises will students go home inwardly tranquil.

A sample of the "activities" scattered throughout the early history (up to 1870) text will suggest as much. Responses to these learning techniques will be influenced by the presence of students of diverse ethnic backgrounds in the new South African classroom:

> Working in groups, workshop/write a play in which the main character is a trekboer or a Khoikhoi servant who is transported in time into the future and wakes up in a [1990s] wage negotiation meeting. (Or it could be about a modern worker transported back into the past.)

In what ways was the influence of the missionaries good from the point of view of the Khoikhoi, Tswana and others they converted? In what ways might the missionaries have harmed the people they came to convert?

Imagine you are a trekker child. Write down what you would have enjoyed and what you would not have liked about your travels. . . . Imagine you are a Basotho teenager living along the Orange River at the time when the trekkers moved through the land. Write down your thoughts about these people.

Find a South African school textbook from the 1960s or 1970s that deals with the movement of the Dutch trekkers in the 1830s and 1840s. Write a report comparing the view of the trekkers presented in the old book with the view presented in this book.

Imagine that you are [Zulu King] Dingane. . . . Looking at all the information available, decide how much of a threat the trekkers are to you and your way of life. How are you going to handle your meeting with the part of trekkers led by Retief? Think of all the options available to you. [The option taken was to murder Retief and his delegation.]

Imagine you are a child, girl or boy, of the Venda people, and that you have been captured [by trekker raiders] at the age of twelve. You are taken to the market at Ohrigstad where there is a lot of trading going on. You are given to one of the trekker families and they take you back to their farm on a wagon loaded with other supplies. You are too scared to try to escape. The trekker children give you apricots to eat, which you have never seen before. You like them, but you are thinking about your family. You have been indentured to work for the trekker family for fourteen years, so you will be twenty-six when you might be able to leave and return to your people. How will you find them? Will they recognize you? Write about what happens to you. . . .

In the Introduction to this book we said that everyone tells a story differently depending on his or her point of view. In groups, discuss whether you think the writers of this textbook have provided a balanced view of South African history, or whether they show any bias.[71]

Any student who goes on to study the companion volume treating the twentieth century will have no difficulty concluding that the bias of the book is toward the black liberation struggle and its climax in the election of 1994. On the top cover flies the new South African flag, and two photos peer at each other on the left: Cecil John Rhodes and Archbishop Desmond Tutu. This volume, too, begins with questions of elements in the student's sense of identity, with emphasis on immediate family connections and the biographies of parents and grandparents. What was life like for them when they were thirteen or fourteen years old? "Later in this book you will be asked to interview people about specific events and times."[72] Across these 178 pages specific events and times of the twentieth century mark the rise, decline, and fall of apartheid South Africa: hundreds of news articles, portraits, posters, election results, documentary sources, outlines of laws, protests against laws, mass demonstrations, political organization for and against the perpetuation of apartheid, imprisonments, armed clashes, murders, police repressions, forced removals, and other images of change almost invisible in the formats and texts of school histories like *History for Standard 10*. Again, the "activities" sections of this volume underscore the authors' intention to persuade students to become immersed in the changing tides of their society, to test those waters for how others drowned or survived through it all, and to discern how anyone's place and experience in a society influences how they tell their personal and group stories. The book begins with "the South African War" of 1899–1902 and asks the student how that conflict should be named:

> Some people have called this war a 'white man's war,' or the 'Anglo-Boer War' (meaning a war between the British and the Afrikaners). Why do you think they call it by these names? Why does the photo [opposite, showing a 1900 Boer commando unit with two white and five black soldiers] make these names seem wrong?[73]

Most of the ensuing assignments ask about the impacts of apartheid government on cross sections of South Africans in the years 1948–1994. Students are challened to undertake exercises in empathy:

> Imagine that you are working in early Johannesburg at one of these [gold mine-related] jobs. Write a diary entry describing a day in your working life. Include details like:
>
> - how you got to work
> - what you did at work
> - the other people you met
> - anything unusual/horrible, wonderful that happened that day.

> Try to find someone who was moved from their home because of the Group Areas Act. Interview them about how it happened, how they felt at the time, and how it changed their lives.

> Why do you think Source B calls Bantu Education "education for slavery"?

In this unit you learnt that people tried to oppose the Bantu Education Act by setting up independent schools. With a partner, choose any topic in South African history. . . . How do you think that this topic would have been taught in

- one of the government's Bantu Education schools; and
- one of the ANC's independent schools?

How many of the demands of the [ANC] Freedom Charter do you think have been met today?

Find out if anyone in your area took part in the 1956 [women's] march to the Union Buildings. If so, see if you can talk to them about their experiences. If not, write an imaginary account of a woman from your area who took part in the march. Describe your journey to Pretoria and your feelings on that day.

With a partner, imagine that you are a radio reporter interviewing one of the protesters about what happened in Sharpeville. Then act out your interview for the rest of the class. . . . Imagine that you are a young policeman who was present at Sharpeville. Write in your diary about what happened that day and how you feel about the events.

The 1950s, 1960s, and early 1970s are probably the years when your parents were growing up. Ask your parents or neighbors about what life was like at this time.

Get into groups of five. Each person is to play one of the following parts:

- a factory owner
- a wealthy Soweto business person
- a resident of a homeland
- a white mineworker
- an ambitious politician

Each person must decide whether he or she would support or reject each of the reforms [in the 1980s, abolishing some of the apartheid laws], and give reasons. . . . Who would benefit from each reform? Who would not benefit?

Why do you think De Klerk made his speech in February 1990 [unbanning political organizations and announcing the end of politically enforced apartheid]? Discuss which factors you think may have been the most influential in bringing about change. (There is no right or wrong answer.)

Do you know anyone who returned from exile to South Africa in the early 1990s? If so, ask her or him about their experiences. How did hey feel when they heard about De Klerk's speech in 1990?

Some of the problems which faced young people in the mid-1990s are listed below. In groups, try to think of reasons why these problems had developed, and discuss possible solutions. Do you and your friends face similar problems?

- unemployment
- pollution
- AIDS
- violence
- crime
- drug abuse

How do you think people's everyday lives are going to change in the next twenty years? With a partner, agree on five changes that you both think will happen.[74]

In the curriculum that Jennifer Wallace teaches at St. Cyprian's, the two Standard Eight books quoted here preview the more advanced history which she teaches in Standard Twelve. The latter book carries on the process and content of the other two. These are the books that have restored her faith in the uses of texts for history teaching. As a teacher in a private school, however, she is the first to say that new *public* education systems in South Africa face a huge array of obstacles to the coming of effective primary and secondary schools throughout the country. Everything from the cost of texts to the training of teachers in new methods of student-activated learning to the scope of matriculation exams constituted great gaps in 2002. The standard national matriculation exam, for example, a holdover in part from the apartheid era, still asked in 2002 for knowledge of the 1924–1976 period only. Progressive teachers like her are lobbying the government to extend the exam at least to 1994, in step with the texts viewed here. That an ANC-dominated new government has moved so slowly on this matter is puzzling, although flexibility in local school policies has permitted one upper-class Cape Town suburb, Rondebosch, to include a section in its "matric" on the 1996–1998 work of the Truth and Reconciliation Commission.

Meantime, this capable teacher takes her students on tours to Robben Island, the District Six Museum, and the Holocaust Museum. The latter she finds especially important for reducing mass injustice to the scale of individual suffering. She appropriates the psychology installed now in both the Holocaust Museum in Washington and the new Apartheid Museum in Johannesburg: "Enter this history as an individual of old might have to have entered it—as a white, a black, a Jew, or a gentile."[75] She says that discussion and debate have the most effect on the students, but she confesses that getting them to imagine what it was to be a person from another era of history is very difficult. "But I try. I want them to grasp various perspectives, for example that of Steve Biko, a mine worker, and a mine manager." She recommends to students the contemporary works of Alasdair Sparks and Antjie Krog, and with a certain pride she says that her parents, who before 1990 hardly ever discussed political questions, have now visited Robben Island. But some of her students have visited there three or four times. She is sure, with all dedicated history teachers, that young people's investments of their lives in a future South Africa is well served by deep, sober appreciation of its complex, tortured past.

Two Monument Memorials: A Constitution and the Truth and Reconciliation Commission

The distinction between public monuments and public memorials draws a moral-ideological line between celebration and mourning of collective pasts. But the line must not be drawn too exactly, lest one miss the empirical-political complexity of what monument and memorial makers mean to say to future generations, and how the latter bring their own interpretations to these re-collective public symbols.

Ask any informed outsiders what they admire most about the last decade of South Africa's history, and the reply is likely to be "the country's relatively nonviolent transition from a racist to a democratic political order." "Relatively" is a realistic qualifier. At first, 1950–1960, the little-restrained violence of the apartheid government prompted the measured violence of the ANC and other resistance groups. In the "emergency" era of the 1980s, politically motivated murders rose steadily, and then, from 1990 to 1994, the number of deaths from government-instigated and factional conflict doubled and tripled over those of the late 1980s.[76] In those days international news gatherers, as well as visitors like myself, felt that armed revolution was in the air. As of 1986, Desmond Tutu, newly elected Anglican Archbishop of Cape Town, voiced his opinion that "in South Africa it is impossible to be optimistic. Therefore it is necessary to hope." In this very time, however, our visit[77] with the exiled leadership of the ANC in Lusaka, Zambia, fortified hope if not optimism: There in exile, Oliver Tambo, Thabo Mbeki, and their associates conveyed to us a confidence that the future was on their side. Leaders of the Nationalist government, business executives, church leaders, academics, sports administrators, and other prominent whites were already expressing their willingness at last to parley with "the enemy."

Out of the parleys of the next eight years would come a new political order, goaded in part by continuing fear of vast armed conflict. At one point late in the negotiations of 1993, Nelson Mandela would say to the generals of the South African Defence Force:

> If you want to go to war, I must be honest and admit that we cannot stand up to you on the battlefield. We don't have the resources. . . . But you must remember two things. You cannot win because of our numbers: you cannot kill us all. And you cannot win because of the international community. They will rally to our support and they will stand with us.[78]

Mandela and the generals "looked at each other . . . [and] faced the truth of their mutual dependency." The stalemate required compromise.

In the midst of political conflict, compromise is another name for peace. The architects of the new South African political order had to be sure that it would also be another name for justice. They finally succeeded in balancing peace and justice in two political-legal achievements which constituted the roads on which they hoped the country could travel toward a just peace and a peaceful justice: a new Constitution and a Truth and Reconciliation Commission.

Superficially considered, the one might be viewed as the track to the future, the other the healing of the wounds of the past. But the doors of the two institutions opened, in fact, to both the past and the future. They both recovered a past worth celebrating and a future worth hoping for. They were both monument and memorial.

No one in the debates over both the Interim Constitution of 1993–1996 and the final Constitution of 1996 analyzed this combination more eloquently than Lourens du Plessis, professor of constitutional law in the University of Stellenbosch: "A constitution both narrates and authors a nation's history. The potency with which it can mould a politics of memory thus equals the authority with which it can shape the politics of the day."[79] When political leaders reduce to paper their design for a new government, he writes, they bring with them memories of what they mean to preserve and what they mean to avoid from the past. However formal and abstract the legal language, their legal principles bear the marks of particular history. In the short American Constitution of 1787, some six or eight pages long, the Philadelphia convention declared its hope for "a more perfect union" than the Confederation of thirteen colonies had made possible. And in some items of the ensuing Bill of Rights—for example, no enforced quartering of troops in citizen homes and no abolition of jury trials—the authors were vividly remembering complaints against British colonial government. On the whole the anticolonial accents of this 1787 document come across in a bit of a whisper. In the new South African constitution, they fairly shout:

The constitution provides a historic bridge between the past of a deeply divided society, characterised by strife, conflict, untold suffering and injustice, and a future founded on the recognition of human rights, democracy, peaceful coexistence and development of opportunities for all South Africans, irrespective of colour, race, class, creed, or sex. . . .

These words, which open the Postamble to the Interim Constitution of 1993, are a "unique epilogue," says ANC leader Johnny De Lange.[80] Also unique is an ensuing passage of political-ethical philosophy, words which have become justly famous: The baleful legacies of apartheid must now be addressed, on the basis of *"a need for understanding, but not for vengeance, a need for reparation, but not retaliation, a need for ubuntu but not for victimization."*[81] The postamble then turns to the practical question of the place of *amnesty* in the quest for a balance between these high goals. It calls the new parliament to provide for "mechanisms, criteria, and procedures, including tribunals, if any, through which such amnesty shall be dealt with." The "mechanism" that the parliament would approve in late 1995 would be a Truth and Reconciliation Commission. Its basic judicial criterion would be "amnesty for truth." Its hope for justice would be embodied in procedures for securing public knowledge of past victim abuses and perpetrator acknowledgment of responsibility for those abuses.

The final Constitution of 1996 is remarkable for its length, detail, and organizational plan for a new government.[82] Its most remarkable feature is a first twenty-five pages of "Preamble, Founding Provisions, and Bill of Rights." The Preamble resonates with the historical memories and hopes of the 1993 Postamble ("We the people of South Africa . . . honour those who suffered for justice and freedom in our land"). The Founding Provisions encompass the values: human dignity, equality, freedom, nonracialism and nonsexism, the rule of law, universal adult suffrage, and respect for diversities of language. In the next nineteen pages, the Bill of Rights, the mix of memory and aspiration is as dense as is likely to be found in any constitutional document in the contemporary world.

Only minimal knowledge of the life of most South Africans under apartheid is necessary for feeling undertows of recent history and waves of hope for the future in the long enumeration rights and duties of citizens posited in this Bill of Rights. No condensed list does justice to these pages, but their mix of memory and hope reverberates even in a precis:

Equality, Dignity, Security of the person.
Freedom from torture, detention without trial, and slavery.
Privacy.
Freedom of "religion, belief, and public expression, with the exception of propaganda for war, incitement of violence, and advocacy of hatred . . ."

Political choice: party, campaigning, standing for public office.

Freedom of movement, including passport and rights of emigration.

Protection from ill health caused by environmental pollution.

Property: "A person or community dispossessed of property after 19
    June 1913 as a result of past racially discriminatory laws or practices is
    entitled . . . either to restitution of that property or to equitable re-
    dress."

Adequate Housing: "No legislation may permit arbitrary evictions."

Food and health care.

Special protections of children.

Education in one's own language.

Access to courts and "information held by the state."

Then, a last section of this Bill of Rights deals with a matter that was once
a fearsome reality and that may yet again be a form of law and order: "States
of Emergency." This section, reminiscent of the 1980s, is careful, however, to
specify limits on the right of government to declare such a state, especially
limits on its incursion upon certain citizen rights that must be deemed "non-
derogable": equality, dignity, and life, security of the person, freedom from
forced labor, children's rights, and the rights of "arrested, detained and accused
persons."

Three whole pages, the longest section of the Bill of Rights, center on
those latter rights. The history of judicial oppression, before and during the
years of apartheid, rumbles through every page: Persons accused of crime have
the right to remain silent, to be informed promptly of the charge, to appear in
a court within forty-eight hours, to have an attorney, to be treated with dignity,
adequate food, reading material, and medical treatment while in custody, to a
fair trial, to challenge evidence presented, to the use of one's own language in
court, and to appeal a lower-court decision to a higher. These are not abstract
rights invented by logical deduction. They are the precipitate of injustices suffered in concrete places and times, by citizens dead and living, in long South
African history. Post-9/11 Americans might well wonder: Whose constitution—
ours or South Africa's—mandates the surer set of protections of people a government may consider its enemies?

The document is "monumental" indeed, says Lourens du Plessis, in that
it celebrates "a *peaceful* transition to a *non-racial* democracy after more than
three centuries of *mostly violent racial aristocracy*."[83] In text and context, it faces
the past and the future of a body politic. It invites citizens to engage in deliberation together on what duties these rights imply for each other, and it even
invites them—in democratic consistency—to devise improvements of the Constitution in light of the founding values of life, dignity, freedom, and equality.
In all, this sketch of the new basic South African law is enough to confirm
du Plessis's astute summary:

A nation that only celebrates tends to become oblivious of how
meticulous it should guard against the mischiefs of the past. A nation that only commemorates tends to underplay its memorable
achievements; thereby denying itself the inspiration it needs to
come to terms with an undecided future.[84]

Amnesty for Truth, Truth for Reconciliation

Appraisers of constitutions worldwide will find much to discuss in the South
African constitutional achievement. Americans should take particular note of
the 1996 tribute of the text to the authority of international law, a recollective
whiff of the role of international pressures in the final demise of apartheid.
Also worth noting is the insistence of du Plessis that respect for citizen participation in the making of law applies to the making of improvements in the
constitution, too. Not an inert, inflexible high law, immune to input from the
least of citizens, "Constitutional construction is the responsibility of a *public*
and an *open* community of constitutional interpreters," which includes every
citizen and every legitimate public association.[85] As a political, economic, and
cultural society, South Africa remains a work in progress. Around the constitutional skeleton the body politic has many a muscle to grow.

The acid test of any democratic order is its openness to need, concern, and
justice in the life of the individual citizen. The new order in South Africa is
far from realizing concretely the promises of the constitution, for the legacies
of the recent past hang heavy in the ordinary lives of its people, and the architects of the new polity considered this legacy a first order of new business.
Colossal past wrongs haunt the present. For some rectification of those wrongs
the new parliament authorized establishment of a Truth and Reconciliation
Commission.

The task of its seventeen members: to expose past injustice to individual
citizens, to walk a line between vengeance and amnesia toward the victims and
the agents of "gross violations of human rights" in the apartheid era, and to
recommend to government reparations for victims and amnesty for perpetrators who tell the truth about their part in those violations.

ANC leader Johnny De Lange testified that the TRC "was born in the
engine room of political negotiation."[86] Among the precedents for the rigorous
task of the future TRC was a move by De Lange's own party—the Motsuenyane
Commission—a "historic event, insofar as it marked the first time that a liberation movement had engaged in an independent commission to investigate
it own past, of human rights abuses."[87] Unfortunately, this high moral moment—illustrating the ability of a group as well as individuals to "swear to
their own hurt"—was not to be duplicated five years later when the ANC refused to accept the final TRC report with its criticisms of the ANC.[88]

At the heart of the idea for the later TRC was a compromise between the interests of apartheid victims, who wanted punishment, and the interests of perpetrators, who wanted impunity. The resulting mandate for the Commission, as one American scholar puts it, emerged from "reluctant realpolitik and . . . visionary moral ambition."[89] The mandate required balancing acts akin to the steering of a ship through waves roiling with clashing currents. The double-sided principle, "amnesty for truth," for example, was challenged early on in the Constitutional Court by the family of one murdered victim as an offense against justice. In the Court's rejection of the suit, Justice Ismail Mahomed called attention to the political-moral complexity of the TRC's task which required careful navigation between conflicting material interests and moral claims. The task, he wrote, consisted of

> a difficult, sensitive, perhaps even agonising, balancing act between the need for justice to victims of past abuse and the need for reconciliation and rapid transition to a new future; between encouragement to wrongdoers to help in the discovery of truth and the need for reparations for the victims of that truth; between a correction in the old and the creation of a new. It is an exercise of immense difficulty interacting in a vast network of political, emotional, ethical, and logistical considerations. . . . The results may well often be imperfect and . . . support the message of Kant that "out of the crooked timber of humanity no straight thing was ever made."[90]

Much has been written about the processes which led to the TRC, about its achievements over two and a half years, and about flurries of criticism that accompanied its work and its sequels. Of all recent efforts of South Africans to memorialize their negative pasts, the TRC has been the most elaborate, organized, and well known internationally. Inside South Africa in 2002, one was likely to hear the opinion: "Other countries praise the TRC. Here we got tired of it, and we don't much celebrate it anymore." Not always evident to foreign or domestic observers, however, has been the significance of the TRC episode for the posing of political-ethical *agenda* which call for democratic deliberation for a long time to come, not only in South Africa but for many other countries including the United States. Here, in conclusion of this chapter, I want to identify some basic questions in this agenda which I believe must be answered by citizens and institutions that stand in a worldwide crossroad between the injustices of a past and hopes for justice in a future. Almost every careful student of the South African TRC, including especially its members, know that the place of "truth," "justice," and "reconciliation" in human politics is inherently uncertain, unfinished, and forever subject to dispute. The theoretical-practical dispute over the meaning of these terms can no more be settled by a truth commission than it could remedy, in one swoop, the economic and political damages of colonialism and apartheid in all of South Africa. Clashing values and interests roil every society, and societies whose public powers *muffle* public expression of the clash are by definition not democratic. As philosopher Alasdair MacIntyre puts it: "Traditions, when vital, embody continuities of conflict."[91] By this definition the apartheid regime lacked vitality. It treated the answers to some conflicts, endemic to the democratic tradition, as perversely settled: Whose interests deserve decisive voice in public policy-making? Who has the right to define another's interests? How should differences in power relate to differences in privilege? Whose violence is justified, whose not? The apartheid regime had simple, oppressive answers to these questions. The new Constitution and the TRC together raised the level of discourse for South Africans by juxtaposing citizen values, claims, interests, and statuses which can never be easily composed and never should be. How do societies learn to tolerate high levels of conflict between the "ideal" and "material" interests of citizens (Max Weber's phrase) without falling into civil war? One answer is that nonlethal conflict requires ground rules on which most parties agree—protections of life and dignity in constitutions, laws, and enforceable rights not subject to revocation by majority vote. Newly vital conflict became possible in South Africa on the ground of principles flatly denied by the old regime: a definition of "South African" in nonracial terms, human rights law applicable to all, and limits on the power of government to treat diversity of cultures as license for diversity of public privilege.

Truth, Reconciliation, and Democracy: Seven Principles

Below, for the conclusion of this chapter and the setting of my turn toward the history of my own country, are seven principles which, in my reading of recent South African history, challenge the deliberations of citizens in both of our countries, especially around the theme dominant in this book: How does a human society deal with its negative past for the sake of a more positive future?

1. *Where Silence Has Served Injustice, Victims Deserve Special Voice*

> For me, the Truth Commission microphone with its little red light was the ultimate symbol of the whole process: Here the marginalized voice speaks to the public ear; the unspeakable is spoken—and translated; the personal story brought from the innermost depths of the individual binds us anew to the collective.[92]

> Those who made the decisions and issued the orders did so secretly and did everything to cover their tracks. Those who followed the or-

ders, the hints, the nudges, and the winks did so under a cloak of darkness. Neither those who formulated deadly policies nor those who carried them out so cruelly ever imagined that one day the darkness would be dispelled, that voices they thought long silent would speak.[93]

Democratic theory proposes that every citizen deserves his or her "day in court," access to the public press, and claim on the attention of powerful leaders. Ordinary experience in every society, however democratic in form, dims the luster of this theory in countless ways by which some voices are louder and some interests more likely to claim attention from the powerful. Indeed, when the powerful serve their interests at the expense of justice to the weak, the latter's interests are doubly at risk: Not only do they suffer at the hands of power, but power can deny their suffering publicity.

This ordinary truth had notorious reality in apartheid South Africa. For the reversal of its racist principles in theory and in future practice, the designers of the TRC processes gave precedence to the long-silenced voices of victims. Courts are said in western democracies to offer the same opportunity, but courts cost money, time, and professional collaborations—all formidable barriers to a public voice for citizens lacking in all such resources for penetrating the narrow gates of courtrooms. Critics of the TRC note that in taking depositions from some twenty-two thousand people and after conducting public hearings with seven thousand of them, this only scratched the surface of the millions of South Africans who suffered under the former regime. Deputy Chair Alex Boraine notes, however, that the TRC placed no limit on the number of people who would be interviewed by the commission staff. "We never turned anyone away. We even extended our time line."[94] In sum, the TRC opened a wider door of public justice for the voiceless than it is likely to open in any court system on earth. Unjust, unpublicized suffering acquired new public status in this process. As Desmond Tutu commented to Antjie Krog: "Pain and suffering are remarkable things—our universe is very odd. Pain gives a quality to what is happening that nothing else seems able to give."[95] Stories of personal pain help deliver public memory from the abstractions of statistical reports of terror, in much the same way as did newspaper pictures of victims of the September 11, 2001, attacks on New York and Washington. The concrete images linger from the TRC hearings on apartheid-style terror: electric shocks, the paper bag treatment, prisoners pushed out of windows, youths shot in the back while fleeing from police, letter bombs that severed arms, and blows that blinded. The dead who died so unjustly now re-enter the communal memory of the living.

> [T]he biblical figure of Lazarus comes to mind. He represents the
> memories of the dead and persecuted of South Africa's apartheid

past as they intrude on the life of the present. Lazarus represents
the re-animation of South Africa's memory . . . Lazarus walks largely
because of the TRC.[96]

Societies owe to their dead multidimensional memory of their lives—this is a
chief assumption in the work of the TRC and one of its great contributions to
world debate on the classic question: What is truth? An enriched version of
"truth" underlay the Commission's listening to the seven thousand stories
which came in its public hearings. Deputy Chair Alex Boraine said that from
the beginning members knew that they had to search for the *politically service-
able* truth that went from *bare facts* to *knowledge* (historically contexted truth)
to *acknowledgment* of the human agency that makes history to *accountability* of
all concerned for action in the future to heal and curb the evils of the past. It
was a complex, awesome definition. The Commission early expressed its openness to four other ways of describing truth that serves political reconciliation:
rehearsals of *fact*, personal *story*, interpersonal *dialogue*, and finally in proposals
for *restoration* for damages. All of this, commission leaders came to believe,
had to be included in a definition of justice-serving truth in a society that had
so deeply offended that truth.[97]

In African culture, the community of the living has always included communion with the dead. Christians claim that there is a communion of saints.
About them, a line in the New Testament says that "apart from us," the living,
the saints of old "would not be made perfect" (Hebrews 11:40). Given the
silence with which perpetrators mean to drape victims, the TRC mandate added
a corollary: Apart from them and from our memory of their afflictions, the
living cannot be made perfect, either.

2. Past Injustices Must Be So Consigned to the Past as to Build a Barrier Against Their Repetition

We remember history in order to change history.[98]

Dealing with the past is not dwelling in the past—it is part of the
promise of a new future.[99]

The issue is both personal and cultural. Kierkegaard's remark—that, in order
purposefully to forget, one must first remember—can be interpreted in terms
of political ethics: A public has no right to stop dwelling on old injustice unless
it has remembered clearly and done something to remedy that injustice.

Like the view of Richard von Weizsäker that Germany needed changes in
its national life before leaders and citizens felt secure enough to stare unblink-
ingly at the evils of the Nazi era, South Africa experienced a freedom to confront the evils of apartheid once majority rule and a new constitution had
restructured their society. New structures do not guarantee new public mem-

ory, however, as demonstrated in the examples of truth commissions in Argentina, Guatemala, and El Salvador in 1990s and early 1990s. There, in a rush to impunity for all but a few perpetrators, the names of the vast majority of known agents of atrocity never appeared in official reports. Victims were mostly left in ignorance of who tortured their relatives, who threw them out of helicopters into the ocean, and who buried their bodies in unnamed graves.[100] Victims may want to forget their pains. But if they try to silence the memory by burying it in psychic depths, they may have planted a time bomb there. Too painful to forget, too painful to remember: That is the psychological dilemma of victims denied the right to tell their stories out loud to others. In a moving tribute to the testimony of Nomonde Calata, one of the four widows of the murdered Cradock Four,[101] Xhosa Professor Kondlo said to Antjie Krog:

> It's significant that she began to cry [during her testimony] when she remembered how Nyameka Goniwe was crying when she arrived at the Goniwe's house. The academics say pain destroys language and this brings about an immediate reversion to a prelinguistic state—and to witness that cry was to witness the destruction of language . . . was to realize that to remember the past of this country is to be thrown back into a time before language. And to get that memory, to fix it in words, to capture it with the precise image, is to be present at the birth of language itself. But more practically, this particular memory at last captured in words can no longer haunt you, push you around, bewilder you, because you have taken control of it—you can move it wherever you want to. So maybe this is what the commission is all about—finding words for that cry of Nomonde Calata.[102]

Psychologists will argue over whether recovered memory of pain is always healthy. Some who told their stories to the TRC found themselves retraumatized by the horror, haunted above deck by demons once banished below.[103] But on balance, the storytelling seems to have benefited most if not all victim-witnesses. Simpson Xakeka probably spoke for the majority when he said to Priscilla Hayner:

> I still have bullets in my chest, I'm still in pain. But emotionally it has helped a great deal. . . . There's a saying in our culture that "coughing it out relieves everything." I'm not going to forget what happened to me, but talking about it provides emotional relief. When I get together with others and talk about it, it helps. But I must stress that I won't forget what happened.[104]

Care for victims' ongoing health may compete on occasion with public legal and political health, a competition which Nyameka Goniwe experienced when she and the other three widows felt marginalized in the memorial ceremony in Cradock. Tension between public and private good is no stranger to the theory or the practice of democracy. Indeed, the good done a public in the recounting of past injustices may not be unalloyed, especially when it trespasses on a public's limits for absorbing horror, even at once or twice removed.[105] Horror stories make our nightly news; tomorrow we are glad to forget them. A private psyche that wants to forget will have plenty of support from a public that wants to forget. But such forgetting inflicts new harms all around: *Personal isolation in one's own suffering continues to fortify political alienation so long as no human neighbor empathizes with that suffering.* This truth emerged in both victim-perpetrator and victim-neighbor relationships in the TRC hearings.

Alex Boraine records a pair of remarkable openings to new relationships between victims and perpetrators made possible by public storytelling. White South African Johan Smit suffered the loss of a son to a bomb planted by the ANC in a shopping center in 1985. A commissioner asked Smit if telling his story, learning how his son died, and talking to the family of the man who did the killing, enabled him to find "some relief." His answer must have surprised the commissioners, for he proceeded to say how he was beginning to have some understanding of how such an atrocity could occur:

> Yes, it gave me peace because I knew what was happening. I thought that if I placed myself in the other person's shoes, how would I have felt about it? How would I have liked not to be able to vote, not to have any rights, and that kind of thing? So I realized that I would not have liked it, so I realized how it must have felt for them.

Grief, expanded toward empathy, is a remarkable human achievement. It did not always occur in the hearings; but when it did a momentous political change begins. A similar exchange, from the other side of an atrocity, came in the testimony of a colonel who headed the Ciskei Defence Force that carried out the Bisho Massacre. Speaking to a Bisho audience the colonel said,

> We are sorry, the burden of the Bisho massacre will be on our shoulders for the rest of our lives. We cannot wish it away. It happened. But please, I ask the victims not to forget but to forgive us. To get the soldiers back into the community, to accept them fully, to try to understand also the pressure they were under then. This is all I can do.

"After a moment of stunned silence," says Boraine, "the entire audience, which included many of the victims of the massacre and their relatives, burst into applause."[106]

That applause did not necessarily mean the transformation of alienation into utopian reconciliation, and it did not settle the question of how forgiveness serves or mis-serves a knitting up of the torn sinews of a damaged body politic.

But it does mean that one way by which a past atrocity gets *put* in the past is when its victim offers public expressions of grief and a perpetrator offers a combination of fact, remorse,[107] and empathy for victims. The mere concession, "It was wrong, and it should not happen again," clears a first barrier to a different future. Victims assist that opening when they offer, not sympathy, but empathy for the humanity of the wrongdoer. Welcoming both victim and perpetrator "back into the community," on new moral terms, was a chief end of the TRC. At its best, it served that end remarkably, and the achievement, for a deeply fractured society, was profoundly political.

3. Some Are More Responsible, Some Less, but All Are Responsible

> Thou shalt not be a victim. Thou shalt not be a perpetrator. Above all, thou shalt not be a bystander.[108]

Near the deadline for filing applications for amnesty, six young black men in Cape Town entered their application in the TRC office. The application read, "Amnesty for apathy."

> The act says that an omission can also be a human rights violation. . . . And that's what we did: we neglected to take part in the liberation struggle. So here we stand as a small group representative of millions of apathetic people who didn't do the right thing.[109]

If they have made no other contribution to an emerging world consensus about the causes of mass, government-sponsored murder, truth commissions and international court trials have demonstrated that political responsibility is many leveled. Western courts focus their work on the principal agents of crime, truth commissions also; but the latter are free to widen the scope of agents, as did parliament's mandate for the TRC, which distinguished between four levels of responsibility for officially enacted atrocity: (1) those who carry out the torture, the murders, the disappearances; (2) those who issue the orders; (3) those who create a climate in which gross violations of human rights can occur; and (4) those officials who contribute to (3) by neglecting their duty to curb or punish (1) and (2). This is a wide net of responsibility, but the six Cape Town youths widened it to a fifth level: (5) the apathetic bystanders. Significantly, these six black youths confessed apathy toward the struggle of black-led movements. Former University of Cape Town Vice Chancellor Mamphela Ramphele wove the same wide net when she noted that a diminished sense of responsibility for changing the apartheid system afflicted the oppressed as well as the oppressors. "We tend to justify the acts of those who are oppressed. The survival culture during the struggle spawned a particular approach to life that undermines the building of a culture of rights *and* responsibilities."[110]

No single issue generated more philosophic-ethical controversy in the hearings of the TRC than the question of how much responsibility, if any, particular persons in the South African society of 1948–1994 ought to bear for the evils of apartheid. Security police told truths about their treatment of dissidents, but often with the disclaimer, "We were obeying orders." Order-givers sometimes said, "We didn't order them to do those terrible things. 'No president can know everything which takes place under his management—not even an archbishop.' "[111] Some, including President F. W. De Klerk, did acknowledge that some apartheid policies were conducive to human rights abuses.[112] But only a few high officials of any party confessed to sins of omission. For that confession the Cape Town Six offered an example of conscience in citizens that exceeded that of many officials.

Did a great mass of citizens bear *real* responsibility? A certain few TRC witnesses answered an eloquent "yes" to the question in ways that must have caused great discomfort all over South Africa. The eloquence of these testimonies matched their rarity. A former state spy, Craig Williamson, testified in 1997 in Cape Town as follows:

> It is . . . not only the task of the members of the security forces to examine themselves and their deeds. It is for every member of the society we served to do so. Our weapons, ammunition, uniforms, vehicles, radios and other equipment were all developed and provided by industry. Our finances and banking were done by bankers who even gave us covert credit cards for covert operations. Our chaplains prayed for our victory and our universities educated us in war. Our propaganda was carried by the media and our political masters were voted back into power time after time with ever increasing majorities.[113]

A few similar forthright confessions of high-level responsibility came from two officials of the National Party. One was Pik Botha, former National Party Minister of Foreign Affairs:

> I could have and should have done more to find out whether the accusations that government institutions were killing and torturing political opponents were true. Not one of us in the former government can say today that there were no suspicions on our part that members of the South African Police were engaged in irregular activities.

Another was Leon Wessels, former Deputy Minister of Law and Order:

> I . . . do not believe that the political defence of "I did not know" is available to me, because in many respects I believe I did not want to know. . . . Since the days of the Biko tragedy . . . the National party did not have an inquisitive mindset. The National Party did not have an inquiring mind about these matters.[114]

A "turbulent priest" like Desmond Tutu or a disaffected member of Parliament like Alex Boraine might come to tell us about illegal torture, said Adriaan Vlok, former Minister of Law and Order, and we "should have listened to people like that . . . [but] we had all been indoctrinated not to listen to each other"[115]—not to listen, especially, to longtime political opponents like members of the Liberal Party in Parliament. Among them was Boraine,[116] who more than once expressed his awareness that "I who participated in an undemocratic Parliament have to accept a measure of responsibility for the actions of that Parliament."[117] It was only natural for many white people and a few blacks, he added, to remain quiet about the injustice of the racist system when they were the principal beneficiaries of that system.[118] Perhaps the profoundest *absence* in the TRC hearings was that of white South Africans, the principal beneficiaries of apartheid for decades. The economic fact of their benefits lay behind one final recommendation of the commission: a one-time wealth tax, a recommendation which by 2004 Parliament had not adopted.

The idea that political responsibility assumes a wide net of agency encountered in former President F. W. De Klerk a severe countercurrent of ethical and political philosophy. In several settings, including the TRC, De Klerk expressed sorrow that apartheid had hurt some people; he apologized for some results of the policies. But he never conceded that the policies were morally wrong in principle. And in response to the proposal that he apply for amnesty for the crimes committed during his time in parliament and as president, he resorted to the claim that "amnesty" concerns guilt for a legally defined crime, and of that he was never guilty. Not to a truth commission was he required to confess moral responsibility above and beyond the legal. Having disowned responsibility for the crimes of various subordinates, he declared himself immune to amnesty as well as to confessions like those of his NP colleagues Pik Botha and Leon Wessels.

Obvious in much of this debate was ambiguity about whether "gross violations of human rights" consisted sometimes of legal actions that were morally wrong. Many of the horrors that came before the TRC were technically unlawful, and courts of the era who overlooked these horrors have their own accountability to undertake in some future year of South African history.[119] Charging perpetrators with crime that was not defined so in their society became muscular in the trials of Nazi war criminals in 1945–1946. Under the Nuremberg laws, did Nazi functionaries merely do their legal duty? The TRC was not a place where extended discussion of ethical theory was much to be expected; but theoretical standoffs accounted for some of the bitterest clashes in the deliberations. Was apartheid a good idea that had "unfortunate" results, or a bad idea in principle? Are there moral duties which override legal duties? Do leaders really have to take responsibility for much of the behavior of their associates? To what degree were only a few people responsible for the racism in this system, to what degree the many? The deliberations of the TRC left these questions open for many a participant and for many in the national audience. But in these clashes over assumption, once again was demonstrated the dictum of Kurt Lewin, "Nothing is so practical as a good theory." One has to add: or a bad one.

4. Some Must Represent Others

Responsibility thus calls us to stand-in for one another, to act self-lessly for others, in particular for the poor and the oppressed.[120]

The idea of representation has always been subject to much ambiguity and dispute among political philosophers. When a leader, elected by a majority of voters, claims to represent them, should she also claim to represent the minority opposition? Is she free to define constituent interest as she sees fit? Or must office holders continue to subject themselves to the critiques of both majorities and minorities? What is the obligation of officials to interpret the interests of rival constituencies to each other?

In its refusal of general impunity and its consideration of amnesty for some but not all perpetrators, the TRC insisted on uncovering the individual victims and agents of atrocity. But on many occasions it found itself stymied over the resistance of high officials to assume any responsibility for the behavior of lesser officials. A similar public tension surfaced on the side of victims in the hearing. Twenty-two thousand depositions, some anti-apartheid activists noted, only scratched the surface of those who actually suffered from forty-five years of National Party rule. Were the TRC witnesses therefore representative of a great mass of other sufferers? Who has the right and the responsibility to represent the interests, the causes, and the facts pertaining to others?

The question may never be settled in political theory or practice, and the lack of settlement is important. Surely one of the lines between a human-rights culture and the culture of totalitarianism is the freedom of any citizen on occasion to cry: "That guy doesn't represent me!" But, on the other hand, the right and responsibility of some to represent others is mandated by almost any philosophy of public life except radical libertarianism. Furthermore, if the conservative tradition of Edmund Burke has continuing validity, democratic "representation" of interests is two-sided: outward, on behalf of constituents to others, and inward, on behalf of those others to the constituents. In this double role some leaders have heavier, more complex, and more controversial roles than others. When a Willy Brandt knelt before the war monument in Warsaw in 1970, Poles had a right to think that he did so on behalf of Germany, for he was the German Chancellor. Inside Germany, the gesture was very controversial. It took years for most Germans to accept the power and justice of the event, which was all the more remarkable for the fact that socialist Brandt spent almost all the years of the Nazi regime exiled in Sweden.

No frustration and failure haunted the work of the TRC so regularly as the refusal of leaders on many levels, especially the highest, to assume some genuine version of responsibility on behalf of their parties, professions, and the nation as a whole. The frustration and failure came to its most acute climax in the appearances (and disappearances) of the two living former state presidents, P. W. Botha and F. W. De Klerk. The one stonewalled the Commission with unconcealed contempt; the other laid claim to innocence of active or passive collaboration with the mean work of frontline perpetrators.

In an eloquent exercise of a "dream" of a radically different display of representative responsibility, longtime Progressive Federal Party leader Frederik Van Zyl Slabbert fantasized an inaugural ceremony on April 27, 1994, in which new President Nelson Mandela would say publicly, in the presence of F. W. De Klerk, "I have no hesitation in saying to F. W. De Klerk and his people: What I and my people suffered under your party's rule we will never forget, but we forgive you, and I invite you, and them, to build a new country with us." To this, Slabbert imagined, De Klerk could have responded with the words:

> I want to confess today on behalf of my people and myself, before
> you and the world, that we were fundamentally and completely
> wrong. That we almost wreaked irreversible damage on our country
> and its people. . . . For that I ask your forgiveness and that of your
> people.

"My people," De Klerk would say, include youth whom we misled, their parents, and "the police and army who had to stand at the forefront of oppression."[121] It would have been a tour de force of comprehensive representation, what only a head of state has full legitimacy to undertake. It would have been a display of symbolic moral responsibility transcending quibbles of direct, order-issuing administrative responsibility. Such a confession could have brought out some reluctant, healthy sighs of repentance among many white South Africans.

On the other hand, this fantasized speech could have been prompt political suicide for a former President who hoped to protect his NP political base as he entered the new ANC-led administration. But public confession was not to be, either in 1994 or in 1996–1998, when De Klerk and a few other high officials of the former regime did appear before the TRC while most others refused to do so.

Slabbert believed that his "dream" was no mere fantasy. It embraced a realistic public good:

> To bring truth and reconciliation together in our country would at
> the very least require a process of this magnitude. Reconciliation on

such a collective and social scale has to work by means of an awe-inspiring power of example, a cleansing ritual loaded with the symbolism of atonement-forgiveness-reconciliation. The truth referred here is not the truth of law and science, but the truth that comes from confiding and acknowledging, a sort of confessional truth. There is no guarantee that if it happens, there will inevitably be reconciliation. But at least at a leadership level the example of personal reconciliation needs to be made.[122]

Willingness to be seen as representatives of others, it turned out, was much more likely among the victims appearing before the TRC, said one of the commissioners, Richard Lyster.

> We've heard them ask the commission not just to recognize them, but also to recognize the thousands of other people who have also suffered. We've seen these people also caring and nurturing other people and helping them. We have been moved by that.[123]

"That" might be named the *ubuntu* of sufferers. Is there an analogous community of perpetrators, or two perpetrator communities—those who defend each other's crimes and those who have confessed? The history of the TRC leaves the answer hanging. The agents, the authorizers, and the cultural cultivators of wrong are seldom willing candidates for the *ubuntu* of confessors. Though F. W. De Klerk shared the Nobel Peace Prize with Nelson Mandela in 1993, his refusal to accept any responsibility for the crimes of apartheid diminished his reputation in profound contrast to that of Mandela. Of Mandela an American journalist said in 2004: "He is a hero precisely because he always admitted his errors and then tried to rise above them. And he never stopped learning."[124] De Klerk never rose to this stance. As Desmond Tutu sadly remarked of National Party leaders as a whole during a TRC hearing:

> It hurts me when I think of the quiet strength and resilience and magnanimity of the victims, that there is no response from their side. And for reconciliation we need everybody. . . . You see, we can't go to heaven alone. If I arrive there, God will ask me: "Where is De Klerk? His path crossed yours." And he also—God will ask him: "Where is Tutu?" So I cried for him, I cried for De Klerk—because he spurned the opportunity to become human.[125]

5. *Some Power Must Call the Powerful to Account*

How can you report policemen to policemen?[126]

> We had been so intimidated by the system . . . and so we would keep quiet. . . . We said just what the authorities wanted to hear. . . . And

Peter Storey came here and said, "No, that is not what God's dream for you is!" . . . With Peter's leadership, people learned what it meant to speak up, to be assertive.[127]

Among the strongest criticisms of the TRC has been its overconcentration upon individual victims and perpetrators at the cost of concentration on the *systems* that facilitated the racist ideology of apartheid. Hearings of institutional and professional representatives did occupy the docket toward the end of the hearings, and commissioners knew very well that individual responsibility, throughout the apartheid era, rooted in systematic patterns of policy, organization, and enforcement. In its own defense the commission could claim that the various policy evils of the era were already widely known and studied. Everyone knew about the pass laws, forced removals, Bantu education, reserved jobs, and arbitrary imprisonment. The TRC, critics urged, should have done more to denounce these systematic injustices, their legitimators, and their top-level implementors.

One group of crucial top-level officials of the system never brought into the hearings were judges. At one point, a lawyer commissioner, Yasmin Sooka, recommended that judges be subpoenaed and asked about their refusals to question this and that apartheid law or to enforce laws that might have moderated the harms of certain policies. Boraine reports that he opposed the idea out of anxiety that putting judges on "trial" might damage the reputation of the Commission. He was wrong to reject the idea, he says in retrospect. "No other institutions were exempt, and the refusal of the judges to appear before the Commission confirms the view held by many judges that they are in some way superior to other people, and beyond criticism." In its final report the Commission said bluntly, "History will judge the judiciary harshly" for refusing the invitation (as opposed to a supoena) to appear and for "their dismal record as servants of the apartheid state in the past."[128]

Quis custodiet custodes? It is one of the most debated questions in the history of law. If the overthrow of apartheid in South Africa and the subsequent TRC provided an answer, it is: *moral claims*, whose representatives can be as few as a single person or as numerous as in a social movement. The architects of the apartheid regime were proud of its allegedly independent judiciary, but very few judges in the era asserted independence of parliamentary power. When in 1963 parliament passed the law confining Robert Sobukwe to absolute solitude, for example, no judge protested that it was inhumane punishment, or questioned parliament's right to inflict it. Must moral principle sometimes judge positive law? Western lawyers tend to be wary of the idea. In the United States, the notion that the Supreme Court has obligations to consider the supremacy, on occasion, of moral claims will always be subject to sharp controversy. Many South Africans today know that morality and its base in religion can be their only refuge from bad positive law. Among those parliament members who supported the creation of a truth commission in 1995, Johnny De Lange put it unambiguously in 2000:

> Our call for a truth commission did not come from the constitution, or any law, but from our morality as people who want to heal our nation. . . . The international community expected us to deal with our past in a way that derives its legitimacy and morality from the international human rights practice.

He went on to note that the amnesty side of the TRC mandate "derives its authority from the constitution, whereas the human rights component claims its authority from our morality, our humanity."[129] The same argument ought to underlie the ongoing debate in the United States on joining the International Criminal Court.

"Our" morality, of course, suggests a collective moral consensus as much subject to democratic dispute as to affirmation. In the TRC moral norms frequently found overt support in Christian religious terms used by commission members and some witnesses. Not everybody in the country was happy with this phenomenon, for not every South African is a Christian, nor do all Christians articulate their political thinking in the theological terms of Archbishop Tutu. The relation of religious faith to the choice of moral principle is not to be settled in the politics of a truth commission, but in some instances the *lack* of both religious and moral critical leverage on laws and policies evoked some painful moments in the hearings. Not all religious beliefs provide that leverage, as Boraine reports sorrowfully of former State President P. W. Botha: "[He] was a proud and spiritual man, nurtured in Afrikaner nationalism, whose passion for his country was in the end deeper than his religious values."[130] One might put it differently: Nationalism was integral to his religion. On the other hand, there was the poignancy of "a very prominent member of a death squad" who applied for amnesty with the sad *post facto* admission that he had been misled, especially by his Dutch Reformed Church:

> I know now that what I did was very wrong but I believed my political leaders and my church leaders supported me in what I was doing. I believed it was part of God's mission to destroy the ANC who I was told were terrorists and communists who would destroy our country and our religion. . . . What can I do now? I have no place to go to. I can never, ever go back to the church which never criticised me but always supported me in what I was doing as a member of the security police.[131]

He was not alone in feeling bereft of a politically critical church. Politicians who opposed the regime often met with the criticism that they had no right to question the government. Both they and that death squad member found little "place to go" in churches unwilling to say that official power in human affairs must not have the last word.

6. "Truth" Helps Reconciliation, But It Is Not Enough

> Africa is a place of story-telling. We need more stories, never mind how painful the exercise might be. This is how we will learn to love one another. Stories help us to understand, to forgive and to see things through someone else's eyes.[132]

> Was the entire TRC process a failure? Yes, if one wanted to bring truth and reconciliation together. No, if it made us all aware of where we come from and the direction in which we must move.[133]

The argument will go on for a long time to come: Did the TRC harm "reconciliation," serve it, or leave it unaffected? Along with the criticism that it did not address systems of oppression focally enough, this question will remain the heart of many disputes over this monument-memorial event in the recent history of South Africa.

Much depends on a definition of *political* reconciliation, a question I will raise finally below. Without doubt burying the public past in public silence has its short-term benefits. In opening up his own East German *Stasi* files, Timothy Garton Ash discovered that some of his cold War-era German friends regularly reported their contacts with him, a truth that damaged their friendship. Divorces and suicides resulted in some of this "outing." But there was another side, said Ash: "Against this you have to put the many, many cases where reading the files has brought people relief, enhanced understanding and a more solid footing for their present lives. . . . 'At least now I know' is the common refrain." He is the first to concede that "the two wisdoms cannot be easily combined."[134]

Slabbert, among others, believes that personal confession and legal prosecution are the only two ways for getting at the truth about negative human behavior. The first cannot be coerced, and the second has narrower, more trustworthy procedures than those followed by the TRC. He believes that the effects of truth-telling on reconciliation are too various for assuming it to be either asset or liability. He notes that truth in divorce cases seldom leads to reconciliation between the parties, and in TRC cases like that of Steve Biko, the family's resentment at the offer of amnesty to his murderers impelled them to seek reparation from a court. Add to this argument the observation that many white people got tired of the TRC hearings and turned off the TV, and one has in Slabbert the skepticism of an apartheid opponent who, as a lawyer, doubts both the truth and the reconciliation effected by the TRC.[135]

But an equally passionate lawyer, Albie Sachs, speaks for other side. Now a judge in the Constitutional Court, Sachs spent 168 days in solitary confinement in the early 1960s. While exiled in Mozambique in the 1980s, he lost an arm in a car bomb planted by the South African secret police. He had experienced the dehumanizing effects of loneliness and uncertainty under interrogation, and he knew how violence can leave a person damaged for life. The comprehensive truth about human experience in those years, he said, was personal. It could not be reduced to the factual "truth-and-nothing-but-the-truth" demanded by ordinary courts:

> I believe that personalising these accounts, far from having
> been the weakness of the process, was its strength. The oppressed
> are people. . . . We had to make people realise that human beings
> were doing things to other human beings. Perhaps the most difficult
> part of the whole process was to acknowledge that the perpetrators
> themselves were human beings. . . . Reconciliation lies in converting
> knowledge into acknowledgment of the pain, in hearing the voices
> of the victims, speaking for themselves in their multiple voices,
> from all sides, from many different quarters, from all the sections of
> our society. . . . It lies in the perpetrators acknowledging, however
> haltingly in whatever limited way, at least something of what they
> did.[136]

Not to identify "truth" with "the facts" was important for all thoughtful proponents of the TRC process. The courts may settle for "just the facts," but that way lies many an abstraction from lived human experience. Personal stories encompass wider ranges and shades of truth, and a society's history ought to encompass the same. And, beyond this analysis of factual, personal, and social (or "dialogical") truth, the TRC welcomed a fourth dimension of truth: truth that serves rather than destroys community between the oppressed, the oppressor, and the society at large.

This wide-angle focus became a bone of contention between the most acerbic critics and the most faithful defenders of the TRC process. The secrecy and anonymity of apartheid crimes constituted a permanent underground poisoning of many human relationships in South Africa. The issue here is what fortifies, and what restores, *trust* between persons who have endured many reasons to distrust each other. Prior to the fall of the Berlin Wall in 1989, numerous residents of East Germany, they later reported, suffered a collapse of trust in each other, even inside families. Authoritarian governments benefit from this collapse; they want citizens to be frightened enough of speaking up about injustice to protect themselves from being its next victim. Things done in the dark, remaining in the dark, thus acquire powers of repetition. No public power exists to call these things to a halt. For the TRC, *making knowledge public and identifying the agents of wrongdoing for the sake of hindering such repetition*

was the essence of the difference between mere knowledge and "acknowledgment."
Again, here is the distinctive, difficult, complex claim underneath all truth
commissions: depriving old crime of its secretive clothing and re-covering it
with moral whole cloth. Such uncovering of truth is imbued with hope. When
so understood, such truth is an ally to the restoration of trust between the
damaged and the damagers. Nascent trust may be at first a shaky bridge toward
reconciliation, but it can be a beginning. Facts and narratives did not lessen
the weight of trauma in all TRC witnesses nor did they yield firm beginnings
of tangible reconciliation with oppressors. But they did release many into a
new peace in their own personal life and with some of their neighbors, too.
Was it worthwhile to victims themselves to testify to the Commission? Not all
would answer "yes," but one Lucas Sikwepere did. Shot, blinded, and left with
bullets in his neck by the police, he said to Pumla Gobodo-Madikizela: "I feel
what has been making me sick all the time is the fact that I couldn't tell my
story. But now I—it feels like I got my sight back by coming here and telling
you the story."

Even certain perpetrators acknowledged personal benefit from their hearings. One was "Tim," who wrote a letter to journalist Antjie Krog: "Now, with
me having gone to the TRC with my story, it seems almost as if it's all right
to talk about it. Slowly, things are changing. It's as if I have been freed from a
prison that I've been in for eighteen years. At the same time, it's as if my family
have also been freed—my brother is all of a sudden much softer, more human,
more able to talk to me."[137]

7. After Political Nightmare, Reconcilers Have a Long Road to Travel

> The rather naive expectation—at the onset of the TRC's work—that
> once we have welcomed truth in the front door of our house, recon-
> ciliation would slip in the back door, proved to be wrong. . . . [But
> eventually] on one issue there was total agreement. Reconciliation
> was a costly and very fragile exercise. Also that it would be impossi-
> ble to refer to reconciliation without taking into account the issues
> of justice, accountability and restitution.[138]

The word, precious to the Christian tradition, refers in that tradition first
of all to the reconciliation of humans with God. Use of the word occasioned a
split between the theologian and the lawyer members of the TRC. The one
quoted Second Corinthians 5:19. The other exclaimed: "When the dust settles
in the streets, when the shooting stops, when people let go of one another's
throats, be grateful. That is enough!"[139]

The tension between high ethical hopes and resistant empirical realities
is an old concern among both the theorists and the practitioners of politics.

Some break in this tension appears in numerous post-TRC writings about the word "reconciliation." Some wish to abandon the word in political discourse. Others say that reconciliation is a step-by-step process that extends into the far future. Most resort to usage that takes seriously processes with many practical steps on the way to a society more humane than that experienced in the past. For the shooting to stop is one of those steps. For constitutionalized human rights to replace government fiat is another. And for a culture of revenge to begin to give way to tolerance, increasing empathy, and the rigors of forgiveness is yet another. These may all be social possibilities, but they are surely subject to long delay in the face of many injured relationships.

Almost no participants in the deliberations or evaluations of the TRC process ignore the danger of (what Slabbert calls) "sentimental" hopes for truth or reconciliation in the short-term future of South Africa. The great majority agree that the TRC itself was only "a first step of a long process of national and individual healing"[140] and that economic development must make good on the unmet promises of the new South African constitution, itself a document rooted as much in hopes as in achievements. A major post-TRC report from an ecumenical group of theologians goes to great length to link "reconciliation" to a long-term address of economic disparities: "Reconciliation without restorative justice is a mere salve for the consciences of the privileged." There is stolen property to be restored, bad housing to be repaired, employment to be developed, and civic participation to be made easy. For these theologians, reconciliation is far more rigorous than the cessation of the shooting. As John de Gruchy exclaims, "The critical issue is what we *do* with the truth that has been uncovered."[141]

Two other searching perspectives on reconciliation, one from a poet and the other from a theologian, can be adduced here as a help to a definition of reconciliation that cuts through standoffs between the idealism of theologians and the pragmatism of lawyers in South Africa and everywhere. The one is Njabulo Ndebele, poet-literature-scholar and Vice Chancellor of the University of Cape Town. The other is Dirkie Smit, Afrikaner, professor of ethics at Stellenbosch, member of the faculty of the Beyers Naudé Centre for Public Theology, and longtime critic of apartheid from years of teaching at Western Cape University.

Ndebele takes the processes that tend toward justice and new civic community seriously. With the coming of the revolution of the 1990s and the TRC, "the preconditions, for reconciliation," he writes, "were laid by acknowledging a common interest to preserve an imperfect zone of stability, in which the scale of morality was nevertheless seen to be tipped in favour of an emergent order." Such language speaks of process and history; it is neither absolutist nor relativistic but relational. "An imperfect zone of stability" comes as a decided improvement in the quality of life of citizens who have endured the instabilities of racist oppression and armed resistance. Ndebele offers several principles for defining the social dynamics that can lead to deeper reconciliation between alienated citizens: "It is important that we do not arrive at answers to problems too easily . . . It is in the interactive struggle for the solutions that new relationships are forged." Government's service to this interaction will be to preserve a safe public space for it to happen. In that space, "Our ability to shift into several identities in a multicultural society allows us the potential to locate ourselves within questions posed by others."

> The potential of an individual South African to establish relationships across inherited boundaries is a real feature of our national experience today. If there is any one thing the hearings of the Truth and Reconciliation Commission have done, it is to reveal the range of matters that lie at the center of our interactive public space. . . . The TRC, its hearings, and its report on their own cannot bring about reconciliation. It began a process that should continue.

Ndebele goes on to observe that, years ago against the tides of apartheid, reconciliation was already beginning to occur in the "nooks and crannies" of this society, "wherein the daily intricate intimacies of co-operation between master and servant may have created reluctant bonds, particularly in the farming and sharecropping communities." Similar bonding occurred between the negotiators of 1990–1993, who discovered that they were "not total strangers to one another." This history permits one to talk about reconciliation as a goal that is already happening in increments. The same can be said for forgiveness, more a process than the instantaneous act as described by many theologians. Finally, both the negotiated political settlement of the early 1990s and the later TRC

> allowed the country to cross a particular river of time and circumstance. Seen in this light, the negotiated settlement appears to have unexpectedly delivered a will to live with unresolved tension, while seeming to ensure that the painful wound of tension does not fester. Instead, opposite poles can enter into controlled engagements in which fixed positions are gradually abandoned until a comfortable, if imperfect, solution is accepted as a *working position*.

Interestingly enough, Ndebele adds, as of year 2000, social research indicates that white South Africans, who under apartheid "lost very little in material wealth . . . whose rights were never really violated" were pessimistic about their future while the previously oppressed were hopeful about their future. "They have far better access to water, electricity, telephones and houses than before. They experience a great deal more official responsiveness."[142]

This language and this perspective compose a sober, empirically rich, and norms-infused description of how reconciliation might be conceived in contemporary South Africa. It goes far toward warding off false idealism and false cynicism. It is something of a call to diligent, patient, daily work at interpersonal and intergroup bridgebuilding. It combines hope and realism for support of civic engagement and protection against the tyranny of perfectionism and despair. It embraces a rigorous conjunction between political conflict and political peace, as memorably expressed by Adam Michnik, veteran of Poland's democratic struggle of the 1980s. Said he to TRC leaders:

> I am negotiating because I have chosen the logic of peace and abandoned the logic of war. This means that my enemy of yesterday must become my partner and we will both live in a common state. He may still be my opponent but he is an opponent within peace, not within war.[143]

A theological help to the same perspective came in 1996, just as the TRC was beginning, from Professor Dirkie Smit, who draws on the memory-oriented theology of the late H. Richard Niebuhr. In his 1941 book, *The Meaning of Revelation,* Niebuhr described the use and misuse of personal and social memory in ways that could have been a charter for the work of the TRC a half century later:

> We do not destroy this past of ours; it is indestructible. We carry it with us; its record is written deep in our lives. We only refuse to acknowledge it as our true past and try to make it an alien thing— something that did not happen to our real selves. So our national histories do not recall to the consciousness of citizens the crimes and absurdities of past social conduct, as our written and unwritten biographies fail to mention our shame. But this unremembered past endures. . . . Our buried past is mighty; the ghosts of our father and of the selves that we have been haunt our days and nights though we refuse to acknowledge their presence.

To remember our own past in all realism, Niebuhr goes on to say, is "also to make the past of others our own." Faith and its source, God's self-revelation, launches the faithful on a journey of re-remembering that has no foreseeable end. Because it acquires new awareness of the history of others, this "conversion of memory" makes genuine solidarity possible, though only in an ongoing exploration in company with the contemporary descendants of those others.

> The conversion of the past must be continuous because the problems of reconciliation arise in every present. . . . Groups use their separate histories as means of defending themselves against the criticism of others and weapons for warfare upon rival parties. We cannot become integrated parts . . . until we each remember our whole past, with its sins. . . . No mere desire to overcome differences of opinion is of any avail unless it expresses itself in such reinterpreta-

tion and appropriation of what lies back of opinion—the memory.
. . . The measure of our distance from each other in our nations and
groups can be taken by noting the divergence, the separateness and
lack of sympathy in our social memories. Conversely the measure of
our unity is the extent of our common memory.[144]

In May 1997, a year and a half into the work of the TRC, Chairman Tutu
issued an invitation to the leaders of all the major contending political groups—
Nelson Mandela, F. W. De Klerk, Mangosuthu Buthelezi, and Stanley Mogaba.
Would they go, on the same day, to the site of some "notorious atrocity" committed by members of their own parties and there say, "Sorry—forgive us."
None accepted the invitation. Representative symbolic repentance would have
been well served by that gesture.

Then, in late 1997, one member of the TRC, Mary Burton, invited the
ordinary citizens of the country to commit themselves to the long journey
toward reconciliation by personal signing of a "Book of Reconciliation" to be
placed in TRC offices throughout the land. Anjie Krog said, "I decided at once
to take my whole family on Reconciliation Day [December 16], with the idea
of transforming the Blood River ritual of my personal history into a new ritual
of reconciliation and responsibility." But sadly, she reported, "The last time I
looked at the Book of Reconciliation in Cape Town, it had been signed by seven
people. Another forty-five had signed on the Internet."[145]

In the meantime, several commissioners, feeling obliged to support the
TRC recommendation of reparations, joined their colleague Burton to initiate
a movement, "Home To All," which called white South Africans to pledge their
active support of efforts to restore and heal the economic, political, and cultural
wounds of apartheid. Amid controversy, relatively few whites signed up. Some
did, some will. Wrote Burton:

> Reconciliation will not come quickly, but in the meantime peo-
> ple need hope of a better life, and a belief that steps will be taken to
> deal with past injustice. We have to increase our efforts to improve
> matters, to do the best we can—for the sake of South Africa, and for
> the sake of other troubled parts of the world, which look to us for
> guidance.[146]

Museums, statues, history texts, a constitution, a truth commission: They
all grasp the past for the sake of letting it go. They all have urged South Africans
onto the long road to reconciliation. Some are joining the pilgrimage, some
hang back. But other "troubled parts of the world" do look for guidance out of
similar troubles. If we Americans are wise, we will count ourselves as having
something to learn from these remarkable attempts of a new country to remember, to forget, and to become a country indeed.

3

Old Unpaid Debt

To African Americans

Modern people know better than to think that the sun needs a fresh [human] heart to rise each day. Funny, though, we keep on killing one another. We just don't have any reasons that would make sense to an Incan priest.

—Jerry Adler[1]

You get a sense of white Americans thinking, "Damn, that really happened."

—Richard Roundtree, commenting on the impact
of the 1977 television series Roots[2]

[F]or memory to function well, it needs constant practice: if recollections are not evoked again and again, in conversations with friends, they go. Emigres gathered together in compatriot colonies keep retelling the same stories, which thereby become unforgettable. But people who do not spend time with their compatriots . . . are inevitably stricken with amnesia.

—Milan Kundera[3]

"I ain't what I oughta be, I ain't what I'm gonna be, but I ain't what I was."

—Sign over a Western bar, admired by
Martin Luther King, Jr.

Genuine history teaches that things *could* have been different. Had Nazism never been defeated in war, public images across the German landscape would now feature monumental celebrations of Adolf Hitler and German armies. German children might be growing up, even if they knew enough to ask, with only vague answers to the question, "Whatever happened to the Jews?" Were the apartheid regime still in power, it would still be illegal to counter the Voortrekker Monument in Pretoria with statues of ANC leaders in a nearby public park. South Africa's schoolbooks would still report as unalterable fact the virtues of "separate development." White families would still be assuming that the best jobs remained in reserve for the future of their children.

Dramatic shifts in political power prepared the way for these revisions of public culture and concomitant education of children. Societies educate their young early. Long before they enter formal schooling, children have learned a lot about "how things are." They slip naturally into believing that what is, is what ought to be. The "normal" becomes the normative.

As we have seen, one constant theme in the commitments of memorial makers worldwide is their determination that a coming generation will not be deluded into captivity to such axioms. They mean to shape new social futures for their children by posting "Do Not Repeat" signs over doorways into the past. We have observed how, in modern Germany and South Africa, this determination issued in ongoing political struggle and shaping of new institutions. To be sure, children who enter a society different from the one their parents entered will eventually have their own opportunities to distinguish between social *is* and moral *ought*. They, too, will have to learn that things ought to be different. Such critical capacity has to wait a while. One is not born with it.

Why some of us acquire it, and some do not, philosophers and social scientists have long pondered. One of the more profound psychological mysteries is how present experience shapes and misshapes personal memory of what was and what ought to have been. How trustworthy is memory concerning what "really" happened? As all historians know, memory fractures, ignores, selects, and reselects from times past. No personal human memory qualifies as history. But, like journalism, memory often writes the first draft of history. Collective public memory is not merely an accumulation of personal memories. Nonetheless, we have to treat the memories of some citizens as credible, else we might never trust the outcomes of any court trial. Furthermore, unless we absolutely insulate individual recollection from institutionalized social memory and both from the histories academics write, we have to reckon with the complex relation between all three.

It will be the contention of the next two chapters that, here at the beginning of the twenty-first century, some Americans are learning to offer each other more honest versions of our national history than many of us were taught as children. A foray into my own childhood may help document this contention.

Black and White: 1927–1975

On a wall in the new Apartheid Museum in Johannesburg hangs a picture of a black housemaid holding a white child. Underneath is the caption, "I love this child, though she'll grow up to treat me just like her mother does."

White children born in the American South have long been taught to revere the first four words of this testimony—but not the final twelve—in memories of their own relation to a black servant in their households. In 1923 the United States Senate appropriated $200,000 for erecting in Washington a monument to the "faithful slave mammy." Fortunately the proposal failed to pass the House. Sentimental celebration of affectionate relations in their households insulated many southern white memories from awareness of what that South African woman meant when she added bitterly, "She'll grow up to treat me just like her mother does."[4]

Human hope for a better world hinges on the possibility that we all can learn, with the Apostle Paul, to give up at least some of our "childish ways" when we grow up.[5] I was the first child of parents born in the upper South in 1900 and 1901, respectively, my mother in rural Virginia and my father in Maryland. Both lived in Norfolk, Virginia, for most of the next eight decades. My father was an attorney, proud to have graduated from the University of Virginia and much involved in the civic life of Norfolk and lay leadership of the Methodist Episcopal Church South. We were middle-middle-class and sub-urban, with enough family income to employ Mary Oakes as our household maid for five and one-half days a week. In those preschool years of mine, a walk to the park was an adventure, invariably accompanied by Mary. (Never, to my memory, did anyone in our home call her "Mrs. Oakes.") Washing and cleaning were her regular chores. A segregated society had its exact duplication in the society of our house: separate bath and eating arrangements, knives, forks, and dishes. Every night she left us for a segregated bus trip of five miles across town to a segregated housing area which, years later, I would learn, was one of the worst slums in the United States.

I remember that her 1930 wage was $10 a week, translatable, perhaps, into $140 in today's economy. That calculation would make her income about half the official 2003 poverty line of $14,000. I do not remember ever asking my father, "Is $10 a week enough to live on?" As I grew into adolescence, the *unasked* questions were legion: Why no black students in my high school when there was a black community directly across the street? Why an absence of blacks from the city council? From our large Methodist church? From homes in our neighborhood? What was wrong with the radio program, "Amos and Andy"? With the minstrel show presented by my seventh-grade class? With the fact that, as a 1946 draftee, my Alabama training camp was thoroughly seg-regated? With the absence of any black student from Davidson College?

During my sophomore year in that college, Mary Oakes died in her sleep, asphyxiated by gas from a leaking stove pipe in her home. By that time I was beginning to know what there was to *grieve*, not only in the injustices afflicting the black woman whom I knew best, but in the lives of millions like her in the society that had raised me.

Breaks in that raising began to accumulate in my life that very year, 1948. By then I had become a Presbyterian and an officer in its state youth fellowship. In that capacity I was sent to an interdenominational conference in the mountains of North Carolina. A substantial minority of the conferees were black young people my own age, and one of the major adult leaders was a black minister named Lucius H. Pitts. Fifteen years later he would be president of Miles College in Birmingham during the notorious civil rights struggle there. Pitts spoke candidly and ironically about what daily life was like for black people in the South, and, at the conference end, he presided over a communion service that still sticks in my mind as the first time I had ever received that bread and grape juice from black hands. When, at the end of the service, Pitts said, "Go in peace, brothers and sisters," something changed in me. A fork in the road opened up. I was on my way into alliance with forces in American society already at work tearing down the political-institutional monstrosity of racial segregation.

That road would be a long one. For me the end is not yet. One communion service on a hillside in North Carolina was a kind of conversion for me, but, as a contemporary South African white theologian has observed, "conversion" need not be "a sudden act of moral insight." It can rather be a key moment in "a process of learning . . . the beginning of a new way of living."[6] From that beginning I would go on in 1957 to invite Lucius Pitts and James McBride Dabbs to spend a summer conference week with young people at my North Carolina presbytery camp, to stir discomfort in a congregation over these issues when I preached about them, to serve in an official community relations committee in Raleigh, to march behind Martin Luther King, Jr., in Selma on the very day that Lyndon Johnson ended his voting rights proposal to Congress with the words, "We shall overcome," to walk from house to house in a Raleigh black neighborhood soliciting voting registration, to make the sad observation that there were more black people in rallies of the local Democratic Party than in any church in town, to join a coalition of southern Presbyterian ministers intent on challenging racism in its many forms, and, finally, to assume the presidency of an ecumenical seminary in New York, where I not only discovered how pervasively *national* is racism in America, but also how education for the eventual cure of racism requires the voices, spirits, intellects, and experience of African American colleagues who have not given up their hopes for the humanization of white Americans.

I derive from this reconnaissance into my own pilgrimage some confirmation of what the word "repentance" can mean in personal-social terms. The word in the Hebrew Bible is *shuv,* to "turn," in the Greek New Testament, *metanoia,* a pervasive "change of mind." Clearly my new turns of mind, in all of these years, owed much to a complex of influences stemming from certain *persons* (like Pitts and Dabbs), certain *institutions* (like the church and the Democratic Party), certain public *gatherings* (like a march from Brown Chapel to the Sheriff's office in Selma), and certain highly symbolic *rituals* (like a Christian communion service). In all of these experiences, white Americans like me have been traveling from private and public amnesia into private and public mourning of a childhood past that educated us only too well. We are being re-educated, and occasions that promise our re-education are worth celebrating. In the rest of this chapter I recount some contemporary public events that mourn the racism that has afflicted African Americans for four centuries and that, by public remembering of that past, become events akin to ones already recounted of modern Germany and South Africa.

Three Cities

For how far back into history should anyone repent of the sins of ancestors? Historians will differ over how far into the past lie the roots of a society's racist institutions, and ordinary citizens will differ in their tolerance for what is "ancient history" for some and "persisting reality" to others. In our American case, the candidates for repentance occupy a disconcerting variety of locations in time. Christian scholars now study the two-millennia-old roots of anti-Semitism in certain passages of the New Testament. Such is the authority of that book that few of its modern readers dismiss that research as pedantic. Seeming textual legitimations of slavery and the subordination of women in the same book are like candidates for "revisionist" scholarship. *A fortiori,* if religious people can change their understanding of the Bible, they may well be open to changing their understanding of ancestors nearer in time.

The presence of slavery in American society is a "mystery of iniquity"[7] that deserves careful study of how the social reputation of an evil waxes and wanes. The makers of the U.S. Constitution inclined to the belief that one day slavery would have to be abolished. But how was it that Virginians had more antislavery societies in the 1820s than any other state but quickly abandoned them all in the 1830s? Thomas Jefferson seems to have assumed that one day slavery would have to go. A gathering storm of mid-nineteenth-century abolitionists assumed the same. But abolition waited years until loud, quiet, and violent national forces came together. During my lifetime I have never encountered in a fellow American enough temerity to say out loud, "Slavery was good." But many in my generation have said, "Segregation is good, and also white supremacy." The latter opinions are direct derivatives from the history of slavery, and they constitute warnings against the easy assumption that long ago this country learned to call that institution evil and to slough off its burdens. Not so: The weight of the thing still hangs around. No sooner does it get exiled into our collective amnesia than it pops up again, demanding new, accurate memory, acknowledgment, and memorial. Or so the agents of the following four local events have steadfastly claimed.[8]

Richmond, Virginia

Rivaled only by citizens born in Massachusetts, those of us born in Virginia early internalized an affection for the connections of our state to both the "Founding Fathers" of the United States and the "War between the States." The geography, landmarks, tourist attractions, and history books of Virginia overflow with contradictions between these two streams of our regional history. We did not often talk about it, but the questions were always there: Can pride in Thomas Jefferson and Patrick Henry join with pride in Robert E. Lee and Stonewall Jackson? Can Virginia, the first importers of black slaves with the eventual largest state population of slaves, surf so easily over this past? How did Virginians come to play such a key role in the revolutionary creation of "free" America, Lincoln's "last best hope on earth," and join in a war in 1861 to undo that creation? How could they argue so vociferously that, in going to war with the Federal government, *they* were the upholders of the original U.S. Constitution? How for decades did southern historians promote this latter view in virtual neglect of the fact that the "peculiar institution" of slavery was the foundation of southern economic and political power and therefore the insti-tution which war had to protect? How is it that few Virginians say out loud what most surely believe: that it was best for Americans all that the "Lost Cause" was lost?

The superficial answer to all this has to be that we humans are experts in internalizing ambiguity, contradiction, and forgetfulness. Who of us, raised in Norfolk in the 1930s and visiting Jamestown upriver from us, have any mem-ory of being told that 1619 is as portentous a date in the history of that settle-ment as 1607? Both years antedated the famous 1620 landing on Plymouth Rock, and Virginians have never been shy about saying, "We were here first." But the conscious content of the "we" seldom includes those twenty Africans unloaded on the Jamestown dock in 1619, nor focuses attention on Powhatan's people, who really *were* "here first."

If there is a city in the United States whose local culture combines memory and amnesia about this ambiguous history, it is Richmond, Virginia. On a site surveyed in 1607 by Captain John Smith himself, Richmond is the last upriver natural navigable point before the falls of the James River. This was Richmond: state capital since 1779; capital of the Confederacy from 1861 to 1865; destroyed not by the Federals but by the retreating Confederates in 1865, home of the FFV (First Families of Virginia), the UDC (United Daughters of the Confederacy), and the SCV (Sons of Confederate Veterans), and host to a Confederate Museum in the former home of Jefferson Davis; built first on old river plantations to the east, aging cotton and tobacco farms to the south, and flourishing orchards in the western valleys; rebuilt after 1865 on tobacco manufacturing, railroading, and commerce; home of a twentieth-century Harry Byrd-dominated state legislature meeting in a Jefferson-designed capitol; known in the 1950s as a southern center of "massive resistance" to school desegregation.

No less than Berlin and Charleston, Richmond is a city that remembers. Any visitor unaware of that has only to walk down Monument Avenue on the western side of the downtown. There, since the 1890s, has stood the proud equestrian statue of Robert E. Lee, followed soon down the avenue by Stonewall Jackson, J. E. B. Stuart, Jefferson Davis, and Matthew Fontaine Maury. On the base of the columns around an erect Jefferson Davis, inscriptions still proclaim the Confederate version of liberty. Like the idea of the "Lost Cause," as David Blight has recently written, these statues were born out of white southern grief but were "just as importantly . . . formed in the desire to contend for control of the nation's memory."[9]

Traditionally, black Richmonders lived east and north of the center city, whites north and west. By the 1950s half of the local population was black. Oliver Hill, first black member of the City Council, was elected in 1948. In 1977 a black majority finally came to the city council along with a first black mayor, Henry L. Marsh, as a local news headline announced: "Richmond, Former Confederate Capital, Finally Falls to Blacks." By this time two-thirds of white students in city schools had left for either private or exurban county schools. Various leaders sensed that the 1970s were "a time of growing racial polarization."[10]

The new Mayor Marsh, however, announced his intention to make Richmond an urbane example of economic growth and civil unity through new commercial development of downtown. Already a scattering of civic leaders, black and white, had begun to talk with each other about declining finances of public schools, the segregated housing market, and unequal employment opportunities. Quiet new partnerships had sprung up between individual couples in neighborhoods, parent-teacher meetings, and local civic associations. But from the 1970s to the early 1990s, the move from talk to institutional change was slow. A growing vocal minority agreed that, if Richmond was to overcome its longtime contentment with being a racially divided city governed by an elite white business establishment, it had to dismantle some institutional walls. The election of 1977 had tumbled one of them and set the stage for others. Like South Africa in the 1980s, though with a less radical sense of crisis, a cross section of citizens began to envision and build some bridges between various shores of the racial divide.

In almost every case the bridges required new experiences of each other from the two sides. One such experience was that of a Virginia-born woman,

Cleiland Donnan, who in the early 1970s was the director of a ballroom danc-ing school for white suburban teenagers. Her growing social-historical aware-ness in the 1990s spoke volumes about what white southerners could learn about their segregated society and its rootage in history once they began to engage in candid conversation with black neighbors. By 1972 she must have known that the local crisis over school desegregation was a warning that Rich-mond could be on its way to becoming a hostile central-city black enclave over against blissfully isolated rich county suburbs. In that year, she said, "I decided that I wanted to become part of the answer rather than part of the problem of Richmond." In her first participation in meetings of black and white citizens, she discovered that getting over race prejudice is like peeling an onion, "and it is tempting to rest content with reaching a particular layer of skin, when there are yet other layers waiting to be discovered."[11] In 1985 came a personal breakthrough that altered her estimate of Virginia history:

> In that year I heard a black man explain about our state's past, and suddenly I saw clearly my own false pride in all those beautiful to-bacco plantations along the James River. Standing out now was the hurt and pain and suffering of slavery. But most of all stood out the seemingly small continuing hurts—my own arrogance, slights, and my thinking that blacks had their place in the East End of Rich-mond and I deserved my place in the West End.

Soon after this new awareness she invited a couple, Janene and Winston Jones, who had moved into a previously all-white neighborhood, to pay her a visit. Said Mrs. Jones: "I remembered the first time Winston and I visited the Don-nan home. Black Richmonders usually visited the West End as servants. We wondered if the lady inside really wanted us." Said Mrs. Donnan, "the lady inside was as nervous as the Joneses."[12]

No student of interracial conflict in the cities of America is likely to sup-pose that new interpersonal relations will alone transform the social, economic, and ideological structures that have so constrained justice for black people from centuries back. But interpersonal relations have always had an important place in southern culture, and over the past quarter century structural change has partnered with interpersonal to effect some significant shifts in this city's pub-lic life. For purposes of this study, the reformation of Mrs. Donnan's Virginian *memory* is critically important. Growing up and living in this city had little equipped her to perceive the reality that lay, like a huge underground deposit, at the base of interracial rumblings in her city. It was an archeological site waiting to be dug: the Richmond legacy of slavery.

Like Monument Avenue, nothing in the architecture, statues, or other signs on the Richmond cityscape of the 1950s would have reminded locals or visitors of Richmond's key roles in the fostering of slavery in pre- and post-Revolutionary America. Virginians were pioneers in developing many facets

of the "peculiar institution"—from the importation to the sale to the distribution to the legislated devices for controlling a growing slave population in
the years from 1619 to 1860. The James fall line made Richmond the natural
site for unloading Africans who survived the Middle Passage and the markets
of the Caribbean. As capital of the pre-Revolutionary colony, the Virginia legislature invented "Black Codes" that would shape the relations of the slave
black and the free white in all the South and some of the North well into the
nineteenth century.

In Virginia and the other twelve original English colonies, "civilization"
began with agricultural and commercial ambition which entailed systematic
denial that the people called Indian were either civilized or capable of real
farming. For planting and harvesting of crops for competitive world markets,
no resource finally proved so valuable as black slave labor. Without supposing
that mere economics inexorably determined this preference, in his mid-
twentieth-century classic history, John Hope Franklin summarized this development:

> The answer to the vexing problem [of farm labor] appeared to be the
> perpetual servitude of Negroes, whose supply seemed inexhaustible
> and who apparently presented none of the problems that white [in-
> dentured] servants presented. If they ran away, they were easily de-
> tected because of their color. If they proved ungovernable they could
> be chastised with less qualms and with greater severity than in the
> case of whites, because the Negroes represented heathen people
> who could not claim the immunities accorded to Christians. By the
> middle of the seventeenth century Virginians realized the possibili-
> ties that lay in the exploitation of black labor; and all that was
> needed was the legislative sanction to give validity to the practice
> that was already developing.

So it was that

> [b]efore the end of the seventeenth century the slave code of Vir-
> ginia was well established. No slave was allowed to leave the planta-
> tion presumably on an errand for his master without the written
> permission of his master. . . . Slaves found guilty of murder or rape
> were to be hanged, and their masters were to be compensated by the
> colony. For robbing a house or a store a slave was given sixty lashes
> by the sheriff, placed in the pillory with his ears nailed to the posts
> for a half hour, and then his ears were severed from his head. . . .
> The pattern which the pioneers set was to be followed in subsequent
> years, as the institution became more deeply entrenched and as
> fears regarding the reaction of Negroes to their status increased. Be-
> fore the end of the colonial period Virginia, like her neighbors, had

become an armed camp in which masters figuratively kept their
guns cocked and trained on the slaves in order to keep them docile
and tractable and in which the assembly, the courts, and the custodians of the law worked for the maintenance of peace and order
among the black workers.[13]

Absent though many such facts were from the Virginia history book which
primary children of the 1930s were expected to study, it would be unfair to say
that none of this history was known to educated Virginia whites in the mid-
twentieth century. But it is fair to observe that in its public architecture, statuary, and other memorials the history of slavery in Richmond had virtually no
public visibility before the 1990s. Not until then did a cluster of citizens decide
that the time had come to remember, unearth, publicize, and make peace with
this past in some dramatic ways.

A poignant occasion in February 1993 offered many locals, black and
white, a chance to engage in shared celebration of achievement and grief: the
premature death of a Richmond-born hero, tennis champion Arthur Ashe. His
talent for the sport had been nurtured on the segregated courts of city parks.
Discriminatory athletic facilities and opportunity impelled him to leave Richmond to pursue his athletic career. When he won at Wimbleton, the U.S. Open,
and the like, he put Richmond on the international sports map, and local media
duly celebrated. Tragically, in the early 1980s, when the world of medicine was
only beginning to understand the transmission routes of AIDS, Ashe became
HIV-positive from a transfusion of infected blood. From then until his death
in February 1993, he became twice over heroic in his worldwide work against
the disease and his regular use of his status as a champion to draw children
and young people into participation in his sport and into commitments to
education.

That Richmond was proud of Arthur Ashe came to eloquent expression
in two events: The first was the display of his body in the state capitol, the first
time of such a display since the body of Stonewall Jackson lay in that quasi-
sacred Virginia place in 1863.[14] Behind this honor, of course, lay the political
fact that a majority of Richmond voters were now black. For their farewells to
him and with waits up to an hour, a long line of people black and white wound
up the hillside to the two-century-old classic Roman building to view Ashe's
body.

It was the beginning of a public movement for a more permanent local
memorial to Arthur Ashe. Why not a statue in his honor, and why not erect
it—of all places—on Monument Avenue? Local debate gathered in the conversations, the media, and public meetings over the next two years, the climax
of which came in 1995 in a long night meeting of the Richmond City Council.
At issue was not so much the appropriateness of a statue but its location. "Build
it near one of the now-desegregated public tennis courts where he once learned

to play," said many participants. "Monument Avenue was designed, well, for something different." The spirit of the debate, said witnesses afterwards, was civil and not rancorous—as one might expect among soft-spoken Virginians. All told, 128 citizens stood up to testify. One of them, a white, is said to have furnished a turning point in the deliberation with his statement, "If we locate it on the Byrd Park tennis courts, it will say to the public: 'He was a great tennis player.' But if we locate it on Monument Avenue, it will say, 'He was a great man.'"[15]

A few months later, that is where they located it: in a street crossing on Monument Avenue, not far beyond the pillared monument to Jefferson Davis, in company with that line of Confederate generals on horseback. From the 1890s Richmond had celebrated them as its "great men." Without arguing that those equestrians should be pulled down in deference to a new estimate of what the War between the States was all about, justice-minded Richmond citizens black and white knew that they were introducing to Monument Avenue an important bit of historical-cognitive dissonance. A statue of Arthur Ashe embodied a new slant on that Civil War: General *Grant* had liberated *his* ancestors.

In its very design, the Ashe statue spoke in a way also dissonant with the men on horseback down the street. Here was a hero of peace: In one hand he proudly raises a tennis racket. The other he extends toward a cluster of several children at his feet, and on that hand rests a book, symbol of his commitments to the education of black young people. The pedestal bears a sports-allusive quotation from the New Testament: "Since we are surrounded by so great a cloud of witnesses, let us also lay aside every weight, and sin which clings so closely, and let us run with perseverance the race that is set before us."[16]

If nothing else in its present urban landscape, the Ashe statue marks a new expansion of Richmond's "monumental" memory.[17] But there was a prelude to this event in another event in the year of his death: what the organizers called "A Unity Walk Through History." The idea grew from discussions between community leaders like Cleiland Donnan, Janene and Winston Jones, East End ecumenical retreat center director Ben Campbell, Baptist minister Paige Chargois, mayor Walter Kenney, and Susan and Robert L. Corcoran of the local Moral Rearmament Movement.[18] Coming together in a new association to be called Hope In the Cities (HIC), they decided that it was time for Richmond to look beneath the surface of its modern streets, river banks, office buildings, and parks to acknowledge that many of these acres once bore the prints of thousands of slave feet. A distinctive mark of the organization was to be acknowledgment of racial history. Ben Campbell said that in his estimate Richmond was "ground zero for race relations in the United States," given facts like its 1857 gross income of $4,000,000 from the slave trade.[19] Leaders of the project called in historians to survey the extant records of that era. An approximate map was drawn up to mark the places where slaves were unloaded, chained, and marched across a river bridge into a temporary warehouse on the north side, thence to the market auction block and plantation workplaces in Virginia and all the South.

HIC leaders then planned a two-mile path through these key locations, beginning with the south side of the river where the ships once unloaded human cargo and continuing to the north side whose market once hosted an estimated 350,000 slaves.[20] Invitations went out to fifty U.S. cities and twenty foreign countries to send delegates to the conference that would include a walk through the sites of this history. On a sunny June day in 1993, three hundred people assembled to follow the path where once trudged those Africans. Along this trail, the hike was punctuated with history lessons offered by an array of professional actors, storytellers, musicians, and Native American dancers. Among the somber locations were:

- remnants of the former southside docks.
- the cross-river old marketplace.
- a symbolic site of a now unlocatable old well, into whose deep water a black mother once threw her two small children and herself, as their only possible escape from slavery.
- Church Hill, on the east side of town, where still perches the St. John's Episcopal Church, National Historical site of Patrick Henry's famous "Give Me Liberty or Give Me Death" speech, which some historians believe to be the site of an original Native American burial ground.
- a platform on which a story teller, dressed in shabby plantation clothes, testified to incidents of slave resistance, and an actor, dressed quite differently, recited the Patrick Henry speech.

Presumably nobody in the audience that day needed reminding of the irony that Patrick Henry delivered his speech within shouting distance of a slave market. After the walk, a prominent African American columnist for the local *Times-Dispatch* reflected that Richmond might, after all, be readier to turn a corner than he had always supposed. The partnerships that would soon form for proposing the Ashe statue must have gathered some strength along this trail, and the embarrassing contiguity of bondage and liberty in the Patrick Henry speech may have stirred some observers (including this author) to open the history books and to inquire about Patrick Henry's views on slavery. It turns out that, like Thomas Jefferson, Henry had a profoundly guilty conscience in the matter. In commenting on a contemporary book attacking the slave trade, he wrote to a friend:

> Is it not amazing that at a time when the rights of Humanity are
> defined and understood with precision in a Country above all others
> fond of Liberty: that in such an Age and such a Country, we find

Men, professing a religion most humane, mild, meek, gentle and
generous, adopting a Principle as repugnant to humanity, as it is in-
consistent with the Bible and destructive to Liberty. . . . I believe a
time will come when an opportunity will be offered to abolish this
lamentable Evil.[21]

The celebrations in Richmond, between 1890 and 1920, when the statues
to Confederate heroes were raised on Monument Avenue, left few recorded
indications that the generation of that era remembered this divided conscience
among great Virginians of an early time.[22] In fact the guilt of the great Virginians of 1775–1820 turned into forgetfulness twice over in their immediate
southern descendants from 1840 through 1900. Samuel Morison comments
wryly about Patrick Henry's letter: "Except in South Carolina and Georgia,
almost every Southerner looked upon slavery as an evil, but a necessary one;
in time it became so necessary that it ceased to appear evil."[23] Later, by 1900,
one could say that slaves had publicly disappeared from Richmond's statuary
history.

In the midst of their countermovement, as some white Richmonders began to absorb the immemorial, unmemorialized suffering of slaves in the past
history of their city, Paige Chargois called for new empathy for the need of
some whites to honor the courage and suffering of their Confederate ancestors.
How to honor the sacrifices of leaders of the "Lost Cause" without honoring
the cause itself requires moral-historical discrimination not easily achieved by
anyone white or black in modern America. As one ponders the likelihood that
the equestrian Confederates will never disappear from Monument Avenue, one
thinks of Oliver Tambo's refusal to dynamite the Voortrekker Monument. Citizens need time to learn hospitality to each other's feelings about their diverse,
painful pasts, especially when one ancestor's triumph was another's humiliation. But suffering itself, whatever its nature and circumstance, can evoke a
powerful communal bond. As a German theologian wrote recently, "Suffering
is an experience common to all humans, indeed it must be suffering that unites
humans most profoundly."[24]

The achievement of accurate public memory of an embattled, ambiguous
good-and-evil past is a work in progress in Virginia as this is written. An emblem of fractured feelings about "the" war erupted in year 2000 when, on the
site of the old Tredegar Works, now a national historical site, the Bureau of
National Parks proposed to erect a statue of Abraham Lincoln,[25] seated with
his young son Tad, in commemoration of their visit to devastated Richmond
on April 4, 1865. A banner portrait of Robert E. Lee had already flown on these
acres, only to be burned by protesters. On the opposite ideological side, the
National Parks proposal to make Lincoln a companion to Lee roused other
citizen anger. As of 2004, however, a prospect of reconciliation of memories
was evident in the success of H. Alexander Wise and his associates'

proposal for a Tredegar National Civil War Center on this same site, where, for the first time anywhere in America, a museum will combine stories of the Confederacy, the Union, and the role of African Americans in that traumatic war. Wise is former president of Richmond's Museum of the Confederacy. Sixteen of his ancestors were Confederate officers. His black partners in the project include ninety-five-year-old Oliver Hill and John Motley. For twenty years the latter has been collecting Civil War artifacts in the basement of his home in Connecticut. Like James McBride Dabbs, Wise believes that it is time to remember the centrality of African Americans in the whole history that led to and flowed from the Civil War. On her side of the history, Virginia Legislator Viola O. Baskerville, vouches for the proposal with enthusiasm: "The beauty of the Tredegar project is that now African Americans can begin to understand that we weren't just acted upon, but that we contributed to our own freedom. When [black visitors] see reflections of themselves on exhibit, they'll understand that we too were participants in history." Wise is equally sure that white visitors will find that the museum will honor all participants in the war along with reasons to doubt that the Lost Cause was altogether honorable or the Union cause altogether heroic.

> My great-granddaddy always said that slavery was a curse to the
> South, but that we just didn't know how to get rid of it. Today it's
> time to deal with this. The war happened 137 years ago. That's
> enough time to step back and see where we are. We can let it screw
> us up forever or we can begin to move forward.[26]

In 1990, on New Year's Day, Virginia inaugurated the first black governor of any state in the country, L. Douglas Wilder, grandson of ex-slave grandparents who moved to Richmond in 1880. Virginia-born Supreme Court Lewis E. Powell, Jr., administered the oath of office. A long preinaugural church service at St. Paul's Episcopal Church had preceded. It was the church that Jefferson Davis attended during the war. The service had ended with congregational singing of "The Battle Hymn of the Republic."[27] No one who knows Richmond can assume that a new museum can turn the clashing currents of its history, like the falls of the James, into a smooth-flowing river of civic composure. But many once-suppressed tributaries of the history are now visible in the public mainstream of this city. Like few cities in the United States, Richmond can now host a civic conversation that involves virtually the whole of the American story.

From this partial profile of a modern Southern city one cannot conclude that the tentacles of racism have been exorcised from every dimension of its politics, economics, and culture. Some of it has certainly been removed, but Mrs. Cleiland Donnan's racist "onion skins" are still being peeled away. No Richmonder interviewed for this account believes that the city has no more peeling to do. But they all testify that the city, in its shifting complex of public forgetting and remembering, "ain't what it was." Nor is it what they hope it may yet be.[28]

Rosewood, Florida

The suffering of slaves in western history may never be adequately compre-hended by even the most empathetic of historians. Nor will the scale and depth of suffering among millions of native Africans transported across the Atlantic likely to be remembered accurately by any future generation of Americans. But, like history in general, there will always be occasions for reassessments and re-remembering of ancient evil. In a visit to a slave-export castle on the coast of Ghana, the horror of the thing reduces many African Americans to angry tears and some white Westerners to angry shame. Visitors to the German camp museums know these reactions well.

Common sense might assume that recent injustices are first and most likely candidates for public remembering. But in fact initial surges of attention to an atrocity can collapse into stark recession. The next two cases illustrate how, locally and nationally, a public can bury an embarrassing recent event in a grave of amnesia marked by not so much as a stone.

In the 1970s a poll of residents of Florida or Oklahoma concerning what happened in Rosewood and Tulsa in the early 1920s, would have found only a small minority who remembered, and most of them would have been African American. By the end of the 1990s, however, the polls would show a sharp increase in the number of citizens, white and black, who could at least respond: "It was a race riot." Like wide public recognition of the word "Holocaust," large numbers of people in Florida now know what "Rosewood" means. Indeed, by the end of the 1990s, seventy years after the event, aids to memory had surged: a book-length history, magazine articles, national television news magazine features, documentary films, museums, organized local tours, a well-financed partly fictionalized movie, a burgeoning Website, teaching materials for schools and—most notably of all—official Florida state legislative reparation for living survivors and descendants.[29]

Whatever facts about the Rosewood Massacre may still be disputed, the basic story can be summarized as follows.[30] A tiny village, nine miles from the Gulf of Mexico in Levy County on the west coast of Florida, Rosewood was only one of a dozen local American communities that saw a renewed eruption of lynching in years following World War One.[31] Trigger of these bouts of lawlessness was often an alleged assault of a black man on a white woman. Between August 1920 and December 1922 at least eleven black men were murdered by mobs of whites in towns near Rosewood. Gainesville, thirty-five miles to the northeast, hosted a 1922 New Year's Eve parade of the local Ku Klux Klan, only a few hours before the beginning of the Rosewood riot. Some twenty-five to thirty families, most of them black, lived in the village.

In the early morning of January 1, a white woman, Fannie Taylor, reported that she was assaulted by a black man. That afternoon vigilantes captured and killed Sam Carter, who became the first of at least six black men and women to be killed over the next six days of riot, which ended in the burning-down of every black residence in the town and the death of an uncertain number of others besides the six. Joined eventually by recruits from Georgia and South Carolina, a crowd of four to five hundred whites fanned out into the woods to look for the man believed to be guilty of an attack on Mrs. Taylor. By midweek a cluster of fifteen or more blacks barricaded themselves in a home, offered armed resistance to the attackers, and killed two of them, both local white businessmen. The official death toll remained at six blacks and two whites, but forever after black survivors would report that an unknown number of other neighbors were murdered and buried in an open field. In some lulls in the gunfire, a few black adults gathered the town's children together, fled to the woods, and—with the help of two Seaboard Railroad conductors—carried the children by rail to Gainesville.

Two or three days into the week, newspapers local and national began to carry stories of Rosewood. Alarmed, Florida Governor Cary Hardee in Tallahassee telegraphed Sheriff Robert E. Walker to inquire if the situation required National Guard help. The sheriff replied that "the situation is under control," in spite of the fact that two to three hundred vigilantes were still roaming the area and torching black homes. By January 8, "the Rosewood community as African American residents knew it had been obliterated from the map of Florida.... Today [1993] there is a small green highway marker with white lettering that reads 'Rosewood.' What once was the village is now overgrown with trees and vines, and scattered about are a few bricks and parts of buildings. Little other physical evidence remains."[32]

What remained in the rest of January and two weeks of February 1923 was some belated attention of the Florida governor to legal investigation of the Rosewood horror. On January 29 he appointed a grand jury to inquire into "certain high crimes that have been committed by unidentified parties" in two west Florida counties. So far as the records show, no black was appointed to this jury, which apparently heard some two dozen witnesses, a majority of them white. On February 16 the jury foreman "reported that the jurors regretted being unable to find evidence on which to base any indictments," but "deplored mob action and declared that they were speaking for the best people of Levy County."[33] By this date the flurry of Florida news coverage of Rosewood was dying down, while the event continued to get attention in newspapers throughout the United States. Southern papers ran Associated Press reports, and in a scattering of editorials almost all assumed that, while the initiating cause of the riot was in fact the rape of a white woman by a black man, legal process should have had its way. Northern newspapers criticized the passive role of the state government, and many black-owned papers took heart that African Americans under armed attack in Rosewood had fought back.

By some calculations, between 1829 and 1992, the United States saw forty-five "race riots," some of them far more costly in human life than the Rosewood affair.[34] Were numbers alone to be the measure of murders most to be lodged in public memory, Rosewood might well deserve the obscurity embodied in those empty green fields beside the modern highway marker. But neither judges nor moralists consider murder a crime to be relativized and drowned in swamps of statistics. In 1993, a committee of Florida state legislators heard a petition for redress from a small company of Rosewood survivors. The committee then persuaded their colleagues to vote an appropriation of $50,000 for the employment of five academic historians to recover the facts about 1923. An overdue practical question prompted this measure: What, if anything, could the state of Florida do to remedy the harms done to the former residents of Rosewood and, in addition, to their lineal descendants?

From the resulting academic study most of the summary here has been drawn. In its wake, first came the Florida legislature's decision to award $2.1 million to the living survivors, their children, and their grandchildren as compensation for lost property or as scholarships for education in Florida colleges. Major sponsor of the bill was Senator Daryl Jones of Miami, who observed in 1997 that compensation for every instance of racial violence could not become the responsibility of the state government:

> Our history is replete with similar situations. We had to find a way
> to distinguish Rosewood from most other flash acts of racial vio-
> lence. In this case, the sheriff was well aware of the rising senti-
> ment. People from as far away as South Carolina had come to par-
> ticipate in the carnage. Because there was a clear opportunity to
> intervene and because the governor and other state officials were
> well aware of it, Rosewood was a unique case.

"But," he added, "that bill would have had no chance of passage with a Republican majority [new as of 1997] in the Senate. That bill would not have even been heard" on the senate floor. It had been only narrowly reported out, by a 14–11 vote, from the then-Democratic-dominated Senate Judiciary Committee.[35]

Unearthed, the basic facts about Rosewood 1923 are now ensconced in many public places and Florida citizens' awareness. Thanks to flurries of full-scale historical monographs, newspaper articles, television news magazines, tourist buses, a burgeoning Website, and—in particular—a movie based on the research of the five Florida university historians, the name Rosewood is not likely anytime soon to disappear from widespread recognition in Florida and elsewhere in this country. The 1997 movie *Rosewood,* directed by John

Singleton, provided a full-scale cinematic version of the story, prompting re-viewers to ask a range of searching questions. Does a mixture of fiction with fact—a requirement for financially successful historically based films—really serve the reputation of survivors of such an event? Are African Americans emerging now from the comforts of forgetting such history into a new freedom to acclaim ancestral courage and endurance? Are black historians, actors, and film directors at last exercising the privilege of telling such stories on their own terms and not through the eyes of whites? What about the quarrel which some aged survivors have with twisted facts they see in the film? Can film persuade an upcoming generation of white Americans to take this history se-riously enough to endure the pain of viewing it, remembering it, and under-standing it as vital to the identity of their neighbors? Or will most white Amer-icans turn aside from such films as not belonging to their history?[36]

Concerning the two audiences, journalism professor E. R. Shipp wrote that "many black moviegoers are entranced, by this [Rosewood] tale that has its roots in a past about which they know very little." On the other hand, in some white viewers the movie "stirs feelings of guilt." A scattering of historians may say that Rosewood was, after all, one incident among many in America of the 1920s. Perhaps its new prominence is overblown? "Events like it most certainly took place elsewhere in that area and in that era."

To this latter dismissal of Rosewood, a moralist like myself has to reply: An iceberg tip, 10 percent of the whole, suffices as warning of danger to all navigators. Written history is forever incomplete in all of its volumes, but even an incomplete recovery of the Rosewood story prompts both warning and cel-ebration. About the Singleton film, Shipp comments: "When a people's history has been deliberately obliterated, how can anyone question attempts to piece together that history from shards that remain, using artistic license to fill the gaps?"[37]

To this one may add: The Rosewood story is so incomplete that, like all stories of ancient evil still infesting a society, memory recovery remains as work for new generations. Such work belongs in many other locations. One is Tulsa, Oklahoma.

Tulsa, Oklahoma

In 1955, Don Ross was fourteen years old and a student in the segregated Booker T. Washington High School in Tulsa, known in the United States as headquarters of numerous oil companies. He had a popular history teacher named W. D. Williams. One day Williams told the class a story. Ross will never forget that day:

> In his slow, laboring voice Mr. W. D. as he was fondly called, said on the evening of May 31, 1921, his school graduation, and

prom were canceled. Dick Rowland, who had dropped out of high school a few years before to become rich in the lucrative trade of shining shoes, was in jail, accused of raping a white woman Sarah Page "on a public elevator in broad daylight." After Rowland was arrested, angry white vigilantes gathered at the courthouse intent on lynching the shine boy. Armed blacks integrated the mob to protect him. . . . [A] shot rang out. A race riot had broken out. . . . All of the black community was burned to the ground and 300 people died.

More annoyed than bored, I leaped from my chair and spoke: "Greenwood was never burned. Ain't no 300 people dead. We're too old for fairy tales." Calling a teacher a liar was a capital offense. Mr. W. D. snorted with a twist that framed his face with anger. He ignored my obstinacy and returned to his hyperbole. He finished his tale and dismissed the class. The next day he asked me to remain after class, and passed over a photo album with picture and post cards of Mount Zion Baptist Church on fire, the Dreamland Theater in shambles, whites with guns standing over dead bodies, blacks being marched to concentration camps with white mobs jeering, trucks loaded with caskets, and a yellowing newspaper article accounting block after block of destruction—30, 75, even 300 dead. Everything was just as he described it. "What you think, fat mouth?" Mr. W. D. asked his astonished student.[38]

It was a pivotal history class. Ross, the "astonished student," went on in 1982 to become Tulsa's first African American representative to the State Legislature. Unearthing the Tulsa race riot of 1921 became a burning lifelong cause. In 1971, fiftieth anniversary of the riot, at age thirty he helped to found a magazine, *Oklahoma Impact*, one of whose aims would be honesty concerning Tulsa's history.[39] As they were looking for a way to break open the city's collective memory of 1921, an article, "Profile of a Race Riot," by Ed Wheeler, came to the editors' attention. Wheeler was host to a local radio program that specialized in recall of history. The young editor of the local Chamber of Commerce magazine *Tulsa*, Larry Silvey, had commissioned the article, only to have it banned from publication by senior chamber officials. Reflected Silvey in 1999, "The men who controlled the Chamber of Commerce were in their 70s in 1971. Which meant that they had been in their 20s during the riot . . . it is likely that these men had something to hide." But not only these members of the business elite; while Wheeler was writing, he began to receive anonymous threats by phone and in person. One threat, scrawled across the windshield of his car, read: "Best Look Under Your Hood From Now On."

After the article had also been refused by two local white-owned newspapers, Ross, with a group of black neighbors, met with Wheeler "but only at night, in their churches, accompanied by their ministers." "Profile" then became a cover story for black-owned *Oklahoma Impact* in an issue sold out to customers in the black community and ignored in the white community.

After a chasm of a fifty-year silence, a restoration of the city's public memory had at least begun. Under Ross's subsequent leadership, his state, the United States, and the world would now find it as easy to think "race riot" as to think "oil" in connection with images of Tulsa, Oklahoma.[40]

Historical studies of the riot now abound.[41] Since the purpose of this book is to portray how citizens and governments as well as scholars engage in public recoveries of negative social memories, I will concentrate here on the successes and failures of Ross and his supporters up to 2004 in their efforts to rectify local public memory and to achieve belated justice for the survivors from 1921.

Historians testify that many details from 1921 remain obscure, and a local Tulsa public now argues over whose memories and what records from 1921 accurately portray the event. Hardly anyone would say that the story achieved regular conversational prominence in the city before the 1990s, though one contemporary newspaper editor testifies that "I came here in 1979 and learned about the riot immediately."[42] That there was a long relative silence seems unquestionable, however. Nothing is more characteristic of public preservation of radically negative fact about the past then the instinct to inter it. For decades South African whites either disbelieved the tortures and murders in the prisons or decided not to know about them. Germans took forty years for a second and third generation to construct indelible public education about the Holocaust. The shower of Holocaust images descending on Germans in the 1980s occurred relatively sooner after the event, than did the upsurge of publicity about 1921 in Tulsa in the 1990s. Had they waited equally long to inform their grandchildren about the meaning of "Kristallnacht," the word would have begun to appear in the high school history books in about the year 2000. (Brent Staples of the *New York Times* heard Ross retell the story, and afterwards he thought of the ravages of lethal anti-Semitism—"the pogroms that were carried out against the Jews in Europe.")[43]

Like other accounts in this book, Tulsa now offers examples of what citizens, their institutions, and their governments are doing to memorialize the sinister side of their collective pasts. Four book-length studies of the 1921 event were published between 1982 and 2002,[44] plus hundreds of newspaper articles and television interviews both national and international. For my purposes here, detailed accounts of Tulsa-1921 are less to the fore than an account of how the rediscoverers of the event have both succeeded and failed, so far, in establishing a fairly stable, coherent institutionalized public memory.

We will never know precisely how to measure the spectrum of sharp memory, fuzzy memory, and forgetfulness among Tulsans as a whole as the decades passed from 1921. But we can empathize with young Don Ross's astonishment and incredulity at W. D. Williams's summary of the riot one day in a history class. In 1999 Ross said to Brent Staples, "I thought my community was a proud community that would never have let whites get away with burning us down."[45] This is an interesting reflection of one young black Tulsan's perception of the capacity of his neighborhood, past and present, for resistance to armed attack. According to the official records of the time, armed defense of the community took the lives of ten white attackers. Officially the toll of black deaths was then and is now twenty-eight. The validity of these statistics became a cause for bitter controversy in the 1990s, as black Tulsans scoffed at so low a figure while whites resisted being told that more than twenty-eight blacks died. In fact, militant blacks of the time were sure that more than ten whites died in the riot. Many were secretly proud to claim this higher total. Rarely in this debate did a white voice raise the question: "Why are African Americans inclined to accept a higher figure and white Americans inclined to accept a lower?" Not only dusty coroner records but identification with certain ancestors over others is an answer. One resists a history that casts aspersion on the people of the past most "like us." How could these things be? *Surely*, many German Americans said to themselves in the early 1940s, Germans could not be murdering Jews *en masse*. . . . Surely no American soldier would spatter bullets on women and children in My Lai. . . . Surely white citizens of sophisticated Cape Town would not stand by as 66,000 local people got transported fifteen miles away from their longtime homes. . . . Surely . . . Bosnia, Rwanda, Chechnya, Sierra Leone. But young Don Ross's incredulity rose from another "surely": Were not my ancestors brave defenders of themselves? Yes, but to no avail.

One does have to ask why black parents and grandparents talked so little, around their own dinner tables, about this courageous side of their community's defense. Some in the 1990s said that they kept quiet because they could not know if such a riot might erupt again. Others said that they did not want to discourage their children from believing that with hard work they could build a bright future in spite of enduring white racism. Yet others wanted to instill the pride that says, "No one can take our lives and our dignity away from us, no matter how many of us they murder." By whatever amalgam of caution and pain, it is still remarkable that, thirty-four years after the event, a black high school student could accuse his much respected history teacher of lying about the past. Surely our Tulsa forebears would never let whites do that to them!

Embarrassment at what whites in fact had done had spread through many strata of Tulsa's white residents hours after the riot. Many were prompt to vow repentantly that the city must move quickly to restore all possible damages inflicted on one of the wealthiest black communities in the United States. Thirty-five blocks of Greenwood homes lay in ashes, a total of 1,256, "along with virtually every other structure—including churches, schools, businesses, even a hospital and library."[46] At least five thousand people had become refugees. Financial losses alone came to at least $2 million in 1921 dollars. Faced with all of this evidence of what mob violence did to their city in thirty-two hours, board members of the Tulsa Chamber of Commerce Board promptly mingled moral outrage with moral commitment:

> Leading business men are in hourly conference and a movement is now being organized, not only for the succor, protection and alleviation of the sufferings of the negroes, but to formulate a plan of reparation in order that homes may be rebuilt and families as nearly as possible rehabilitated. The sympathy of the citizenship of Tulsa in a great way has gone out to the unfortunate law abiding negroes who have become the victims of the action, and the bad advice of some of the lawless leaders, and as quickly as possible rehabilitation will take place and reparation made.
>
> Tulsa feels intensely humiliated and standing in the shadow of this great tragedy pledges its every effort to wiping out the stain at the earliest possible moment and punishing those guilty of bringing the disgrace and disaster to this city.[47]

The words "rehabilitation" and "reparation" have seldom sprung so quickly to the public vocabulary of an urban American elite. Unfortunately, subsequent local exercises of power would soon paper over this language and replace it with distorted versions of fact. In a move that advertised the growing value of city land that now lay covered in the ashes of Greenwood, the city council passed a "fire ordinance" on June 7 requiring new building in the area to include expensive fire-proofing. Subsequent white defenders of the ordinance would claim that it favored the future quality of life in Greenwood by raising standards for the reconstruction. But in June 1921 the council put forward two quite different justifications of the new law: It would help expand the industrial area near the railroad, and it would be "desirable, in causing a wider separation between Negroes and whites."[48] The more segregated, the safer the city—District Six comes to mind. Though its police force had failed to protect black residents of Greenwood and may even have aided the murderers, leaders of city government would henceforth breath no suggestion that tax funds should go to Greenwood's rehabilitation. Soon after, insurance companies let themselves off the hook by pointing to a clause in policies that exempted losses from riots. No insurance claims were ever honored for any Greenwood policyholder, and talk of reparation among "leading business men" soon died down.

Tulsa's leading black lawyer was attorney B. C. Franklin.[49] In response to the June 7 fire ordinance he immediately went to work with colleagues to have the ordinance overturned. He was successful. But as for rehabilitation and reparation, in spite of support for such measures in state and national newspapers, no local success would be forthcoming. Alfred L. Brophy writes that the case for *governmental* reparations in Tulsa was very strong. Recent precedents in Illinois and Kansas had granted reparations for riot damages and lynchings, on the ground that governments had failed to provide victims with the protections to which they were legally entitled. The damaging evidence against local and state police and national guard systems was very strong. The Oklahoma Supreme Court eventually acknowledged that "a great number of men," wearing police badges of dubious official status, had been "engaged in arresting Negroes."[50] They had been engaged in killing, too.

> It is very difficult at this point [2001] to reconstruct the instruc-
> tions from the mayor and police chief to the deputies. That difficulty
> arises in large part because the city refused to allow a serious inves-
> tigation of the riot. There are, however, a substantial number of re-
> ports of those instructions and the pattern of destruction certainly
> fits with those reports. Quite simply, it is difficult to explain the sys-
> tematic arrest of blacks, the destruction of their property, and the
> timing of the invasion of Greenwood without relying upon some co-
> ordination by the Tulsa city government, with the assistance of the
> local units of the National Guard.[51]

This conclusion is a basic element in any argument on behalf of govern- mental reparations in the United States or any other country. The assumption, of course, is philosophical: What a government *permits* or *authorizes* by action or inaction of its officers has implications for the continuing liabilities of that government *transgenerationally.* The arguments, "times have changed" or "those guys are no longer in office," or "our political party had no responsibility for these atrocities"[52] give government a cheap exit from concern for old in- justices. A government that facilitates or fails to prevent murder should be no more protected by statutes of limitation than individual murderers. For gov- ernment and every other collective human affair, time does not heal all wounds. Only some institutionally enacted therapy—rehabilitation, compensation, rep- aration—heals.

Time, in fact, can inflict new wounds, especially when it gives successive elites the chance to bend memory and history to the service of their own exculpation. Brave and forthright as was the Chamber of Commerce pro- nouncement of June 7, 1921, there was one suggestion in their text which was soon to become the full-blown official version of the origins of the riot: "bad advice of some of the lawless leaders," that is, Greenwood black leaders. On June 14, Mayor T. D. Evans set the myth in motion with a summary version of the event replete with moral justification that blamed the victims:

> [T]his uprising was inevitable. If that be true and this judgment has
> come upon us, then I say it was good generalship to let the destruc-
> tion come to that section where the trouble was hatched up, put in
> motion and where it had its inception.[53]

A grand jury also convened on June 7. Over the summer it would issue a few indictments, mostly against blacks; but no one, white or black, would ever be convicted of a felony connected with the riot. Eventually, says Brophy, "the legal system failed to hold [any] Tulsans criminally responsible for the reign of terror." Instead, in a final report, the jury issued its judgment that black leaders had indeed instigated the riot, that "there was no mob spirit among the whites, no talk of lynching and no arms." This version of truth left Tulsa blacks enraged and racist whites comforted. Two factors accounted for the riot, concluded the grand jury: the breakdown of law enforcement (true enough), and "agitation among the Negroes for social equality." Black leaders were the culprits. "Thus," concluded Alfred Brophy, "the grand jury recast its evidence to fit its established prejudices. And as it did that, as it confirmed white Tulsa's myth that the blacks were to blame for the riot, it helped to remove the moral impetus to reparations."[54] In a grim double sense, it was a whitewash.

The repair of history and the cause of reparation would now persist quietly in the memory and the eventual work of the Tulsa black community. Just as one second-generation professional, Don Ross, was to take up the reparation cause beginning in 1971, another son of the first generation was to make distinguished contributions to the repair of the shadowed history. B. C. Franklin had led and won the fight against the duplicitous fire ordinance of June 7. But substantial success in the eventual rectifying of Tulsa's and many another chapter of African American history would await the work of his son, John Hope Franklin, six years old in 1921.[55]

One of the first thorough histories of the event would come in the work of the third-generation work of Scott Ellsworth, who wrote his doctoral thesis at Duke University under Distinguished Professor Franklin. Published under the title *Death in a Promised Land: The Tulsa Race Riot of 1921*, the study ushered in flurries of publications that by 2003 would number in the hundreds. Ellsworth supplied a long, updated chapter to the Commission Report of 2001 which concluded, "In the 1920s Oklahoma courtrooms and halls of government, there would be no day of reckoning for either the perpetrators or the victims of the Tulsa race riot. Now, some seventy-nine years later, the aged riot survivors can only wonder if, indeed, that day will ever come."[56]

As this is written in 2004, days of reckoning have come in fits and snatches. The 2001 *Commission Report* ends with a passionate claim for the justice of reparations from Oklahoma state and local governments. It summarizes a wide spectrum of legal offense to justice in the lives of Oklahoma black citizens: early-century disenfranchisement, segregation of schools and housing, police passivity in the face of twenty-three lynchings statewide, and (among other petty-apartheid laws) segregation of public telephones. "Stand back and look at those deeds now," urged the report:

> In some government participated in the deed.
> In some government performed the deed.

> In none did government prevent the deed.
> In none did government punish the deed.[57]

The issue of reparations divided the Commission, however, and that division was to carry over into debates in the state legislature well into 2002. In that spring, Don Ross's long efforts bore fruit in a bill for a scholarship fund for up to three hundred "linear heirs" of riot victims and survivors. Unsettled in the debate was the question of whether the recipients of this educational reparation would have to live now in the Greenwood community or might live anywhere. Meantime, a cluster of local Tulsa church leaders collected a modest fund of $28,000 for distribution to 131 known living survivors. The oldest of them, Otis Clark, aged 99, received $214.03. It wouldn't replace his grandparents' house, their vegetable garden, or the lives of his stepfather and his bulldog, said Clark to a reporter, but "you have to be grateful for whatever you get. . . . It's better than nothing."[58]

Better than that token, however, in 2002 and into 2003, would be more substantial fund proposed by a former chair of the Tulsa Chamber of Commerce, John Gamberino. He offered to raise 1.5 million private dollars for awards of $5000 to each of the 118 African Americans known to have survived the riot and for scholarships for young descendants of all victims. By early 2003 Gamberino had raised almost half of the goal in cash and pledges; he blames 9/11 and the economy for coming up short. This material gesture by private citizens goes far, in this writer's opinion, toward making good on the outburst of moral indignation and commitment to reparation of those early leaders of the Tulsa Chamber of Commerce: eighty years later, no match to two million 1921 dollars, but better late than never, and better $5000 than $214.03.

Meantime, the efforts of Senator Don Ross to convince the Oklahoma legislature to do its part in materially repairing the damages done to Greenwood community had foundered in arguments over the responsibility of one generation for the sins of another. The 1997 legislature had asked the Commission to make specific recommendation about the city and state's responsibility for reparations. By divided vote the Report answered "yes" and clothed the answer in passionate concluding rhetoric:

> Why does the state of Oklahoma or the city of Tulsa owe anything to anybody? Why should any individual tolerate now spending one cent of one tax dollar over what happened so long ago?
>
> The answer is that these are not even the questions. This is not about individuals at all—not any more than the race riot or anything like it was about individuals
>
> This is about Oklahoma—or, rather, it is about two Oklahomas.
> . . . The riot proclaimed that there were two Oklahomas; that one

claimed the right to push down, push out, and push under the other; and that it had the power to do that.

That is why the Tulsa race riot . . . can be about making two Oklahomas one—but only if we understand that this is what reparation is all about. Because the riot is both symbolic and singular, reparations become both singular and symbolic, too. Compelled not legally by courts but extended freely by choice, they say that individual acts of reparation will stand as symbols that fully acknowledge and finally discharge a collective responsibility.

Because we must face it: There is no way but by government to represent the collective, and there is no way but by reparations to make real the responsibility.[59]

In her epilogue to its 178 pages, Tulsa Senator Maxine Horner, African American, vouches for the *Commission Report* with the caution that its righting of history must now be complemented by some material righting of lingering wrong: "We can be proud of our state for examining this blot on our state and out conscience." But, she added, "There are chapters left to write . . . The Oklahoma legislature is now the caretaker of this past and may disperse to the future forgiving, fair, kind, deserved and decent justice."[60]

As of 2001–2002, the Legislature had decided not to write a very substantial "dispersion to the future." It passed a "1921 Tulsa Race Riot Reconciliation Act," which (1) acknowledged the "staggering cost" of the riot, (2) authorized the construction of a memorial to the event, and (3) set up a structure in the state education department for awarding scholarships to descendents of the victims. In addition the legislature auhorized the awarding of medals to all the known survivors. Except for the medals, it authorized no funds for these measures. Proposals for money or educational reparations to survivors never made it out of committee. In the wake of these slight legal gestures, some local consciences, like that of John Gamberino, turned to voluntary citizen forms of reparation while others shifted their hopes from the state legislature to the Federal courts. With endorsement by a group of prominent black citizens, including John Hope Franklin and Don Ross, and with national support from Harvard Professor Charles Oglevie and attorney Johnny Cochrane, the litigants were pursuing the case as these pages are written. In the spring of 2004, the United States District Court declined to honor litigant claims; but the case, now on appeal, may yet reach the Supreme Court.

Whither Tulsa in its reckoning with its most scandalous past? The end is not yet.

INTERLUDE: HOW DO COMMUNITIES COME TO RECKON WITH THEIR NEGATIVE PASTS?

The stories of modern Richmond, Rosewood, and Tulsa, spelled out in modest detail here, offer some bases for a summary answer to an important general question: by what processes do members of a local body politic come to public awareness and action regarding a negative past? These three American cases, plus analogies to the German and South African cases, occasion a pause in this chapter for suggesting certain conditions and dynamics which the cases have in common. Every student of memorials notes that the provocations and contents of collective memory are unique to particular times, places, histories. But the cases here are not so individually unique as to defy some generalizations of how they came to pass.

Above all, the cases illustrate the necessary collaboration of citizens, scholars, the powerful, and the weak in effecting these rediscoveries. Like the discovery of the Dead Sea Scrolls by a shepherd in the cave of Qumran, it is possible simply to stumble upon a buried past. But whole communities are not likely to do that. Seldom does the process begin by chance. Changes in public memory require intentional individual, small group, institutional, political, and conceptual collaborations extended over time. The collaboration requires some preconditions in the forgetful society itself. Remembering Richmond, Rosewood, Tulsa, and international illustrations in chapter 1 and 2, one can identify requirements like these:

I. A SOCIETY MUST BE SOMEWHAT OPEN TO THE VOICING OF MINORITY MEMORY. The control of public memory is an old story in totalitarianism. Notoriously, the Soviets wrote and rewrote their encyclopedias to fit their political needs of the moment. A totalitarian regime never finishes plugging loopholes into its past evils. Under the Kuo-min-dong Taiwanese government, for forty years after 1947, it was a criminal offence to speak of the "2/28 Massacre" in either a public place or in private conversation.[61] In Nazi Germany, public speaking about the concentration camps could land you in one. In democratic America, we have seldom experienced so radical a restriction on free speech, though the experience of Ed Wheeler in Tulsa showed quite clearly in 1971 that the exercise of that freedom can be a risk to life and limb. "Freedom for the thought we hate" is now under considerable siege in the United States in wake of 9/11 and the 2001 Patriot Act. That freedom can only become real when some loophole remains open and individuals of courage shout through it.

2. HOWEVER SMALL, SOME GROUP MUST KEEP THE MEMORY ALIVE. With modern tools of surveillance and communication, totalitarian government can

quash memory in even the most intimate of family settings, as happened under the *Stasi* system in the East Germany which instilled fear of dissident conversation even between husband, wife, and children.[62] But even an authoritarian government may find private pockets of resisting memory hard to control. For some 250 years, by all visible signs, the Christian church in Japan, under the Tokugawa emperors, ceased to exist in Japan. With the coming of tolerance in the mid-nineteenth century, dozens of Christians came up from underground in Nagasaki, the product of ten generations of secret practice. American society, so far never that tightly controlled by any government, has had enough loopholes to facilitate the illegal formation of worship services in slave quarters, a plethora of resistances to the Jim Crow era, and family-passed-down memory of atrocities that white people could remember if they wanted to, in contrast to black people who could not forget. Because it was so small a place and its destruction so complete, memories of Rosewood-1923 were perhaps more fragile, even among blacks, than memories of Tulsa-1921. Even in Tulsa, with family and social relations far more numerous, a young Don Ross could be unaware of 1921. But many Tulsans, black and white, were neither unaware nor completely silent about it from 1921 on. Some 175 years after his death, certain descendants of Thomas Jefferson began to speak publicly about the fact of their genetic relation to him through his mistress Sally Hemings. It requires a very determined, organizationally and technically equipped regime utterly to squelch such intergenerational memory of families, churches, and backroom conversations among friends.

3. AN INDIVIDUAL MUST SPEAK UP, AND AN INSTITUTION MUST SUPPORT HIM OR HER IN DOING SO. Senator Ross could hardly have escaped stories of the 1921 riot in his adult years. But in fact a high school history teacher introduced him to that past, and the rest is modern Tulsa history. Institutions with power to escape captivity to political and cultural orthodoxies can be seedbeds for germinating myth-challengers. Oppressed so effectively and so long by the institution of slavery, Tulsa's African American leaders instinctively knew that their freedom rested on soft ground without the fortifications of black-owned and black-managed institutions. Their success in building Greenwood Avenue was so obvious to whites across the tracks that in some it inspired fear and jealousy. Racist rhetoric in the 1920s, in cities across the country, spit out the word "uppity" as badge of blacks who obviously were refusing to stay in their "place." Even when displaced to north of the tracks, they built Black Wall Street. They fought in France, sent children to college, built churches, organized civic associations, and purchased guns to protect their neighborhood. In all of these initiatives they supported each other's memory and—more important—each other's resistance to oppressions of the past. Democracy requires hiding places for dissidents. African Americans have long since been building them.

4. SOME DEGREE OF LAW AND LAW ENFORCEMENT HAS TO FACILITATE THESE FREEDOMS. From slavery through Reconstruction into the "Second American Revolution" of the 1960s, law was often the enemy of black Americans; but in spite of irregular enforcement, law can protect dissidents against the lawbreaking disposition of majorities. The long-range horror of 1921 for Tulsan blacks was the utter breakdown of law on the side of city government and city police. Soon after, nothing embarrassed many members of the white establishment more than the probability that "deputized" white men wearing police badges had stood by while murder and arson spread across the Greenwood community for a lethal eighteen hours. Some of the deputies, blacks would always maintain, were themselves murderers. The first post-riot expressions of horror came from elitist white leaders who testified to the inaction of government as one cause of the riot's unchecked rampage. Many of these same leaders soon fell quiet as media and court support of the myth of *black* irresponsibility gathered steam. In subsequent decades, whites refused to hear that police officers were capable of murder. Blacks knew better; they remembered differently. In 1971 they at last took advantage of a legally free press and a black-owned press to publish the differences. That press, too, was one of the loopholes.

5. A COALITION OF THE FEW, FROM BOTH SIDES OF DIVIDED MEMORIES, MAY HAVE TO MEET TO STRATEGIZE FOR CORRECTING PUBLIC CONSCIOUSNESS. That meeting in a church basement—between Ed Wheeler, black editors, and ministers—resulted in the publication of Wheeler's account of the riot in the magazine owned by Don Ross. It was a tiny coalition, but it presaged some opening of a public mind to the negative past on a scale that would grow, fitfully at first, to become a deluge of public information and public debate in the 1990s. Margaret Mead once heard the remark, "Change can begin with only a few people." She replied, "That is the only way change begins." She exaggerated, perhaps, but for turns of public attention to an unpleasant past, a resourceful few can finally stir the many. Fiftieth, sixtieth, and even seventieth anniversaries of the riot passed in Rosewood and Tulsa with little acknowledgment in the media or public speech. But the seventy-fifth in 1996 was different. Twenty years of revived academic history writing, the integration of a local historical society, a pamphlet written and distributed to some church study groups, and finally a coterie of legislators had brought the matter into the public arena. Soon the whole country took note. A petition of Rosewood survivors to the legislature had begun a similar process in Florida.

The case was not different in the politics behind the Steglitz and Schöneberg Holocaust memorials in Berlin, nor in the District Six Museum in Cape Town: From the few to the many to the officials—seldom the other way around.

6. POLITICAL INSTITUTIONS MUST BE PRESSURED TO PUT A STAMP OF LEGITIMACY ON THE NEW MEMORY. The recent history of national truth commis-

sions underlines the importance of governmental sponsorship to some inquiries into the past. In the South African case, a truth commission had to be mandated before the parties to the formation of a new government could compromise their differences. Even where a functioning democracy is underway, however, politicians and administrators are seldom the originators of new public attention to negative history. Not until the spring of 2003 did the South African government yield to public pressure for carrying out the reparation recommendations of the TRC. Custodians of national pride—that is, official collective representatives—need prompting by the quiet work of historians, the feature stories in the media, and the agitation of voluntary pressure groups. Roads to state and national capitols are paved with political resistances, as many narratives here illustrate. A truly tiny minority of citizens is not likely to have much initial success in the centers of power; but combinations of media attention, political party interests, and accumulations of voter opinion polls can bring representative bodies into the act of certifying that "yes, this new version of history is nearer truth than the old, and it is time we all said so publicly." When presidents, governors, and legislators do say so, new memories acquire new legitimation and tenure. On the fortieth anniversary of the end of World War Two, a German president catalogues the evils of the Nazi era before a hushed Bundestag in Bonn; and something official has occurred to make harder either the forgetting or the smoothing over of those evils among Germans generally. Just so, the State of Oklahoma authorizes scholarships and a monument to 1921. Even without the money for carrying them out, the proposals honor long overdue recovery of the real past. Before the dignity of that recovery, myth, at least, will officially have to bow.

7. PUBLIC CONTENTION MUST CONTINUE, BUT THE ISSUES AND BURDENS OF PROOF HAVE CHANGED. Supporters of reparations in Tulsa and Oklahoma look with some traces of envy on the Rosewood actions of the Florida State Legislature. Opponents say that the two situations differ so much that Oklahoma cannot imitate Florida. The latter's black population, its higher number of black legislators, and its greater state wealth, they say, brook little comparison with Oklahoma. The number of Rosewood survivors and descendants are smaller; and Florida's political culture is older and less fractured by the pioneer-territory mentality:

> Most of the whites living [in Oklahoma] belong to families that
> came after 1921, or are the children and grandchildren of the Joads.
> The former feel no responsibility for what happened 80 years ago.
> The latter have their own family histories of hardship and misery
> that make it easy to say, "So what?" The larger Indian population,
> most of whose ancestors were marched here at bayonet point (in the

"Trail of Tears," 1830 and after), is not particularly sympathetic either.[63]

Competition between oppressed minorities, refusal to identify with a past unconnected from one's direct ancestors, and pragmatic getting-on with the future: These are all very American arguments. At the end of this chapter I will attend to them again.

For the moment here, to be underscored is the crucial emergence of new resources and motives for a vastly enriched public *deliberation* over the loose ends, the unanswered questions, and the uncertain facts about a contentious past. The present discussion no longer has to bear the same former freight of myth and once-hidden primary truth. This is a great political-ethical gain. It builds a platform of public agreement on grounds of which contending parties can redefine their disagreements. Now, few citizens of contemporary Tulsa dare to *say* out loud that blacks were the principal instigators of the riot, that the burning of Greenwood was inevitable, or that local government did everything in its power to quell the anarchy. A new history has come into being, and there is enough agreement on it to drive underground celebrations of white superiority, the Ku Klux Klan, and the old days of segregation. An intervening civil rights movement and changes in local and national law, of course, influenced this shift of balance between public silence and public conversation. Americans, Floridians, Oklahomans, and Tulsans now have to look back on the 1920s as an awful time in the history of white-black relations in democratic America. To be publicly nostalgic about that time can be as disastrous for a political reputation as was the 2002 nostalgia of a Trent Lott for 1948.[64]

In twenty-first century America, local recoveries of shameful history are on the rise. For highlighting the kinship as well as the differences in these country-wide community struggles, one more illustration is instructive.

The State of Oregon: Ceremonial Day, 1999

A fourth illustration of collective reckoning with long-ignored negative history centers on a state legislative initiative rather than on (as in Tulsa's case) a local community's petitions to a legislature. A look at Oklahoma's history of racial intolerance provides a useful background for understanding the attitudes prevalent in Oregon when it achieved statehood.

Not a member of the Confederacy, Oklahoma was "Indian Territory" during the Civil War, one of areas to which President Andrew Jackson ordered all Indians east to the Mississippi to be removed in the 1830s. In the postwar era, before its statehood in 1907, Oklahoma acquired the reputation as a place of refuge and opportunity for freed slaves and their descendants. All-black towns sprang up in some locales. Tulsa's Greenwood flourished. But early twentieth-century Oklahoma belied its reputation as a safe place for blacks to live. Between 1907 and 1920 thirty-three lynchings occurred in the state; twenty-seven of the victims were black. The white leaders of several small towns conspired to expel blacks, and one postcard picture of the Tulsa riot had written over it in white ink, "RUNING. [sic] THE. NEGRO.OUT.OF.TULSA.JUNE.TH. 1. 1921."[65] Indians and freed slaves to the contrary, many Oklahomans considered their state "white man's country."

Early and late, that was the view of the great majority of white settlers of the trans-Mississippi west, and no state illustrated this more consistently than Oregon, which was admitted to the Union in 1859 as a free state. The "Oregon Trailers" of the 1840s made clear in their first legislation as a U.S. territory that black people, slave or free, were not welcome. An 1844 law forbade Africans or mulattoes to enter the territory under penalty of being hired out "at auction to the lowest bidder." A more elaborate 1849 law to the same effect was prefaced:

> WHEREAS, situated as the people of Oregon are, in the midst of an Indian population, it would be highly dangerous to allow free negros [sic] and mulattoes to reside in the territory, or to intermix with the Indians instilling into their minds feelings of hostility against the white race.
> SECTION 1. That it shall not be lawful for any negro or mulattoe to come into, or reside within the limits of this Territory: *Provided,* That there is nothing in this act that shall be constructed as to apply to any negro or mulattoe now resident in this Territory.[66]

That Indians and blacks might have common cause against racist Europeans was a reasonable surmise.

In 1926 the Oregon legislature, with little fanfare, revoked the 1849 law, long a dead letter and never strictly enforced. In 1997, however, a small group of white and black citizens decided that the time had come for fanfare. Looking at race relations in the state and finding them little different from those of many another region, they set to work to persuade their legislature to mount a "Day of Acknowledgment" which would signal to the state and the world that Oregon means to be, at last, a place where people of every ethnic group on earth were welcome as full fledged citizens: Indians, Japanese, Filipinos, Chinese, Mexicans, and—above all, given Oregon's discriminatory legal focus on them—African Americans.

The ceremonial day—April 19, 1999, the 150th anniversary of the 1849 law—came about via political processes much like those in the other three cases described here. Significantly, the idea germinated in a conference on human relations at Portland State University led, in part, by leaders from Richmond's Hope in the Cities. This transcontinental influence testified to a recognition on both coasts that the ligaments of racist bonds to the past existed in analogous forms, east and west, south and north in the United States. Three leaders of this November conference—Steve Freedman, Richard Baldwin, and Michael Henderson—with a small group of other conferees set about recruiting support for the proposal. Among those recruited were a half dozen ethnic interest groups, a Portland newspaper, key legislative leaders, and the state's most famous, nationally known politician, now-retired Senator Mark Hatfield.

Catalyst for support of the state legislature was Anitra Rasmussen, Oregon native and recently elected member of the House of Representatives. She says that she became alert to the issue during a two-week trip to South Africa in company with other young political leaders. They visited Robben Island. There, she says, their black guide spoke of his seventeen years in these cells. To this international collection of tourists, he exclaimed three times over: "Ladies and Gentlemen, do not be afraid of me! For I do not hate you. I love you. I did not do this time in prison for my mother or my father or my aunt or my uncle. I did this for you so we could all be free!" Testified Rasmussen, "The first time he said this, I thought, 'Gee, how nice.' The second time, I thought, 'Oh my, this is real.' And the third time, I knew what the face of Christ looked like. I knew I was looking at the incarnation of God, of Grace and Redemption."[67] From this near-conversion experience on Robben Island, Representative Rasmussen went to a planning meeting in Portland for persuading the Oregon Legislature not only to revoke the 1849 law in high public visibility but to make the action an occasion for a new public promise of "liberty and justice for all," for every ethnic group of Oregonians.

By 1999 Oregon already had a mixed record of progress and resistance in race-related legal justice. Its Supreme Court was the first in the country to declare an "Alien Land Law" unconstitutional—a law directed chiefly at Japanese immigrants, including those confined to internment camps during World War Two. The 1950s saw repeals of the state's antimiscegenation law, the law forbidding the sale of alcohol to Indians, and insurance surcharges for non-white car drivers. In 1953, under the leadership of a young Mark Hatfield, the legislature passed one of the country's first public accommodations laws. In the same year it eliminated the word "white" from laws governing legislative voting apportionment. In 1959 it passed a fair housing law, and in 1974 Portland mandated equal opportunity employment in companies doing business with the city.

But acknowledgment of the mixtures of justice and injustice in the state's history hardly appeared in its public school history books, and not many observers disagreed with the assertion that Oregon and its cities were among the most segregated in the country. Commitment to the rights of all citizens still stood in the shadows of half-reformed policies of the past. The quiet revocation of the 1844–1849 laws in 1926 needed amplification, said the designers of the Day of Acknowledgment.

Some of them believed that the legislature would pass the resolution of acknowledgment without a dissenting vote. That was the case with the state Senate, 27–0, but unanimity failed in the House of Representatives, 50–7. In a long morning of debate, House members both defended and repented of Oregon's history. A taped record of the debate portrays a range of personal philosophy and experience that influence lawmaking more often than some politicians admit. At issue on April 22, 1999, was a resolution of some 290 words which began with a confession of "discrimination, exclusion, bigotry, and great injustice toward people of color, including native Americans, African Americans, Latinos, Chinese Americans, Japanese Americans and Pacific Islanders." The text goes on to identify the law of 1849 as a signal example of injustice and to propose a future public dialogue on the "lingering effect" of this history. It then calls for individual citizens to examine their own personal attitudes and the discriminatory structures still in place in local society. The end of the resolution celebrates all those citizens responsible for Oregon's progress in these matters, and it commits the legislature to future measures that will facilitate "full participation of racial minorities in all aspects of Oregon life."[68]

Introducing the debate, Representative Rasmussen conceded that "it is easy for us to deny any connection to the actions of people long dead, for it is part of our culture to believe that we can always start fresh, to start over without obligation to the past"—a social philosophy, she might have added, associated often with the history of the American West. We serve in a lawmaking body, she said, that embodies a contradiction to this attitude:

> We are, by the nature of our office, connected to the actions of a previous generation's legislature—the 1849 Oregon Territorial Legislature. From them, our power, our office descends through generation after generation to the people on the floor today. Long before we were born, the office we hold today existed—and long after we pass away from this earth, this office, this institution will exist without us. Our votes, our actions, our words are a part of something that is larger than any one of us. . . .
>
> Colleagues, facing the history of race in Oregon is not pretty, nor pleasant. Nor is it taught in our schools. But mark my words, it is remembered, and it lies close to the surface waiting to be told. . . .
>
> Our history, once acknowledged, is not our destiny, and from here, with this vote, we resolve to start over, to start anew and more forward with mutual respect and as one people.[69]

As if to make good on the assertion that Oregon's racial history was indeed neither "pretty nor pleasant," African American Joann Bowman rose to second the resolution in an eloquent rehearsal of the history, beginning with the reflection that white immigrants into Oregon "transferred white European moral values from east to west." She then catalogued exclusionary laws affecting blacks, Chinese, Indians, Eskimos, Mexicans, Filipinos, and Japanese down through the years since 1849. She noted the 1868 legislative opposition to the Fourteenth and Fifteenth Amendments to the United States Constitution. (Oregon had declared itself a free state in 1849 and therefore favored the Thirteenth Amendment. It did not formally approve the Fifteenth until 1959!) Through their newly organized NAACP chapter, black Oregonians began in 1919 to petition for a public accommodations law, passed finally in 1952. In the same year the legislature permitted women to own property. We finally rid ourselves of these laws, she concluded, but not without the influence of national trends.

Over the next hour, several of the seven final "nay" voters explained their opposition to HR3. Representative Krummel complained that it "continues to foster a sense of victim rather than victor." He then lauded those African Americans whose reputation represents victory over racism—Harriet Tubman, George Washington Carver, Booker T. Washington, Jackie Robinson ("one of my all-time favorites"), and Dale Hale Williams, MD: "Let us honor this form of activity rather than continuing to look for the victims." The victims, promptly replied white legislator Piercy, include her own son, "who faces racism every day" in his school and neighborhood. Black colleague Winters then testified, "I may be the one person here born in Oregon and who experienced the discrimination of not being able to eat in a downtown restaurant. . . . We need all to decide if once and for all we are going to see ourselves as one people, the American people." Two white male opponents then explained that they too abhorred racism; but, said Representative Wilson, "we don't serve ourselves well by recalling a painful past, for what really counts for today and the future is not engaging in symbolism but in substance."

Not a single woman legislator, white or black, spoke for the negative in this debate; and two white male opponents pled that, not legal "symbols" but a changed "heart," was the only antidote to racism. Representative Walsh, a Bible in hand, quoted Matthew 22:37–39 on the "great Commandment" of love for God and neighbor: "If this country doesn't move forward with this in our heart, we will continuously have racial conflict." Even the U.S. Constitution, to which he swore allegiance in 1995, including the Thirteenth through Fifteenth Amendments, will be to no avail unless we take all of it "to our hearts, without which all our laws and papers will make no difference."

A final voice of support came from Representative Shetterly, who stated that from his Jewish wife he had learned the importance of memory in observing the ritual of Yom Ha-Shoah in annual memory of the Holocaust. Such memory, he testified, fortifies the commitment, "Never again." Soon after the question was called, and HR3 passed the House of Representative 50–7.

The 1.5-hour-long debate evoked currents that had recently swirled around similar debates in Virginia, Florida, and Oklahoma. Especially clear in the

Oregon deliberation was overt appeal to religious argument for one position or the other. In her closing statement after the vote, Representative Rasmussen repeated this note in remembering that it was in a church that she first met the idea of the Day of Acknowledgment. She reaffirmed the importance of the South African example for the changes hailed in HR3. South Africa is "a country that should be in ashes today. But it isn't because of people like Desmond Tutu, Nelson Mandela, and unnumbered white and black people" devoted to peaceful transition to a nonracial definition of citizenship. As a coda, she said: "But I apologize for any pain which I have caused colleagues today" in pressing for this resolution. It was a gesture to the seven "nays" in deference to the healing democratic wisdom: No permanent resentments. We will need to work together in the future.

There ensued an afternoon of high celebratory ceremony in the House chamber. Both houses convened with eight hundred people from all over the state filling up the balcony and, by an inspired invitation, sitting on the floor between the delegate desks. The ceremonies began with the presentation of national and state flags by two Buffalo Soldiers, dressed in their nineteenth-century uniforms,[70] two members from the Umatillo and Grand Rond Indian nations in full dress, and a uniformed member of the Northwest Veterans Association. After the Pledge of Allegiance and singing of the Oregon state song, the audience settled down to hear a series of notable speeches.[71]

Former Senator Mark Hatfield led off, striking notes of confession and regret for his own implication in numerous legacies of racism in his own lifetime: "I grew up in Salem and once welcomed Paul Robeson and Marian Anderson to our Junior High School. But we knew that they had to drive all the way back to Portland to find a hotel that would accept them—and those hotels in Portland were not all that posh. . . . And my generation saw the impossibility of carrying out the dreams of the American Indians as based on treaties which were not honored." He went on to remember segregation in the Navy in which he served in World War Two, parades of the Ku Klux Klan down the main street of Salem, legal discrimination against the desire of Roman Catholic parents to send their children to parochial schools, and anti-Semitism in the schools, social clubs, businesses and professions of the state:

> The old myth of the West was its egalitarianism. But in fact everyone then was not getting a new start. . . . Today's Oregon is much better than "the good old days," for serious efforts are now being made to correct old injustices. . . . Now Paul Robeson and Marian Anderson can obtain a hotel in the capital city of Oregon. . . . Congress has issued a formal apology to Japanese Americans, and today in our schools we are doing intercultural and historical studies.
>
> But the unfinished agenda of justice is each generation's responsibility. The virus of racial injustice continues to be highly con-

tagious with many mutations against gender, disability, and sexual orientation. . . . Each of us is part of the human race.

At the last sentence the citizen audience broke out in loud, sustained applause. Hatfield chose to add a footnote:

> I remember this as a truth that no person is too young to learn, and I can recall very quickly where I learned it—in a Sunday School class, where we sang, "Red and yellow, black and white, they are all precious in His sight."

It too brought sustained applause.

Hatfield was followed by former Chief Justice Edward Peterson, who also confessed at length his own immersion in racist attitudes and practices parallel to most white Americans of his generation, northern and southern. Wisconsin-born, he knew

> by age seven that African Americans, Jews, and Catholics were not as good as me. . . . I was taught this by people who loved me . . . but also by movies, radio, and friends. . . . In law school I saw the wrongs perpetrated on African Americans, but I did nothing. It took years for knowledge here [pointing to his head] to move to knowledge here [pointing to his heart]. Today most racism is no longer so overt. Recently I was driving down the street and was cut off by another driver, and I exclaimed, "You Latino bozo!" It came into my head unbidden. If it is not people like me who cause racial discrimination, who does? Blacks, Indians, other minorities? No, it's because of white people like me. I have learned that I can change, but it is not easy to unlearn the deeply ingrained, unwelcome thoughts I learned as a child. . . . I celebrate this resolution about to be signed for increasing *public* awareness of racial discrimination; but I must say to the white people here that our first step must be to increase *my* awareness of racial discrimination. Then and only then will we be able to take giant steps toward a future of racial equality in Oregon.

Governor John Kitzhaber then stepped forward for official signing of the resolution. In his short statement he echoed an awareness that "this aspect of our past is not pleasant, and for some to come here was not easy." It was not easy, he implied, for descendants of either side of a racist past.

Five speakers then concluded the event to represent the new broad ethnic-cultural spectrum of modern Oregon—Native, Latino, Japanese, African, and European—Americans all. Rose High Bear, Athabascan from Alaska, addressed the assembly as "our relatives." She described her nation as created by the Great Spirit "to be a suffering people" but living "with connectedness and harmony." As such, she said, "We acknowledge the many contributions of our relatives, African Americans, your sacrifice and suffering. We know that from your suffering comes the healing power of empathy . . . and we remember our Bosnian relatives who are on their own trail of tears. . . . We are all related!"

Susan Castillo, first Latino state legislator, then reminded the assembled that Oregon was already a land of immigrants four centuries ago as Spanish ships sailed the Pacific coast, as Mexicans in the eighteenth century established cattle ranches here, as their descendants harvested crops amid the labor shortages of World War Two, as they struggled against the insult of local shop signs ("Dogs and Mexicans Not Allowed"), and as they joined Cesar Chavez in demanding civil and economic rights for migrant laborers down to the present moment. Quoting Chavez, she noted that justice is like education: "Education does not change things overnight. It makes change possible and irreversible. It cannot be stolen or taken away. It can be given away without losing any of it. It is something to hand down to children and grandchildren."

Attorney Peggy Nagai then confirmed the "not overnight" nature of the justice struggle as she recounted the beginnings of the forty-year process by which Japanese Americans finally received presidential and congressional apology and modest reparations for their internment in the 1940s.[72] NAACP national president Merlie Evers Williams then testified, with pride and passion, "I live here. This is my state . . . and I wish it to reach its full potential." She closed with the memory of how the murder of her husband in Mississippi in 1963 epitomized her longtime alienation from the United States of America: "On the day the government buried Medgar Evers in Arlington Cemetary, *Taps* were played, and they handed me the American flag that covered his coffin. For years I had not felt patriotic at all, but that one moment made me feel American again."

The last words of the afternoon came from Senator Avel Gordy, African American and chief protagonist of SR3. She shared the contents of a message she had recently received from one Virginia Smith, who told of her "Oregon Trail" white ancestors and a family letter read to her as a child thirty-five years ago. "The old letter revealed that my ancestors were slave owners. [When as an adult I read the letter for myself] I was shocked to see that my parents had left out some details . . . that our ancestors were slave owners who used the 'n' word. . . . When I read in *The Oregonian* newspaper of this special Day, I thought it might be a new starting point. What can I do to help?"

Senator Gordy answered: "Not to forget but forgive, correct, heal, move forward together."

The long official day ended with "The Battle Hymn of the Republic." The real end, for many, was a possible beginning of accelerated change in citizen relations in Oregon. In articles before and after April 22, *The Oregonian* quoted a cross section of citizen attenders. Some were optimistic, others cautious:

It was a long time coming. It's good to make everyone aware of what happened to all our brothers (Marcus Luke, 61, Umatilla color guardsman).

I want my kids to know that there were laws that kept black people from succeeding. But today is a day of calm and peace (Loretta Smith, African American of Portland).

I will celebrate [only] when they give me my 40 acres and a mule (Brenda Phillips, representing "those who could not make the journey," including her ninety-two-year-old grandmother).

It made me think about a massacre of Native Americans outside Roseburg in the mid-1850s (Sue Shaffer, chair of the Cow Creek Band of Umpqua Tribes of Southern Oregon).

Good things come to those who wait. But they come sooner to those who act. . . . This is not exactly a joyous occasion. It is something I feel is late in coming. But I'm glad to see it. We've still got a lot of work to do (Bobbi Gary, African American great-grandmother of two).[73]

Perhaps the simplest, most direct evaluation of the event came from an anonymous African-American-Oregonian as he boarded the chartered bus for going home: "At last they've told our story." They had told it publicly, officially, repeatedly, all day long. Perhaps it really was a harbinger of change.

One Way into History: High School Texts

You don't have to be Jewish to weep for the men, women, and children who were shepherded into gas chambers during the Holocaust; you don't have to be black to share the despair of men, women, and children who were crammed into slave ships, bound for a lifetime of slavery in an unknown land.[74]

What Do Our Seventeen-Year-Olds Know?

Chief Justice Peterson echoed the experience of many of his contemporaries in his admission that "by the age of seven" he had learned the catechism of ethnic hierarchy in Wisconsin. Family talk, neighborhood society, and casual slurs among peers educate us early to perceptions of history saturated with feeling and attitude anything but empathetic. It can happen long before religion, official political doctrine, and grade school try to teach us how we ought to feel about this or that neighbor. Psychologists and counselors know that feelings, like glaciers, do not melt instantly in temporary warmth of a Fourth of July oration or one of those Sunday school classes that stuck in Senator

Hatfield's memory. Seeds do get sown in such occasions, but the conditions under which they can sprout may take years to arrive.

In the 1950s and 1960s conditions did begin to exist that would re-educate the head and the heart of many of Justice Peterson's white American peers. This re-education would reverberate in classes where school systems confronted the young with the history of America in books. To what degree history books equip the young with fact that they never forget or with attitudes different from those of parents has been a subject of polls and other studies over the last twenty years. On the whole they have concluded that high school graduates in America do not remember many "basic facts" about our history. One of the most systematic of the studies—testing 7,812 seventeen-year-old high school juniors drawn from all fifty states and concentrating on three major ethnic groups—was reported in 1987 under the title, *What Do Our 17-Year-Olds Know?*[75] No comparable previous test had ever been administered to American high school students, so the results of the study had little to say about how previous generations had mastered historical fact The five scholars who devised the study had all grown up in the latter half of the century and had all engaged in the debates over *whose history* should be most prominent in the books and memories of modern Americans. They agreed from the beginning, they said, that certain facts about the past are important for civic and political discourse among adult Americans, and—implicitly contradicting post-modernists—that the answers to some questions of history are not subject to dispute. Thomas Edison did or did not "invent the light bulb" (among 141 questions this one gained the highest number of correct scores [95 percent] from students male and female, white, black, and Hispanic). John Winthrop and the Puritans did or did not "found a colony in Boston" (only 19 percent of students answered correctly, the poorest score among all 141). And Columbus did or did not "discover the New World before 1750" (72 percent of whites knew that, but only 47 percent of blacks and 54 percent of Hispanics). But there was no room in the test for students to reflect that the country had already been "discovered" by peoples who had lived here for thousands of years. Only one of the 141 items mentioned Native Americans ("Indians were put on reservations after the Civil War").

As all accounts of social science method have to concede, categories of important versus unimportant knowledge have to be chosen according to norms that are ultimately controversial. Who is to say that widespread awareness of an Edison, fuzzy memory of 1492, and ignorance of a Winthrop tell us whether a student will "use" history well or poorly in, for example, thinking about a career or voting in an election? This skeptical question gets some put-down, however, when one asks whether it makes any difference if white and black students diverge considerably in awareness of histories that affect their present interests and relation to each other. What difference does it make if

- Less than a third of either group knew what Jim Crow law was all about.
- Only one in four black students know about the "three-fifths" clause in the original U.S. Constitution.
- Only a third of whites and only 43 percent of blacks knew what the Emancipation Proclamation did.
- Only half of whites and less than half of blacks knew that there was a national debate over slavery before the Civil War.
- Less than half of whites but almost three-fourths of blacks associated Martin Luther King, Jr., with the Montgomery Bus Boycott.
- Two-thirds of whites but less than half of blacks could locate the area of the Confederacy.

To excerpt scores on just twenty such questions[76] is to open a window on the different histories which American whites and blacks begin to carry around in their heads as young people. Many variables in American educational systems are at work here, but the most striking critique derivable from this data is *how often history study among African American and Euro-American youth fails to alert them to the events of the past which most decisively have shaped their mutual and conflicting interests, aspirations, and opportunities in their society.* Ignorance about these events feeds the roots of racist misunderstanding on both sides. Race *matters* in America 2003 in part because history matters.

The five historian-designers of the 1985–1987 study knew all of this. They chose their 141 questions through screens at once philosophical, political, ethical, and educational. Their prefatory statement set forth convictions which virtually summarized their vocation as history teachers:

> The committee agreed that students must understand basic chronology; that they should know the most important provisions of the Constitution and Bill of Rights; that they should know the major events that shaped the nation and formed its character; that they should know both the achievements and the frailties of the American political system; that all students, not just blacks, should be familiar with the history of civil rights issues and court decisions. The committee sought to construct a bare outline of an American history that belongs to all of us, not just to groups whose ancestors were involved in particular issues or episodes. . . . [The committee agreed that:] It is possible to define American history, with all of its complexity, controversy, and variety, as the story of a people forged from many different pasts, but joined together under a common political system. There is, in short, an American people, not just a mosaic of unrelated groups, each with its own story, disconnected from the whole. Perhaps it was the factionalism and the contentiousness of the previous quarter-century that had made such a synthesis possi-

ble, but no one [among the five of us] questioned the inclusion of questions drawn from women's history, black history, and social history as an integral part of the American story.[77]

Leaving for my next chapter the embarrassing omission of *Indian* history from this catalogue, one can easily surmise that the assumptions in this statement are the stuff of huge controversy in American universities, political interest groups, local school boards, parents, and teachers. Historians who peruse high school history books of the past forty years are likely to observe that, as the books have introduced greater and greater variety and detail in the stories of the many American peoples, "the" story of "the" American people becomes less and less coherent, synthetic, and consensual. Deconstructionist disdain for the myths of consensus is easy; but not so easy is the complex of intellectual, political, and normative questions which must be answered for the writing, the selling, and the adoption of textbooks for the school systems of the United States. We have fifty state public systems, hundreds of private schools, and thousands of local school boards, all of whose leaders have powers to decide what should and should not be taught about American history to young citizens. Textbooks in science, social studies, and history arouse great political and religious passions across the United States, a phenomenon which suggests that education, after all, is never "merely academic."

One axiom which infused the discussions of the above five test designers is basic to the present book: Ethics and democratic politics, as well as intellectual integrity, have large stakes in the ability various groups of Americans to appreciate in depth each other's history. Social psychologist George Herbert Mead once remarked that, for democracy to work, citizens, upon stepping into the voting booth, must vote for someone else's interest in addition to their own. To do so they must have some accurate knowledge of what those other interests might be. Debate over "common" and diverse goods is at stake here. Citizens need time and communication for discovering what in fact they have in common. Infinite clash of competing interests kills commonality and coherence in the body politic. Doubtless the mutual understandings which link diverse groups will always be incomplete, subject to correction by the groups' own voices. Interest groups must be free to define themselves. But what difference will it make if others pay no attention? When clashing memories of the past haunt the perceptions of this or that group of citizens, deep alienation may exist alongside surface placidity. When African American philosopher Cornel West exclaims, "A profound hatred of African people . . . sits at the center of American civilization," or a journalist like David Shipler speaks of the United States as "a country of strangers,"[78] the least that ought to greet such claims is recollection of certain historical events that render these opinions understandable. Indeed, one had better understand those events before one ignores their impacts on the present, else public argument is likely to go nowhere. Worst of all, the uncompromisable "glue" of society will disappear along with the society's very ability to compromise. As T. V. Smith reminded the ethical-ideological critics of compromise, "It is the uncompromisable which compromise exists to safeguard."[79]

The more reason then, for the continuing education of a public, among all of its parts, about each other. This is the democratic, practical case for expanding anyone's awareness of the trail along which a neighbor arrived on the perimeters of your life and you arrived on theirs. The study of history has to be one door to that awareness, especially when history is (1) taught by teachers who aim at such awareness, (2) with the help of texts that feed it, and (3) in the company of peers who are the living descendants of ancestors who walked into American history via those separate trails.

An Intergenerational Tour of One High School History Series

In celebration of certain visible, positive changes in all three of these elements of a class in history—the teacher, the text, and the student neighbor—I want next to compare some examples of American high school history books from four decades, 1960–2002. Others have studied this "history of history" more thoroughly than I mean to do here. In parallel with the above excerpts from high school texts in contemporary Germany and South Africa, here and in the next chapter I want to identify concrete *improvements* in the attention of high school history books to the negative American past as regards African Americans and Native Americans. Historians may quarrel over the superficiality evident in history as taught to the very young, and ideologues may decry various omissions of positive or negative evidence for the virtues of ancestors. But these necessary quarrels ought not to obscure the fact that high school students in 2003 were meeting varieties of American experience in their history books in ways absent in the books of one and two generations ago.[80]

The friends of "multicultural history" have to concede that it is hard to write the many American stories and to connect them with one American story. How contested is the idea of "one story" can be gathered from a visit to the contemporary Museum of American History in Washington, D.C. Times, peoples, and themes multiply in great profusion along the walls of this museum. The impression is not even kaleidoscopic, for even a kaleidoscope has patterns. But at least the raw material of a more coherent national story is there in stories of human tributaries to the national river. Whatever the future of the one story–many stories debate, on one modest relative observation we ought all to agree: We are the better educated as Americans if we know and acknowledge the many ways by which our ancestors and our contemporaries arrived in the American neighborhood.

A glance across the multiple editions of one popular set of high school history books, 1960–2003, turns up some sturdy evidence that, relatively speaking, the present generation of young people has less excuse than did their parents and grandparents for coming to believe that 1492 was a date decisive only for white Europeans or that "Reconstruction" had no impact on the current relations of black and white Americans.

From 1950 to 1995, one succession of texts appeared under the initial authorship of Lewis Paul Todd and Merle Curti. Over these forty-five years the book went through some ten editions, acquiring in the process new authors and new titles.[81] The series offered changing answers to the question, "What should all high school students learn about the history of African Americans?" Vast new work of professional Black History scholars lies behind many of the changes and, most powerfully, the civil rights movement. Among the visible changes are these:

- The 1961 edition contains six columns of text on slavery in the Americas and six on the history of the abolition movement. It describes few of the conditions of slave life, little about the work they did, little about slave resistances, and nothing about the importance of their economic contribution to the "rise of the American nation" (the title of this edition). But the account of the abolition movement has some biting paragraphs, for example, a quotation from William Lloyd Garrison: "I found contempt more bitter, opposition more stubborn, and apathy more frozen" in New England than in the South. The text notes conflicts between economic interests and moral feelings expressed by slaveholders George Washington and Thomas Jefferson. Relatively benign pictures of southern plantation life appear here in a Currier and Ives print, but on an adjoining page is a photograph of a tunnel used in the Underground Railroad. The 1966 edition is not greatly changed except for the addition of a photo of Frederick Douglass, a sidebar biography of Harriet Tubman ("Moses of her People"), and a painting of a slave family on horseback making "a dash for freedom." But these additions are harbingers of more radical ones in the 1972 edition.
- By 1966 the civil rights movement, as led by Martin Luther King, was eleven years old. Its impacts are drastic on the 1972 Todd-Curti. A diagram of the Middle Passage portrays the international scope of the slave trade in vivid, searing language. All regions of the country are said to share blame for this "evil":

> New England slaves, like slaves everywhere, rebelled against the central evil of slavery—the total and permanent ownership of human beings by other human beings. Many New England slaves fled from their masters, no matter how kind their masters might be. (1972:65)

Five full columns, replete with moral condemnation, describe slavery in the Thirteen Colonies. "Denied their humanity, Africans became

slaves and most remained slaves for life, as did their children." Few of
the colonists, we are told for the first time in the series, knew or cared
that Africans came from civilizations hundreds of even thousands of
years old; and, by being put ashore in America, black newcomers were
forced to abandon "all that they had held dear in the lands of their
birth" (1972:64). Supplementing this perspective, subsequent pages
describe the artistic cultures of West Africa ("Ghana, Benin, Mali,
Songhai, Ashanti, Dahomey"). And then appears the fact that not all
ancient African culture disappeared among these coerced emigrees. In
music, for example, the spirituals replicated African musical forms
and "poignantly expressed the slaves' deep longing for freedom" (1972:
314). Readers are asked to remember that an estimated fifteen million
people were taken captive from Africa over three centuries of the trade—
though they are not asked to ponder the possibility that, according to
some scholars, the number should be fifty million. Thus "Africa was
drained of its most valuable resource—its people" (1972:306). Slaves,
the text notes, made the American Cotton Kingdom economically profitable; and one should not forget the frequent slave resistances in
these centuries, epitomized by the names Denmark Vesey, Gabriel
Prosser, and Nat Turner. The latter appears in a drawing depicting his
effort to recruit fellow slaves to his revolt.

Much has happened in the political and academic culture of the
United States between 1950, when this book was first published, and
its third edition of 1972. The emerging tradition of black-authored academic history, begun long ago in the work of Carter G. Woodson,
Charles Wesley, and W. E. B. Du Bois, begun anew by John Hope
Franklin and greatly expanded in the work of a new generation of
black scholars, has finally affected high school history writing. Some
schools across the land are newly integrated, and black high school
students are less likely than ever to tolerate a papered-over past of their
ancestors.[82] Detail and moral passion now infuse these accounts of
slavery. Students white and black might now detect the unmistakable
non-neutrality of some history writing. As concerns slavery, at least,
the new editions will no longer tempt the careful reader to gloss over
an evil past under the influence, as in the 1960–1980 South African
parallels, of passive verbs and mere "happenings."

• The 1977 edition repeats much of the approaches of 1972 with some
  new details on the moral and physical horrors of slavery. With the
  1982 edition arrive a twelve-column account of abolition, yet more details of horror and resistance, vivid pictures and maps of the Underground Railroad, an account of the role of religious revivals in contrib-
  uting to Abolition, the role of women in the same (exemplified by the
  Grimké sisters), quotations from and a portrait of Frederick Douglass,

mention of Henry Highland Garnet, Sojourner Truth, and William Wells Brown, and an array of vivid photographs—tags worn by different classes of plantation slaves, an attic stop on the Railroad, Harriet Tubman and six freed slaves, and Harriet Beecher Stowe. The 1961 edition describes Stowe's *Uncle Tom's Cabin* as full of "melodramatic distortions." But 1982 adds that, while the characters come across as "often moralistic," they nonetheless "come alive in a way readers never forgot." Many nineteenth-century southerners, we are told, protested the book as failing to acknowledge the "kindness" displayed by many masters toward their slaves (1982: 374–382).

• At the end of all three editions between 1977 and 1986, students read about the twentieth century civil rights movement. Lacking in these texts, however, are critical accounts of the Reconstruction and post-Reconstruction eras of 1865–1955, that is, how in those ninety years American society enacted legal and social discriminations which so hobbled the "rise" of African Americans as to make indispensable for them the civil rights movement of 1950–1970.

In sum, Frances Fitzgerald could concede sarcastically in 1979 that "the history texts now hint to a certain level of unpleasantness in American history," enough unpleasantness, doubtless, to raise the hackles of many patriotic critics of multiculturalism in public education. But she shrewdly observed that for African Americans to enter history texts in the 1960s and 1970s was to begin to see that they had been part of the history all along since 1619:

> [E]ither the blacks belonged to American history or they did not, and if they did they belonged to all of it. To include a section on the civil rights movement meant that the whole of American history had to be rewritten to include blacks and their perspective on events. It was as if Tolstoy had first written *War and Peace* without the character of Pierre.[83]

By their new attention to the history of minorities in American history as a whole, the texts of the 1960s and 1970s, she says, "contain the most dramatic rewriting of history ever to take place in American school books."[84] In the 1960s, political society "discovered" blacks, Hispanics, Asians, Indians, and women. Then history book authors discovered them, too. Fitzgerald acknowledges this political context of texts as inevitable. She understands the problem of the "add-on" strategy for bringing history up to date—the descent into miscellany at the expense of coherent narrative. Unfortunately, in her acerbic criticisms of textbook politics she largely fails to celebrate these changes as relative gains in knowledge and justice for students of this nation's "rise." The United States is a country whose perpetual openness to immigrants means that its self-conscious collective identity is never quite up to date. But at least by 1990, history as available in high school texts did more justice than ever to a variety of real stories of real people in our national past.[85]

A final sampling of evidence for this assertion, regarding the place of African Americans in some contemporary secondary school texts, can be drawn from the most recent descendant of the Todd-Curti series—*The American Nation,* published in 2001 under the supervising authorship of Paul Boyer.[86] This book, 1184 glossy pages long, weighs six pounds, costs $75.00, and on the first thumbing-through displays remarkable modern advances in the arts of printing, format, color reproduction, maps, and—above all—educational method. If the barb "as dry as a high school history book" is much deserved by some of the books which previous generations of Americans studied, this book hardly deserves the same.[87] We are a long way from the history which Donald Shriver studied in high school in the mid 1940s.

Indeed, the hooks to learning here are so various, colorful, and inviting that a casual reviewer will know immediately that the book demands a lot of students but even more of teachers. Like the contemporary German and South African texts already described, this book expects a teacher to involve students in multileveled approaches to multicultural history. On two preface pages the authors identify fourteen dimensions of history study to be pursued in the thirty-six chapters:

1. Using Historical Imagination
2. Understanding Geography
3. Recognizing Point of View
4. Comparing and Contrasting
5. Identifying Cause and Effect
6. Analyzing
7. Assessing Consequences
8. Distinguishing Fact from Opinion
9. Identifying Values
10. Hypothesizing
11. Synthesizing
12. Problem Solving
13. Evaluating
14. Taking a Stand (2001: xxii–xxiii)

Among these formidable intellectual and empathetic demands, particularly striking is the aim of combining 1, 6, and 11. The first of ten "Great Debates" featured in sidebars from time to time asks if Columbus's expeditions to America were good or bad for Europeans, Indians, and Africans. It sets the debate in the context of public quarrels in 1992 over celebration versus mourning of the event. Was Columbus a curse for Native Americans? Some say yes, some no, and "some historians try to balance these viewpoints," as does this text, which aims at "synthesis" (2001:xxiii). In the next thousand pages students are frequently asked to imagine themselves as members of one or another historical group and to write, picture, or otherwise undertake an exercise in empathy for people of the past. Early on, many of these exercises concern Native Americans. Not until almost three hundred pages into the book do exercises multiply around the lives of black slaves. But meantime the whole text of the Declaration of Independence has been reproduced, and a sidebar quotes Jefferson's original draft protesting the institution of slavery and asks the student: "Why do you think the Congress deleted this passage?" A few pages later, after the story of the framing of the original U.S. Constitution, with its "three-fifths" clause, a "historical imagination" assignment reads: "Imagine that you are a legislator voting on the ratification of the Constitution. Will you vote for or against it? Why?" (2001:148)? One measure of educational success of this book will be whether teacher and student will follow the chain of events, over the ensuing seventy years, that will lead to the Civil War. On the whole, the text competently portrays the economic, political, moral and cultural collisions that will swirl around the fatal issue of slavery from 1790 to 1860.

When *The American Nation* takes up "The Cotton Kingdom" on page 263, for example, its next hundred pages, leading up to the Civil War, offer extensive opportunities for the student to enter into the viewpoints, issues, class conflicts, human ambitions, and human suffering that abound in nineteenth-century American history. Nothing in any of the previous volumes of the Todd-Curti ancestors of this book compare with these chapters. As of 1987, Frances Fitzgerald complained that most high school books obscured the realities of class conflict in American history,[88] but section 2 of this 2001 book begins by noting the parties to the "irrepressible conflict"—southern yeoman farmers, poor white farmers, planters, and slaves. One assignment asks for an essay on "what life was like for most free African Americans in the South" and "what cultural traits white southerners of different classes shared" (2001:263). Soon after come the projects:

> [I]magine that you are a slave escaping the South with Harriet Tubman's aid. Write a fictional account of your journey.
> To what extent can it be said that many slaves protested their condition every day and in every way possible?
> *Consider:*
>
> * how slave culture was a form of resistance
> * what other forms of resistance slaves practiced
> * the limitations of direct resistance (2001:279)

In a true display of "the irony of American history," page 187 scatters three photos down the margin: the original manuscript of the 1790 Bill of Rights, a pair of slave chains, and a "Votes for Women" lapel button from the women's suffrage movement. Women populate this text in greater number than in any previous Todd-Curti edition. Links between the women's movement and abolitionism get noted from time to time. Nine pages on "The Slave System" and six on the abolition movement include the pictures: a slave nurse of a white child ("Proslavery advocates argued that slaves like this nurse were very well treated"[89]), an 1860s Georgia slave log cabin, a painting of an auction of a slave family, a slave gathering for worship in the woods ("Why . . . there?"), a poster ad for capture of a runaway, Nat Turner, Harriet Tubman, Henry Highland Garnet, Sojourner Truth, and the 1837 burning of Elijah Lovejoy's printing press in Illinois. In its commitment to synthetic balance, the text observes that

> Northern opposition to abolition arose from fear and prejudice against African Americans. Many northern wage earners feared competing with free African Americans for jobs. In addition, northern merchants and mill owners were afraid that abolition would disrupt cotton production. (2001:301)

On average, history textbooks devote fewest pages to remote centuries, most to recent. The first third of this mammoth text takes us into the Civil War, but already it has considerably redressed the invisibility of African Americans in many another book about the first three centuries of American history. Chapters on the Civil War tell us that 180,000 freedmen fought on the Union side of the war, 32,000 died, and 20 received the Congressional Medal of Honor (2001:387). Then follow thirty pages on the Reconstruction and post-Reconstruction eras.

Among comparative gains of this book over the contents of its ancestor editions, its treatment of Reconstruction is probably the most significant; for, as many recent historians have insisted, treatment of the eras 1865–1876 and 1876–1955 has consistently been short, superficial, and ideologically slanted against accounts of the real injustices—amounting virtually to a reimposition of slavery—done by this society to African Americans in the long decades before the twentieth century civil rights movement. Whether Andrew Johnson or the Radical Republicans of Congress served the interests of the newly freed slaves is at least posed for student debate, against the impressions left by any who have seen the film *Gone with the Wind*, not to speak of *The Birth of a Nation*.[90] No student is likely to leave this debate ignorant of Jim Crow laws. The text devotes seventeen pages to the attempts of Reconstruction Congressional leaders, 1865–1876, to transform slaves into citizens. It asks, in a sixth "Great Debate," for an assessment of successes and failures: Did freed slaves get the "forty acres" suggested by General William T. Sherman? Should the assaults of the Jim Crow era on rights promised in the Thirteenth, Fourteenth, and Fifteenth Amendments be balanced against the institutions which the newly freed men and women built for themselves as counter to these injustices? Should the three amendments be seen as legal leverage waiting for the day of a revived Civil Rights Movement of the 1950s (2001:419)? By page 427 we are in the 1890s, and the text proposes the empathetic project:

> Imagine that you are an attorney representing Homer Plessy [of
> *Plessy v. Ferguson*]. Prepare a closing statement arguing that segrega-
> tion, as practiced in "separate but equal" facilities for African Ameri-
> cans and whites, violates the Fourteenth Amendment.

Over the next 135 pages African Americans do not much appear as the text turns to the "Manifest Destiny" era of U.S. continental expansions, industrialization, and war with Native Americans and Spain. But when, on page 562, a famous 1903 quotation from W. E. B. Du Bois appears for the first time in this 1950–2001 series, a latter-day careful reader already has at hand the history that renders Du Bois's pained words plausible:

> One ever feels his two-ness—an American, a Negro; two souls, two
> thoughts, two un-reconciled strivings. He [the African American]
> simply wishes to make it possible for a man to be both a Negro and
> an American, without being cursed and spit upon by his fellows,
> without having the doors of Opportunity closed roughly in his face.

Opposite this page is a multicolored chart of lynchings in the United States, 1889–1918, showing that in only six of forty-eight states—five in New England and Utah—did no lynching occur.

The twentieth-century half of the book offers a cross section of samples of the cultural contributions of African Americans to national life: jazz, poetry, novels, sports, science, and fine art. Data and pictures profile the role of African American troops in World War One, the upsurge of the Ku Klux Klan in the 1920s, race riot and murder in Chicago, Detroit, Boston and Tulsa,[91] continued job discrimination in factories across the land, sluggish progress in economic opportunity under the New Deal, the million African American soldiers of World War Two, Japanese American internments, Holocaust, Hiroshima, and twenty pages on the civil rights movement of 1950–1970. Accounts of the explosion of human rights activism follow as the text tries to do justice to the multitude of ethnic and other groups who found precedent in the civil rights movement: women, Chicanos, Native Americans, persons with disability, the retired, and children. Pictures, population charts, and protest events crowd these pages, so that by now, this late in the semester, a high school student should know very well that he or she lives in a rainbow country, matched by this rainbow history book. The story to date may be confusing and incoherent. Students may be hard put to tell "it." But they should not by now doubt that American history is a composite of many stories. A photograph shows crew members of both sexes and three ethnic groups climbing aboard the fateful *Challenger* space capsule in 1986. The one soldier pictured from the Gulf War of 1991 is a black woman. Maya Angelou reads her poetry before the Capitol in the 1992 inauguration of President Bill Clinton. Through it all have woven more strands of the African American contribution to the fabric of this national history than has appeared in most of the public school books of the twentieth century. The resulting quilt displays good and evil, human achievement and human degradation. One of the last references to the life and death of an African American (2001:1078) is a 1998 picture of the family of James Byrd of Jasper, Texas. The text fails to mention the conviction of his three killers for murder by Texas courts, leaving it to the student or the teacher to observe this event as a hopeful judicial break with the impunities of the lynching tradition documented five hundred pages earlier.

In pursuit of its "synthetic" aim, *The American Nation* tries frequently to raise issues of cultural and political controversy by alluding to two sides of a historic argument. It never gives explicit quarter to the defense of slavery or segregation, but it does record that these racist institutions had their defenders. "Many" teenagers loved Elvis Presley and how he learned from African American music in his invention of rock 'n' roll, but "many" adults disliked it. It upset "many" that black and white musicians began to appear together on stage. Furthermore, as television grew in popularity in the 1960s, "it remained a selective mirror, showing primarily white, middle-class, suburban experiences. Poverty, if shown at all, was treated as a minor problem. Working women, ethnic minorities, and inner-city life rarely appeared. When they were shown, it was usually in a way that reinforced stereotypes." As illustration, there was the 1966 protest of the NAACP against the TV version of the old radio program, *Amos 'n' Andy,* which had entertained millions in the 1930s. "[F]or many viewers the characters represented white stereotypes of the African American community," and the network canceled the program, including reruns (2001:876). There is no project in these latter sections, however, asking the student to identify stereotypes in the media of 2001. That question, perhaps, remains for the teacher to pose.

High school students who study this book in the wake of the Iraq war of 2003 will have some teachers with vivid youthful memories of the Vietnam War. Analogies between Vietnam, the Gulf War of 1991, and Iraq of 2003 will offer much opportunity for class discussion of change and currency in the statistics on black soldiers' participation in these recent wars in the disproportion recorded on page 985: 24 percent of black deaths against 11 percent of blacks in the nation's population. "Polls showed that African Americans were much more likely than whites to consider the [Vietnam] war a mistake" (2001: 991). The twenty-five pages devoted to the Vietnam War end with a photo of two veterans pressing hands against "our wailing wall" in Washington with its "terrible grace." Unmentioned here is the 1998 Pentagon award of medals to the three helicopter crewmen who tried to control the My Lai Massacre. Two "imagine" assignments conclude these pages:

> Imagine that you are a veteran of the Vietnam War. Write a letter to the president explaining how you think Vietnam veterans should be honored. (2001:1003)

> Imagine that you are a Vietnamese veteran of the Vietnamese War. Write a letter to a U.S. veteran explaining how the Vietnamese people's long history of resisting control by outside powers helped them endure terrible hardships and continued fighting. Describe the similarities and differences between Vietnamese history and U.S. history. (2001:1005)

How many students asked to undertake these assignments will have parents who fought in that or a subsequent American war? Will students be urged to interview parents and adult neighbors on the matter? What resistances to the second assignment will erupt in classroom controversy? Will slumbering interracial tensions feed both resistance and controversy? One wonders. But one is sure that, for imaginative study of this and other issues of American history, a history class does not have to be always dry, dull, or irrelevant to the youthful present.

No page among the eleven hundred supports this surmise more directly than the final paragraphs of the 2001 text.[92] This ending comes as close to any passage in the book to being an attempt to knit up the raveled sleeve of multicultural miscellany with a precis of what American history is all about. Students reading these paragraphs in the spring of 2003 and thereafter will have reason, after their long trek through five centuries, to ask if indeed this is what the whole journey is about. Beside a photo of an Indonesian woman casting a vote in 1999:

> In many parts of the world, true democracy remains distant. Democratic nations attempt to convince the rest of the world of democracy's appeal by helping solve existing social and economic problems.
>
> The United States is committed to playing a central role in this effort. Some of the earliest English settlers in America believed they were lighting a beacon that would show the way to a new era in human history. After the establishment of a democratic government, the idea of America as a world leader became a reality. However, the nation has not always lived up to these ideals. Many groups have been excluded from the promise of democracy. Over the years, though, the United States has tried to expand democracy, individual freedom and the privileges and obligations of citizenship to all its citizens.
>
> Global powers may shift, and economies may change, but the appeal of democracy will likely remain. People will continue to strive for individual freedom, self-government, and citizenship in a just

nation. This is particularly true for those people living under unjust rulers or in extreme poverty. The vision of democracy and freedom can still inspire acts of great courage and heroism.

As is true in history, the future will be determined by new gen- erations' willingness to tackle tough problems. In this book you have learned of our nation's history up to the present. The next chapters in this still-unfolding story are yours to write. (2001:1091)

By the time some high school students get to this paragraph, they will need no priming to launch into a discussion of the American presence in Iraq. That their nation "has not always lived up to these ideals" they will have had much evidence from this book and from current news. Does the mix of positive and negative evidence confirm or challenge "the idea of America as a world leader" and as "a beacon that would show the way to a new era in human history"? Nothing in these final four paragraphs suggests that in the rest of the world Americans might look for ideas and beacons not already resident in our own history. What do other national histories have to teach us? Will teach- ers raise this question? This author hopes so. I will pursue the matter in the final chapter of this book.

To Repair Memory: Pilgrimages and Museums

Among unfortunate clichés abounding in contemporary public speech are two: "It's history" and "it's of mere historical interest." The speakers usually mean: it's over, you must consign it to the past, you can't change it now. The writers of history texts, the curators of museums, and builders of monuments and memorials all have investments in resisting these glib dismissals of their work, which intends the message: "What we portray here is important for you, now and in the future."

As we know from Germany and South Africa, every museum carries heavy freight from the past into the present, just as the present brings its own freight to bear upon the past. We would have no Sachsenhausen or District Six mu- seum if the adjective "mere" had ever been permitted to suffuse discussions leading to their establishment.

If they are to serve to portray facts important for a present public to re- member, however, museums, like textbooks, require agreements between their founders and a potential set of visitors who will say: "Yes, this is a display of something we must not forget." The arousal of these constituents may take a long time, especially in a public that presents solid fronts of resistance to re- membering shadow sides of its own past. The product of this resistance, as we have seen in all the local case studies of this chapter, is multigenerational amnesia. The best antidote is likely to come from some persistent, aging minority of survivors who work away at fashioning signs to the past in ways vivid enough to convince upcoming younger contemporaries that, not only did "it" happen, but the happening has practical impacts on you.

Revisiting Selma

Making it vivid, as all history teachers know, is no easy matter. Multigenerational honor to the important past may require multimedia education. Among recent events related to *political* education, there was one in March 2003 that brought a group of elected American politicians, some family members, longtime activists, a company of students, and some curators of museums into a walk into the history of the civil rights movement in Alabama. Organized by the Faith and Politics Institute in Washington, D.C., the occasion brought twenty-seven members of Congress, including two senators, to three cities whose names will always carry association with a major change in legal justice for African Americans: Montgomery, Birmingham, and Selma. The first was the scene of the "Montgomery Improvement Association" wherein Rosa Parks famously refused to sit in the back of a city bus and Martin Luther King, Jr., first came into leadership of a new surge for civil rights in post-1876 America. The second was the city where police dogs, firehoses, and jails brought new national government support of the movement. The third was the place where, out of clashes between police billy clubs and nonviolent demonstrators, there finally came a national Voting Rights Law which would make good at last on the Fifteenth Amendment to the United States Constitution. Selma is the right place for locating a National Voting Rights Museum: In direct response to demonstrations there of March 1965, a president of the United States addressed a joint session of Congress to propose a new voting rights bill. It would pass the next August.[93]

One of the young leaders of the events of 1963–1965 was John Lewis, since 1986 a congressman from Atlanta. Lewis helped lead the famous "Bloody Sunday" march over the Edmund Pettus Bridge, suffering a concussion from police clubs. Thirty years later, he began to invite congressional colleagues to join him in a return to Selma. Locals joining them in the spring of 2003 included Selma black mayor James Perkins, Jr., several black police officers, and seventy-three-year-old George Sallie of Selma with his billy-club scar from that Pettus Bridge crossing in 1965. Sallie fought in Korea in the early 1950s. Said he: "I was fighting for somebody else's freedom in Korea, and did not even have my own. I figured voting could give me the chance to choose who would lead me."[94] Then there was thirty-five-year-old Artur Davis, African American congressman from nearby Montgomery, who after the bridge and voting museum visit remarked:

> Frankly, the struggles that we face pale in comparison to the enormous obstacles that were thrown at John Lewis's generation. All the

opportunities I've had . . . are a function of a fairer and more equal
America [and are] a direct product of the civil rights movement.
There would literally not be a 7th Congressional district [my West
Montgomery district] without the Voting Rights Act.

And there would have been no Representative John Lewis, either, nor predecessor Representative Andrew Young apart from the Voting Act of 1965. This
fact turns Lewis's commemorative marches across a bridge from a mournful
memorial into a celebratory monument.

In the midst of the March 2003 ceremonial bridge crossing, Lewis shed
some tears. "Some of it," he explained to reporters, "is tears of hurt and pain,
but some of it is tears for joy, to see how far we have come." The great satisfaction of the day, he said, was the change evident in the feelings of younger
people—Congress members and students—about this particular past. "One
person said that this is the first time that he sang, 'We Shall Overcome.' "
Several Congressional participants suggested a nonviolence workshop for the
entire House. Kansas Senator Sam Brownback said that the pilgrimage "helps
me feel what I've read about. You can get the sense of despair at that time, the
hope that's come since then and the distance it's yet to travel." Old enough to
have been there in 1965, another prominent Republican participant, Jack
Kemp, remembered a visit of his football team to Alabama in the 1950s and
asked himself why, in 1965, had he not been there in Selma? In particular,
"Why hadn't I protested the treatment of my black teammates in professional
football?"[95] Actor Chris Tucker, too young for that particular regret, said that
for him the event was pure joy. "It's like I'm experiencing some lost presence,
coming here and being connected with the past." And Charles Gushue, a high
school student from Washington, D.C., said that the experience would help
him to introduce to some friends "the empathy that's missing" in their relation
to the past.[96]

New intergenerational empathy may have been the salient achievement in
this weekend Alabama visit. In his remarkable echo of the philosophy of Martin
Luther King, John Lewis testified that his numerous annual trips to Selma left
him still concerned for those white citizens who had cheered that police brutality. It was his version of intergenerational hope:

I often think: Where are those people now? What is it that made
people do what they did? What did their children and their grandchildren think about what they did? Did they try to . . . make up or
amend for what their fathers and grandfathers and mothers and
grandmothers did?[97]

Personal Pilgrimages to Public Repentance

The 1990s saw some phenomenal personal quests for answers to Lewis's questions. The personal often led to the public and the institutional.

Sigmund Freud did more than any other modern theorist of the human mind to formulate the notion of suppression, repression, and the reality of the unconscious. Freud once compared the urge to protect oneself from unpleasant memories to the stationing of mental "troops" at this and that anxious juncture of one's past. We peel off some of our available troops as guardians against the conscious outbreak of pain which we want never to experience again. The problem with this mental strategy, he said, is that eventually everyone gives out of troops, leaving one defenceless against new pain. Freud believed that, with careful listening, he could help push the troops aside for a while and bring the original painful events into the open, where they could lose some of their crippling power.[98]

Among pertinent illustrations from the 1990s are these three:

- African American historian Roger Wilkins said to a *New York Times* reporter in 1995 that "for people of my generation slavery was pushed away." He "recalled a day when his mother told him stories of their ancestors that he had never heard." He asked her, "Why didn't you tell me that when I was growing up?" to which she replied, "Well Roger, I guess it is like the old folks used to say: We didn't like to clank our chains." But attitudes are changing among many blacks, he said. "[They] have come 180 degrees, and they look at slavery with pride. They say, 'I must be descended from some extraordinary people to have weathered that hideous storm.' "[99]

- Richard Rusk is son of a famous Georgian, Dean Rusk, Secretary of State under Lyndon Johnson in the 1960s. He is a newspaper columnist in Oconee County, sixty miles east of Atlanta. In 1992 he learned from an Atlanta newspaper about a 1920s lynching of four black persons by a dozen white men five miles from his home near Moore's Ford Bridge. An elderly man, aged ten at the time of the murders, came forth to identify four of the perpetrators, now all dead. "I was just stunned," said Rusk. "That same day, I drove to the bridge and got up on the bridge and just stared into the muddy water of the Apalachee River. I just tried to imagine what could have led to such horror." His interest in the event soon lapsed. Then, in 1997, he heard a speech by Archbishop Desmond Tutu, who was visiting Atlanta. Tutu said that the United States might need a Truth Commission. At that he remembered the Moore's Bridge murders and decided to organize a "Moore's Ford Committee." He said, "It was a spooky feeling. You're talking about dragging up a racial atrocity like a lynching in your community, where the descendants of victims and killers are all around you." His committee found the victims' graves, set up a memorial, started scholarships in three counties, and held art exhibits "to raise public awareness of the tragedy." He went on to investigate the toll of lynching in Georgia—542—from 1880 to 1930. Not everyone in his neighborhood, white or black, applauded these efforts. One older black protested, "It was bad enough living through those years. I don't want to be reminded of them." A year or so later, members of Rusk's Committee began to hear of similar efforts around the United States: Price, Utah; Wilmington, N.C., Orangeburg, S.C., Chatanooga, Tenn.; Rosewood, Fla., and Duluth, Minn. "In this country," he said to a reporter, "hundreds of communities have their acts of lynchings. Something significant is taking place here and across the country. It leads me to think America at the grassroots level might be ready to finally face this history."[100]

• Something significant was taking place also in the connection of white southern historians to the buried memory of their own families and professions. In his address to the bicentenniel of the University of South Carolina in April 2002, Professor Dan Carter of Georgia State University meditated on the "shared past" alongside the "separate memories" of southerners black and white. "[S]ome our our most intense reflections on the past are shaped in an intensely private and familial context. But it is also true that even personal memories are often interwoven with that larger history and particularly our group identity with that history."

His family told lots of stories, he continued. His grandfather liked to hand on stories from his father, who fought in the Civil War. At the young age of twenty-seven, in the 1890s, the grandfather became postmaster of his impoverished community of Effingham. Almost a hundred years later, Carter's own son undertook research for a master's thesis in local history, and only from that research did it dawn on Carter "that my grandfather had been appointed postmaster by a Republican President at a time when virtually all whites had closed ranks in the Democratic Party and most Republicans were black; that—in this small close-knit community—he had almost certainly known his predecessor, a local black political activist named Frazier Baker. Baker then moved from Effingham to a larger post office in Lake City twelve miles away and had been brutally murdered by a white mob the next year for daring to keep what had become a 'white man's job' in the late 1890s. This I learned from my son's research. But I had heard nothing of this from my grandfather, only silence."[101]

By contrast, Carter suggested, it was not likely that the descendants of Frazier Baker had forgotten, any more than the family of Richard Puckett in nearby Laurens County, S.C., forgot his murder in 1913 "at the hands of a huge mob." Hardly anything appeared in print about this latter incident. Local Laurens whites professed to knowing nothing about it. But black families knew. Puckett's grand nephew David Kennedy learned about it in the 1950s in a front porch conversation with his grandmother and aunts. "I relived it on that porch that night. . . . Nobody could tell it like the sisters sitting together telling that story . . . the look they had in their eyes, the anger and the frustration. . . . And almost in the words of James Weldon Johnson in *Lift Every-Voice and Sing*, 'Hope unborn had died.' I saw that in their faces. Also their warnings to me: Be strong, but be very careful. They will kill you."[102]

The Museums

By a recent authoritative count, as of 2003 there were 238 museums in the United States devoted to aspects of African American history in thirty-nine states. On top of this array of local memorials, in the spring of 2003 there appeared a proposal from a President-appointed commission for the building of a National Museum of African American History and Culture on the Mall in Washington. In December 2003, President Bush authorized that museum for a still-undetermined site.[103] Such a museum on the Mall was first proposed in 1915 by black northern Civil War veterans as they celebrated the fiftieth anniversary of the war's end.[104] For the next eighty-five years [105] the proposal languished in various private and government quarters, while in the meantime memorials appeared on the Mall to Washington, Lincoln, Grant, the Holocaust, Korean War Veterans, Vietnam War Dead, World War Two, Japanese American internees of the 1940s, and American Indians. The new museum of American Indians, opened in September 2004, fills almost the last space in or around this American "front yard."

For some years the national capital did have an African American museum related to the Smithsonian Institution, but its location in suburban Anacostia puts it off the track of most tourist visitors to Washington. Housed in a fine building in a largely black neighborhood, the museum focuses on stark portrayals of the Middle Passage in charts and an hour-long film that have undoubtedly contributed to many a public school project in classes brought here by teachers. One day, the guides tell you, these exhibits could become part of a Mall museum. But a visit to Anacostia should leave any citizen worried by the question: Why, 140 years after the Emancipation Proclamation and almost 400 years after Jamestown, are African Americans the last to be the subject of a museum in the shrinking site-spaces between the U.S. Capitol and the Lincoln Memorial? After regular congressional proposals between 1929 and 1991, why did it always take back seat to other official interests?

It is hard not to offer the blatant answer: anti-black racism, which has put African Americans low on many a list of priorities throughout the history of the United States. One can adduce political disagreements among black leaders and priorities deemed by them to be of greater urgency, but the lag ought to be an embarrassment to any high school student who has absorbed the meaning of the black presence in American history from 1619 on. As this is written, Congressman John Lewis and Senator Sam Brownback seem assured that concepts, coalitions, and money are beginning to coalesce around the careful work of the new Commission. But the long delay in the building of a national museum to African Americans should disturb every American.

Perhaps the only fortunate element in this delay is that it gives supporters the chance to take advantage of astonishing recent developments in the design of museums worldwide. Museums are sometimes thought to be inert, dumb witnesses to a long-gone past. But modern designers now know how to make a museum visit into an emotional as well as an intellectual experience. They aim, through various interactive media, to introduce visitors to the reality of humans once as alive as the visitors.

For example, the Detroit museum, opened in 1997, displays a model of a slave ship with life-sized human figures below decks. By way of modern contrast, in an adjoining gallery is the suit worn by Mae Jemison, first African American member of a space crew.[106] James Petty, now of Gulfport, Mississippi, a former California talk show host, has collected some fifteen thousand material remnants of slavery. His ambition is so to display them in a museum that "you'd walk in and you'd be standing on a beach of white sand, the West Coast of Africa. And [in] this part of the museum the heat would be 100 degrees. And you'd step into the slave ship and smell the smells and hear the screams."[107] Already, a church-related museum in upper westside Manhattan adds sound to its portrayal of the Middle Passage.

A multitude of media displays is not always required to trigger a shock of recognition in many museum visitors. Sometimes a single small item will do— as when a Howard University professor said that she broke down in tears when she looked at a single tiny manacle meant for a black child on a slave ship. Oswald Sykes, former New York State health administrator and amateur diver, went looking for such items inside the slave ship *Henrietta Marie*, discovered sunk off the Florida coast. His wife Marion Sykes had the same experience looking at a pair of shackles on display at the conference of scuba divers: "It was the reality of seeing those shackles and knowing that someone wore them 300 years ago. . . . It still affects you. All the shackles bother me, the small ones especially."[108]

Empathy for human beings of the past, by definition, requires vulnerability to emotion, some participation in feelings akin to those of the real people of the real past. Textbook history study can easily insulate readers from this experience, and here a museum can have supplementing educational advantages. A bare space will do. In 2001, after their classroom study of the Underground Railroad, a class of Brooklyn third and fifth graders accompanied teacher Elaine Purvis on a visit to the Lafayette Avenue Presbyterian Church, whose building, from the early 1860s, harbored escaped slaves. Led in darkness through that space and singing "Oh Freedom!" as they shuffled along, the experience became more than a footnote to their book study of Harriet Tubman. "I wasn't feeling it," said ten-year old Daynesha Vicks. But in that basement, "I felt like crying. Like we were slaves trying to run away."[109]

No single generation exhausts human understanding of a former one. A number of southern whites have begun to acknowledge the likelihood that whites and blacks in their region share more than a little historical genetic kinship. In the 1960s, a third-grade student in Durham, North Carolina, Mackie Alston, began to wonder why some of the black students in his newly desegregated school also had the name "Alston." In the late 1990s, as a theological student, he turned the question into research and a film that documented the probable relation of forebears on both sides of the racial divide to an eastern North Carolina white plantation owner. The film won the documentary prize in the 2000 Sundance Festival and was recently broadcast on PBS.[110]

Another current piece of pioneering focuses on the *names* of a people whom history books render nameless. While they lived slaves were valuable property, and their (owner-given) names often entered the legal records of their locales as regularly as did real estate. Such was the case in Louisiana where, for 150 years, lists of slaves have moldered in the basements of parish courthouses. Gwendolyn Midlo Hall, a professional but not a conventional historian, has spent fifteen years investigating such records in her native Louisiana and in Europe:

> Aided by several research assistants, she amassed computerized records on more than 100,000 slaves—the largest collection of individual slave information ever assembled. . . . In one courthouse, she said, someone had tried to burn the records, apparently afraid they would expose a black family that had been passing for white for several generations. . . . "I'm hoping [she said] this database will help smooth the path for others to make Africans concrete as human beings."

Whites in this research can acquire some new concreteness, too, not all of it welcomed by their descendants. Hall's data enabled the *New York Times* to discover that the great-grandfather of the current governor of Louisiana owned fifty slaves in 1860.[111]

Akin to this naming-project is the work of Julianna Richardson, founder the organization HistoryMakers. She seeks to recover five thousand names and biographies of the people, many still alive, who made possible the moves toward justice for African Americans in the past century. Among her "noncelebrities" is ninety-three-year-old Alonzo Pettie, believed to be the oldest living black cowboy. Building on the interviews of two thousand former slaves by staff of the Works Progress Administration in the 1930s, Richardson expects to complete her work by 2005. Howard Dodson, director of the Schomberg Center in Harlem, believes that her research embodies a growing emphasis in the formation of museums of African American history: "History is made not just by the Martin Luther Kings and the Malcolm X's but by every individual who has the consciousness to take responsibility for their lives and seek to shape and form their world."[112]

A summary observation about museums: The very fact that African American museums are now present in 238 American places means that, like the case of the numerous Holocaust memorials on the streets of Germany, some window on these painful and hopeful pasts is likely to be right around the corner from the local streets where many Americans live. But, as this author knows, and Germans know, too, one usually *decides* to go to a museum. One can always pass by on the other side.[113] But Richard Rusk may have been right: "Something significant is taking place across the country" if so many "grassroot" Americans "might be ready to finally face this history." The test case of this readiness may be readiness of some of us go to a museum we would, deep down, prefer not to visit.

In the summer of 2000 a small private one-room art gallery on the East Side of Manhattan put on display a collection of some seventy postcard photographs of a few of the five thousand-plus lynchings in the United States in the period 1880 through 1946. These photographs, some of them gruesome, were collected by Atlantan James Allen in the hope that, once displayed, they would provoke a "never again" response from contemporary viewers. Remarkably and beyond expectations of the sponsors, this mini-exhibit drew so many visitors that it was transferred to the larger spaces of the New York State Historical Society. Diverse reactions to the smudgy pictures surfaced. Said collector Allen: "White people feel guilty and reticent; black people look at these pictures and just get angry." Columnist Brent Staples feared that "with these horrendous pictures loose in the culture, the ultimate effect could easily be to normalize images that are in fact horrible."[114] It is no minor fear. Horror-hardened viewers of old Auschwitz pictures, not to speak of horror movies and video games, fall into the same "normality." In the spring of 2004, some Americans feared that the same numbness might diminish public disgust at the photographs of torture in the Abu Ghraib prison in Iraq.

This Virginia-born white has to testify that viewing those seventy post cards has therapeutic potential. One organization specializing in Holocaust studies entitles its work, "Facing History and Ourselves." For me, the ultimate *moral* threat in these pictures erupts from the faces in the *white* mobs, including the faces of young children, assembled here in a spirit of festivity and glee. The sender of one post card writes to his friend, "Well, John, this is a token of a great day we had in Dallas [Texas] March 3. A negro was hung for an assault on a 3-year-old girl. I saw this on my noon hour. I was very much in the bunch. You can see the negro hanging on a telephone pole."

Moral anger must fasten, in the first place, on the suffering of victims. It belongs, secondly, to the susceptibility of human being to collaboration in such crime. Transmuted into anxiety, the latter opens one's consciousness to the realization that I, who am angry at how humans treat humans, am also a human being. That third dimension was both a moral reason to visit this "little" collection and a psychological reason not to visit it: Do I really have the inner strength to face the possibility that I am a potential recruit to such a mob? Am I ready to specify the old Christian concept of original sin to my own vulnerability to joining the crowd that commits such an awful crime, or to standing by while others commit it? Reinhold Niebuhr used to say that the only *empirically* obvious Christian doctrine was the one expressed in Romans 3:23: "All have sinned and fall short of the glory of God." As a general surmise, it may be bland and nonthreatening. As concretized in an Auschwitz, a Vlakplaas, a New York draft riot, or five thousand Americans lynched in every American state but six,[115] it induces personal fear and trembling.

Evildoers are a warning. Robert Lifton, MD, ended his account of his extensive interviews of the Auschwitz doctors: "[M]ost of what Nazi doctors did would be within the potential capability—at least under certain conditions—of most doctors and of most people."[116] To resist this thought may be the essence of moral-intellectual cowardice in face of the atrocities that litter human history. Not to resist may be the essence of courage vis-à-vis the dumb artifacts of a museum. Rightly seen and absorbed, they speak volumes and they speak personally.

They can also speak to an oncoming future. An arresting example is the sophisticated Studio Museum in Harlem, near this author's Manhattan home. A compact, two-story place on busy 125th Street, it warns visitors of "the impending gentrification of Harlem" as its property values escalate. "This four square miles," says one display, "provides black people with the roots of our existence in America outside of the south. The stakes are too high for us just to walk away."[117] One message of this museum: "Citizen, remember District Six!"

Can the Past Be Repaired?

In a phenomenon that historians may eventually find important to understand, the 1990s did see an outbreak of new interest, across the United States, in facing the country's negative history, especially in regard to slavery and its legacies. When in 1992 a slave graveyard was uncovered on the construction site of a new Federal building in lower Manhattan, almost no public leader objected to designating a portion of that space as sacred. As many as twenty thousand skeletal remains, many of them of children dead from disease, lie in this ground. In the fall of 2003 a six-city, five-day pilgrimage from Washington to New York paid tribute to the slaves who once worked in these cities and escorted 419 caskets bearing remains from Washington to the New York burial ground. The fenced green grass of the one-acre site, shadowed by skyscrapers, is not yet the site of a permanent monument, but it has already been declared a national landmark. Howard Dodson, Chief of New York's Schomberg Center and sponsor of the these events, believes that the best symbol of the burial ground will be a African Adinkra symbol, Sankofa, which means "return to the past to make the future."[118]

In response to the burial ground discovery, scholars began to probe anew the history of slavery in New York City, and political leaders from Ghana came to visit and to "beg forgiveness for African involvement in the slave trade."[119] In the same years graduate students at Yale University uncovered its early financial gains from donors who were slave traders or owners,[120] the *Hartford Courant* confessed that it had once advertised for the return of escaped slaves to slaveowners, and the Aetna Life Insurance Company of the same city admitted that well into the nineteenth century it had offered insurance against losses sustained by owners from escaped slaves.[121] As Brent Staples observed, the year 2000, in Germany, Switzerland, and the United States, "has been a big year for institutional contrition."[122] The year 2002 was potentially even bigger. In that year

> when nine lawsuits seeking reparations were filed in New York,
> New Jersey and other states against FleetBoston, Aetna, J. P. Morgan
> Chase, and other companies, lawyers involved in the cases said
> Brown, Yale, and Harvard Law School were likely defendents in fu-
> ture suits. So far, rulings have gone against the plantiffs.

But Ruth J. Simmons, newly elected president of Brown and first African American president of an Ivy League university, has directed Brown to undertake "an exploration of reparations for slavery and specifically whether Brown should pay reparations or otherwise make amends for its past." That past includes the office building in which she works, constructed by laborers who included slaves.[123]

In the late 1990s, a notable upshot of all these acts of long-delayed, public institutional contrition was the growing awareness of Americans north, south, east, and west that slavery in the history of the United States began, continued, and survived in many forms on a *national* scale. No commercial center had more to do with importing, owning, selling slaves than the country's preeminent metropolis, New York City. "New York City was a capital of human bondage, with more slaves than any other city with the possible exception of Charleston, S.C.," said Staples, writing in the wake of an op-ed article by Columbia historian Eric Foner. Like all historians who know more embarrassing facts about the past than most members of a public have ever wanted to know, Foner took advantage of the new tide of interest in slavery to inform readers of the

Times that it is quite a historical error to associate slavery with the sins of the southern planter aristocracy and not with the sins of the northern commercial aristocracy:

> Nowhere did the connection go deeper than in New York City. How many New Yorkers today know that when the South seceded, Mayor Fernando Wood proposed that New York declare itself a free city, so as to be able to continue to profit from slavery, as it had from its beginning?
>
> Slaves built New York—and the rest of the country—from their earliest arrival here at the beginning of the 1600s. In 1750, slaves represented more than 10 percent of the city's population. . . . Accounts of the city's rise to commercial prominence in the 19th century rightly point to the Erie Canal's role in opening access to produce from the West, but they don't talk about the equal importance to the city's prosperity of its control over the South's cotton trade.
>
> Elsewhere in the North, too, textile factories relied on slave-grown cotton, shipping interests carried cotton to England, and banks and merchants financed cotton production.
>
> On the eve of the Civil War, the economic value of slaves in the United States was $3 billion in 1860 currency, more than the combined value of all the factories, railroads, and banks in the country.

Will these truths come to occupy a prominent place in the teaching of history in New York public schools? In a permanent city museum? Foner hoped so. Then he ended with a word to the nation as a whole. In his Second Inaugural Address, Lincoln "was asking Americans to consider the obligations created by slavery. The first of those obligations is to acknowledge the full truth."[124] If the second is honest history teaching, and the third a museum, is there yet another? Foner did not say. But an answer to the potential fourth question was already coming in renewed public debate in the 1990s: "Yes, reparations."

The Reparations Debate

In January 1989, not long after Congressional appropriation of symbolic reparations to interned Japanese Americans of World War Two, Congressman John Conyers, Jr., Democrat of Michigan, introduced a bill, H.R. 40, "The Commission to Study Reparations Proposals for African American Act." As of 2003, he had introduced this bill to his Judiciary Committee fifteen times. It has never emerged from the committee for debate on the House floor.

Conyers says that he chose the number "40" as a symbol of "forty acres and a mule" which the United States initially promised freed slaves.[125] "This unfulfilled promise," he writes, "and the serious devastation that slavery had on African-American lives has never been officially [acknowledged] by the

United States Government."[126] His proposed bill would confess the "fundamental injustice and inhumanity of slavery," would establish a commission to
study its subsequent effects on freed slaves and their descendants, and would
recommend to Congress "appropriate remedies to redress the harm inflicted
on living African Americans."

These measures would surely feed the impetus for the establishment of
the new national museum of African Americans and would also set the stage
for a slow renewal of a reparations debate which, since 1865, has never completely lapsed among African Americans but which has been mostly smothered
among white leaders and citizens. Conyers's 1988 submission was a precursor
of the remarkable upsurge of "political apologies" in the world of the 1990s.[127]
President Bill Clinton traveled to Africa in 1996 and in a Uganda airport apologized for the weak response of the world community to the Rwanda genocide
of 1994. Similar regret, amounting to shame, came simultaneously from
United Nations General Secretary Kofi Annan. Clinton then visited Guatemala
and expressed regret for the role of the CIA. in overturning a democratically
elected government there in 1954 and in U.S. training of death squads who
would murder two hundred thousand native Indian peoples of Guatemala over
the next several decades. In a domestic apology, Clinton invited to the White
House a remnant of survivors of the long-secret 1937 experiments conducted
by public health scientists in Tuskegee, Alabama, on the effects of treatment
versus nontreatment for syphilis. All the subjects of that experiment had been
African American men. In the face of tragic, notorious wrongs, subsequent
apology by perpetrators or their representatives can be a small step toward
Tikkun olam, Hebrew for "healing the world." From 1865 on, for the healing
due African Americans, the United States took step after episodic step toward
some just healing and some healing justice to freed slaves and their descendants. In the great hiatus of 1876–1955, however, varieties of racist law and
custom overwhelmed the limited justice for freed slaves installed by Reconstruction law. From the first days after the Civil War, legally "free" African
Americans have pressed the claim privately and publicly: "You owe us, and you
have not paid." You, American society, owe more to the work of slaves over two
and a half centuries than your history books, your laws, or your institutions
have ever admitted or compensated for. Well that Abraham Lincoln, a month
before his assassination, should view "all the wealth piled by the bondsman's
two hundred and fifty years of unrequited toil" as "paid" back in the blood of
war and the loss of much of that white-accumulated wealth. But is that all the
"requiting" due? What about the debt, as real to us as invisible to most whites,
which accounts for some of the wealth of modern American society? Would
this society be as rich as it is now without the contribution of all that 250 years
of unpaid-for, "unrequited toil"?

Among those who have now brought the question again to the public fore,
none was more eloquent than Randall Robinson, a leader of the successful

1980s campaign for U.S. divestment from South Africa. He begins his book, *The Debt*, with a description of his visit to the rotunda of the United States Capitol in Washington, D.C. Very few white Americans, including this author in early family visits to Washington as a child, have ever viewed this great, iconic building through Robinson's eyes:

> To erect the building that would house the art that symbolized American democracy, the United States government sent out a request for a hundred slaves. The first stage of the Capitol's construction would run from 1793 to 1802. In exchange for the slaves' labor the government agreed to pay their *owners* five dollars per month per slave.
>
> I thought, then, what a fitting metaphor the Capitol Rotunda was for America's racial sorrows. In the magnificence of its boast, in the tragedy of its truth, in the effrontery of its deceit.
>
> This was the house of Liberty, and it had been built by slaves. Their backs had ached under its massive stones. Their lungs had clogged with its mortar dust. Their bodies had wilted under its heavy load-bearing timbers. They had been paid only in the coin of pain. Slavery lay across American history like a monstrous cleaving sword, but the Capitol of the United States steadfastly refused to divulge its complicity, or even slavery's very occurrence. It gave the full lie to its own gold-spun half-truth. It shrank from the simplest honesty. It mocked the shining eyes of the innocent. It kept from us all—black, brown, white—the chance to begin again as co-owners of a national democratic idea. It blinded us all to our past and, with the same stroke, to any common future.[128]

Any American who reads Robinson is likely to see the U.S. Capitol through new historical spectacles. One direct result of this powerful prose, published in 2000, was a small event on the steps of the same building in the early summer of 2001. Three months later that soaring white dome was to become one of the likely targets of 9/11.[129] Taking a leaf from the Richmond organization Hope in the Cities and its "Walk Through History,"[130] some two hundred participants in a conference at Howard University engaged in a "scrubbing" of the Capitol steps—a symbolic gesture toward removing the stains of slavery that Randall Robinson intuited in the very stones. In company with pantomimes by the Ayinde Dance Troupe of Richmond, we scrubbed and scrubbed, well aware that something more would have to happen if ours was to be something other than an idle gesture. Among other international participants in the event was Joe Devaney, retired mayor of Liverpool, the principal English port in the transatlantic slave trade. He was joined by the ambassador of Benin, a west African country that held down the third angle of the trade. Liverpool already has a museum displaying its profits from the commerce, which helped fund the British Empire. Devaney said that he was giving his scrub brush to Prime Minister Blair.

Apologies unaccompanied by remedial action can be received as hollow. In no small sense the coming of a new, humbled consciousness about this architectural monument to American history is itself something of a remedy. Robinson's view of the Capitol makes it, in minds that do not forget his pain-filled pages, a memorial as well as a monument. But, important as books, museums, and memorials may be as forms of patriotic repentance, the history of slavery in America calls for something more than a sad new sobriety of citizen consciousness. Anonymous slaves helped the "rise" of the American Republic—as that early edition of Todd-Curti termed it. Can—should—the Republic also rise to the persistent demand of living African Americans for new public acknowledgment of this past and new concrete remedies for enduring impacts of slavery on some of the living?

The committee imprisonment of Congressman Conyers's bill for fifteen years testifies vividly to the stubborn "no" which comes from the majority of American national legislators. Some would observe pessimistically that a public majority never repents, and a Congress that represents the majority will never repent, either. But the recent success of the reparations movement for tiny Rosewood and its persistence now in the courts of Oklahoma are the flickers of a national debate that will not go away. Indeed, the debate is now so newly vigorous among a growing cluster of African American leaders that the country should count on hearing the rumble of reparation-talk for many years into this new century. At the end of his book, Robinson sees this debate, especially as it is surfacing among African Americans themselves, as a great public gain:

> The catharsis occasioned by a full-scale reparations debate . . . could launch us with critical mass numbers into a surge of black-self discovery. . . . We could disinter a buried history, connect it to another, more recent and mistold, and give it as a healing to the whole of our people, to the whole of America.[131]

Immediate resistance to the very idea of reparations has long evoked spontaneous protest from many Americans: "Hey! We've been doing something to rectify slavery down through the years. A war that cost six hundred thousand lives, three constitutional amendments, the legislative success of the civil rights movement, affirmative action, and the advances of blacks into all sorts of occupations. Look at the growing black middle class in 2003, and say then that African Americans need reparations!" This retort closes the door on the debate that Robinson has in mind. At stake are conflicts of value and ways of thinking which have divided Americans for centuries and which are subject to no such simple dismissive rhetoric. A House Judiciary Committee may treat the Conyers bill with either fear or skepticism or both, but the reparations debate now underway will find increasing public voice whether or not Congress is one of those voices. That there *is* something to debate remains as a first step toward the new democratic dialogue that Robinson is calling for.

In his 1984 book *After Virtue*, Alasdair MacIntyre quotes fellow philosopher John Anderson of Australia as urging that we "not ask of a social institution: 'What end or purpose does it serve?' but rather, 'Of what conflicts is it the scene?' "[132] American society is the scene of many political-philosophical conflicts. The most famous is that between "liberty" and "equality." No less famous is "individual" and "society." More subtle is a conflict of preferences for "past" and "future." Pairs and triplets of such conflicts abound in the subsurface of much political contention in this country, and books on political philosophy explore them at length. Without doubt many of us in this early twenty-first-century America have slight patience for conversation that circles *ad infinitum* around these abstractions. But we mis-hear the rising tide of passion among a growing number of African American leaders for *public debate* over reparations if we dismiss it as merely abstract. In its new body of literature, its academic support, its organizational clout, and its combination of legislative and judicial initiatives, the reparations movement is clearly not about to disappear. Randall Robinson foresees a fundamental advance of the movement if and when advocates and opponents enter into serious talk about the issue. The advocates will count it a preliminary gain if they can convince a substantial minority of us that there really is something to talk about here, out loud, at length, until the majority of us hears what African Americans have been trying to say in company with William Faulkner: "The past is not dead. In fact, it's not even past."

If we acknowledge that the reparations debate, episodically begun in 1865 and subject to waxing and waning ever since, is beginning anew in this century, we must further acknowledge that it has to be a debate with no forgone conclusion. In this book I celebrate those recent incidents in American life when citizens have engaged in authentic mourning of the negative sides of our national history. As a debate taking on new vigor, the reparations movement can be so celebrated. It will not be received as cause for celebration among those who greet the idea with anger, impatience, or prompt dismissiveness.

Real dismissiveness consists of refusals to stop and listen. Real democratic dialogue requires listening on all sides. Robinson and other leaders of the movement are well aware that this debate has to take place among African Americans themselves as well as between them, other Americans, and people of other nations. Easily forgotten in the emerging controversy is that the reparations idea is flexible. It never was reducible to "forty acres and a mule." It does not come down to a money payment to every living descendant of slaves. Its philosophical kin is the question, "What is justice?" a debate old as Plato and never worth ending.

Arguments on both sides ought to be identified and taken seriously. For the sake of clarifying both sides and for help in distinguishing basic from superficial disagreements between the two, I end this chapter with a sketch of issues in the debate over which citizens will have to argue, perhaps long into the night, before mutual understanding yields a vision of reparations-justice that the majority of African Americans and other Americans can accept.

Issues and Arguments in the Debate

I. CAN TRAGEDY, BY DEFINITION, BE RECTIFIED? Money awards for tragic damages are no stranger to American courts. Professional malpractice, accidents leading to injury or deaths, and charges of mental suffering flood our courts, so much that some legislators are trying to place "reasonable" caps on the size of these awards. Behind their concern may lie a wisdom which optimistic American culture often hides from public conversation: Death is the tragedy for which there is no adequate remedy. If ten to fifteen million Africans died on the Middle Passage, we should rightly mourn them, but there are no right material compensations for this massive tragedy.

True enough, most proponents are likely to reply, but there is *some* repair of this tragedy when America's history books tell this story with increasing candor and detail. For clearing the ground of false comparisons with other mass deaths in world history, our books can at least point out, relentlessly, that Africans who did make it alive to American shores were the only major group of future Americans who were being brought here utterly against their wills. They were virtually the only group whose living conditions here cut them off from their given names, native languages, cultures, and family connections. Getting this history straight does not compensate for a tragedy, but it does rectify one condition that makes it even worse: amnesia.

2. WHO IS RESPONSIBLE FOR FEASIBLE RECTIFICATION IN THE PRESENT? Reparations advocates insist that the object of their project is not the dead of the past but the living of the present. At stake here, as the debate deepens, are issues of intergenerational responsibility. Again, legal analogies are not far-fetched: Before an estate is released to heirs, debts of the testator have to be paid. Ought not a new management of an established institution be liable for correcting the correctable errors of predecessors? Institutions link generations while leaving new work for the next one. The very amending of the U.S. Constitution suggests this linkage and this responsibility. The argument, "I am not guilty for the crimes of the Nazis," heard often from young postwar Germans, stirred an answer from some of their peers: "No, guilt belongs to the perpetrators, but responsibility for repair of the enduring damage belongs to us all, insofar as repair is possible." The same distinctions underlay the reparations recommendation of the South Africa TRC. When, in the spring of 2003, that

government finally awarded some $3900 to each of twenty-two thousand persons given hearing by the TRC, the money conveyed both economic and symbolic value. It was a something better than a nothing.

Opponents, at this point, are likely to draw a philosophical line: "In law there are statutes of limitation. Otherwise we would be infinitely liable for all the crimes of our ancestors. We have long since stopped burning witches, heretics, and homosexuals. Our only responsibility is being sure we don't tolerate that again." "Well," say the advocates in reply, "we want repair of the damage that a past is still inflicting on a present. If your father and grandfather perished in that Tulsa massacre, if your property-owning uncle had his farm stolen from him after Reconstruction, or if your aunt was raped by a white man who never went to jail, your family in year 2000 suffers impacts. How far back should a statute of limitations go? It's debatable, but remember that in most American law there is no such statute for murder. The ghosts of the murdered haunt many living African Americans. Be careful about insulting them by minimizing the tangible effects of murder on the living."

Especially pertinent on this level of the debate is the temptation of Americans black and white to celebrate economic progress of some while turning blind eyes to the economic entrapment of others in this society. Roger Wilkins, who began his education in a one-room segregated school in Mississippi in the 1930s, is now a full professor of history at George Mason University in Virginia.

> I have had the great fortune to see and participate in an astonishing American effort to adjust life as it is lived to the ideals proclaimed by the founders. . . . But what I have seen surely doesn't mean that I am free to accept a separate peace and turn my back on the most vulnerable people in the country. This includes, most notably, the poorest blacks and the poorest Native Americans and Latinos, who, because of their beaten condition, often seem unattractive and frightening to most Americans, even me sometimes. But instead of recoiling from them in rage and fear, we should allow our intense reaction to their near (or in some cases total) defeat to motivate us to change our culture so that the cascade of destruction from generation to generation may be slowed and finally halted.[133]

3. DO ANCIENT, BROKEN PROMISES OF A GOVERNMENT DESERVE TO BE HONORED STILL? The question will be taken up again in the next chapter in connection with the only other crime in American history which is truly comparable to that of slavery—the one against Native Americans. Objection to reparations for African Americans comes frequently from citizens whose forebears came to the United States well after the Civil War. In order to slough off a feeling of responsibility for the legacies of slavery, Polish immigrants of the

1880s might suppose that the history of American slavery is not their history. The question comes down to social-political philosophy. Can one become a citizen of any country without inheriting the burdens as well as the benefits of its past? How can immigrants swear to support the U.S. Constitution and take pride in the Declaration of Independence without implicating themselves in all our national past? Further, given the willingness of white European immigrants to benefit from the preferences handed whites over blacks in American legal and social history, how can Euro-Americans claim that they have not benefitted from the legacies of slavery in this society? The Irish workers who rioted in New York City in 1863—only to be controlled by the quick arrival of newly victorious troops from the Battle of Gettysburg—were afraid that the emancipation of slaves would produce competition for their industrial jobs. As history turned out, they had little to worry about: Discrimination in employment would persist everywhere in the country. An Irish immigrant coming to late nineteenth-century America soon heard the message: "You are on the low end of our social scale, but you are not so low as the former slaves."

Not alone among institutions but uniquely, governments represent intergenerational continuity. That was Anitra Rasmussen's message to her Oregon legislative colleagues. Some redresses belong peculiarly to governments whose predecessors, as in Florida, Oklahoma, and Oregon, implemented the past injustices. Only governments make and change laws. They are responsible for remedying the continuing damages of old unjust law. The same argument applies to broken promises of government. By permanent disregard of its promises, government acquires a reputation for fraud which eats away public trust. Then the reputation of law itself suffers.

4. ARE THE IMPACTS OF REMOTE EVILS CALCULABLE IN THE PRESENT? Undoubtedly some of the impacts are incalculable. No one will ever measure precisely the most serious of all the impacts of anti-black racism in American society: the inbred, debilitating suspicion of some black people that they really *are* inferior to whites. Social scientists offered empirical evidence of this self-deprecation in arguments before the 1954 Supreme Court which reversed the 1896 law declaring the legality of segregated public schools. As the resistance of Roger Wilkins's mother to "clanking the chain" illustrates, black educators, religious leaders, and parents have long sought to protect their charges against this virus of internal consent to inferiority. The achievements of Richard Allen, Frederick Douglass, Sojourner Truth, Harriet Tubman, Mary McLeod Bethune, Martin Luther King, Jr., Malcolm X, Andrew Young, John Lewis, James Hal Cone, Ruth J. Simmons, and James A. Forbes ought to be lifted up as proof of how much self-respect black Americans can inherit from history.

But there are ways to calculate. One is economic. Robinson made the following observations about conditions in the late 1990s:

College-educated whites enjoy an average annual income of $38,700, a net worth of $74,922, and net financial assets of $19,823. College-educated blacks, however, earn only $29,440 annually with a net worth of $17,437 and $175 in net financial assets.

American capitalism, which starts each child where its parents left off is not a fair system. This is particularly true for African Americans, whose general economic starting points have been rearmost in our society because of slavery and its long racialist aftermath.[134]

Thus, middle-class white Americans who have inherited more than $175 from their parents already have a financial asset exceeding that of most black neighbors. Calculations like this can be multiplied, but underlying them all will be the claim that from slavery right though much of the twentieth century, a black skin *systematically* kept an American "rearmost" in economic terms throughout his or her lifetime. One can sidestep the salience of this fact by reverting to the individualism of American culture that says, "You get what you work for." But it is a large detour around formidable economic truth to settle for this cliché. Within a twentieth century context alone, Robinson calculates, the cumulative differential between white and black wages from 1929 though 1969 was $1.6 trillion. That sum, were it to have been invested in 1929 in an Educational Trust for young blacks (one of Robinson's favorite concrete suggestions for a national reparation), it would have grown by a multiple of trillions.[135] Equal work has not always led to equal economic gain in this country. One has to be blind to economic reality not to know that.

5. IF THE DEBT IS SO LARGE, CAN SOCIETY AFFORD TO PAY IT? We know the price of slaves in nineteenth-century America, and economists can estimate the value of their labor above their minimal living expense to their owners. Indeed, some of the newly freed slaves knew how to make just such an estimate.[136] Before the debate dissipates in sands of true incalculability (what is a human life really worth?), modern analyzers at least have to conclude that the exercise yields an important conclusion: The profit from slaves was very large and not utterly beyond measurement, for example, in the recorded profits from cotton exports in the nineteenth century, the largest among all American exports in the period. The very fact that sums of money involved here are intimidating calls for recognition that, excluding absolute justice, one might have to settle for some form of relative justice in view of ascertainable economic fact.

No government has practiced that justice more consistently in the past century than Germany. In paying reparations to the State of Israel and individual Jewish survivors of the Holocaust, representatives of the Federal Republic often commented, "No matter how large the sum, no amount of money will ever suffice to compensate for National Socialist [Nazi] persecution."[137] Whatever the uselessness of money for compensating true tragedy, it can still carry heavy symbolic meanings; and, when offered with integrity, meanings matter. "We are meaning-hungry creatures."[138] Without meaning, money can be insulting. Without money, meaning can be cheapened.

6. WHAT MIGHT CONSTITUTE CONCRETE, FEASIBLE, ACCEPTABLE REPARA-
TION? The answer to this question has to be a product of a political process whose participants are honestly seeking an answer. Any sample of the growing literature on reparations shows that there are a variety of measures which in combination might compose a compromise that neither denies justice nor pretends to be a perfect version of it. In 1997, Tony Hall, white Congressman from Ohio, joined John Conyers in asking Congress to issue an official one-sentence apology for slavery. Construction, at last, of that national museum on the Washington Mall would go far, one supposes, toward concretizing national gratitude for four centuries of contribution by African Americans to the "rise" of the United States. Robinson's proposals center on a new national effort to ensure that all young African Americans have needed scholarship help for education. And Lillian Kamura, former president of the Japanese American Citizens League, proposes a well-financed public education effort that will lift the history of African Americans into public awareness comparable to the gains in public awareness of the harms done Japanese Americans in the 1940s.[139]

The reparations in that very case in 1990, however, underscore a distinction which has recently been made by Dr. Pablo de Greiff, a native of Columbia now serving as Research Director of the International Center for Transitional Justice. It is one definition of "justice," he says, that specific compensations should be granted individuals "in proportion to harm"—the classical legal concept of *restitutio in integrum*. It is another to speak of groups who, as a whole, have suffered various injustices originating in a near or a remote past. Should the idea of just reparation be focused, by definition, on the first sort of harms and, for the second, should proponents depend on a wider concept of justice as compensatory and distributional? Such a widening might introduce more sobriety and less dismissive rhetoric into the current debate. When discussion of reparations comes down to such concrete proposals, proponents will be found to advocate a range of specifics, some of which are symbolic and cultural, says de Greiff—public recognition of publicly forgotten history, the renewal of civic trust, and social solidarity that affirms the obligations of the rich and the poor in new forms of finance of education and job training.[140]

According to Conyers's annual Congressional Forum publication, American whites oppose the idea of reparations by two to one. Even the one, however, should encourage advocates. Reduced to specifics like the above, general public support might grow, especially if money reparations focused on the one-third of black citizens who are poor along with the 11 percent of whites who are so.

"At last they've told our story": If the great majority of America's black citizens could echo that Oregonian from April 22, 1999, they might agree that *Tikkun olam* is actually happening between blacks and whites in this country. To reach this conclusion, the debate must abandon talk about "mere symbolism." If symbols were so "mere" in political life, controversy over the raising of a Confederate flag over government buildings in South Carolina, Georgia, and Mississippi would not still be generating controversy in those states. Symbols are "mere" when they are hollow alternatives to, rather than accompaniments of, tangible embodiments of justice. Japanese Americans in 1990 usually acknowledged that government payment of $20,000 to each camp survivor alive in that year was largely symbolic—far from the value of years stolen from them in the camps and property stolen from them in West Coast locales. But $20,000 was evidence of real official regret, real apology, real political repentance on the part of legislators who, proud of much in their predecessors' achievements, were not proud of it all.

7. WHAT ABOUT CLAIMS BY OTHER GROUPS OF AMERICANS? The question comes with great force from one other group in particular: Native Americans, whose case I ponder in the next chapter. African and Native Americans have similar and different arguments to press upon the governments and institutions formed by Euro-Americans. Each has reason to follow the reparations debate as it unfolds in relation to the interests of the other. But they are not the only abused people and their descendants in American history. One thinks of the white residents of Appalachia who have suffered long neglect at the hands of corporations and governments; the discriminations in wages and living conditions of migrant workers; and the assorted injustices to Asian immigrants who before 1965 worked for industrial America while facing formidable legal barriers to their desire to become U.S. citizens. In the rich American society of the twenty-first century, a cry for new dignity for the American poor would draw encouragement from the argument for African American reparations. Almost every proponent among middle-class and wealthy blacks stresses the need of the argument to focus on the poorest African Americans. The latter have many other companions in the American underclass.

In addition to these candidates, there is another whose claim has long been summarily dismissed by a federal government little inclined to remedy the damages done to a rebellious people in America's one internal "just war," that of 1860–65. White southerners' claim to reparations for Sherman's property-destroying March to the Sea, for example, as well as for decades of rail tariff rates favoring northern industry, will always be afflicted with ambiguity on all sides. There was justice in the destruction of wealth "piled high under the lash" of slavery, though the war losses of Southern whites were deepest among poor white farmers who never had owned slaves. For the injustice of post-1876 racist law, white-dominated state governments all over the country bore shared responsibility. That is one reason why self-proclaimed innocence in the memory of many white Northerners to this day can raise surges of resentment among many Southerners. It is not only Sherman's invention of "total war" that rankles contemporary Southern memory, but forgetfulness of the passive and active Northern collaboration with slavery before the war and with racist institutions afterward.

To quell some of that resentment, honesty on the part of white Northern politicians might be enough "reparation" for white Southern memory. The same might be said about memories of injustice among other ethnic contributors to our national history. What Chinese and Irish laborers suffered in building industrial America should never be minimized. That said, opponents of reparations for African Americans need to hear this persistent, historically realistic word from the advocates: *history, law, politics, economics, ideology, and social custom have imposed discriminations on African Americans as a whole which cannot be equated with other systematic discriminations.* In the wake of a great urban riot of 1992, *Los Angeles Times* editor Jack Miles put it precisely and painfully when he observed that white Los Angeles residents seem always to prefer hiring a newly arrived Mexican to any member of a "fifteenth generation" African American family. "This is what slavery has done to us as a people. . . . My deepest, least argued or arguable hunch is that everything in America begins with that old and unpaid debt."[141] With the exception of Native Americans, no one who looks at American history since 1619 ought to deny that black slaves and their descendants have suffered the unique fate of being always relegated as a group to the bottom of America's social hierarchies.

8. DOES THE IDEA TEMPT AFRICAN AMERICANS TO IDENTIFY THEMSELVES CHIEFLY AS VICTIMS? Some are saying so. The history of slavery is vast, complex, and depressing to remember. Slight regard for the humanity of slaves was no monopoly of white Europeans. African tribal leaders were essential to the trade. Even today some Africans recollect enslavement as somehow the fault of those who "let" themselves be captured.[142] More to the point: Preoccupation with injustices done your ancestors can blur your focus on the new opportunity open to you in twenty-first-century America. Given the examples of Japanese American and Holocaust-surviving Jewish parents who often fell silent before their children about the awful injustice in their past, is it really better to liberate new generations of African American youth from much dwelling on the past?

Proponents have two strong replies to this worry: There are heroic stories as well as victim stories to be told of the four centuries of African presence in American society, and a recent generation of scholars has made this very clear. The very survival of the black family, black resistance to discrimination, black contributions to American culture, and black affirmation—in spite of all—of the American democratic dream are all species of the heroic. But secondly, say advocates, a vigorous reparations debate can call African Americans to new dignity in the public sphere as they claim payment of the "old unpaid debt" as a matter of *justice and not charity.* Says Robinson: "Even the making of a well-reasoned case for restitution will do wonders for the spirit of African Americans."[143]

Might it do the same for the spirit of Americans all? That is a great, final issue.

9. WHAT BENEFIT, FROM REPARATIONS TO AFRICAN AMERICANS, TO US ALL?
Akin to Randall Robinson's visit to the Capitol was Roger Wilkins's visit to Jamestown, Virginia. The museum guide took note of the 1619 unloading of twenty black slaves on the river dock there and, turning to Wilkins and his family, was moved to exclaim, "Blacks were among the First Families of Virginia!"[144] Wilkins heard the remark with considerable ambivalence. Jamestown guides have not always mentioned that 1619 human cargo, nor until recently did guides in Mount Vernon or Monticello mention the fact that those plantations were sustained by slave labor. Very few contemporary Virginians who know the initials "FFV" include in their images of those "first families" a black face. In echo of John Hope Franklin, Wilkins notes that American slavery was virtually invented in the colony of Virginia. The tragic irony in the "FFV" tribute of that guide is that there are now few surviving names from millions of Virginia slaves to list alongside names like Spotswood, Carter, Ruffin, Berkeley, Washington, and Jefferson. Wilkins quotes from the autobiography of his Uncle Roy:

> We have been Americans for well over two hundred years, but for much of that time we were a family without a name and for most practical purposes without a country. Up to the time of the Civil War the branches of our family tree rustled with bills of sale, not birth certificates. We were sold by sex, age, and weight, not by name, and as a consequence of this loathsome traffic in human flesh, my ancestors from the third generation back are as lost as any missing tribe of Israel.[145]

Wilkins's book focuses on four famous Virginians (Washington, Jefferson, Madison, and Mason), on their troubled feelings about the institution of slavery, and on their ultimate unwillingness to convert their slave "property" into free citizens. Wilkins writes with profound appreciation of what "Founding Fathers" like these men did to fashion America's unique constitutional democracy. Their political beliefs about freedom were sources of the very passion for freedom that their own slaves yearned to enjoy. In an irony with hardly an equal in American history, those slave yearnings "were rooted in the social and political physics of freedom, set in motion by the founding generation to which Mason, Washington, Jefferson, and Madison, despite their slaveholdings, made massive contributions." Hence, he confesses, "I don't need this nation to be perfect for me to love it." But he knows that it would be far more lovable in the twenty-first century if Americans in general would acknowledge the imperfections of these heroes and would learn to appreciate African American anger at the baleful legacy of hypocritical idolatry of patriotic hero-worship. Wilkins thinks of four of his known ancestors and, toward these four famous Virginians, feels

> a rising rage that men so distinguished and so powerful could have been so timid about using that power in the cause of freedom and justice for America. I want to take those four lives [of my family]— as emblems of millions of others like them—and push them in the faces of those four founders and say, "Look at the pain you might have avoided and the potential you might have liberated had you had the capacity to care for human beings like these as deeply as you cared for yourselves and for people like you." But that's the rub, of course. They couldn't because they were morally crippled by their culture and politically shackled by the grating chain that snaked through the new republic and diminished every life it touched.[146]

To love the United States of America, as Wilkins does, and yet to be angry with its sins past and present, is his form of patriotism. It is a form worth imitation, especially if it embraces Wilkins's like acknowledgment that the America he loves is one that black people helped to build:

> For me to aspire to be something other than American would be to renounce all their contributions to this country, all their struggles for space in which to live their lives, all the things they built, all the wealth they created, all the love they passed down the generations that came down to me.[147]

African Americans, Honest Patriots

Author James McBride Dabbs of South Carolina liked to tell the story of the Confederate soldier who marched wearily at the end of a column belonging to the army of Stonewall Jackson. The general himself rode up to the man and, for encouragement, asked, "Think you'll make it, soldier?" The soldier replied: "Ah'll make it, general. Only ah hopes to God ah never loves another country."[148]

Over the centuries African Americans have had many reasons not to love the country that treated them and their ancestors so unjustly. It may take a long time before Americans appreciate the combination of "patience in tribulation"[149] with stubborn hope for liberation from oppression that so consistently marks the African American spirit. The reparations movement may yet succeed in evoking some tangible remedies for the legacies of slavery that continue to cascade through the nation. But after some such justice has been distributed, we all might find new reason to continue to love this country because its citizens are honest enough to know how unjustly some have treated others at many a turn in our history. And some of us, white European descendants in particular, might learn to marvel that the sons and daughters of slaves have hardly ever ceased to love the country that enslaved them. With that learning might come a new depth of chastened respect for anyone who not only loves a country in spite of its grievous misdeeds but loves it enough to remember the misdeeds and to work for their remedy.

That remembering and that work continues in the United States as these pages are written. Among the most serious attempts of other local American communities to address their traumatic pasts is Greensboro, North Carolina, where, on November 3, 1979, five labor union leaders were murdered in a standoff with the local Ku Klux Klan. Advised and helped by veteran leaders of the South African TRC, including Desmond Tutu and Alex Boraine, the seven-member Greensboro Truth and Community Reconciliation Project (GTCRP) came into official being on June 12, 2004, in a community ceremony attended by hundreds of citizens. Their task was to recover the facts of "The Greensboro Massacre" of 1979. It will be the first formal American version of the South African TRC.

The stories in this chapter demonstrate that parallels to the South African model are under development in this country. The Richmond, Rosewood, Tulsa, and Oregon precedents presage other stirrings of local Americans' collective commitments to discover painful truth about their pasts and to blend that truth into quests for new depths of civic reconciliation. We will hear more about Greensboro in 2004–2005. As this is written, two African American businessmen in Greensboro, owners of the vacated Woolworth building where four university students began the sit-in movement on February 1, 1960, have announced plans for turning the building into a museum. Business, foundation, and state legislative funding now ensures the success of the project. Its sponsors believe that it will annually attract 100,000 visitors to this stop on the South's new "civil rights trails." The North Carolina state government has recently published a fifty-two-page picture-rich pamphlet identifying 167 state sites of significance in local histories of resistance to slavery and post-1865 racial discrimination.[150]

A survivor of the Greensboro massacre, whose husband was among the five people murdered, voiced her hope for the future of this event when she said to a reporter, "I always hated going back to Greensboro, and I always felt people there hated me, and us. But if we can speak our hurt, our pain, and ask our questions and seek truth . . . then I feel there a real opportunity for reconciliation."[151]

No witness before the South African TRC would have put it more precisely. She is one of a host of African Americans who have come in recent years to agree with James Baldwin's eloquent urging that they find their past and let it speak to them and all Americans:

> Go back to where you started, or as far back as you can, examine all of it, travel your road again and tell the truth about it. Sing or shout or testify or keep it to yourself; but know *whence you came*.[152]

1. Sachsenhausen, "Work Makes Free."

2. Berlin-Zehlendorf, 1960, "To the Victims."

3. "Locations of Terror which we must never forget." Berlin, Kerfurstendamm.

4. "The Room," Great Hamburgerstrasse, Koppenplatz, Central Berlin.
Memorial to the unannounced invasion of a Jewish home by the Gestapo.

5. The Schöneberg Lamppost signs:
"All Jews older than six must wear the
yellow star with the inscription 'Jew'."

6. The Schöneberg Lamppost
signs: "Aryan and non-Aryan
children are forbidden to play
any games with each other."

7. Ferdinand Reihlen-Boergers, age 8,
at the Spiegel-Wand in Steiglitz.

8. Gate inscription, Wannsee Conference Center, "In this house took place in January 1942 the notorious Wannsee Conference. In memory of our fellow Jewish human beings murdered by the National Socialist dictatorship."

9. Ground-level Mahnmal installed in 1988, fiftieth anniversary of Pogromnacht. "God's true name/the insulted Schem Ha Mphoras/which the Jews prior to the Christians/held unexpressable sacred/died in six million Jews under a crucifix." Next to the *Stadtkirche* in Wittenberg, where Luther often preached.

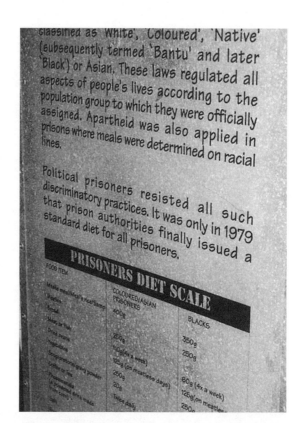

classified as 'White', 'Coloured', 'Native' (subsequently termed 'Bantu' and later 'Black') or Asian. These laws regulated all aspects of people's lives according to the population group to which they were officially assigned. Apartheid was also applied in prisons where meals were determined on racial lines.

Political prisoners resisted all such discriminatory practices. It was only in 1979 that prison authorities finally issued a standard diet for all prisoners.

PRISONERS DIET SCALE

FOOD ITEM	COLOURED/ASIAN PRISONERS	BLACKS
Mealie meal/Mealie rice/Samp	40'0g	350g
Bread		
Meat or fish	200g	250g
Dried beans	(4x a week)	
Vegetables	120g (on meatless days)	
Coffee/puzamandla/gravy powder	250g	80g (4x a week)
Coffee or tea	20g	125g (on meatless
(A powdered drink made from corn)	Twice daily	250g

10. The apartheid prison diet: "blacks need less food." (Robben Island)

11. Black maids sitting on the ground below "whites only" bench, while tending a white child. *Cape Town Holocaust Museum.*

We learn about the Holocaust so that we can become more human, more gentle, more caring, more compassionate, valuing every person as being of infinite worth so precious that we know such atrocities will never happen again and the world will be a more humane place.

Desmond Tutu
Archbishop Emeritus
August 1999

12. Wall inscription at exit of the Cape Town Holocaust Museum.

13. A history class at St. Cyprian's School, taught by Jennifer Wallace

14. "Washing slavery" from the U.S. Capitol steps,
Initiatives for Change Conference, July 2001.

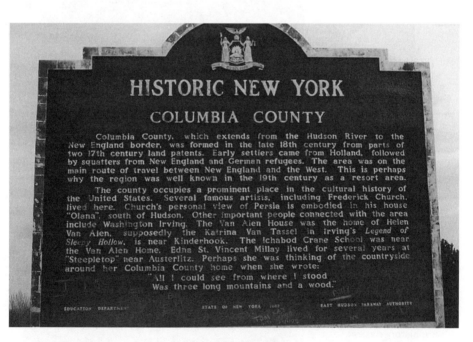

15. A sign alongside Indian-named Taconic (Taghkanic)
Parkway, which makes no mention of Mohicans.

16. Congressional gathering before the Edmund Pettis Bridge, Selma, Alabama, 2001. *Courtesy of the Faith and Politics Institute.*

17. Senator Sam Brownback (R-KS) in light jacket leads pilgrimage participants in prayer at the Civil Rights Memorial in Montgomery. To the left of Senator Brownback is Senator George Allen (R-VA). To the right are Senator Norm Coleman (R-MN), Senator Richard Shelby (R-AL), Senator Bill Frist (R-TN), Harrison Frist, Representative John Lewis (D-GA), Senator John Corzine (D-NJ), and Senator Mike DeWine (R-OH).

18. Stonewall Jackson and Arthur Ashe—neighbors on Monument Avenue, Richmond, Virginia.

19. Fire hose and archway statue, Kelly Ingram Park, Birmingham.

20. Statue of a dog attack, Kelly Ingram Park, Birmingham.

4

Unreflected Absences

Native Americans

All life was cheap in the late seventeenth century, but Indian life was cheaper.

—Helen C. Rountree[1]

If your king have sent me presents, I also am a king and this is my land. . . . Your father [James I] is to come to me, not I to him.

—Wahunsonacock, the Powhatan, to Captain John Smith, 1607[2]

I have listened to a great many talks from our Great Father. But they always began and ended in this—Get a little farther; you are too near me.

—Creek Chief Speckled Snake, 1829[3]

As this is written in early 2004, a commission of artists and museum professionals has just chosen a design for the New York City World Trade Center Memorial to the 2,982 persons killed in the terrorist attacks of 9/11. Central to the design will be two thirty-feet-deep reflecting pools at the site of the former two towers, hence the memorial name, "Reflecting Absence." Commented the chairman of the selection panel, Vartan Gregorian, "The voids left by the destruction [are] the primary symbols of our loss."[4]

If the territory of the modern United States were ever to reflect the absence of the original human settlers of the continent, our landscapes would have to be covered with a vast profusion of such memorials. African Americans, then called "colored people," are so much present in my earliest childhood memory that, along with most white southerners, I never imagined a society in which they were not visible members. Not so with the people we now call Native Americans. "Indians"[5] entered my life in Norfolk, Virginia, in books, Halloween costumes, Tom Mix movie serials, two or three grade-school assignments, and homemade bow-and-arrow–stick-gun neighborhood games of cowboys and Indians.[6] But as a child I never met Indians, nor did I have reason to recognize a place where they used to live. Like the majority of Americans, I felt their presence in my past chiefly as an absence, a people who once were but are not now. James Loewen begins his chapter on the matter with characteristic acerbity:

> Historically, American Indians have been the most lied-about subset of our population. That's why Michael Dorris said that, in learning about Native Americans, "One does not start from point zero, but from minus ten."[7]

In my case, one exception in this miseducation was a visit which my family made to Jamestown Island when I was about eight years old. Jamestown was only thirty miles up river from Norfolk. In grade school they taught us the story of how the Indian princess Pocahontas saved the life of Captain John Smith, leader of the first permanent English settlement in North America. Mythical that story may be, but it was the one image of 1607 which most Virginians absorbed. There was not much else to remember from a visit to Jamestown Island in the 1930s. A damaged brick church—not contemporaneous with the old settlement—an old well, a river shore, and a souvenir kiosk: That was about it. No one told me that on this shore in 1619 those first twenty Africans arrived, nor did I acquire there any concrete images of the Powhatan people who greeted those 104 English yeomen and gentlemen who disembarked there in 1607.[8]

Such ignorance is a major barrier to concreteness when east-coast-born, European-descended Americans like myself begin to study, think, and write about the original inhabitants of this continent. Throughout our lives we have had few actual human relationships with their descendants. In all the years since my childhood, nobody told me that, in fact, some three thousand assimilated residents of Tidewater Virginia identify themselves as Indian. Nor did anyone note that the river inlet on which we lived in the early 1940s was probably inhabited once by a tribe after which the Chesapeake Bay was named.[9] East Coast Americans, in particular, know that Indians once were, but we have few experiences to tell us that they still are.

It would be many years before I came to appreciate the reasons why people living west of the Mississippi were likely to have at least glimpses of Indians in their daily rounds and why the name "Cherokee" signified more than the name of a town in western North Carolina. I remember quite well a few instances in early grade school when we looked at pictures of the Seminoles in

Florida or made amateur models of a Navaho hogan. But Indians were more profoundly absent from that school than were the still-segregated descendants of those twenty Africans of 1619. Who among our teachers was brave enough to tell us the story of the "Trail of Tears," wherein thousands of eastern Indians were forced by a Federal government, under the command of President Andrew Jackson, to remove themselves westward in the 1830s to far-off Oklahoma and other trans-Mississippi places? What did we know of the forty-year devastation of the power, the places, the population, and the culture of the Powhatan Indians who once lived in and around Norfolk, Virginia?

In this chapter I undertake modest celebration of some changes afoot in the opportunities Americans now have for belated understanding of this history, not only from books but also in public places, public events, and public law. For most of my life I have been an educator, but in this matter I have to confess that, like the case of most European Americans, I am the one who needs the education.[10]

Basic, large, and growing assistance in filling this hiatus has been available for many years now in the work of historians, anthropologists, and the writings of Indian authors. Their published works fill many shelves of libraries and academic book stores. To sample these works is to know the stories which were omitted or mistold in one's own decades of education from primary to graduate school. Like even the best academic studies of long-neglected peoples, the formal public availability of this knowledge is one thing. Its absorption into the public mind is another. To be sure, the content of a "public mind" will always be imprecise. Public attention to the past fluctuates, attends to this and that event for a while, then moves on. The experience of Germans, South Africans, and African Americans already to the fore in this book, however, testifies to the injustice of a public that forgets the damages its predecessors inflicted on a great numbers of its past members, descendants of whom are still "around." American public memory has a lot of growing to undertake before it is rich in accurate, balanced, and just awareness of the "Indian experience" in America since 1492. As he writes, this author is participating in that growth. The primary spirit of this book is celebratory: how some of us, somewhere, recover facts and images of painful historical pasts for the sake of honoring those who suffered then and for committing our societies to "never again." But anyone who, at a late age, tries to fill the hiatus here confessed to will embark on an intellectual-emotional journey that will take one only a few miles into a forest of truths which extend further than one will ever live to explore. Loewen is right: "Our journey into the history of Indian peoples and their relations with European and African invaders cannot be a happy excursion." There are some happy facts to record about the contemporary state of relations between Euro-Americans and Native Americans, but four-hundred-year negative backgrounds haunt this hunt for positive change. The change due is far from complete. For most Americans like myself, we may have to begin Loewen's "journey" at a prekindergarten level in hope of advancing to third grade. That advance cures some illiteracy, but it portends a longer trek we hope our grandchildren may someday undertake.

Again I should emphasize that literature on this history is monumental in size and, empathetically read, it composes a memorial for which my grandchildren may someday be grateful. Like the flowering of Black History in the past fifty years, books about Native American-European "contact" in the past five hundred years have multiplied in numbers impossible for any scholar to master. So, even for an advance to grade-school level of awareness, most of us who try to write on the subject do well to undertake modest goals. Mine will be to imitate the movements among many citizens in Germany, South Africa, and the United States for discovering *local* acknowledgments of this negative history. Every contemporary American lives in places where once lived members of one or another of the 550 Indian nations who we know populated the current bounds of the United States. One large category of those nations was the Algonquian, who lived in woods and mountains spread from North Carolina to the Arctic Circle and west to the Rocky Mountains. The Powhatans were Algonquians, as were the Munsees who inhabited Manhattan Island in 1624. Anyone like myself who has lived many years in Virginia and in New York might suppose he has some obligation to nourish intellectual inquiry into a history that lies hidden in familiar names like "Appomattox" and "Manhattan."[11] New York City, observes Evan T. Pritchard, was "one of the first European towns to be developed in North America, and one of the first to forget its Native American roots." But then, there is the Algonquin Hotel at 59 West 44th Street, "which has not hosted many Native Americans elders since it opened its doors in 1902, but it has done one thing for the aboriginal people of the island: reminded the world of who lived in New York before first contact" with Europeans.[12] But then, too, there is Jamestown Island—not now remembered for its Indian name.

What windows on Native Americans, past and present, might be fashioned from patient inquiry into their presence in certain localities that have hosted one's own American life from birth to maturity? In my case, the east coast of America has to be the broad beginning. For these pages, I will narrow my attention to Virginia and New York, the geographical bookends of my autobiography.

The Jamestown Settlement Museum, 2003

To visit Jamestown Island, sixty years after one's first visit as a child, is to find encouragement in the development of the historical and political culture of one's home state. Since 1957, when the Jamestown Museum first opened, no eight-year-old Virginian visitor was likely to depart with only two or three images of those first English colonists and their Powhatan Indian neighbors. A private foundation, state government moneys, and a large staff of guides well educated in history and anthropology have now produced a museum that, expanded for the year 2007, will celebrate the four hundredth anniversary of that first permanent English colony.

The main museum building and outdoor reconstructions cover many acres. Along paths wandering down to the river shore is a model Powhatan Indian village with homes ("yehakins") and the artifacts of Stone Age daily survival. Guides demonstrate tools for the tanning of deer hides and invite you to try your hand at it. Further on is the stockade of the old James Fort with its English-style thatched-roof living quarters, cannon-punctuated stockade, and large church building. All 104 first white settlers were required, a guide will tell you, to attend church three times a day, token of life habits brought from England which would occasion a multitude of conflicts with local neighbors. Down at the docks are life-sized models of the three ships that carried them, in a voyage of four and half months, to Virginia. A guide tells you what they ate at sea. Children clamber over the decks and wiggle the rudder post. There is something in this museum to intrigue all ages.

Privately the guides, a few of them Indian, say that their employment as public educators has required study of a thick book of historical and anthropological materials. Many of them hold graduate degrees in the two fields, and in candid moments they will express both pride and reservations about their work: "We had to study a lot, and we are expected to be good marketers of the museum. We are told not to offend anybody." There is room in these displays, however, for combinations of visitor admiration, pain, and offense at the history of one's ancestors on all sides, Indian as well as English. New England visitors may not like the frequent insistence that "it all began here" in 1607 rather than 1620. Descendants of Nansemond Indians, who once occupied land that is now Norfolk, are likely to find that statement provincial. Evidences of the original cultural clashes abound on these walls and in the display cases.[13] For example, one is apt to wonder: Why did the English build that ten-foot stockade when no such wall enclosed the Powhatan village?

Other clashes peek out in the formal exhibitions. The film, texts, maps, documents, and anthropological data here strike a balance between idealism and cynicism about both the English and the Indians of early Virginia. A twenty-minute professionally produced documentary film makes clear that, without Indian help, starvation and disease would have killed all the colonists (instead of only half) in that first winter of 1607–1608. No wonder that Captain John Smith would write of the Powhatans in 1612, "victuall [food] is their chiefest riches."

The Powhatan himself, an early wall display makes clear, must have assessed his "riches" in terms of political reach. By military and diplomatic means, by 1607 he had brought some thirty Eastern tribes under his control. "His subjects were required to make tribute payments and to work his fields."

He compelled some neighbors to pay tribute with as much as 80 percent of their resources of food, clothing, and ornaments. He was a rich, powerful chief, in contrast to even the most aristocratic among the 104 new arrivals, who, by the standards of his people were grossly uncivilized. "To them," says the film narrator, "*we* were the savages."[14] By English definition a culture with no written language had to be "uncivilized," against which assumption was Indian humor at the English love for writing things down: What was wrong with their memories?

Had they known all the conditions which these English men were fleeing in their native country, one display suggests, the Indians might have be yet surer that the English were the savages. A panel here describes seventeenth-century England as a land of "startling contrasts: a world of poverty, disease, superstition, and ignorance which coincided with a golden age of cultural, scientific, economic, and political achievement"—Shakespeare and Francis Drake on one side, the squalid streets of London on the other. But England had just defeated the Spanish Armada, and its contest for control of the Americas was now well underway. It had cannon, seagoing ships, and entrepreneurial lust for wealth. With their firearms, metal tools, and written documents, the English would soon report to home that the Powhatan people were as "inferior and salvage" [sic] as the Irish.[15]

Of all the walls in the exhibitions, the one that displays most vividly the impacts of this "first permanent English settlement in North America" is a map which, with little red lights, contrasts the Virginia locations of the Powhatan Indians in 1607 with those of 1646. In the earlier year Powhatan's hegemony extended over all of eastern Virginia. Less than forty years later, by war, deception, treaty abandonment, purchase, or squatter-right, English "settlers," now better termed invaders, had pushed the Powhatans out of virtually all of the bay and river coasts of the area, portent of the day in the twentieth century, when the State of Virginia would honor treaties with survivors of eight tribes out of an original thirty and would grant small land reservations to only two. Jamestown was where "it all began," but this provincial, presumptuous "all" includes the inexorable retreat of eastern Indians before the oncoming tides of European arrivals. Like Columbus before them, they presumed that English sovereigns had the right to lay claim to this land. Had not Sir Walter Raleigh named it after his queen? From their English manor experience, did they not know better than these locals how to make full agricultural use of this land? Even if the locals did supply the colonists of 1607–1608 with life-saving food, how could their agricultural practice compare with that of Europeans? And when they demanded reciprocal gifts from the colonists, were they not making a bold claim of equality with the new arrivals? Add to this their pagan religion, and what reason did an Englishman have to consider Indians fully human? By 1624 Captain John Smith, initially a mediator between the clashing cultures, was quoting a contemporary theologian convinced that Indians were "greedy and perfidious devils," who rightly should be dominated or killed.[16] Accordingly, by 1622, Powhatan and his advisers had come to believe that the English would show no regard for local interests, so they launched a deadly attack on several new settler villages. In self-defense the Jamestown assembly responded in kind. The ensuing twenty years of war, plus new tides of immigrants, led to so complete a shift in power that "after 1646 all the surviving Powhatan groups were inundated by English settlers and left on separate islands of tribal territory." A treaty of that year banned Indians from entering their former homes south of the York River, and contradictory legislation adopted the same day made provision for the treaty's abrogation should "further order" require. It was the first of hundreds of treaties, breakable at their convenience, which English colonists would make with American Indians over the next three hundred years.[17]

With the shrinking of Powhatan homeland came rapid shrinkage of their numbers. Helen Rountree estimates that some 5,000 Powatans lived in the region in 1607, only 2,900 in 1669, and a mere 600 in 1699. When, by 1669, 30,000 English had arrived in Virginia, their eyes began to skip over the presence of those remaining 2,900 Indians in their midst:

> There was never any real chance of holding the English back after 1646, even had their government wanted to do so. There were simply too many of them, and they all were too determined to make their fortunes raising tobacco. They flooded Indian lands at a rate and on a scale that. as Edmund Morgan, put it, "transforms crime into politics." . . .
>
> By the end of the century the Powhatans were as oppressed as free Afro-Virginians. . . . No Englishman foresaw, however, that they would survive; in the decades following the 1646 treaty, it looked to everyone [of the English] as though the Powhatans were a vanishing people. That idea was a self-fulfilling prophecy as far as Anglo-Virginians were concerned. It led them to pay less attention to and make fewer records about the Indian groups that continued peacefully to survive in the late decades of the century. This near-disappearance from the English records has long given historians the erroneous impression that most of the Powhatan tribes "died out" by 1700. In reality, the second half of the seventeenth century was a time of culture change for a fringe [of the Indians] that continually grew, while the core people stubbornly hung onto their old ways as long as possible.[18]

Virginians of my generation need no other explanation of why we hardly ever consciously rubbed shoulders with human beings who might be called Indian. While three thousand citizens of the metropolitan Norfolk area now assert Indian identity, this is simply a new fact for most of us who look back to childhood in that city. The original Powhatans of eastern Virginia had long since been quickly subdued and pushed westward in the 1830s or into the two tiny reserves that are still protected by the Commonwealth of Virginia. The remaining broad landscapes host many monuments to the "First Families of Virginia" but hardly any to those who really were the first.[19] Now, at least, a museum at Jamestown opens a door on this history for all visitors willing to explore it.

Before the exit from the exhibition galleries, one passes a panel which salutes a segment of that early non-Indian population who did not arrive until twelve years after 1607. Some dozen photographs here are portraits of modern-day African Americans whose successes mark their status as a long way from that of their ancestors of 1619. The museum makers want to make clear that from then on, Africans had been among the original Virginians—as Roger Wilkins and his family would one day proudly assert. Not until 1705 would that Virginia House of Burgesses—also founded in 1619—systematically legalize the inferiority of these black immigrants. With a little imagination, a museum visitor will perceive that the combination of land for the taking from the Powhatans and black slaves for import laid the foundation of Virginia's early colonial economy. In 1705 the legislature solidified this system with another sort of pioneering: the invention of "black codes" after which other of the thirteen colonies would model similar legislation. As one looks at a tiny precis of this history on that pre-exit museum wall, one remembers that "no offense" rule which the guides here are supposed to obey:

> After 250 years of slavery, blacks in Virginia finally won their freedom in 1863. Even then, they faced a long struggle for political rights and economic equality. Today the descendants of those African slaves actively promote a better understanding of their history and culture.

The blandness of this inscription is striking, but the fact that the curators insist on mentioning Afro-Virginians before exhibition's end, is another invitation to a visitor to reconnoiter a history which he or she may have once learned but can now recall in contexts which museums can make newly vivid. No mention here of a war which, in 1863, still had to be won by Virginia's enemies before its slaves were free, nor any specific reference to new outbreaks of legalized anti-black and anti-Indian racism that would flourish in proudly democratic Virginia for another hundred years. But, as far as it goes, this museum does promote an understanding of the past that mixes celebration and admiration with a critique of cultural and military imperialism. It is more than once was taught young white Virginians. For that, their descendants can be grateful.

Native Americans, too, can be grateful that, for expanded understanding of their ancestors' four-hundred-year conflicts with Europeans, history *books* are now telling the story at a depth of detail never before available to scholars, students, and the public. In a recent public meeting the designer of the new Tredegar Museum in Richmond remarked that he hoped it would "educate its visitors without their knowing it." In another meeting related to the same project, a prominent German remarked that museums do more: They give visitors "the opportunity to confront physical objects that make you think, or to sit in a room and talk with people who will remind you that there are things out there that we normally do not talk about so much." The latter speaker, born German in 1946, knew very much indeed about how a national public learns to face a negative past.[20]

If Americans in general are to become well educated about the history of the Indian presence among us, we will need more than museums. We will need, at minimum, devotion to resources that are usually available in a museum room which may be the most important room of all: the book store. To pick up just one book at the end of the visit to the Jamestown Museum—as I did—is to walk back into a history to which the museum merely opens a door. If, in our schools, universities, churches, and mass media we are not encouraged to move into the study of books, we will have scarcely have begun to do justice to Native Americans past and present.

Virginia's Checkered, Belated Attempts to Heal This Fractured Past

This book so far has attempted to celebrate constructive, positive present responses of publics to their negative pasts. One has to search persistently for these responses in the case of Native Americans. The faithful studies of a historian-anthropologist like Helen Rountree are perhaps the best of the monument-memorials. Her book on the Powhatans is marvelous therapy for the ignorance of most visitors to the modern Jamestown Museum. Below is a sketch of her record of the struggle for increments of justice for the Powhatan and their descendants as they found themselves drawn unwillingly into the laws, the institutions, and the public culture of what was to become the Commonwealth of Virginia.

A PARENTHETICAL DISCLAIMER. The theme of this book has been the attention which citizens of nations have finally granted victims of injustice in their own past and present. But the "victim-perpetrator" polarity is doubly tempting. We dehumanize "victims" if we remember them only as victims and not as human persons. We also dehumanize them if we attribute to them a moral innocence on grounds that they were objects of colossal injustice. No human being is a mere object. Even in face of gross persecution, humans remain agents. Our behavior exhibits response-ability. Our responses are often weighted with hatred, violence, and counterviolence which deserve moral blame. The Powhatan Wahunsonacock's punitive dealings with his enemies and his demands for tribute were already history when John Smith first met him. War the European understood only too well. Conquest was in the air of contemporary politics on both continents. In tribute to their moral agency, both European and Indian rules of war disparaged the murder of women and children. Prudence, if not moral principle, should have persuaded many Indian nations early on to make peace with each other for making more effective war with Europeans. Furthermore, though war between Indian nations was seldom as violent as the warfare practiced by their new white enemies, the destruction of the Chespeakes in 1608 carried out the Powhatans' own version of scorched-earth imperialism. If one wanted to support the idea that human beings are basically weapon wielders and warmakers, one could turn for evidence to Indian history before and after the European invasions.

In sum, as a Native American staff member of the Smithsonian Institution once said to me, "Indians have their own sins to account for. We should not idealize them." She was alluding to the old, typical nineteenth-century oscillation of white Americans between Rousseau's myth of the "noble savage" and John Smith's "greedy and perfidious devils." This duality does scant justice to the reality of Indian humanity or Indian behavior over the centuries. The same is true for humans of every culture.[21]

That said, it is time for the popular imagination of Americans to concede that any honest account of this five hundred-year history abounds in so much devastation of Indians by Europeans that the moral scales are heavily—heavily, heavily—weighted against us Europeans. One does not have to make Indians into saints in order to raise the historical-moral question of who might first qualify for the badge "greedy and perfidious devils"—or whose history abounds most with evidence that lethal weaponry is the most typical human tool. Tragedy consists of goods and evils locked in inexorable conflict, and people on all sides of this tragic history mixed much good and evil in their treatment of each other. But naming the history as "tragic" offers no excuse for an easy slide into the surmise, "Everyone was equally wrong." Not so. In almost any comparison, Native Americans were more sinned-against than sinning. When we refuse to agree with this conclusion, white Americans are preferring comfort over painful acknowledgment of historical fact.[22]

Let me return to my native Virginia.

The Treaties

Early and late, Jamestown colonists and their descendants made treaties with Indians, but in doing so they planted seeds of many future misunderstandings. Historian James Wilson writes that between the European-borne diseases that would devastate Indian populations all over the Americas and conflicting interpretations of treaty-making, the grounds of tragedy were prepared from the earliest connection of the two sides. "What drove it ultimately out of control was a lethal combination of alien diseases and an encounter with people who, inconceivably, did not live in a reciprocal universe"[23]—that is, a social world in which equals negotiated to achieve balances of power and interest. From the beginning, few east coast English colonists brought with them a readiness to see Indians as equals to themselves. Over every negotiation loomed the vast, arrogant assumption that an English monarch had already laid claim to this land, so that Indian claims to it were a priori invalid. Their future right to sell any of it was equally invalid. Theologians defended the theory, as did one Charles Wolley, an English clergyman, who solemnly proclaimed in 1670 that the first discovery of a Country inhabited by Infidels, gives a right and Dominion of that Country to the Prince in whose Service and Employment the discoverers were sent.[24]

The arrogance here is worth long pauses for reflection among us Earth people. What if, one day, a science-fiction-anticipated, armed host of invaders from outer space actually arrives in some Midwestern corn field and proclaims: "Hear now: Your planet belongs to us." The logic behind the claim should be anything but strange to Earth ears. Columbus said as much to the Indians who met him on the shore of Guanahani.[25]

A culture of reciprocity was not altogether lacking in early and late dealings of Europeans with Indians, however. A survey of some of the early treaties between the Jamestown "settlers"[26] and the Powhatans suggests that some notions of justice and promise keeping attended the English side. Contemporary with the settlement of Jamestown and Plymouth-Massachusetts Bay was the life of John Locke (1632–1704). One suspects that before the seventeenth century was over, some English read his religion-tinged writings on natural law and human rights. If they did not, they at least had in their minds some traces of ancient Jewish and Christian ethics of truth telling and promise keeping between people equally deserving of respect as children of God. Early and late, Europeans kept laying the basis for the skepticism of the Sioux elder who would say in 1891, "They made us many promises, more than I can remember, but they never kept but one; they promised to take our land and they took it."[27]

The treaty history of early English America is suffused with the assumption that in any agreement the English were the superior party and so could break the agreement with impunity. They did not assume reciprocity. Indians expected it. It took them a decade or so to revise that expectation. After the disastrous wars of 1622, for example, Jamestowners wrote a treaty in 1628 in which they stated candidly that its provisions would stand "until ye English see a fit opportunity to break it." The opportunity came three months later.[28] Finally, in 1646, the General Assembly passed a pair of contradictory laws which allocated land north of the York River to Indian settlement "until further order therein" and, probably on the same day, mandated that all the land north of the York belonged to the colony.

We can conclude only that the settlement law was, in effect, an agreement among the English that they would move northward again when Indian rancor over the recent war had diminished, and that any protests made later by the nonliterate Powhatans would be pushed aside.[29]

Like other treaties, that of 1646 assumed the sovereignty of the Virginia government over the Powhatan. In token of this political assumption the Powhatan agreed to present to the Virginia governor an annual tribute of wild game, a provision reconfirmed in 1686 and practiced by one or another of the Powhatan nations for the next three centuries down to the present. There is a glimmer of reciprocity in this remarkably enduring custom. The governor was often the court of last resort for Indian complaints. As "father," he had duties to his children—a pattern that would persist well into the twentieth century as Indian leaders made their treks, often futile, to lay their cases before the Great White Father, the president of the United States.

If one is looking for glints of justice and acknowledgment of the interests of Indians in this early Virginia history, an event of some apparent promise would be the Treaty of Middle Plantation of 1677. Its ten articles spelled out a mixture of paternalism and reciprocity which, ironically enough, would not see much official repetition until the twentieth century. Eighteenth- and nineteenth-century legal and social relations between the burgeoning immigrant population and the shrinking numbers of the Powhatans would increasingly demean the latter. But as of 1677, Anglo-Virginians agreed to certain balances between the rights of both. A first provision—always first—acknowledged that the Powhatans were now subjects of the king of England. Second, they were to hold their lands "by patent" and at a tax of only twenty beaver skins deliverable every March to the Governor. Further, if and when their leaders came to see the governor, they were to be fed and housed at colony expense. Separation between the two peoples would be protected by a three-mile rim around Indian land into which whites were not supposed to intrude. Complaints of ill treatment were to be taken directly to the governor "to receive justice as though they were Englishmen." Indians were to have access to wild game and fruits that did not happen to be used by the English; and the government was to protect the Powhatan against any invasions by "foreign" Indians. Trade relations between all groups were to be controlled by the governor. And—in an early legal distinction between Africans and Indians—Indians were never to be enslaved by their employers. Ceremony and celebration attended the signing of this treaty, whose "good will . . . was to be reinforced by crowns for the Indian signatories." Unfortunately the crowns were subsequently withheld and then lost at sea;[30] but at least in this treaty, seventy years after John Smith's arrival in Jamestown, the idea of reciprocity had survived in diminished forms.

The next 250 years of Virginia's legal dealings with its Indians offer very few additional glints of such reciprocity. Ironically, the colonial and state legislatures of 1700–1800 were often under such pressure from land-hungry and racist white immigrants that to some extent the "will of the people," that is, English people, often overrode the glimmers of legal treaty rights in the decisions of legislators. The latter were readier to enforce treaty provisions "than did those settlers living near the Indians, and [the legislature] did its feeble best to restrain the settlers." Back in 1677, for example, the Virginia Assembly had nodded to traditional Indian understanding of land rights by granting the Pamunkeys freedom to hunt and fish on the unfenced land of the English. In 1705 the Pamunkeys had to petition the governor to enforce this right.[31] Protections of such rights would erode steadily over the next century, and the legislature itself would legally bar the door to the one basic right that sustains all others: the right to be considered as fully human as one's neighbors.

Virginia's Long Struggle Against Legalized Human Inequality

Racism in the service of land acquisition and land cultivation is the dominant theme of relationships between Anglo-Virginians and Indians over the next century. Exploitation of black slave labor—especially for the profitable cultivation of tobacco—complicated and overshadowed Indian interests right through the Civil War era. Though the cause of human rights for African Americans in the twentieth century would eventually spill over into rights for Indians, the latter meantime tried hard to distinguish themselves from Africans. It is not too much to say that racism was refined among Indians in defense against the racism of the Europeans. In the early twentieth century, for example, Indians would successfully claim the right not to ride in segregated rail cars designated for blacks. The 1705 laws were the first of many attempts to segregate the races, European, African, and Indian, according to their respective ancestry. As early as 1691 the legislature forbade marriages between whites and both Indians and blacks, and subsequent law against "miscegenation" steadily tightened pseudoprecise measurements of a person's racial identity. Ninety-eight years after 1607, the legislature passed its "Black Code," which scooped up Indians and blacks into the inferior side of a biracial society. Indians could now sue for redress of grievances with the governor but not in the courts. They were forbidden to lift a hand against white squatters on their land "on pain of getting thirty lashes." And as late as the 1920s the legislature was struggling to specify how to distinguish "real" white people from Indians and blacks. Twentieth-century racist law in Germany and South Africa rested on identical logics.

This sad story began with legal energy as early as 1691, when the legislature forbade marriages between "Negroes, Mulattoes, and Indians." In 1705 a "Mulatto" was defined legally as anyone with a black great-great-grandfather

(=one-eighth black). The definition changed in 1785 to one-quarter—a great-grandfather. Down to the 1920s, the Virginia legislature was issuing law for defining genuine whites as those having only one-sixteenth or less of "Negro blood," and local Indians were at pains to prove by that measure that at least they were not Negroes. On the side of glimmering eventual change, the record shows that "in 1699 several Englishmen petitioned unsuccessfully that the law [against intermarriage] be repealed." Not until 1967 and 1975 would that petition be legislatively answered in the affirmative.[32] The long trail following myths of "blood" was to extend into 1954 when the Virginia Assembly declared that an Indian grandfather made one a tribal Indian but only on the condition that he or she had "less than one-sixteenth Negro blood." Thus, one could be "white" or "Indian" if one could prove that one was not descended from a black great-great-grandfather or -grandmother. In postwar 1866, in anticipation of the Jim Crow era, an unreconstructed Virginia legislature tightened the definition to make anyone with a black or Indian grandparent a "colored person," catching Indian Virginians in a bind between the privileges of whites and the continued subjugation of blacks. "Henceforth," comments Helen Rountree, " 'racial purity' would be a major issue in defining Indians; it would be a veritable cornerstone of the Indians' self-identity."[33] The historical cement in that cornerstone was white racism, without which the language of "half blood" would never have entered American talk.

Laws governing marriage, the most personal of contracts, reflect the contract law and majority prejudices of their eras. From the perspective that finally gained legal expression in the 1975 Virginia cancellation of all its discriminatory laws, one can only celebrate the ancient *lack* of prejudice among the Powhatans against "interracial" marriage. When John Rolfe contracted his famous marriage to the Indian princess Pocahontas, it was no break in her cultural tradition, but the precedent would not achieve much honor in future Virginia law. As late as 1924, in a "Racial Integrity Law" that codified the "one drop rule," Virginians were told that "every person in whom there is ascertainable any Negro blood shall be deemed to be a colored person," although the one-fourth rule remained for the designation "American Indian." There was one loophole in this legalism: A person of one-sixteenth Indian ancestry could still qualify as white.

> The exception was inserted for the benefit of those Virginians who claimed descent from Pocahontas and planter John Rolfe. A number of them were from influential families, and they wanted to be able to boast of their distant link to the Powhatan "princess" without having to use separate bathrooms and other inferior facilities designated for non-whites.[34]

This narrative of racist law traces its own "trail of tears." It will be a sign of some liberation from racism in modern Virginian white culture if the irony of the Pocahontas exception summons smiles, if not laughter, from members of the FFV.

In 1924 the United States government declared that Indians could be American citizens and thus permitted to vote in Federal elections. Only in 1948 did Virginia followed suit for its state elections. And only under the impact of the civil rights movement of the next two decades did racism finally disappear from its law books in 1975.

In counterpoint to this dreary history, Virginians should remember those white settlers who protested the stranglehold of expanding racist law and who voted against it by marrying into Powhatan communities. But these were few. In some contrast to New England, Virginia's Christian missionaries seldom managed to read from their faith its equalitarian potentials. Thus cultural conflict and mutual disrespect went their tragic way. Helen Rountree describes the unrealized potential of the settlers for entering a "reciprocal universe" in these poignant words:

> A continued sore spot with the Powhatans was English people's steadfast refusal to consider Indians as marriage partners. The English who wrote on this subject were probably right in surmising that the Powhatan would have been more receptive to English culture had English people given this evidence of considering Indians as fellow human beings. As it was, even well-meaning English missionaries were going out to the Powhatan reservations to assure the people of English esteem while trying to convert them. . . . [T]he Indians' English neighbors, most of whom were from the poorer strata of English society[,] were apt, in their struggle for prosperity, to maltreat Indians. The "Christian" example set for the Powhatans was not a good one.

She goes on to describe some of cultural habits on each side which each found "peculiar" in the other: Why did the English keep their wives at home and the Powhatans expected them to work the fields? How could one eat with the small English spoon when the half-pint-sized Powhatan spoon was so much handier? Why use wine to get drunk when rum did the job more quickly? Why did the English bathe so seldom, much to the offense of the Indian nose? And why was an Englishman so prompt to give advice to others?[35]

The answer to the last question was the English confidence that they were better, wiser, and more "civilized" than their Indian neighbors. Had the answer been otherwise, the details of cultural conflict, like those above, might have been explored and rendered into mutual learning and adaptation on both sides. But domination-subordination assumptions in social norms systematically poisoned inclinations to learn from the "other." By building barriers to reciprocal relations with Indians, the colonists and future white Americans could only

experience that Other at increasing depths of estrangement. Indian collaboration in this evolution of racism makes it doubly tragic. Much to be regretted
is that both parties preferred myths of "blood" to a view, from another side of
Indian culture, beautifully stated by the Navaho medicine man White Feather:
"Native American isn't blood. It is what is in the heart. The love for land, the
respect for it, those who inhabit it, and the respect and acknowledgment of the
spirits and elders. That is what it is to be Indian."[36]

A Rebirth of Indian Status, Rights, and Dignity?

The recent half-century history of Native Americans and Euro-Americans contains more occasions for provisional celebration than almost any of the four
preceding centuries. As was suggested by the presence of Indian drummers
and dancers in the 1993 Richmond "Walk through History," Virginians are
now participants in larger nationwide movements for justice to Native Americans in the wake of the civil rights movement of the 1960s. Belated but real,
by 2004 new magnitudes of political organization, public communication, and
economic effort characterize the life and work of the some two million surviving Indians of this country. Later in this chapter I return to these recent events
and to some reflection on these new, more promising relations between American governments, Americans of all ethnic origins, and the surviving descendants of the original inhabitants of the continent. For now, if any member of
the Powhatan nations reads these pages, he or she will surely mark it down
that white Americans still have a long way to go before they even imagine what
it might mean for the English to have attempted to build, on the western shores
of the Atlantic, a "new world" based on reciprocity.

Pondering a Second Locale: The Mohicans of Columbia County, New York

> According to the vision of a Mohawk dream catcher of long ago, the
> secret spiritual masters of the four races of men will come together
> around their wisdom fire, in the effort to restore what is dying. The
> power they will assemble will be immense, but the task may be be-
> yond even their resources. It will require the participation—the
> awakening to the spiritual life—of a great many more people in a
> society in which so many of our "best and brightest" are habituated
> to living as if they do not have a soul, or have forgotten where they
> put it.
>
> —Robert Moss, Chatham, New York[37]

They have all disappeared now. The trails they walked have gone. No markers honor their burial grounds. The woods are silent to their battle cries.

—Dominic C. Lizzi, contemporary resident of
Columbia County, New York[38]

It is to be admired, how strangely they have decreased by the hand of God.

—English colonist Daniel Denton, on the decline
of Indian population in Manhattan by 1670[39]

I am a summertime resident of a woody hill in Columbia County, New York, a hundred miles north of Manhattan. The psychological rule, "out of sight, out of mind," would easily explain why the residents of Columbia County have little reason to think of Mohican hunters whenever they glimpse the deer and the turkeys which still roam these woods. We may sometimes think ruefully that the burgeoning deer population could use more regular Mohican hunts if the crops and shrubs of the land are to prosper. But the Mohicans are as profoundly *absent* from Columbia County as the Powhatan are from Tidewater, Virginia, at least in the eyes of us who have lived in both places. The public reminders of their one-time long presence here are few and far between. Local students of the history speculate where a dozen of the villages might have been, where a cave for hiding against a subzero winter, where perhaps former burial mounds. But aside from a few place names, for the untutored modern resident the visible traces are rare on both banks of the Hudson River, a rarity that underscores the profundity of the absence.

The Mohican name for the river was *Muhhekkannatuk,* "Great Waters," a name which was extended to "Great Waters which are never still, flowing back and forth," in view of the Atlantic tides that reach all the way to present-day Albany. With the Powhatans of eastern Virginia, one could think of them as a tidewater people.[40]

In 1609, along these banks and tributary streams, lived at least three thousand Mohicans, perhaps as many as twenty-five thousand. As the American Revolution was beginning 165 years later, their numbers would shrink to about three hundred.

Up the great river in September 1609 came a ship captained by Henry Hudson. His compatriots would rename the river after him, in the fashion of Sir George Grey, Namer-of-Ten-Rivers in South Africa.[41] A few Mohican place names survive on the modern map,[42] but everywhere in Columbia County now are names, mansions, and land histories associated with the flood of Dutch and English who, during the next two centuries, would buy, claim, and otherwise occupy this valley for the building of huge estates along both banks of the river. For most of the tourist brochures and highway markers, the history of Columbia Country begins with the voyage of the *Half Moon* to an anchorage just south of present-day Albany.[43] A nineteenth-century artist pictures Indians in canoes welcoming the Dutchmen and bringing aboard corn, pumpkins, and tobacco. A crewman, Robert Juet, wrote that these were "very loving people and very old men." They welcomed him as many Indians, from 1492 on, welcomed Europeans, by offering them presents in expectation of presents in return. Like the Powhatans, they lived in a universe of reciprocity.

Their ancestors had lived on these river banks for a very long time—perhaps as long as 12,000 years. The late Kenneth Mynter, one of a cluster of local residents who have made career-long studies of Mohican history, observed in 1986 that "Indians were living here in this county before the building of the great pyramids . . . at a time when our own ancestors were living in the Neolithic or New Stone Age in Europe—hardly any further advanced in culture than the Indians."[44] One local county landowner recently found arrow heads which tested out as 1,500 years old. However many centuries ago the migratory relatives of the Mohicans came to this river valley, their era lasted at least as long as any the Dutch and English would bring with them in their own cultural memory of several thousand years. They owned the east and west banks of the Hudson River as surely as the English owned the Thames.

The year 1609 would mark the beginning of the end of the Mohican era in the Hudson Valley. "In about 150 years or less, they were gone."[45] James Fenimore Cooper would have every reason from their scarcity in his region to write a novel about the supposed "last" of them.[46] The story of the Mohicans' displacement from these hills, forests, and riverbanks is complex, but its central theme coincides with that of the rest of the Native American story right up to 2004: *land*—its buying, selling, appropriation, stealing, occupation, and occasional sharing in four centuries of European and Indian relationships.

A second Columbia County scholar, Shirley W. Dunn, has undertaken an exhaustive investigation of recorded local land transfers from 1609 through 1730. In theory, the Dutch approach to land purchases was morally superior to that of the English. The former had instructions from their Dutch sponsors to purchase, but not to preempt, land acquired from Indians; the latter assumed that as migratory people the Mohicans had no permanent title to land to which now the King of England laid total claim:

> Wouter Van Twiller wrote in 1633, "I have . . . taken possession of the aforementioned river . . . Itt's not the intent of the States [General of the Netherlands] to take the land from the poore Natives as the Kinge of Spain hath done . . . but rather to take itt from the said Natives at some reasonable and convenient price, which, God be praysed, we have done hitherto."[47]

The moral superiority of the Dutch to the English diminishes, however, when one reflects that they assumed the right to establish the colony of New Netherland whether or not the natives assented; and, further, whatever the fair or unfair price they paid for land, they had ideas about ownership quite parallel to that of the English and quite in contrast to that of the Indians. Stephen Comer, Mohican, says that the moral difference between the Dutch and English in these matters is minuscule. They were, in his view, "equally criminal, or, if you will, evil."[48]

Given the proclivity of the Dutch and the English for keeping property records, Dunn's research yields a vivid, painful picture of what happens when a traditional, barter-based economy collides with a commercial global economy driven by human thirst for money wealth. Captain Hudson's successors brought with them kettles, hoes, knives, cloth, alcohol, and guns, most of whose uses Indians could promptly appreciate. Not much appreciated, as numerous accounts make clear, was the difference between European and Indian concepts of "property" and "ownership," especially as these terms related to land. Indians have never deserved the prejudicial slur implied in remarks about "Indian givers" in popular American talk. Once a metal pot was bought or sold, Indians knew that the seller had no right of arbitrary repossession. But land was different. It was home. It was the place where the ancestors had lived from time immemorial and where they were buried. It was host to the wild animals that sustained human life through the winter. It could sustain a variable number of human lives, as migrants came and went, as one tract of land declined in its usefulness, as it underwent some years of natural restoration, after which it could be reinhabited. This complex of concepts combined with Indian belief in the spirit and ancestral presences in the land to render the European, especially English, idea of *possession* ("fee simple") as absurd. It was so absurd that it took a long time for many Indians to understand how, for the English, an absoluteness attached to land purchases entailing fences, laws against trespass, and refusals to permit anyone but the "owner" to use a vacant piece of land for hunting, firewood, or temporary agriculture. "Worldwide," says Comer, "indigenous peoples do not sell their lands; that is what makes them indigenous. If they 'sold' their land it was because ultimately they were forced to."[49]

Add to this basic conflict definitional differences over what constitutes a "contract" and a "deed of sale"; add also the sharp practice of new settlers and Indians themselves in selling land that someone else had already sold; and one has a formula for mischief and misunderstanding which would corrupt European-Indian relations for five centuries from the Atlantic to the Pacific. Finally, add the concept of perpetual *land inheritance* by the purchaser's lineal descendants, and one really has moved into a truly "new world" of land tenure. How reasonable, to Sir William Johnson, to remind some River Indians in 1754 that "most of the lands concerning which you complain were patented when you were children, some before any of you were born." To their mystification, notes Shirley Dunn, "the Mohicans were caught in the web of deeds which they had been signing in exchange for products since 1630." How *un-*reasonable to think that a piece of paper a century old forever determined who could use a piece of land! It was a momentous collision of cultures.

> It was not unusual that these sales were sometimes in conflict with each other. This was true for many reasons. Perhaps the most significant one was that the Indians believed that land sold reverted back to them if not occupied or farmed. Secondly all the Indians who may have had some claim to a piece of land may not have been signatory to its deed of sale. Or, in some cases, a previous Indian landowner could be seduced by an unscrupulous buyer into selling the same piece of land again.[50]

In sum, the Mohican case, like that of the Powhatans in contemporary Virginia and the Wampanoags in Massachusetts Bay, was a cameo of what would become continentwide exploitation. In Virginia a colonial government invented the first Indian reservations in America only to stand by while "colonists let their livestock graze on Indian crops and attacked Powhatans who protested; squatted on tribal land; purchased lots and then refused to pay for them; or used corrupt interpreters to manipulate Indians into selling land when they thought they were signing documents that simply confirmed their right of possession."[51] In the Hudson Valley, when the land being purchased encompassed thousands of acres and hundreds of square miles, when ideas of "just price" were wildly diverse in two cultures, and when no party to the transaction was sure what future needs might rise up to justify a descendant's quarrel with the terms of the trade, some similarly great tragedies were in the making. A well-documented example was the formal sale of a large portion of modern Columbia County—some 700,000 acres—to the Rensselaerwyck family on May 24, 1649. Mohican Chief Skiwias and an agent of the Dutch patroon presided over the transaction. The surviving record shows a payment of "10 fathoms [sixty feet] of cloth, 10 kettles, 10 axes, 10 adzes, 10 swords, 10 hand sewant (strung beads), 10 knives, and1 firelock gun."[52]

Says Kenneth Mynter: "I have read the deeds, and [I doubt] if the Indian grantors of the land realized what they were doing, when they marked their clan totem and an X on a piece of parchment."[53] One might concede that a heft of European hardware had very large comparative value to the Mohicans as long as they could exercise their rights of land residence and use. That, of course, was the catch. Perhaps the Dutch negotiators did not know what the Mohicans did not know. Nonetheless, the stage was set for many a future refusal of Dutch and English owners to tolerate either residence or use on the part of Mohican neighbors.[54]

Comprehension of this Columbia County history has recently been taken up as a public duty for the cluster of devoted historians quoted here. As this is written, one wonders if we are on the edge of a belated new day of public awareness of the mixed goods and evils of this local past. The current evidence, too, is mixed, says Robert Moss:

> Talking to friends and neighbors, I have found that, while everyone
> is aware, on some level, that long before the county had dreamed of
> a real estate broker, it belonged to Indians, few people have any ex-
> act notion of who these natives were, or the kind of world—social
> and spiritual—they inhabited.[55]

But as of the late 1980s, he adds, "I find that many of my neighbors are increasingly alive to these things," and slowly but steadily, more than fifteen years later, that impression has had reason to grow. As accounts like the ones quoted here come to the attention of neighbors like myself, one's imagination gets invested with sobering statistics. Take the scale of these early land contracts. The Rensselaerwyck transfer of 700,000 acres (at 640 acres per square mile) came to just under 1,100 square miles, the larger part of modern Columbia County. This stretch of land would be equal to a rectangle ten miles inland from the Hudson River and a hundred miles downriver from Albany, that is, almost to New York City.

Then there is my immediate summer family residence in Austerlitz Township, an area now just west of the Massachusetts state line.[56] Two-thirds of the township, some 20,722.5 acres, or thirty-two and one-third square miles, were eyed by a group of twenty or more squatter-settlers in the early 1750s. In 1756 they paid four supposedly representative Mohican leaders the sum of 230 English pounds for the whole tract, or about 7 pounds per square mile. A year later, the number of settlers had grown to at least seventy, and the leaders applied to the colonial government of Massachusetts for formal title to the land, which was granted. From then on 100 acres was assigned to each family, which meant that for each such farm a settler had paid Mohicans about 1 pound. As of 2002, modern economists calculate, that pound would have multiplied by a factor of ninety-six, putting its dollar value at $147, which means that the 1760 purchasers paid the equivalent of $1.47 per acre for an acre which, in 2004, was selling for over $10,000.[57]

One of those settler families was named Spencer, who gave our local town its name.[58] In 1760, in Spencertown, a Congregational church was organized which would later become Presbyterian. In 2003, its 1771 building achieved national landmark status, complete with highway marker. There is a sad aspect to such markers. Most New England towns have early settler date signs on their highways, each implying more prestige the closer to the year 1620. By virtue of these signs, residents of these northeastern places have reason to grow up assuming that real local history began at these dates. Against this cultural prejudice, there is nothing to prevent public pressure, one of these days, for some highway markers to call our attention to the presence of another people on these acres long before some of us assumed our right to claim them.

So far, few such markers dot our county landscape. An exception is a pair of markers south of Columbia in Dutchess County. One notes the location of the burial ground of the village of Shekomeko, the other the home of Prince Quack Mannessah, "the last known Indian resident of Gallatin." Another is the Pasoquack Preserve, a small area in Valatie near Kinderhook Creek, set aside by the town in year 2000 as a park.

To be sure, the hazards that had already diminished the Mohican population by 1756 were complex. They included costly wars with ancient Mohawk enemies living to the west, devastations of smallpox, ups and downs of the fur trade, addiction to European goods and to alcohol, and defense against these threats by the selling of more and more land. The Mohican nation would disperse for a while to a new center along the Housatonic in Connecticut, then to a gathering in 1735 around Christian missionaries John Sergeant and David Brainerd in Stockbridge. Along with the Moravians, those two English missionaries had more respect for Indian interests than did colonial governors and fur traders of Massachusetts and New York. The Moravians were so effective in defending the integrity of their Mohican converts that the colonial government decided to shut down the mission. As Kenneth Mynter summarizes this sorrowful incident:

> The Moravians, who alone of all white men, had shown the Indians true Christian spirit, had labored long and hard among them. . . . David Brainard performed like services among the Mohicans at Stockbridge. There is no record of early Dutch or English clergymen doing any work among the Indians, but the English finally rewarded the kindly Moravians by arrest and a forced abandonment of their efforts. The story—never told in school history books—was that the traders, whose traffic in liquor was materially reduced as a result of Moravian teachings, lost no opportunity to misrepresent them, and accuse them falsely . . . of being emissaries of the French.[59]

The Moravians and a number of their Mohican converts then left for Pennsylvania and the land of the Delawares, as did David Brainerd. Soon after, angered by their treatment by the British, the Mohicans largely sided with the Americans in the Revolutionary war, fighting in the battles of Bunker Hill and White Plains and furnishing "over 300 bushels of corn by snowshoe and pack-basket through snow-covered forests" to the winter-beleaguered army of George Washington in Valley Forge:

> At the close of the war General Washington sent a special message to Congress, highly praising the contributions of the Hudson River Indians and their brothers at Oneida and Stockbridge who had served under his command. He recommended that just compensation be rewarded for their services. . . . [T]hey had hoped that with

victory would come aid to recover lands or adjustment previously denied them by British courts.

But the new [federal] government appears to have been too busy for such matters, leaving disposition of Mahikan claims to the new State of New York. The New York legislature, well-known for its failure to settle Indian claims amicably, had quickly and conveniently forgotten the sacrifices made by their allies in the recent struggle. Legislature members were too busy making deals with big land companies and influential businessmen for the disposition of Indian lands.[60]

Scattered now in Connecticut, Pennsylvania, Ohio, and Ontario, and little rewarded with justice from the new Americans, the remaining Stockbridge Indians accepted the offer of the Oneidas in central New York to settle there on a tract of land. A generation later that tract, too, fell under pressures from white settlers, so remnant Mohicans decamped for a far-off tract purchased from the Menominee nation near modern Green Bay, Wisconsin. It was the 1830s, the years of the "Indian Removal Act," enforced by President Andrew Jackson over the famous constitutional objection of Chief Justice John Marshall. Today, in Bowler, Wisconsin, the Red Springs Reservation numbers some 1600 Mohicans.[61] The identity of the Mohican nation would formally survive with official recognition of its status by a twentieth-century Federal government. But, some 140 years after Henry Hudson, the Mohican story in the future Columbia County of the State of New York had virtually ended. As the Mohicans had moved away, Europeans had "quickly moved into the cleared areas and started farms. Only a few Indians were left behind, those who had European spouses, and some who stayed to work on the settlers' farms."[62]

In late 1996, a cluster of local historians, some of them quoted here, gathered in support of the establishment of an Institute of Native American Studies at the local community college. Its current work, in 2004, promises some new justice, at least in the form of a design for a new curriculum for grades four and seven in the New York State public schools. Perhaps their efforts will motivate local citizens to erect some new public postings of the life once lived here by the People of the Continually Flowing Water. One notable improvement on public memory would be a revision of state markers on the north end of the Taconic Parkway, whose Mohican-derived name might better be transliterated "Taghkanic." Ironically, the markers summarize in two hundred words the history of Columbia County beginning only with the Dutch. Looking past the marker across the Hudson Valley to the Catskills, few tourists are prompted to remember who first lived here.

Merely sketched here, the Mohican story, like that of the Powhatans, was a baleful anticipation of things to come. A precious personal, positive residue of this foray into a much-neglected history I must offer here. Having acquired a new appreciation of the Mohicans who once roamed "my" hillside in Columbia County, I look with new eyes out across the landscape between my front porch and the Catskill Mountains beyond the river. The mountain chain stretches fifteen miles along the river. Buddhist monasteries, retreat centers, and campsites dot the area now. For over a century hotels in these mountains have been a resort for what we moderns call "recreation." In that tradition, Indian-owned casinos are about to come to the Catskills. Did the Mohicans ever climb these hills for a very different form of re-creation? We do not know.

For me, at least, there is something re-creating about the sun's setting behind those mountains thirty miles away. As I ponder the silhouette of those hills, the words of Psalm 121 come to mind. But in a new way now, the Mohicans come to mind. All the land between here and there once was home to humans not of my lineage. Their history stirs in me a new suspicion of what we Westerners mean by "owning." My government assures me that I own this hillside with its view of the Catskills. But the Mohicans assure me that, in a deeper sense, it owns me, that it is a gift for which the only human response is: "Thank you." I am inclined to add: "Forgive us our trespasses."

History Learned, Unlearned, Revised: A New Public Education?

Late nineteenth and early twentieth-century writers sometimes referred to Indians as the "vanishing americans." As a participant in the low level of Euro-American awareness of histories like the above, this author celebrates the scholarship that assures us that Indians are no longer vanishing in life or in books. Their continentwide population had shrunk drastically by 1900 (to 237,000) from a probable 7 million in 1492.[63] The figure now is about 2 million.

In response to this newly accessible history, how much improved is public education in the United States, compared to one or two generations ago? The answer is not easy to ascertain. Thanks to explosions of mass media, "public education" now takes place as much outside of schools as inside. By the beginning of the twenty-first century, both television and film have begun to portray Native Americans with accuracy and humanistic realism that are great improvements over the stereotypes of the cowboy-and-Indian era. Films like *Dances with Wolves, Soldier Blue,* and *Little Big Man* have provided millions of viewers with the relatively unprecedented American cinematic experience of cheering for the interests of the Indians rather than for the cavalry coming to the rescue of beleaguered settlers.[64] These pages have already saluted similar media changes in images of African Americans, along with changes over decades of high school history books. Whatever their corrected images of Indians in the past, the new books will not serve their civic purpose if they do not open students and teachers to corrected images of Indian peoples in the present.

That is why one scholar suggests to teachers that they subscribe to one of the more independent Indian newspapers.[65]

How have high school history books fared in regard to Native Americans? To what extent have the books of the past forty years benefited from the scholarship that has made possible the advance of this author, for example, from James Loewen's "minus 10" to perhaps a "minus 1" level of knowledge of this past? Using the sample of high school history books studied in the previous chapter, let me return to questions of the general history of Indians on this continent, in contrast to the two very local histories just sketched. Once again I want to concentrate on editions of one book widely used in the American public school systems of the past forty years.

From "The Rise of the American Nation" to "The Triumph of the American Nation" to "The American Nation"

Diplomat Joseph Montville, veteran of many international conflict negotiations, observes that parties to most hostile relations begin with the assumption that some have been the victims, some the victimizers:

> [V]ictimizers traditionally employ the psychological mechanisms of avoidance and denial of unpleasant truths about their behavior and that of their forebears. And victims are ordinarily so intensely absorbed by their own losses that they rarely understand the complexities and moral ambiguities their oppressors might have experienced in the past. It is especially important to take into account the fact that the victimizers may also have been victims at some point. This is why revision of history books—getting the story straight—is common in successful political reconciliation processes.[66]

The political reconciliation of Native Americans with the descendants of European Americans is far from complete in this beginning of the twenty-first century, and "getting the story straight" to the approximate satisfaction of both sides of a five-century conflict will take many more decades of patient effort by scholars, political leaders, educators, artists, and the general public. "Victim" and "oppressor" are slippery categories. Any admission (as in the "disclaimer" above) that Indians were more sinned-against than sinning will surely anger some descendants of European immigrants who fled poverty and low social status to make for themselves a new life in America. Those who dared to climb aboard the covered wagons to head for Oregon often had their own oppressions to resist at the hands of established easterners. The courage to cross those Rocky Mountains before 1869[67] should never be underestimated. In a recent documentary, former Governor Ann Richards of Texas spoke passionately about her identification with pioneer women who endured hard winters, sod-packed soil, the threat of childbirth death, and hope for material wealth which only their children would live to enjoy. How long will it be before prominent politicians like her add a note of regret for the cost borne by Mexicans and Indians for the American settlement of their part of the country? As Montville suggests, asking any sufferer to remember suffering which they, in turn, have imposed on others is asking a lot of morally finite human beings. We humans do not readily digest mixtures of hurt and guilt. Texans and Californians, the two largest markets for high school texts, expect from their state school boards decisions about text adoptions that pay due honor to the Alamo's defenders and the Forty-Niners. Much dwelling on the questionable justice of the Mexican War and the murder of the California Indians can stretch the tolerance of students—and of their parents. Nonetheless, honest history must take account of as many parties to the real past as research makes possible. History writers must be open to the claims of marginalized peoples whose stories have been wrongly told or missing from their discipline. In this sense they are obliged to become "revisionists," which is not a synonym for "political correctness." Therefore, one sure measure of improvement in the writing and teaching of history will always be, *Does it portray with increasing depth the "complexities and moral ambiguities" on all sides of a conflictful human past?*

History may have to remain an unending argument, not only about the facts, but about the beneficiaries and the losers in human conflict. The "victors" in any conflict do have power to write history according to their interests, but if this rule alone determines what historians put on paper, their scholarly enterprise sinks into ideology. It may also sink into the suggestion that the winners of wars usually deserve to win. A careful German theologian has warned Americans to beware of this surmise. "A culture that idolizes the winner and shames the loser will always tend to suppress the vulnerable parts of life because it cannot accept the fact that winning is bound up with guilt."[68] Not all winning is guilt-laden, perhaps, but surely, "How the West Was Won" by hard-driving white pioneers deserves to be paired in American history books with "How the West Was Lost" to Indian peoples. Not for them a textbook with the title, "The Triumph of the American Nation."[69]

By this measure, relativists to the contrary, historians and other memory minders can always improve the inclusiveness of our perceptions of our past, and a survey of high school history books in my lifetime makes the case vividly. The books of year 2000 tell a much richer, more inclusive story of the American past than do texts of fifty years earlier. Both as monument and memorial, some of these new texts are occasions for modest celebration. They are likely to offer students and teachers wider lenses into the American past than were ever offered their parents or grandparents. They do not come up to the standard posed so crisply by Howard Zinn at the beginning of his *People's History of the United States,* but they are closer than standard high school history books used to be:

I prefer to tell the story of the discovery of American from the viewpoint of the Arawaks, of the Constitution from the standpoint of the
slaves, of Andrew Jackson as seen by the Cherokees, of the Civil War
as seen by the New York Irish, of the Mexican war as seen by the
deserting soldiers of Scott's army. . . . And so on, to the limited extent that any one person, however he or she strains, can "see" history from the standpoint of others.[70]

Any survey of history books will detect the influence of contemporary circumstance on the writing. This fact can be both positive and negative. In her biting
1979 critique of high school American history books, Frances Fitzgerald notes
that, beginning about 1960, the texts reflected demographical and political
change in their increased attention to immigrants, African Americans, Indians,
and other non–Anglo-Saxon contributors to American society. Over the past
two centuries, she says, Indians come and go and come again in the contents
of public education in the United States. Early nineteenth-century books paid
tribute to the virtues of Indian culture. They sometimes conceded that Europeans had treated Indians "rather badly." Beginning in the 1840s, notes Fitzgerald, stories about Indians deteriorated into stereotypes and angry descriptions of their violence against settlers. Emma Willard, pioneer in the education
of women, wrote a history that for many pages "describes an almost uninter-
rupted sequence of massacres, rebellions, Indian attacks, border skirmishes,
and major wars. . . . In these sanguinary conflicts, the only real virtue that
[white] Americans seem to have is the negative one of not behaving quite as
despicably as everyone else." Americans in the 1840s were energetically "con-
quering" the West, and for the next fifty years stories of wars with the Plains
Indians would fill newspapers and novels. For decades into the twentieth century, images of Indians as warriors became the standard stereotype in the
history books and the infant cinema industry. By 1930, Fitzgerald observes,
attention to Indians in history books and popular media subsided into virtual
neglect.[71]

Then came the 1960s. In the wake of the civil rights movement, as we
have seen, blacks entered the texts, along with Latinos, Asians, women, and
Indians in far more pages than had ever been devoted to them. "Multicultural"
education began, sometimes under organized pressures on state education
boards. Minority constituencies became players in the politics of text writing
and text adoption, along with ideologues of various stripes. One of the costs
paid by the writers, Fitzgerald believes, is that now they had to observe the rule
of blandness—"the inclusion of nasty information constitutes bias even if the
information is true."[72] That is the edited message that Jamestown Museum
guides are supposed to convey, too.

A sampling of references to Native Americans in the widely used Todd-
Curti series does not wholly confirm this view. "Nasty" data about the behavior,

policies, and claims of white settlers of the West does appear in these texts, and as the editions advance from 1960 to 2000, they include sides of the story that offer the student reasons for Indians' resorting to violence in defense of their lands and cultures. The most important change in style and educational method of the newer books—parallel to a similar change in South Africa—are pauses in the narratives which invite students to imagine themselves into this and that side of economic, political, and military clashes between the "settlers" and the natives of the Western "frontier." (Questions about the viewpoints implied in these very words do not abound, however.) On the whole, the newest South African texts are much more demanding in introducing students to the philosophical questions that text writers had to face in assessing what constitutes "facts of history." (Were they settlers or invaders? Should the frontier be imaged from its eastern side as moving ahead or its western side as moving backward? Eastern expansion or western shrinkage?) One wonders: Will some high school history teachers supplement these texts with a chapter or two from Howard Zinn?

Nonetheless, despite shortcomings in text portrayal of a heroic, violent, often shameful, and always morally mixed continental expansion of the United States, by year 2000 the books displayed some impressive new fairness to the Indian side of the story. Below are some benchmarks in these welcome changes.[73]

HISTORY BOOKS AND HISTORY TEACHERS. James Loewen ends his critique of high school history texts with a salute to teachers who teach "against the text," that is, who question the authority of alleged facts and the assumptions which lead this and that historian to tell stories of the past from their own particular points of view. As we have seen in the work of Jennifer Wallace in Cape Town, this mode of teaching puts heavy demands on teachers and students. Not all are up to it. The texts studied here move in this direction by asking students to examine different sides of historic conflicts and to make up their own minds about mixtures of right and wrong ways to describe events of the past. The editions of 1950–1961 speak conventionally of the "discovery" of America by Columbus, and few paragraphs dwell on the millennia of Indian settlement of the continent prior to 1492. Only one sentence (1961:446) notes that the western lands of the Nez Perce had belonged to them "from time immemorial." Though the Vikings get noted as pre-Columbus "discoverers" of America, the American story, for the 1961 reader, really begins with 1492. Prior to the 2001 edition, in 1992, a national controversy has erupted over whether this European discovery was good or bad for the ancient inhabitants of the continent. The 2001 edition poses the question to students on a very early page. This book, says the text, will consider both the good and the bad effects of Indian-European contact, and you, student, should know that this is one of a series of "Great Debates" to be featured from time to time in this book. You are expected to join the debate.

History teachers in public schools know that they can become embroiled in acrid controversy with parents and community leaders over issues like this. Post-9/11, while biology teachers treaded carefully around the issue of evolution, history teachers had a more treacherous sets of issues around criticism and admiration of things American. Texas high school teachers have always needed to think twice about questioning the right of Texans to revolt against Mexico, and a text that dwelled much on the slaves owned by Washington and Jefferson might have difficulty getting adopted by a Virginia school board. Historians are likely to resist the idea that history must have the purpose of fortifying the patriotism of young citizens, but state school boards and parents can be forthright about that goal. So how critical of your own country are you free to be in a public school classroom? In no consistent way do any of these texts prompt the question, but one can be sure that the question enters many post-9/11 high school classrooms, demanding of teachers skills akin to those of international conflict negotiators. How does one tell young people "the" story of their country's past when many stories vie for inclusion in the narrative? Is there a single unifying story or just many stories? The books examined here settle for the latter, but under titles and names which give a very strong impression of what high school history is supposed to leave in the minds of teenage students: admiration for the ideals, the successes, and the continuing promise of the American people past and present. The *Rise* of the nation in early editions of Todd-Curti becomes *Triumph* in the 1986 edition but yields to the neutral *American Nation* in 2001. As we have seen, the last page of the 2001 book states the authors' candidate for the unifying theme of the United States' story—the rise of democracy—and then they propose the question: "What is the role of the United States in spreading democracy throughout the world?" (2001:1091). Students in 2003–2004 would have a plethora of data from the newspapers for discussing the questions about the American war in Iraq.

More broadly, at least four issues pop up, from era to era, in treatments of Indian affairs in the Todd-Curti series.

STORY OR STORIES? A "multicultural" view of American history does require the telling of many stories from many times with many beginnings. That is one reason the twentieth-century high school books get longer and longer. But length in the latest books comes with a prolixity of colors, typefaces, maps, photographs, paintings, graphs, time lines, charts, sidebars, and chapter summaries designed to attract students of the television generation. The 2001 edition adds references to the Internet and CD-supplements that offer details geometrically advanced over resources of two decades ago. How many students make use of this array of paths to "learning more" may not be known. If the textbook publishers do know, they are likely to be secretive about the matter.[74]

One significant gain for the Indian story in the latest editions is their attention to prehistory. The 1950–1961 Todd-Curti books pay scant attention to pre-1492 events, but beginning in 1986 ten pages display how the ancestors migrated from Asia as long as ten to twenty-five thousand years ago. In 2001 a picture-laden time line portrays events in European history contemporary with that of "650 distinct groups . . . living in the Americas" by the year 1400 C.E. Multicolor maps locate two hundred native homelands. Indian myths get told, along with a sidebar noting the U.S. Congress's acknowledgment of Indian reverence for ancestor burial sites in its 1990 law for "Native American Grave Protection and Repatriation Act."

Pasts impact presents: History teachers know that, but they have the burden of proving it to the young. They have to demonstrate "relevance". The 1966 volume, in contrast to 1961, does so in a sidebar, "A Legacy from the Indians," which acclaims "the amazing truth that more than half of all the agricultural goods produced in the world today came from plants originally discovered and cultivated by American Indians." The list is long: from corn and tomatoes to chocolate and maple syrup (1966:22).

Were the Todd-Curti series to be compared to an arctic ice-floe, one might characterize these decade-to-decade changes as a breakup of a whole into pieces that lose connection with each other. This movement gets momentum in the 1972 edition, which introduces "case studies" which invite the student to analyze combinations of fact, political perspective, and even ethics, for example, "Jacksonian Democracy—Myth or Reality?" By this time the story of the Cherokee "Trail of Tears" has acquired new length and detail, though a famous painting of the event does not appear until 1977. One suspects that by the 1970s "Trail of Tears" is a phrase which students have little excuse to forget. Too bad it was not included in the list of 141 fact-questions in the 1987 student survey.[75]

Changes in philosophies of history writing and teaching make their most assertive appearance in 1986. This edition marks a decisive turn in the expectation of writers and teachers: here they invite students into the problems of historical *method*. On what sources does history depend? (What does the "Vision of Peace" by the great Iroquois leader Daganawidah tell us about Indians?) What "study skills" should you be developing as you read this book? (What do the cartoons reproduced here mean? What bias do various sources show? What viewpoints, these quotations? Do you know how to read a time line? Can you connect the ideas in a series of paragraphs? How do you evaluate decisions made by leaders mentioned here?)

By 1986, ten pages on the "first Americans" of millennia ago continue to introduce the volume. On the assumption that human history does flow from complexes of leaders and followers, the 1986 edition introduces "Americana," consisting chiefly of forty-three profiles of leaders from Crispus Attucks (African American, first casualty of the Boston Massacre) and Tecumseh (leader of a confederacy of Indian nations in the Midwest in the early 1800s) to Coretta Scott King. The two Indian profiles include the Navaho Code-talkers of World War Two. When, in 2001, the list of biographies expands to almost a hundred, only four Indians are featured: Pocahontas, Sequoya, Sitting Bull, and Sarah Winnemucca.[76] By the 1980s multicultural narratives had multiplied. We have longer versions of the Trail of Tears and have a special box on the Black Hawk War of the 1830s. Language describing such wars has become harsher: "In the final battle, at the Bad Axe River in Wisconsin, nearly 1,000 Indians—including women and children—were slaughtered by artillery mounted on the [U.S.] steamboat *Warrior*." The student is now asked to compare the treatment of Indians by the Spanish, Mexican, and American governments, and to ponder "in what ways was the nation still undemocratic" in the Andrew Jackson era, when blacks, Indians, and women "were still treated as inferiors in law and custom" (1986:292—293).

In the 1961 volume, the "Indians" index makes references up to page 451, the midpoint of the book, but none thereafter. By 1986, however, not only have the stories increased in number, length and detail, but the "Indian Story" has acquired new modern prominence from the political work of Indians themselves in the 1970s. In 2001, episodes in the story continue into page 963. They are now far from "vanishing Americans."

SETTLEMENT, CONQUEST, OR INVASION? The Time-Life video series *How the West Was Lost* would make a cogent supplement to a section in Todd-Curti 1986 which lifts up "the concept of the Frontier." Rare is the modern American who pictures that frontier from the experience of people on its western side. If we are easterners, like this writer, we ordinarily image that frontier as moving from "us" on the Atlantic to "them" on the Pacific. Todd-Curti 1961 speaks consistently of the "conquest" of the West. To my knowledge it never uses the word "invasion" in any page up through 2001. In 1961 we read that "no organization of Indians could hope to stop the Westward Movement"—a sentence remarkable not only for its capitalizations but also for its assumption about the nature of human initiative and human hope. A 1961 blend of fact and ethics improves, however, when that volume states that "from time immemorial [the Nez Perce] land had belonged to the Indians," but then white "newcomers began to look with greedy eyes at the Nez Perce hunting grounds." (1961:440, 446). Not often in any high school histories do brave western settlers get tags in American history as "greedy." Equally rare is an idea of "frontier" as both a retreat and an advance.

More eloquently than words, the appearance in the 1972 and 1977 volumes of a famous painting of the Trail of Tears invites the student to read the expressions on the faces of men, women, and children and to remember that

Federal soldiers enforced this "Indian removable" of the 1830s. (How many teachers in the 1990s would have the nerve to compare this event to the "ethnic cleansing" of the Balkan wars of that decade? Or to the forced removal of the people of District Six?) By 1977 the text expands into a five-page account of the "westward advance" of the United States but with considerable empathetic attention to the cost of this advance to Indians. Some strong language here, describing the suffering of Indians, contrasts with the blandness which Fitzgerald found in most of the earlier texts and which, strangely enough, returns in 1986. (What happened in the meantime? Did state school boards complain that the 1977 edition was too sympathetic to Indians and too negative about the United States?) The 1977 text abounds with negative descriptions of what Americans soldiers and Indian agents did to "tame" the western Indians:

> Indian resettlement was often marked by dishonesty and brutality on the part of government officials. Sometimes Indian removal took place at gun point.

> Andrew Jackson refused to listen to missionary groups who wanted to help Indians achieve orderly, settled lives.

> [W]hite settlers in Georgia were determined to crush the Cherokees, especially after gold was discovered there.

> In the 1820s and 1830s, most Americans shared Andew Jackson's attitudes toward Indians.

> As in the past, treaties were broken, and the better lands of the reservations were reallocated to greedy settlers. Also, as in the past, each side often sought indiscriminate revenge when the other side violated its code of conduct.

> Some agents in charge of the reservations were honest and well disposed toward the Indians, but many profited from corrupt deals with traders. . . . The Indians were commonly treated with contempt or, at best, as children might be treated. (1977:239, 392, 394)

The writers do not cast all the blame for the violence of the western movement upon the Americans. "There was brutality on both sides" and indiscriminate revenge. The characters of Indian leaders varied as character in any society. In their victory over Custer at the Little Big Horn, "The Sioux and Cheyenne warriors had two outstanding leaders. One was Sitting Bull, able, honest, idealistic. The other was Crazy Horse, uncompromising, reckless, a military genius and the most honored hero of the Sioux." The same paragraph takes pains to peel some of the luster from the nineteenth-century reputation of Custer, who, prior to Little Big Horn, "attacked a peaceful Indian village on the Washita River in Oklahoma, killing unarmed women and children as well as warriors" (1977:394). In response to such events, some Americans are said to have reacted with "horror." But government restraint or rebuke of aggressive generals and local western political leaders seldom comes into play. Not until 2001 does the awful Sand Creek massacre get highlighted with a quotation from Colonel John M. Chivington, who commanded the seven hundred Colorado volunteers and who ordered the slaughter of the women, children, and elderly men of the Cheyenne camp. "It is right and honorable to use any means under God's heaven to kill Indians," say Chivington. The event stirred a Congressional investigation and calls for reforms of the government's Indian policy (2001:435). But students would have to ask a teacher, "What happened to Chivington?" to get the informed answer, "Nothing." The 2001 text neglects to mention that neither the Army nor the Congress issued an official rebuke for his behavior.

Sarah Winnemucca appears for the first time in 1977 in a description of her public campaign against "injustices to her people." In public lectures on both sides of the continent she "denounced the corruption of agents of the Bureau to Indian Affairs, and called for better distribution of lands to Indians. [Civil War] General O. O. Howard, for whom she was a scout and interpreter, declared that she 'should have a place beside the name of Pocahontas in the history of our country' " (1977:396).

Pleased as they must have been with this tribute, her fellow Paiute may have reflected ruefully that few Americans had yet sensed the sting in the white American term "our country."

The rectification of the east-to-west perspective on the "frontier" is not radical in the 2001 much-revised Todd-Curti text, but a chapter headed "The Lure of the West" offers the student a chance to consider whether Americans really had a "Manifest Destiny" to "conquer" that half of the continent. Perhaps the greatest educational gain of the post-1986 texts in this series is their posing of great historical issues that deserve reflection and evaluation by students. Twice in two pages the famous 1845 declaration of John L. O'Sullivan gets highlighted:

> Away, away with all these cobweb tissues of rights of discovery, exploration, settlement. . . . The American claim is by the right of our manifest destiny to overspread and to possess the whole of the continent which Providence [divine guidance] has given us for the development of the great experiment of liberty.

Most Americans, we read, "found debates over manifest destiny of little practical concern. Land and opportunity interested them more." But on the next page students are asked to "reconsider" the O'Sullivan quotation.

1. What indicates that the statement is an opinion [and not a fact]?
2. How does the text use facts and opinions to explain the popularity of O'Sullivan's statement? (2001:316–317)

In some post-2003 edition of Todd-Curti, the authors could renew the debate for their twenty-first-century students by adding a third question: "Are such statements still popular among Americans? In our politicians' speeches?"

Hardly popular in most school history texts is a feature concerning the Mexican War in the 2001 chapter, "American Expansionism." A sidebar on the war notes that few Americans think of it as a turning point in their nation's history, but for Mexicans the war is "a critical historical event" which they memorialize on their modern currency and in the large Mexico City memorial to their dead of 1846–1847.

> Why do the Mexican and American views differ? To answer that question, we need to look at the war through Mexican Eyes. Mexico saw the United States as a land-hungry aggressor and Zachary Taylor's troops as an invading force. Thus, most Mexicans believed that they had no choice but to defend their homeland against what they considered the "Colossus of the North" . . . even today, the Mexican War remains an important part of Mexican consciousness.[77] (2001: 326)

To see the enemies, victims, and losers of conflict with one's own country through their eyes requires moral effort and imagination. If American high school history books of the coming century ask students systematically to "see ourselves as others see us," they will be developing sober versions of patriotism. Whether state boards of education will look kindly on such texts remains to be seen.[78]

"SAVAGERY" OR "CIVILIZATION"? In a section of the 1972 and 1977 editions, "The Indians—the clash of differing cultures," the contributions of anthropology to history writing stand out with a clarity hardly equaled in any subsequent edition of Todd-Curti. In some harsh criticisms of the colonial ideologies of the Spanish, French, and especially British, we read:

> Only the British . . . regarded the Indians as a constant threat to the way of life they were trying to create in the New World. In the British colonies, the Indians were even less a part of colonial life than black colonists.

> The British believed that property could be bought and sold by an individual. They did not understand that, for the Indians, property

was held collectively by the tribe. . . . The Indians felt that they had no more right to sell the land than they had to sell the sky.

Eventually, the colonists decided that they must exterminate the Indians or give up the whole purpose for which they had journeyed to America.

Most colonists made no effort to open the doors of opportunity to the Indians. Instead, they despised and feared them. . . . Nor were the Indians able to understand why the colonists feared and hated them so intensely.

With such profound misunderstanding on both sides, a long-lasting pattern of conflict between the Indians and the settlers was laid down in colonial America.

[It was, in James Wilson's term, a profound failure of *reciprocity*.]

Benjamin Franklin offered to supervise the education of some Indian boys. He was courteously told that Indian methods of education were better suited to the boys' development. The Indians offered instead to take some white boys and teach them Indian arts and skills. The colonists declined the offer. (1972:68–71)

[At the end of this chapter, students are given the assignment:]

(a) What Indian ideas might have been useful to the British settlers?
(b) What British ideas might have been useful to the Indians? (c) Why did such an exchange of ideas become impossible? (1972:71)

Such misunderstanding, the 1977 edition notes in its expansion of this section, "was to haunt relations between the settlers and the Indians throughout America's development. In many ways it still exists today" (1977:66). Later in this volume, the famous painting of the Trail of Tears appears for the first time, plus a more explicit critique of Andrew Jackson than any student would have read in 1961. Even that earlier volume, however, makes it hard for any reader to adopt the old colonial ideology that posed Indian "savagery" against European "civilization." No, says 1961, "There was savagery on both sides." In 1977 the words are "brutality on both sides." And in both editions we read that "[U.S.] army leaders fought not only with guns but also with broken promises." No less than President Rutherford B. Hayes is then quoted as confessing to Congress in 1877: "Many, if not most, of our Indian wars have their origin in broken promises and acts of injustice on our part." This was a rare presidential confession of wrongdoing by his own government. The persistence of this quotation in multiple editions over some two decades is a tribute to the determination of writers to inject some balance and justice into accounts of war between Indians and their white American enemies. (Not all of their military enemies were white. In 1977 we read for the first time about the 1866 recruitment of four all-black regiments, or one-fifth of the war-fighting U.S. western cavalry.) Not once, to my knowledge, does any text over this period of forty years adopt Thomas Jefferson's phrase "merciless Indian savages" for any group of native Americans.[79] Teachers, as ever, have the provocation here to pose the question at the head of the Jamestown Museum film: Who were the civilized? Who, the savages?

The question comes down to a case, first mentioned in 1972, which Indians would remember as cultural aggression and contemporary white Americans would promote as cultural progress: the Indian School Movement, with its Ben Franklinesque goal of "educating" young Indians away from their native culture into Euro-American culture. Criticism of the schools expands in the next edition (1977:396) in response, no doubt, to growing public protests against culture-thievery by numerous Indian groups themselves in the United States and Canada. By 2001, there appears a pair of nineteenth-century photographs of three young men "before and after" their reeducation—hair and clothes, as well as language, thoroughly westernized. Alongside is the poignant account: "The schools were places of misery for most students. Luther Standing Bear later recalled, 'How lonesome I felt for my father and mother!' " (2001: 440).

One could capsule all these issues by asking of American history: Should Indians and settlers be seen as *innocent victims, hostile aggressors, or defenders-against-attack* in their conflicts with each other? The answer, of course, is that, at one time or another, both sides were all three. The memory of each side will always tend to selectivity. A Texas governor remembers the brave settlers who farmed the plains and endured poverty, drought, and blizzards for the sake of their progeny. The Plains Indians remember the land they lost to those settler farms. Out of the growing portrayal of these clashing points of view came many of the educational controversies of the 1975–2000 era, as "the rise of the American nation" collided with the destruction of the five hundred nations. In Todd-Curti 2001, students are peppered with questions about this conflict, implicitly prompting them to question the "standard history" which their parents may have studied.

On the whole, the Todd-Curti series deserves relatively high grades for the growing empathy of the successive authors with the dismal experience of America's Indians during the five hundred years of their contact with Europeans. Adult grumbling about "revisionism" will not make the work of high school history teachers easier in their use of these books, especially its 2001 edition. Friends of a history that only celebrates the strength, courage, and virtues of one's national ancestors could find many paragraphs in these texts to protest against: What about the cruelties of Indians to settlers and each other? Their intertribal wars? Their resistance to economic benefit as defined by a white society of increasing wealth? What's wrong with turning mostly unpopulated land into farms? What about Indian failure to live up to their own ideals of care for the earth, the buffalo, the rights of women? And then this history book: Does the text tilt toward the just interests of Indians or the just interests of white settlers? Were/are the two interests incompatible? If a teacher is brave enough to pursue these questions in a class of sixteen-year-olds, he or she may find that the line between facts and ethics, between past and present political argument, will be decidedly blurred.

INDIAN PROBLEM OR SETTLER PROBLEM? Early volumes of Todd-Curti only begin to fund this argument. Like the image of frontier, the language of "Indian problem" suffuses the 1961 descriptions of the advance of Americans across the continent (1961:39, 450). But in 1972 the phrase acquires quotation marks (1972:395), and in 1977 we read that "no minority has had to face more problems than the American Indians" (1977:720). The problems have become reciprocal. Now, in accounts of the settlement of California, the text of 1986 contends that, if the Spanish and Mexican treatment of the California Indians was "unhappy," their "fate" under American settlers was disastrous: "From 1848 to 1871, more than 50,000 California Indians died of disease, starvation, and violence" (1986:361).

By the time a history class in the late 1980s reached this point in the "conquest" of the West, heroic slants on the story have suffered some erosion, and some actors in the story have their traditional heroism rubbed thin. A crucial case is General George Armstrong Custer. In a 2001 sidebar, historian Paul F. Hutton summarizes a hundred years of conflicting popular perpectives on Custer. In the late nineteenth century, poems, plays, novels, and circuses pictured Custer as "a hero who gave his life to end Indians' domination of the American West. . . . In the 1900s, filmmakers produced nearly twenty movies before 1941 that portrayed Custer as a defender of the settlers." But midcentury historians, makers of popular culture, and Indians themselves now began publicly to tag that image as a myth:

> Novels such as Frederic Van de Water's *Glory-Hunter* depicted Custer as a brutal man. Films such as *Sitting Bull* (1954) portrayed the American Indians as courageously defending their homelands against a cruel Custer. Histories that offered the Indian perspective of the wars on the Plains further eroded the Custer myth to such a degree that in 1991 Congress passed legislation removing Custer's name from the national monument at Little Bighorn. (2001:438)

That 1991 name removal came at the behest of descendants of the coalition of Indians who killed Custer and his 215 men. Indians look back on that battle with pride in their ancestors' ability to resist. One wonders if, in their receptivity to this "revisionist history," members of Congress had some groundwork laid by high school history courses of ten and twenty years earlier. One can guess, however, that not books but *films* had been the leading edge of their conversion to a revised image of Custer. Twenty years before, perhaps as teen-agers, had they seen the film *Little Big Man*, starring Dustin Hoffman and Chief Dan George? If so, they had viewed a satirical version of George Custer: politically ambitious, militarily foolish, advocate of preventive war against In-dians, tolerant of massacre of women and children. Here in 1991 was a clear instance of historical revisionism turned into the politics of public naming.

Reparation and Indian Voice: The Beginnings of a New Justice,
1970–2000

Todd-Curti 1977 ends its section on nineteenth-century "Indian wars" in the following paragraph:

> Thus the lot of the Indians became more and more desperate. The late 1800s and early 1900s were in many ways the Indians' darkest period. Yet their vitality and spirit were reflected even then in the continuing insistence by many of them that they be regarded as separate, self-respecting peoples with worthy ways of viewing hu-man relationships, of understanding their part in the environment, and of sensing their place in the universe. (1977:396)

These words echoed national events in the late 1960s and early 1970s. In those years, Indian leaders countrywide began to take a leaf from that era's ferment of protests against racial discrimination and the Vietnam War. By the 1970s Indian population had grown to 750,000, in 2000 to about 2,000,000.

The 1969–1973 era was a turning point for augmented Indian voice in a cacophony of cries for justice throughout America. At last, says Paula Marks, reservation Indians "had experience in shaping their environments in signif-icant ways and in making themselves heard in the world beyond."[80] In 1968 Kiowa N. Scott Momaday won a Pulitzer Prize for his first novel, *House Made of Dawn*, and in 1969, lawyer-historian Vine Deloria, Jr., a Standing Rock Sioux, published *Custer Died for Your Sins: An Indian Manifesto*, "which became the thesaurus of Indian political issues of the time, as did his second book, *We Talk, You Listen*."[81] That latter title symbolized a new day of Indian response to four hundred years of contact with Euro-Americans. "It is up to us to write the final chapter of the American Indian upon this continent," Deloria exclaimed at the end of the first book; and thousands of younger Indians, in particular, took up that challenge in an unprecedented series of political demonstrations at famous locations: Plymouth, Mount Rushmore, Alcatraz, and the Bureau of Indian Affairs in Washington. Some of the first initiatives for the new activism grew out of the 1961 American Indian Chicago Conference and its breakaway National Indian Youth Council. In 1968, alongside the cascade of civil rights and anti-Vietnam protesters in the cities of America, came the American Indian Movement (AIM) which earned the title "domestic insurgency" from the FBI, "shock troops of Indian sovereignty" from their Indian supporters, and leaders in "the continuing Indian wars" from history-minded journalists.[82]

These events provoked much controversy among Indians themselves, their organizations, members of the U.S. Congress, and Americans generally, but above all they embodied a new, strident *Indian voice* in the country's public life. Speaking to the "white man" on Indians' own terms had been rare for many years. U.S. officials had long dealt with the assorted nations paternalistically as "wards" of the government, an improvement on sheer neglect and massacre but often an affront to the dignity of Indians. Long ago defeated in battles, Indian petitioners in the 1970s now refused to be bound by conventional liberal democratic institutional procedures. The courts and legislatures of the previous two hundred years had violated and voided treaties at will, setting precedents that persuaded Congress and the president in the 1950s to adopt policies called "termination" and "relocation" designed to put an end to the government's "Indian problem." One law cut Federal subsidies to at least sixty tribes. Another aimed at scattering Indians of coming generations into the workforce of the country at large. Assimilation, not respect for the cultural and political integrity of surviving Indian nations, was the watchword of this legislation.

Not to be forgotten in this history is the role of citizen "settlers," especially in the nineteenth century, in opposing efforts of Congress, the courts, and the military to secure even minimal justice for beleaguered Indians. The notorious precedents of a Custer and a Chivington casts more blame on the U.S. military than it may deserve. As Paula Marks observes of the soldiers who manned the frontier forts:

> [They] held the cultural prejudices of the era, but did not generally have a political stake in Indian-white relations and were not seeking Indian lands or Indian trace. In this sense, contrary to the stereotype of army aggression, the military in Indian Territory "usually represented the interests of the Indian more conscientiously than any-other frontier institution."[83]

Hence the accuracy of General William Tecumseh Sherman's famous definition of a "reservation": "a parcel of land, set aside for Indians, surrounded by thieves."[84]

Presidents and the Congress began to repent of this history in the late 1960s. Beset by the failures of both termination and removal, the Nixon Administration ended these policies in 1970. "[A] wide opening to win major reforms from Washington hadn't existed for forty years."[85] In response to growing organized Indian protests, Congress passed a flurry of new laws, sum-marized below, which would hardly have been possible politically without the new activism of Indian leaders and the slow erosion of ignorance among Americans generally concerning vast backlogs of injustice that needed tending to. Some measure of reparation inhered in these Congressional acts. Few were the Indian activists, however, who believed that these measures did more than scratch the surface of debts still owed their peoples. By the 1990s, any non-Indian interested in reparations to Indians had to learn a lot of history, tolerate much complexity, and face a mix of symbolic and tangible claims still accumulating in a growing Native American agenda. Public discussion of reparations for an unjust past and feasible corrective action for the future seemed to have advanced significantly by year 2000, but the advance was glacial. As the Lakota Website summarizes this past and hoped-for future:

> It took almost the entire 20th Century for Americans to begin to re-spect and appreciate the cultures and traditions of Native Ameri-cans. And American Indians have themselves become more vocal in expressing their concerns and beliefs. Perhaps the 21st Century will finally see the dawn of understanding at a deeper level.[86]

In search of understanding as well as tangible reparation, the American public, including this author, has a long way to go. A comprehensive summary of the agenda on all sides is hardly possible for ending this chapter; but two sorts of issues are worth pondering by any non-Indian American who is willing to participate in the awkward, perplexing search for justice against a background of so huge a set of injustices: (1) Can we at least begin to remember and understand the *depth* of the injustices? (2) What restorations of land and political independence should the United States accord Indian peoples in a country and world of growing interdependence?

Wounded Knee

There may be no better place to begin. The Trail of Tears, the Sand Creek Massacre, and the unsuccessful flight of the Nez Perce to Canada would all do for study of events that "peak" in the enduring Indian memory. But Wounded Knee has its own depth of tragic sorrow in that memory. By the late twentieth century sharers of that sorrow had begun to include many Americans who had read the high school history books, seen the Ken Burns documentaries, and read the post-1965 Indian authors. Of all entry points to Indian resentments of the United States, Wounded Knee comes as close as any to a peak of the mountainous range of resentments. A peak image haunted the memory of Black Elk, an observer at age twenty-seven from from eight miles distant. He lived on the Pine Ridge Reservation of South Dakota. Said he to John Neihardt in 1930:

When I look back from this high hill of my old age, I can still see
the butchered women and children lying heaped and scattered all
along the crooked gulch as plain as when I saw them with eyes still
young. And I can see that something else died there in the bloody
mud, and was buried in the blizzard. A people's dream died there. It
was a beautiful dream . . . the nation's hoop is broken and scattered.
There is no center any longer, and the sacred tree is dead.[87]

Of all the *symbolic* embodiments of Indian resentments over five hundred
years of devastation, no event still stuck in Black Elk's memory more stubbornly than this. His successors are many. In the 1995 Ken Burns documentary, *The West,* one young Lakota remarks sadly, "I think of Wounded Knee
every day."

The outlines of the event are familiar: It was the last[88] military engagement
of the U.S. Army with Indians. The army's Seventh Cavalry, the reconstituted
Custer division, was eager for revenge—at least according to a December 10,
1890, article in the *Nebraska State Journal.*[89] Without an attempt here to re-
hearse the details of a story which is, or should be, well known, the meaning
of Wounded Knee to Indians can be summarized by two other quotations from
survivors quoted at the end of the Dee Brown book of 1970. A best seller, this
was the book that enabled millions of non-Indian American readers to hear, at
last, "Indian voices [that] sear the heart":[90] The first comes from Red Cloud,
alluding to the rallying of 350 men, women, and children for performing the
Ghost Dance, with its promise of a miraculous, messianic deliverer who would
finally come to the aid of beleaguered remnants of the Lakotas:

> The people . . . snatched at the hope. They screamed like crazy men
> for Him for mercy. They caught at the promise they heard He had
> made.
>
> The white men were frightened and called for soldiers. We had
> begged for life, and the white men thought we wanted theirs. We
> heard that soldiers were coming. We did not fear. We hoped that we
> could tell them our troubles and get help. A white man said the sol-
> diers meant to kill us. We did not believe it, but some were fright-
> ened and ran away to the Badlands.

The second, Louise Weasel Bear, took pains to concede that not all white people
sought revenge on Indians:

> We tried to run, but they shot us like we were a buffalo. I know that
> there are some good white people, but the soldiers must be mean to
> shoot children and women. Indian soldiers would not do that to
> white children.[91]

White Americans in 1890 knew many stories, some true, of enraged Indians who did kill women and children; but U.S. Army rules of engagement, then and now, forbade such indiscriminate killing, and at least a few of the white soldiers that day remembered the rules.

> One Lakota survivor reported that after one soldier, shouting "remember Custer," shot an elderly woman and . . . a child, one of his fellow soldiers shot him. Similarly, not all of Lieutenant William Calley's men participated in murdering the 347 Vietnamese . . . in the My Lai massacre.[92]

Memory abstracts and simplifies events. Artists, historians, filmmakers and teachers do so out of their need for specific persons and notable incidents for highlighting complexities of the past. Most of all, leaders of aggrieved peoples need particular events for interpreting their grievances to other leaders who have some powers of redress. As Little Bighorn signifies Indian courage and military prowess, Wounded Knee stands for cumulative, colossal, multi-century injustices. Like the proverbial iceberg tip, peak events stand for larger stories than can appear above any particular surface of private or public awareness. When the Lakotas and their allies pressed Congress for taking Custer's name off the Little Bighorn battlefield, they were partners to the Germans, East Europeans, and South Africans who changed the names of places, streets, and buildings in the wake of regime changes in their countries. In effect, the new leadership revised the public silhouette of the mountain ranges of the publicly recollected past.

In Paul M. Robertson's conclusion to his article on Wounded Knee in the 1996 edition of *Encyclopedia of North American Indians*, he writes: "Some people retain their humanity. Nations need to retain theirs, too. The Lakota people have asked the United States for an apology, but to date none has been forthcoming."[93] This is mostly but not quite true. Regret and anger, public and private, did ensue among some Americans soon after December 29, 1890, and in the early 1990s the U.S. Congress would "acknowledge the historic significance of the Massacre at Wounded Knee [and] express its deep regret to the Sioux people."[94] Immediately after the 1890 event, Army General Nelson Miles "was outraged by the deaths of women and children and he removed Colonel [John] Forsyth from command." But subsequently the secretary of war overruled the general, and Forsyth was promoted. Then Congress decided to award its Medal of Honor to three officers and fifteen enlisted men for their "heroism" in the Wounded Knee "battle." No other single engagement in the history of the U.S. Army ever moved Congress to award this many Medals of Honor. Lakota leaders in the 1990s were bent on revocation of the medals, and in response, in 1995, a few U.S. Congress members proposed a bill for a Wounded Knee memorial and funded it to some $5 million. By 2003 Indian leaders themselves had yet to agree on the appropriate nature of such a memorial, but they were agreed that the site itself should be preserved and administered by themselves.

Meantime, in 1973, Wounded Knee had burst into national and world headlines with the occupation of the town and Pine Ridge Reservation for seventy-one days by members of the American Indian Movement under the leadership of Russell Means. Hopes for land recovery and protests against policies of the Bureau of Indian Affairs had prompted local Pine Ridge residents to ask for AIM help. Behind the event lay the accumulated rage of the Lakotas at the racial prejudice and violence they encountered in nearby white towns like Gordon, Nebraska, where they were "cheated, harassed, disrespected" by white citizens and "waited on by rednecks who hated Indians and who probably hated themselves because they made their living from the very Indians they despised." In the wake of a suspected murder, a rally of Indian demonstrators flooded Gordon in early 1972 with the loud message: "We're tired of being cursed on the streets, tired of being beaten in the alleys." A year later, from the courage engendered in that event, some three hundred Lakotas further vented their rage by occupying the Trading Post at Wounded Knee, "a holy place of bitter memories and trashy souvenirs."[95]

The armed occupation was soon followed by a seven-week siege by Pentagon-assisted U.S. Marshals, FBI agents, and pro-BIA Lakota police. Indian deaths in the standoff—perhaps a dozen—were only a prelude to subsequent murders of some sixty local people over the next three years, largely by BIA police and a self-appointed vigilante group called Guardians of the Oglala Nation. During these years hundreds of FBI supervisors had stood by doing nothing to contain intratribal violence;[96] but in June 1975, when two FBI agents died in a firefight near the village of Oglala, two AIM members were tried in Cedar Rapids, Iowa, for the murders. That court, through an all-white jury, acquitted the defendants on grounds of self-defense, "given the FBI's performance on the reservation since 1973."[97]

The Wounded Knee occupation of 1973 will always be an event subject to great controversy inside and outside local and national Indian communities. Smith and Warrior say the event "marked the high tide of the most remarkable period of activism carried out by Indians in the twentieth century."[98] The movement soon faded amid a welter of internal conflicts and government legal prosecutions, but for Indians the symbolism of Wounded Knee would not fade. In 1998 the Oglala Sioux Tribal Council voted 15 to 1 to declare the day the occupation began, February 27, an annual "Day of Liberation and Human Rights for the Lakota People but as well for all Indigenous people in both Americas."[99] Without doubt the 1973 event publicized Indian grievances to a generation of Americans who were either celebrators of, and fed up with, the demonstrators of the 1960s.

Among modern Indian movements, none exceeded in comprehensiveness AIM's agenda: "economic independence and control over natural resources, the political autonomy of tribal reservations, the revitalization of traditional culture and spirituality, and the education of young Indian children. The latter often takes the form of challenges to the public school system to employ more native teachers, abandon stereotypical 'Indian' portrayals in American history courses, and consult with elders over curriculum issues."[100] No movement has been more adept at staging symbolic events that have challenged Americans to give up images of Indians as silent, passive victims of history. Among the protests it helped to organized were the 1969–1971 occupations of Alcatraz Island, Ellis Island, the *Mayflower* replica in Plymouth, BIA headquarters, and the Black Hills. The results of this "guerrilla theater" were debatable among friends and enemies of AIM. In retrospect both can probably agree with Smith and Warrior that the occupations "illustrated both the vast possibilities and the stark limitaiton of a politics based on symbols and media." But their deeper assessment is that these events ushered in

> a season of struggle for power and respect, for treaty rights and per-
> sonal validation, for economic and political justice. Most impor-
> tantly, it gave thousands of Indians a *raison d'etre*, an opportunity to
> be important in their own communities.[101]

To many readers of newspapers, this upsurge of events may have re-called incidents in the history more numerous in their injustices than even the Trail of Tears and Wounded Knee were likely to signify. In some of the demonstrations Indian capacity for irony and humor went on display—as when the occupiers of Alcatraz offered to buy it for glass beads and red cloth worth $24, in imitation of the Dutch "purchase" of "a similar island."[102] But the urban and reservation Indian occupiers of Alcatraz were serious about turning that American version of Robben Island into an educational and cultural center. Like thousands of their fellow Indians, they were determined to keep Americans aware that, in spite of devastation, "Indians are still here," that they intend always to be here. If the overall achievements of the demonstrations were ambiguous or sometimes negative, "the occupiers, representing numerous tribes, successfully brought Native American issues to the forefront of American politics during a highly volatile time in American history."[103]

In June 2004, the most forthright official apology ever offered to American Indians—for "a long history of official depredations"—emerged from a committee of the United States Senate. As of November 2004 the Senate had not voted on the resolution, which decries broken treaties, extermination, forced removals, and destruction of sacred places. As the *New York Times* comments, underlying this gesture, in part, is the new electoral power of Native Americans. Indian reaction has ranged from "words on paper" to "a good first step."[104] The delayed vote, however, suggests that this text may suffer the fate of the apology for slavery so stubbornly submitted since 1989 by Congressman John Conyers.

What Reparations for Native Americans?

With glacial slowness but increasing attentiveness during the past thirty years, American political institutions have been responding to Indian claims for redress of their grievances. Steps backward have vied with steps ahead. For Indians to be declared eligible for U.S. citizenship in 1924 seems, in retrospect, a strangely belated nod of a Federal government toward "first peoples" in our midst. Likewise, for the majority of employees of the BIA at last to be Indian in 1975 seems just as belated.

On the side of retrogression, the "termination" and "relocation" policies of the 1950s echoed old political hopes that Indians would simply dissolve into the American mix or go their own way outside any attention from Washington. But the past, littered with broken treaties and unfulfilled legal commitments, would not go away. In 1970 the Nixon Administration launched a new policy of "self-determination without termination," that is, a new degree of self-government in reservations along with continued Federal assistance for economic development. Angered by the tactics of AIM, neither Nixon nor the Congress implemented this new policy, and Indian organizations for redress continued to multiply. To say that the modern record of redress is "checkered" is therefore an understatement; but one might exploit the metaphor to say that, in concrete ways, the number of red squares on the American "justice" board has visibly increased over the past several decades. They are likely to increase more in the century to come.

Indian claims for tangible redress have long clustered around two daunting issues: *sovereignty* and *land*. A tangle of philosophic, political, ethical, and practical questions besets these two, and citizens like this writer are not likely to offer much persuasive guidance to lawmakers who are newly concerned to weave some approximate new threads of justice from the tangle. But like other pages in this book, one can celebrate certain acts of justice that official and unofficial American institutions have managed to undertake in recent years. These actions offer hope that the twenty-first century really will see not only a dawn of new understanding between Indians and other Americans but also some sunlight of new tangible justice.

Like the question of whether Indians want to be called "Americans," future inquiries into that new justice will be afflicted by ambiguity, clashes of interests, and ponderings of acceptable compromise. Most democratic politicians know that one test of a just compromise is whether it leaves all sides both losing and gaining. That was the gist of T. V. Smith's classic definition: "Compromise is the process . . . whereby each party to a conflict gives up something dear, but not invaluable, in order to get something which is truly invaluable."[105]

Smith goes on to say that compromise usually involves give and take of multiple principles and interests. The list of local and federal concessions to Indian interests, from 1970 to 2000, is long, mixed, and controversial but more often akin to reparations than at any time since 1700. Congress has often taken the lead in these measures, but so have local courts and citizen negotiations.[106] Among prominent recent congressional legislative illustrations are the following:

- In the 1980s, in northern New Mexico, the Taos Pueblo won back its sacred site, the Blue Lake, 48,000 acres of a national park.
- Indians of Maine, who claimed that more than half of the state had been taken illegally from them, went to the federal courts, resulting in Congressional awards of $81.5 million and the right to future purchase up to 300,000 acres of Maine land.[107]
- The 1968 Civil Rights Act accorded to reservation Indians "full civil rights to individuals living under tribal law," reversing a 1896 U.S. Supreme Court decision.[108]
- In 1977–1978, Congress passed some fifty laws "to correct or settle long-standing issues with many tribes over water rights, fishing rights, land acquisition—both compensation and returning some land to certain tribes."
- The 1978 Indian Child Welfare Act qualified Indians, for the first time, to become foster and adoptive parents and authorized family service programs for reservations.
- The 1978 American Indian Religious Freedom Act declared certain religious rituals, along with the use of peyote, to be legal, a right upheld by the U.S. Supreme Court in 1991.
- In 1980 the Supreme Court ordered interest to be paid the Lakotas on the fund offered in 1877 for U.S. appropriation of the Black Hills. The Lakota have refused this payment. "They want the Black Hills returned."
- The 1989 National Museum of the American Indian Act ordered the Smithsonian Institution to return all its Indian remains to any tribe requesting them.
- Building on a 1935 BIA effort, the Indian Arts and Crafts Act of 1990 guaranteed trademarks and other proofs of authenticity of the work of tribal artists.
- A new Museum of the American Indian opened in September 2004 on the Washington Mall, "front yard" of America, occupying one of its last available sites, in anticipation, one hopes, of a nearby companion museum to African Americans.
- Finally and momentously, in 1988 Congress passed the Indian Gam-

ing Regulatory Act, which opened the legal door to casinos on Indian reservations.

The latter law was momentous, for, fourteen years later, 290 Indian casinos in twenty-eight states would dot the land and would report a 2002 revenue of $12.7 billion. Of all forms of reparations to Native American nations, this has now become the best known and most contentious inside and outside of the tribal world. The development is replete with the irony that a taste in white culture for gambling can now feed the wealth of some Indians at levels little imagined by anyone several decades ago. Among the casinos now operating or planned in upstate New York alone are that of the Oneidas in Syracuse, the Senecas in Niagara Fall, the Mohawks in the northern Adirondacks, and the Mohawks and Stockbridge-Munsees in the southern Catskills.

It seems certain, then, that this resident of Columbia County can soon add to his contemplation of the Catskill range an image of Mohicans, long exiled in Wisconsin, at last claiming compensation for lost New York land in a casino on one of those southern hills. They will be only one of at least 204 tribes in the gambling business.[109] Is it all a "scandal"[110] or the ultimate massive reparation? Is it just for surrounding communities and states to have no tax income from casinos for their public services like fire and police protection? Even if casinos provide jobs to many non-Indians and make large purchases from non-Indian suppliers, is it just that no casino profit can be taxed locally?[111] Inside and outside the Native American world, ethical and legal answers to these questions are fraught with the irony of new forms of justice that yield new injustices. With sovereign control of who qualifies for tribal membership and how casino profits are to be distributed, some tribal governments share profits with casino-less poorer fellow Indians in places like Pine Ridge, while others maximize personal incomes by mandating arbitrary limits on who can qualify as a "real" member of the tribe.

On the whole casino question, the conclusion of Eleanor Randolph seems fair and accurate:

> The casinos have been a boon to many Indians, lifting a number of communities from the abject poverty of 40 years ago to the heady power and wealth they enjoy today. The tribes and the states have to make certain this new wealth does not breed new resentments among poorer Indians and neighbors living near these golden casinos. Such disparities do not provide a healthy future for either community.[112]

As this is written, one other justice-related history competes with casinos for notoriety: the legal suit (*Cobell v. United States*) of the National Congress of American Indians, charging that the Bureau of Indian Affairs has, since 1887, so mismanaged and squandered its Indian Trust Fund that a fund that should be $137.2 billion has now shrunk to $3.2 billion. The sympathetic judge in the case, Royce C. Lamberth, said in September 2002 that "he has never seen greater government incompetence than the department [of the Interior] has displayed in administering the Indians' money," accumulated for them from reservation oil, mineral, timber, and grazing leases.[113]

Given all the history so partially summarized in these pages, only an audacious moralist would pretend to explore this agenda forest without the fear that he or she will trip in dense thickets of rights and wrongs. The trail that has led to the current state of "Indian affairs" in the United States is daunting for moralists, lawyers, politicians, and citizens. Like other attempts of this society to recover from its collective evils, this one will long continue to be fraught with ambiguity, simmering resentments, resistance to memory, stubborn defenses of vested interests, and limits of human ability to do anything adequate to compensate for death and other tragedy.

Most complex of all will be continued Indian-Federal debates over the interlocking issues of sovereignty and land rights, and ambivalence among Indians themselves over their independence from, and dependence on, the American national government. As one historian said in 1984, "It is impossible to expand [federal] trust responsibility without also expanding paternalism, however devoutly the Indians and their spokesmen in government wish it were not so."[114] Without my claiming comprehensive wisdom about these issues but in order to be concrete, let me conclude by pondering the longstanding dispute of the Cayuga Nation with the State of New York. Let the reflections of this chapter come to focus in a case still confronting the state and the people of my home state.

The Cayuga Case: Lands that Once Were and Lands that Are

> Cayuga is the biggest of New York's Finger Lakes, a 40-mile-long glacial gash through a rolling landscape of forests and fields. Today the lake is lined with postcard villages and vacation homes. Two hundred years ago it was Indian country. Some people say it still is.[115]

Historian Daniel Usner of Cornell University observes that "if people understood the legal foundation of this [case], they would better understand why these claims exist and why they need to be settled."[116] If the conflict is ever settled, however, more than law will have to be accounted for. Like the larger national picture, this one is an intersection of history, law, economics, ethics, politics and political philosophy.

In the early 1790s the new U.S. Congress mandated that all treaties between individual persons and state governments must be approved by Congress in order to be considered legal. The backgound of this mandate was the long experience of Indians and their colonial allies with their colonial enemies—especially land-hungry colonists who had the habit of making treaties or simply taking possession of Indian land without benefit of any government's permission. Diverse interests and political powers competed in these transactions. In 1789, New York State had invited the Cayugas, then scattered after their alliance with the British in the Revolutionary War, to occupy a reservation of 64,027 acres in the Finger Lakes region. But in 1795 and again in 1807, the state made treaties for the sale of all that land to itself, never asking the U.S. Congress to ratify the transaction.

At stake was a political argument which would take many forms in the future of the country: When is local authority primary, when not? In 1980, citing this history of illegality, the Cayugas, one of the famous six Iroquois nations, sued the State of New York for compensation and for the right to repossess land around the lake that bears their name. By that year the Cayugas had a formal tribal membership of 450; citizens who owned land around Lake Cayuga numbered 7000. For the Cayugas, numbers did not count: Did not Americans always say that "the law is the law"?

The 1980 case issued in a 1984 decision of a federal court-appointed panel that the Cayugas should have some eight thousand acres of publicly owned land awarded them along with a compensation of $15 million. No private owners occupied this land. But, as reported by *New York Times* columnist Bob Herbert in 2002, "The bitterness provoked by that proposal was stunning."

> Local residents threatened to use guns to keep Indians off the land. People complained at public meetings that they did not want their children going to school with "dirty" Indians suffering from dysentery and infected with lice.
>
> The opposition was led by a retired Tufts University professor named Wisner Kline, who said, "People have no conception of how frightening it was fighting them when the country was new." Pointing to a visitor, he remarked, "It was nothing for them to pick up someone like you, and put you in a fire, slowly, a couple of inches at a time until you'd be dead."[117]

Against these gross prejudicial objections, a more radical court decision was to come. In 1994 District Court Judge Neal McCurn ruled that the Cayugas had every right to claim all 64,015 acres which New York State had illegally bought from them. In 1999 a mediator proposed a settlement of $125 million, which the Cayugas accepted and the state refused. Federal courts contined to decide in favor of the Indians, and in October 2002 Judge McCurn ordered the state to pay the Cayugas $247.9 million, "which is believed to be the largest resolution of an Indian land claim in U.S. history."[118]

As of mid-2003, it was also one of the longest-running unsettled court cases in New York history. Central to the continuing political struggle and less overtly racist than Professor Kline but as politically determined, is an organization called Upstate Citizens for Equality, defined in their website as

> composed of concerned citizens that stand against discrimination, and supports the continuation of free enterprise and equality in our communities. UCE was formed in early 1999 to serve as an active and prominent voice for 14,000 residents, landowners, and taxpaying citizens who reside in Seneca and Cayuga counties and are affected by the Cayuga Indian Land Claim.[119]

The multiple interests, clearly tagged here, are an accumulation of policies from a century of federal government relations to Indians: reservations for their exclusive residence, self-government with ambiguous relation to U.S. law, rights guaranteed by the U.S. Constitution plus other rights guaranteed only to Indians, sales-tax-free businesses for selling gasoline and tobacco, and freedom from taxation of reservation property. Not all of these policies are focal in the court case, but they are focal for the politics now surrounding it and many another such dispute across the country. "Citizen" anxiety, resentment, and hostility vie with Indians' ancient memory, treaties, and passion for redress.

Persuasive issues of justice arise on all sides of the dispute, and happy will be the future of Cayugas and other residents of New York if together they—we—arrive at compromises which defuse remnants of the racist violent past that haunts us all. Living together—often as the alternative to dying together—is the great argument for many a political compromise, a truth that Indian leaders themselves have advanced in the public debate of their case. Indian culture has embraced that argument from ages back. Illustrative are the comments of Clint Hightown, official spokesman for the Cayugas in the NPR interview quoted above. Firm claims combine here with equally firm awareness that not everything one may want can be politically secured over against the contrary wants of neighbors:

> HIGHTOWN   This is our homeland. This lake was the center of our territory. You know, I might not live here, but this is still home. . . . If the state of New York did not violate federal law our people would still be here. . . . We've had injustice for 200 years. Now we seek justice.
>
> [Concerning the 2002 court award of $247 million]: It's not what we had asked for. It's not what we feel we're rightfully entitled for. And it's not the return of the 64,000 acres of land that we sought in our lawsuit, either, but it's $247 million to go out and buy land from willing sellers and it'll give us a chance to reestablish our people upon our home lands.
>
> REPORTER JON MILLER   It's unlikely that Congress will see fit to dismantle a system put in place by the Founding Fathers, and in which so

much history, emotion and money are so tightly knotted together. Cayuga spokesman Clint Hightown says that's something the people here
had better get used to.

HIGHTOWN   You know, I do tell them, you know, every chance I get, is
that one day we will be coming back and we will be neighbors, and so
hopefully we can mend those—you know, if there's hard feeling toward
one another. Because one day we're going to have to get along and live
together within the same country.[120]

Martin Luther King, Jr., and Nelson Mandela would not have put it better!
On the other side of the legal-economic-political "knot," UCE chair Connie
Talcott summarized its view:

We have said over and over, everyone's welcome to live here. The
important thing is every one live under the same laws, pay the same
taxes, have the same rights and responsibilities. There is no problem
with the Cayugas coming here. It's all the special privileges that they
are given by the ambiguous federal Indian policy that is the problem.[121]

Retired schoolteacher Joyce Martin echoes the same view: She is willing to sell
her home for a fair price, but "people around here would be very upset because
they think that [Indians] should be paying property taxes."[122]

As this is written, the governor and legislature of the State of New York
remain adamant about their own version of justice in the dispute. No one
knows if even a U.S. Supreme Court decision would alter the balance of political forces or prevent violence around the issue in upstate New York. On some
day in 2005, will the Cayugas celebrate their recovery of their home around
the lake named for them? Will neighbors there admit grudgingly that there is
justice and injustice enough on all sides to permit all to acknowledge that
compromise is better than a new Indian War? Political leadership, not time,
will tell. Meantime, here at the end of this chapter is one citizen's reflection
on the tensions which somehow must be subject to compromise. If these
tensions are to be respected, each side will have to experience some give and
some take.

Law and Justice

One hundred and twenty-six years before the Cayugas entered their suit in the
District Court of central New York State, a Mohican sachem, John W. Quinney,
also a Presbyterian minister, addressed a July 4, 1854, gathering of New Yorkers
in a speech that injected some grim memories into that ordinarily noisy, patriotic occasion. For years Quinney had been an effective mediator between the
interests of his tribe—now called the Munsee-Stockbridge Indians—and the

well established white settlements of the region, many of whom were revolting against the rents charged them by landowners. Debate over abolition of slavery was in the air, and "bleeding Kansas" was in the headlines. Toward the end of his candid speech, Quinney lamented that, amid growing concern for black slaves, "the Indian is left to rot and die before the humanities of the model REPUBLIC!" He reserved his most blistering language for how "law" had become the undoing of his people. Summarizing two centuries of Mohican history, he exclaimed:

> Nothing that deserved the name of purchase, was ever made. From various causes, they were induced to abandon their territory at intervals, and retire further to the inland. . . . To legalize and confirm titles thus acquired, laws and edicts were subsequently passed, and these laws [as] we said then, and are now called justice! Oh! What a mockery! to confound justice with law.[123]

One irony in the Cayuga 1980 case is its central emphasis on two-centuries-old U.S. law. Like most litigation-prone Americans, both sides were pitting the law of one political entity, New York State, against that of another, the United States Congress. Over the two centuries, however, Congress and the Supreme Court have both shared responsibility for "legal" seizures of Indian land in defiance of Indian interests. Occasionally appeal to federal law over state law has played a historic role in the back-and-forth stumble of Indians toward justice. But Quinney was right: Justice and law are not the same. One has to surmise that eventually Indians, the residents of Cayuga County, legislators, and judges will have to cede some authority to concepts of justice not yet embodied in law past or present. Conflict over ideas of justice already agitates both sides of the debate, as it did the civil rights debate of the 1960s. Eventually, one predicts, memories of injustice and new clarities about justice will shape the debate more than legalistic appeals to statute. That was Quinney's hope: "For myself and for my tribe, I ask for justice. I believe that it will sooner or later occur. And may the Great and Good Spirit enable me to die in hope."

Land vs. Money

Native Americans have usually maintained that land cannot conceivably be alienated from them by payments of money. "Our land is everything to us. . . . It is the only place where Cheyennes remember the same things together."[124] Yet time and again they have sold land to Europeans whose idea of private property conflicted with that deep root of Indian culture. This compromise on the Indian side has been more profound than most Americans, with their ideology that money can buy almost anything, tend to perceive. Doubtless there are values for even the most ardent capitalists that for them are not for sale, but land is seldom one of them. The Cayugas have a right to understanding, on the part of their neighbors, that a land-for-money transaction is already a compromise on the Indian side and has always been so.

Actual vs. Symbolic Possession

Indian claims to homelands sometimes sound absolutist. But that is not the tone of Clint Hightown. The statement, "This is Cayuga country," means something to him deeper than "I have a house on Cayuga Lake" is likely to mean to any current resident. So far the Cayugas are not asking for the horseshoe upper rim of the lake to be turned into a reservation for their exclusive occupation. The suspicious among the homeowners may be right that the Cayugas will only be satisfied with such eventual exclusiveness. But that way lies a revival of old American settler belief that you cannot trust the word of an Indian. Trust us, the Cayugas seem to be saying: We will buy your land according to the American real estate market, but we want that land, not just that lake, to bear our name.

Identity, Sovereignty, and American Interdependence

Two-thirds of the two million self-designated Indians in the Untied States live and work outside of reservations. The U.S. government recognizes at least 319 of the nations, and some 120 more are now applying for recognition, which carries economic and political benefits to which "citizens for equality" have great objection. The taxation question for them is as real as it is for any neighbor to national parks, churches, and other untaxed organizations spread across America. Ambiguities and inconsistences abound on all sides of this issue. Members of UCE are not likely to campaign for church property taxation, and reservation Indians are not likely to dispense with neighboring town help, in emergencies, from police and fire departments. Claims of "sovereignty"among leaders of many tribes seems firm and uncompromisable, but the Cayugas, at least, are saying through Clint Hightown that they hope "to get along and live together within the same community." This is not the language of isolation and unmitigated sovereignty. Martin Luther King, Jr., in the 1960s and Rodney King in 1992 said as much about the place of African Americans alongside all other Americans. To be sure, on the matter of an "American" identity, Indian attitudes can be radically diverse. In 1924 Cayuga chiefs advised their constituents not to accept the new privilege of citizenship in the United States offered by Congress in that year. Nonetheless a combination of "separate yet connected" with "similar and different" marks the Indian side of this case. Few seem ready to jettison the "American" side of their identity in favor of complete identification with the "Native" side. If they could completely dissociate themselves from all the rest of America, would they do so? Some would say "yes," but others would not.

We know from the 1950s that a majority of the U.S. Congress was ready to consider all Indians as absorbable into the general population and to cut reservations loose from federal economic aid. Then Congress and the president discovered that the connections could not be so easily cut: Were treaties, lingering injustice, racism, and stark poverty to be no longer of any concern to the government? If so, new injustices would surely arise. Compromise between being "wards" of the Federal government and independent "sovereignty" had to be struck. This country is still trying to discover what that compromise ought to be. The Cayuga case is part of this great struggle.

A Conclusion: Remembering a Terror-filled Past and Letting Go

Opposition leader Professor Wisner Kline rang the changes on old images of the "savage" Indian when he reminded an audience of how cruel Indians could be. Had Cayugas been at the meeting, they could have retorted with like instances of American cruelties. From such a meeting, no overture to compromise and life together around Lake Cayuga would have resulted. As so often illustrated in these pages, there are two ways down which a body of humans can go after its members have experienced gross damages from each other: They can retreat into memory as into a prison, nourish mutual hostility, and make plans for reprisal. Or, having revisited the memory, they can search together for keys that unlock the prison. They can covenant not to repeat the past and can commit mutually to finding new ways of living together.

After some confessions of damage done and damage suffered, after an offer of some restoration to historic victims, a people may have begun to grasp those keys. Some would call it a conjunction of repentance and forgiveness, a combination of honor to each other's negative memories with new covenants of law, balances of interest, and mutual determination not to repeat the old cruelties. The Cayuga Indians and troubled residents around Cayuga Lake seem already on their way down a path toward such a new, sobered relation to each other. Only if they are so, will their old memories and present fears cease to feed the evil spirits of civic revenge.

All these recent events in recent knitting up of the ravel'd sleeves of Native Americans' relation to the rest of America came to a certain symbolic focus on September 21, 2004, as the new National Museum of the American Indian was dedicated on the Mall in Washington. Native Americans numbering almost 25,000 marched to the museum in full traditional dress. The building occupies the last empty space on the perimeter of the Mall. It will be there now as a monument to the Indian certainty: "We are still here." But more: they are here with a new dignity. With tears streaming down her face, Pamela Best Minick of the Cherokee and Pottawattamie tribes put it best when she said to a reporter: "It's more than all the colors and feathers, it's about coming home the way it should have been a long time ago. To come back in the same way and have people not laugh but respect you—it shows we're come full circle."[125]

5

Being Human While Being American

Agenda for the American Future

A patriot must always be ready to defend his country against its government.

—Edward Abbey[1]

The other is the limit beyond which our ambitions must not run and the boundary beyond which our life must not expand.

—Reinhold Niebuhr[2]

I love my country too much to be a nationalist.

—Albert Camus[3]

This book could plausibly end with the author's list of unjustified damages which the United States has inflicted on other peoples over the past two hundred years. The list could be balanced with a list of the benefits which this nation has bestowed on others. Underneath any such listing would be assumptions about measures of justice and injustice, benefit and harms, which constitute elements of an international political ethic. That large task has been and will be undertaken by many thinkers worldwide. From them we all should expect some systematic intellectual help toward the making of a future global world safe for the blessings and safe from the curses which peoples of earth now have unprecedented power to deliver to each other's shores.

This book has focused on the positive steps which citizens in three countries have taken to acknowledge and remedy a collective past which has belatedly evoked their shame and gestures of repentance. The best world would be one in which humans have no sins to repent of; the worst, one in which they never repent. Like forgiveness, the human potential for belated acknowledgment is a hopeful virtue, whose exercise is at its most constructive when it portends a new level of commitment to a more humane future. There is encouragement, for example, in the contemporary phenomenon which Elazar Barkan calls "a new threshold of morality in international politics": victims in numerous locales, entering into intense negotiations with perpetrators and their descendants over how to remember and how to remedy the atrocious past.[4]

An Intra-Military Postwar Repentance: My Lai

Disentangling justified, unjustified, heroic, and atrocious actions on the American side of its wars remains a permanent challenge to this country's historians, public leaders, and citizens. We Americans have scarcely begun a morally mature public debate on the assaults of terrorists on us on 9/11 nor on our assault on Iraq in 2003. But we are almost forty years into debate over the Vietnam War, which, as this is written, has entered the presidential campaign debates of 2004.

Civilians like myself must not forget that it was to the soldiers and veterans that we owe some of our most convincing persuasion that Vietnam was the wrong war for Americans to have undertaken. Whether or not we shall ever have public consensus on reasons for the war, soldiers know that much wrong was committed by all sides. Some explicit governmental testimony to that knowledge came on March 6, 1998, in a ceremony undertaken by the Pentagon in one of the quasi-sacred sites of our national capital: the Vietnam Memorial. There, in antithesis to the Medals of Honor granted members of the Seventh Cavalry for "heroism" at Wounded Knee in 1890, the Pentagon awarded its Soldier's Medal to three helicopter crewmen who, in 1968, turned their guns against their fellow soldiers to halt the slaughter of My Lai villagers.

Almost every critic of the war remembers My Lai as a symbol of American military power run amok[5] in the heat of war. The West Point curriculum now includes analysis of this incident as a warning to future army officers against violating the "rules of engagement." In May 2004, Lt. Col. Dave Grossman, a West Point instructor, said that the army now requires annual troop review of these rules, which include definitions of orders not to be obeyed. "It's the first time in history when an army is instructed in disobedience of orders." (Not true. The Bundeswehr of Germany has had such instruction for over forty years.)[6] In retrospect, the killing of more than two hundred villagers in this assault was to many, inside and outside of the U.S. Army, a gross violation of the "just war" principle of discrimination between military and civilian targets.

Long ago, the present government of Vietnam erected a monument in My Lai to memorialize these deaths and to serve the Communist view that Americans were the perpetrators of numerous such atrocities. To my knowledge there are no monuments in modern Vietnam to atrocities committed by its own soldiers. The Pentagon citations to three helicopter crew members read:

> For heroism above and beyond the call of duty on 16 March
> 1968, saving the lives of at least 10 Vietnamese civilians during the
> unlawful massacre of noncombatants by American forces at My Lai,
> Quang Ngai province, South Vietnam, Warrant Officer Thompson
> landed his helicopter in the line of fire between fleeing Vietnamese
> civilians and pursuing ground troops to prevent their murder. He
> then personally confronted the leader of the American ground
> troops [Lt. William Calley] and was prepared to open fire on those
> American troops should they fire upon the civilians.

The tributes further describe how Thompson and his two fellows—Specialists Lawrence Colborn and Glenn U. Andreotta—coaxed villagers out of bunkers and assisted them to flee. In a pile of ditched dead bodies they found a wounded child, whom they flew to a hospital in Quang Ngai. Together, the citations concluded, the behavior of each exemplified "the highest standards of personal courage and ethical conduct, reflecting distinct credit on himself and the United States Army."[7] The restoration of "standards" to the instigation and conduct of war remains atop the fearsome agenda of modern global society.

The Soldiers Medal event is rare in the annals of countries. But, as Kenneth Boulding once remarked, "If it has happened once, it must be possible."[8] One could skeptically assess the ceremony as part of a Pentagon program for keeping American troops from getting involved ever again in a war with Vietnam-like ambiguities. One could also note that, given the court-martial of Lt. William Calley, his short imprisonment, and the clean bill of military health granted almost every one of his superiors, explicit repentance for My Lai was superficial among high-level military and political leaders. A new generation of leaders now realizes how damaging to American interests is even one My Lai. In May 2004 some were ruefully remembering My Lai as they grappled with the damages to the United States in the abuse of prisoners in Iraq.

As far as we know, no one present that March day in Washington voiced the excusing view, "Atrocities by the Vietcong were greater. And what about all those massacres by the Russians in Chechnya, the Hutus in Rwanda, the Khmer Rouge in Cambodia, and the Bosnian Serbs?" Memorials, medals, and occasions signifying political repentance are best conceived case by case and in one major dimension. Better to leave to other occasions synoptic comparisons between virtues and vices on various sides of terrible conflicts. In the psychology of apology, "We're sorry" gets undercut by the additional clause, "But we had our reasons; and besides, others were worse." One Vietnam veteran, once a helicopter pilot and now a Presbyterian minister, said to his New York congregation in 2003 that in his experience all war is "the Devil's work." He wonders if the rules of "just war" can ever overcome the fundamental injustice of organized killing.[9] He is deeply aware of the hazard in lesser-and-greater evil calculations with their propensity for leading the calculator into moral comfort with the lesser. Lesser evils are still evil. Moral innocence vanishes on a battlefield, which is why Reinhold Niebuhr once cautioned fellow Christians, "We may find it possible to carry a gun, but we must carry it with a heavy heart." To all the evils of war, let no side add the evil of self-righteousness.

In the fall of 2001 and the spring of 2003, the U.S. military portrayed its new weapons in Afghanistan and Iraq as inflicting only unintended, "collateral" damage on civilians. It thereby reaffirmed the old rule of a "just war"—target discrimination. It was also implying that the carpet and nuclear bombing of cities in World War Two no longer has military justification.[10] Was it justified even then? American memory of 9/11 should revive the question. On that day we enrolled anew in a world consensus that unprovoked attack on civilians is wrong. The March 6, 1998, award to that helicopter crew was a military application of a rule which historian Gordon Craig coins for his own profession: "The duty of the historian is to restore to the past the options it once had."[11]

Doubtless, if the whole history of good and evil done by all parties in any war were ever to be told, all their descendants would have large resources for a complex experience of pride and shame. Those of us who did not fight in Vietnam and who opposed the war can look back with our own form of chastened pride when we remember how close many in the antiwar movement came to treating American veterans of the war as scapegoats. "My country sent me to do evil and then hid from me because I reminded them of it. I was a victim of America's arrogance, and I was being blamed for it," lamented one hospitalized veteran.[12] Vietnam veterans have much reason to resent some of the treatment accorded them when they returned to a country whose civilians were blaming them either for losing the war or for fighting it in the first place. This is to acknowledge that America's domestic processing of the Vietnam War is far from over. The awards to Thompson, Colborn, and Andreotta embodied this book's central theme: Next to refraining from collective evildoing, the next best thing is collectively to repent of it. Righteous persons and righteous peoples are those who follow Psalm 15:4 by "swearing to their own hurt."

Agenda for an American Future: The Scope of Mourning, Apology, and Responsibility

> [It] is not too much to say that this was a society unafraid of facing its own evils.
>
> —C. Vann Woodward about Virginia in the 1830s[13]

> The heart has room for many strangers, near and far. There is a global hospitality possible too in the presence of death.
>
> —Rowan Williams[14]

Will the people of the twenty-second century say that Americans of the twenty-first were unafraid of facing their own evil, or, like those Virginians, will we be seen as falling back into the same old sins? The positive evidence in these pages is both promising and discouraging. Political repentance is sluggish work; there is always the chance that we will tire of it, with a dismissive "been there, done that" or an imitation of Germans who say, "We have had it up to here with. . . ."

The ethical language of this book has majored in the declarative mood. It has largely skirted imperatives, in view of the dangers of moralism. Yet the imperative "never again" resides in every act of acknowledgment celebrated in these pages. It is one thing for the German student to declare, "We may never get to the bottom of it"; it was another for her to add, "but we must keep on studying it." Conscious of moral judgment, she knew that her moral finitude did not cancel her obligation to be open to further moral growth. To tire of repentance can be to retire from moral reflection.

Though we cannot plumb the depths of all the unjust suffering among our neighbors past and present, we can grow in comprehending more of it. We can be patient to hear stories that have yet to be told. We can listen to stories of how we or our representatives have been responsible for that unjust suffering. We can do what we can to convey the stories to another generation. And, so far as possible, we can let our memories prompt us to new commitments to change.

"As human beings we have learned, as human beings we remain endangered. Yet we always have the strength to overcome dangers afresh."[15] When President Richard von Weizsäcker said this before a hushed German Bundestag in 1985, the gassing of Kurds, two Iraq wars, Bosnia, and Rwanda were oncoming history. "We shall overcome." Shall we? No realist who had lived through the twentieth century could be immune to deep doubt that "we" do have the strength to overcome our catastrophic addictions to violence personal and collective. The memorials, histories, and acts of public repentance recorded in this book oppose this doubt with hope. But if hope is not to obscure still-waiting agenda of historical-political repentance, it must open us to plausible imperative specifics. Below are my major candidates for the untended agenda of memory, memorialization, and reparation still waiting in the vestibule of the American national house in view of its history as one country among many countries. All these candidates are debatable, but not to debate them would be for us Americans to retreat from reexamination of our national impacts upon our world neighbors, past, present and future.

1. *The Scope of Public Mourning*

> I stated that in times of national stress governments often do bad things and, our government being no exception, that we should try and stop them from doing these bad things in our name, rather than lament them in later years, but that often such belated lamentation may be centuries in coming, e.g., recognizing that killing Native Americans was not such a good thing after all and that Columbus murdered many, many people. Accordingly, it will probably not be until the year 2500 that we will recognize as a nation the millions of Vietnamese, Cambodian and Laotian civilians American bombs killed during the period we know as the Vietnam War. So, by comparison, a few thousand dead Afghan civilians is probably not too big a deal for American sensibilities.
>
> —Haskel Simonowitz, 2002[16]

> Hell is truth seen too late.
>
> —William Sloane Coffin[17]

Along with numerous colleagues across the United States, Professor Simonowitz protests the implication, voiced loudly by various American officials after 9/11, that to oppose any policy of a government's response to that terrible event is unpatriotic, even treasonable. Leaving aside for the moment this defiance of democratic principle, one has to applaud his plea for shortening the *time interval* between collective wrongdoing and its retrospective collective acknowledgment. Publics and their leaders will always turn quickly to observe the wrongs of others, but political prudence can even put a damper on that tendency, too. In the year 2000 the U.S. Congress was about to pass a resolution labeling the 1915 deaths of 1.5 million Armenians a "genocide" inflicted by the Turkish government of the time. The resolution "was tabled in the face of Turkish threats to cut [American] access to military bases."[18]

Ordinarily, in any conflict, we get around to compassion for the enemy side much later than to compassion for our own side. On a space in a memorial garden in Berlin, in the 1990s, there was placed a memorial "To All Our War Dead." Some local group then covered over this inscription with a banner that inserted a German possessive: "To All the Dead of Our Wars," that is, all fifty million humans killed in the war of 1939–1945 of which Germany was a chief instigator. To mourn this expanded version of "our war dead" requires supranationalist moral imagination. It assumes that *enemy* war dead are worth mourning as well as those of one's fellow countrymen.

Most nations on earth have a long way to go before their citizens enter into this widened scope of public mourning. This includes the United States. In company with Dr. Simonowitz, I wonder how long, if ever, there will be:

- a marker on the site of the Washington Vietnam Memorial noting the one to three million Vietnamese killed in their disastrous civil war.[19]
- a similar marker on the nearby Korean War Memorial noting the four million humans killed or wounded in that war.
- a plaque, paralleling the U.S. military's public regret for the My Lai Massacre, expressing similar regret for the 1950 deaths of some two hundred Korean civilians from American gunfire at the bridge of No Gun Ri.[20]
- a tablet, located somewhere in the now-completed Washington memorial to World War Two, which expresses grief for the millions of civilians killed by air power on both sides of that war.
- a global symbol, in the midst of the future World Trade Center memorial, which details the foreign countries represented among the 2,982 deaths there, in Washington, and in Pennsylvania. The number of countries will come to at least eighty.

The mourning of foreigners requires courage and moral imagination not popular in any nation. One can dismiss the idea as simply beyond the capacity of citizens and leaders who understandably have reason to attend, first of all, to next-door neighbors. But there is a deep moral flaw in exclusive domestic grief. In post-1989 Berlin, one could have understood a gathering of public pressure for destroying the huge Soviet war memorial in the Pankow district. In the final battle for Berlin 300,000 Soviet soldiers perished. The East German government erected giant heroic statues and stone-inscribed Stalinist rhetoric to commemorate the event, in which thousands of Berliners died, too. In spite of bitter local memories of how Soviet troops treated Germans (especially German women) in the final months of the war, however, it is unlikely that the city government will ever obliterate this remnant of a Soviet invasion which helped defeat Nazi Germany at terrible cost of human life.[21] One hopes that Germans will increasingly see the Pankow park through eyes filled with grief for "all the dead of our wars." The imagination of many Germans is better equipped than that of Americans to understand what it meant for the USSR to lose twenty million soldiers and civilians in the war.

To the contemporary credit of the American military, however, in the 2004 wake of the Iraq War, its officers in Baghdad were offering compensations between $1000 and $6000 to Iraqi civilians who could make valid claims for family deaths or injuries from misdirected bombs and bullets. "While occasional payments were made to families wrongly bombed in Afghanistan, there was nothing this formalized before." Inadequate and symbolic as this gesture may be, and as little combined with apology or empathy, it set a new precedent of overt military affirmation of the target-discrimination rule along with reparations to the unjustly killed and injured.[22] As this is written, reparatory awards to abused prisoners in Iraq seem also to be intended by the U.S. government.

American presidents, on the other hand, among other representatives of the body politic, have shown little inclination in recent years even to mention the cost of "our wars" to other peoples.

- In his victory speech to the U.S. Congress in March of 1991, President George H. W. Bush expressed no empathy for the Iraqi military dead of the Gulf War, and ever since no official estimate of those dead has emanated from the Pentagon. For years after the war Dr. Beth Deponte, a demographer employed by the Department of Commerce, researched the question, publicized her findings, then lost her job. She concluded that Iraqi deaths in the war, from all causes including deteriorated health care, totaled 158,000, almost half of whom were women and children. Other researchers came to lower estimates, and debate continues, mostly in nongovernmental quarters. Twelve years later, in 2003, one journalist wrote of the Iraq invasion that "the Pentagon said it wasn't possible to estimate Iraqi civilian casualties, and was unhappy that anyone else in government attempted to do so."[23] The principle in this policy is: Keep the public eye focused on war costs to our own people, and forget about the cost to the enemy. News media have largely accepted this principle. "The result is a war in which apparently only 'we' suffer and only 'we' die."[24] More ethically scandalous is the impression left by this policy: "If civilian deaths are not recorded, let alone published, it must be because they do not matter, and if they do not matter it must be because the Iraqis are beneath notice."[25]
- Soon after the formal end of that short 2003 invasion, the surviving Iraqi Ministry of Health proposed investigating the number of Iraqi dead, but on December 10, 2003, the American authority in Baghdad ordered a stop to the investigation, in spite of the fact that, with some

justification, British and American military leaders had talked a lot about smart, precision bombs that limit civilian casualties. In the spring of 2004, one private agency estimated Iraqi civilian dead as between 6,055 and 7,706, or ten times American dead, who by October 2004 had climbed over 1,000. To that total, seldom mentioned in media, should be added the hundred "coalition" dead.

- In the meantime, photos of American soldiers killed in Iraq appear regularly on television screens and in newspapers. We read their names, ages, home towns, and ranks. No such data appears under a headline, "Two Iraqis killed." To the credit of modern journalists, their most striking recent attention to the personal tragedies of mass violence has been the series of portraits and short biographies which appeared, month after month, in the New York Times memorializing every-identifiable person killed on 9/11. This journalistic memorialization reflects the wisdom of many Holocaust survivors who insist, "It's not that 'six million died,' but that a person died, one by one, six million times." Like the names of over 58,000 people on the Vietnam War Memorial, this individualization of mass violence adds to public culture an accretion of moral realism. It rebuts Joseph Stalin's famous cynical remark, "The death of one person is a tragedy, the death of a million a statistic," as well as Hitler's equally famous, "Who remembers the Armenians?"

- Columbus Day 1992 fell under a muffling public cloak when Native Americans protested that Columbus was the villain of their histories. Can Columbus Day be reformed for the purpose of mourning as well as celebration? Americans like their holidays pure and undefiled with negative history. Germans, in their January 27 Remembrance Day, invented a secular form of the Jewish Shoah. Repentance for all forms of dehumanization in the history of the United States needs a national day. Perhaps October 12 can be reformed to become that day. It could be renamed "All America Day," with implicit permission of descendants of Indians to make the holiday a memorial to the deaths of their ancestors at the hands of Columbus as well as a monument to his courage as "Admiral of the Ocean Seas."[26]

The death of people closest to us will always assault our emotions more radically than the deaths of people far away in time or space. Yet, to rest content with this fact is to cut off the possibility that one's own immediate suffering can be a door-opener, not a door-closer, to empathy with the suffering of others. One Manhattan psychotherapist reported that out of the 9/11 event "our empathy bar has been raised. We no longer say, 'Why me?' but 'Why not me?' " We thus exhibit the survivor syndrome. From counseling with people in his downtown Presbyterian congregation after 9/11, Rev. Jon Walton reported, "We are so aware of every life that 10 more deaths in our city add to the loss that we're already borne."[27]

Unforgettable for most Americans will always be how, in the immediate aftermath of 9/11, many doors to *our* losses opened around the human world. Did doors open in new American reciprocation? Four months after 9/11, Claudia Rosett wrote in the *Wall Street Journal*:

> Here, we might look to countries that know far more, firsthand, of the kind of horror we witnessed on September 11. In the week following the attack, [Mayor] Giuliani compared the bravery of New Yorkers to that of Londoners during the blitz. The bravery I would not contest. But—heretical though it feels to say this right now—the blitz was worse. For months, from 1940–41, German warplanes bombed not only London, but a slew of British cities, burying people in the rubble of their own homes and setting off firestorms in the streets. More than 40,000 civilians died.[28]

Amid hundreds of deaths in New York on 9/11 and many thousands in the bombed cities of World War Two, physical remains often disappeared beneath the rubble, leaving statistics of deaths uncertain. And those 40,000 Londoners were only a fragment of British and German deaths in the war. The Germans would lose an estimated 100,000 lives each in Hamburg and Dresden. Chinese and Japanese historians argue even today over the toll of the Nanjing Massacre—300,000 or 20,000?—but for the Japanese there is no doubt that they lost 900,000 lives from aerial bombing of their sixty-seven cities, of whom "only" 200,000 were in Hiroshima and Nagasaki. We Americans are likely to remember, first of all, that our 1941–1945 war deaths approached 400,000, and we are as likely to be shocked when people of other countries minimize that number with the remark, "It was nothing compared to our loss of millions."[29]

Numbers can numb. After the above paragraph, most readers may find themselves skipping the statistics. That is why we will forever need the recorded personal experience of an Anne Frank, a Dietrich Bonhoeffer, or a single Iraqi widow as narrow door-openers into glimpses of evil history. Mayor Giuliani deserves our moral-political salute: He stood on a growing edge of public leadership for expanding New Yorkers' necessarily immediate griefs toward like, larger griefs of neighbors worldwide. Better, after 9/11, to remember the Blitz, and to remember Dresden and Tokyo than to draw tight the perimeters of moral imagination and indignation. Empathy for the "far off" as well as for "the near"[30] belongs in the calling of democratic leaders. It belongs most of all to citizens whose religious faith impels them toward a humanitywide ethic.

Democracy notwithstanding, it is a difficult ethic to translate into political act. When psychologist G. H. Mead said that democracy depends upon voters who vote for the interests of somebody else as well as their own interest, he echoed Edmund Burke. Conservative Burke reminded his Bristol electors that his representation of their interests in Parliament required the reciprocal of representing the interests of the nation back to them.[31] Americans, in particular, now need leaders who will adapt and expand the Burkean theory to an interdependent global human community. Even if domestic acknowledgment of far-off sufferers is accorded only a public token, that token is a supremely important increment of public moral education. There would be no Holocaust memorial in Washington, D.C., if a U.S. president had asserted, "The Jews the Germans killed were not Americans. Let the Germans memorialize them. It is none of our business." As members of a world religious community, American Jews would have protested this claim out of deep religious conviction. John Donne would have protested it out of a similar Christian conviction. His metaphor of Europe and his sexist language may need our updating, but it is time, in the sad aftermaths of the twentieth century, to adapt his famous words to our globalized twenty-first:

> No man is an Island, entire of it self; every man is a piece of the
> Continent, a part of the main; if a clod be washed away by the sea,
> Europe is the less, as well as if a promontory were, as well as if a
> manor of thy friends or of thine own were; any man's death dimin-
> ishes me, because I am involved in Mankind; And therefore never
> send to know for whom the bell tolls; it tolls for thee.[32]

The American politician who best exemplified this rigorous moral perspective was Abraham Lincoln in his Second Inaugural Address. On a March day in 1865, Lincoln addressed a war-weary Northern audience expecting a speech that would blow the trumpets of victory and scourge the South for bringing on a war in which more men in blue died than men in grey.[33] Instead, with great solemnity and an undertone of grief mixed with hope, Lincoln promised "charity for all," for "him who shall have borne the battle" on both sides, "and for his widow, and his orphan." The injection of compassion for the defeated into a victory speech set a new precedent in presidential rhetoric. The assertion of divine judgment on the prayers of both sides also had little precedent. Lincoln knew that this address would not be popular. "Men are not flattered by being shown that there is a difference of purpose between the Almighty and them."[34] Such speech has had few imitators, Democratic or Republican, in Lincoln's successors.

2. *The Scope of Apology*

God forbid that I should claim for our country the mantle of
perfect righteousness. We have committed sins of omission and sins

of commission, for which we stand in need of the mercy of the Lord.

—Harry S Truman[35]

In March 1947 President Truman visited Mexico City. On an unscheduled stop at Chapultepec Castle, he laid a wreath on the monument to six Mexican army cadets who killed themselves rather than surrender to the American army that conquered the city one hundred years before. Numerous local Mexicans rejoiced in the presidential gesture. A local newspaper headline proclaimed: "Rendering Homage to the Heroes of '47, Truman Heals an Old National Wound Forever." A cab driver exclaimed, "To think that the most powerful man in the world would come and apologize." Back home Truman avoided the word "apology," saying simply, "Brave men don't belong to any one country. I respect bravery wherever I see it."[36]

We do not know what combination of justice and injustice Truman saw in the Mexican War. We do know that Lincoln opposed it as a congressman and failed to be re-elected as a result. Many Americans have viewed the Spanish-American War of 1898, the Philippine War of 1899–1901, the Vietnam War of 1962–1975, and the Iraq War of 2003 as national power aspirations rather than "just wars." Truman may not have intended to apologize, but as an avid reader of history he knew that wars are great occasions for "sins of omission and sins of commission," a phrase he surely learned as a member of the Southern Baptist Church. For years after his ascent to the presidency in 1945, various critics challenged him to consider the atomic bombing of Japan as among our recent national sins, but he refused to repent of that decision. Significant for any relevance of religion and moral law to affairs of state, however, was his theological move from sins of individuals to sins of the American nation. Truman's reference to the sins of his country, Martin Marty commented wryly in 2003, was "not the favored form of discourse in these imperial times."[37]

Some will say that a mere apology for ancient collective wrongs has little political impact. The Chapultepec illustration speaks eloquently to the contrary. When, in the second half of the twentieth century, Protestant and Roman Catholic leaders openly confessed the wrongs done Jewish people from early centuries into the present, they took a step toward new relationships with the descendants of an abused people. The same pertinence of apology for collective wrongs in the past to a "righted" relationship in the present appears in many incidents of this book. Perhaps the most dramatic illustration of a thoroughgoing political apology in recent American history was that to Japanese Americans. But there remain on the agenda of history other candidates for apology to descendants of those who once suffered unjustly at the hands of governmental power, either by the latter's "commission" or "omission."

- *The Tories of 1775–1783.* Lest we focus only on very recent history, Americans might start with our Revolutionary War and how Patriots treated Loyalists.[38] The people of modern Nova Scotia number many descendants of the latter. Their memories are vivid with murders, burning of farms, tar and feathers, expropriations. It is a side of Revolutionary fervor about which Americans have little reason to be proud. To my knowledge no government of the United States has ever offered a representative apology to either Canadians or British for patriot mistreatment of the Tories.[39]

- *West European, American, and African collaborations in slavery.* Since slavery always was an international moral crime and is now legally (in the 1948 United Nations Universal Declaration of Human Rights and in the founding statute of the International Criminal Court) a crime against humanity, it would behoove a three-continent coalition of leaders someday to make a collective confession of this wrong as part of a new international commitment to human development on the African continent. Africa lost an estimated fifty million people to the slave trade.[40] Like the stalled proposal for an apology for slavery by the U.S. Congress, opponents of political apology the world over fear that demands for reparations will follow. Were the western world to mount an African version of the 1947 Marshall Plan, along with confession that African slaves helped furnish no small part of western wealth over several centuries, descendants of both perpetrators and victims of slavery, on all three continents, might then look each other in the eye with overdue historical honesty.

- *Presidential apologies.* On February 14, 1995, General John Shalikashvili, chairman of the Joint Chiefs of Staff of the U.S. military, "stood before thousands in the Kreuzkirche in Dresden and apologized for the senseless firebombing of the city fifty years ago to the day."[41] As readers of Kurt Vonnegut's *Slaughterhouse Five* know well, Dresden was a museum city with little military significance. Not profoundly different from terrorist strategies in 2004, civilians were the intended targets of the British and American bombs which killed "at least 35,000 people and perhaps 135,000."[42] The General's apology fitted the reaffirmation of the just war doctrine of target-discrimination in the 1990s in face of its massive violation during World War Two. His words carried weight. But generals are responsible to presidents and prime ministers, whose words carry greater weight. Commenting on belated, ambiguous public expressions of regret for Vietnam by former Secretary of Defense Robert McNamara—never quite rising to the level of apology—Samantha Power says:

Reexamining our reasoning is not something that has come naturally to American statesmen. In fact, Mr. McNamara is one of the very few senior American government officials *ever* to admit major error without being forced to do so. . . . On those rare occasions when American officials have expressed remorse for previous policies, they have tended to do so offhandedly. And while on these shores, such utterances were ignored or derided as insincere, in the countries grievously affected, many victims and survivors welcomed the gesture with surprising grace.[43]

One thinks of the "surprising grace" of audience response that greeted many perpetrator confessions before the South African TRC. A striking illustration of an admission of American political policy mistakes came in late 2003 from an American president not noted for this practice in his first three years of office. An Arab advocate of democracy for his region, Saad Eddin Ibrahim, expressed his astonishment that in a speech George W. Bush "admitted past foreign policy mistakes and vowed not to condone dictatorial regimes, even among close traditional allies." Among obvious examples would be the military help which Reagan and Bush administrations in the 1980s supplied Saddam Hussein's war against Iran. Journalists like Power keep remembering that no less than Donald Rumsfeld negotiated U.S. military aid to Saddam Hussein in 1988 as that dictator was gassing thousands of Kurds.

It is easy, perhaps, to apologize for mistakes of previous administrations—easier, too, when years have dimmed memory of the events. In the 1990s, President Bill Clinton apologized in Guatemala for the CIA's help to General Rios Montt in his coup that overturned the 1954 election there. Tens of thousands of Native Guatemalans died in the subsequent war of Rios Montt against his own people. The faults and defaults of western powers in response to the two outstanding genocides of the 1990s—Bosnia and Rwanda—prompted apologies from Clinton that marked him as a president more open to this verbal gesture than were many of his predecessors. But even he shied away from "humanitarian" missions by American soldiers. As Power writes about his 1998 visit to Rwanda:

With the grace of one grown practiced at public remorse, he issued something of an apology. "We in the United States and the world community did not do as much as could have and should have done to try to limit what occurred," Clinton said. "It may sound strange to you here," he continued, "but all over the world there were people like me sitting in offices, day after day after day, who did not fully appreciate the depth and the speed with which you were being engulfed by this unimaginable terror." But Clinton's remorse came too late for the 800,000 Rwandans who died.[44]

An ounce of prevention is worth pounds of apology. But apologies can still be anticipations of "better, next time." In late 1999, UN Secretary-General Kofi Annan undertook a pair of apologies in his introductions to two long UN studies of the Srebrenica Massacre and the Rwanda genocide. His language had the ring of genuine personal contrition on behalf of UN-related governments who failed to act to arrest these horrors:

> Both Reports—my own on Srebrenica and that of the Independent Inquiry on Rwanda—reflect a profound determination to present the truth about these calamities. Of all my aims as Secretary-General, there is none to which I feel more deeply committed than that of enabling the United Nations never again to fail in protecting a civilian population from genocide or mass slaughter. . . .

> All of us must bitterly regret that we did not do more to prevent [the Rwandan genocide]. . . . I fully accept [the Inquiry's] conclusions, including those which reflect on officials of the UN Secretariat, of whom I myself am one. I also welcome the emphasis which the Inquiry has put on the lessons to be learnt from this tragedy . . . with the aim of ensuring that the United Nations can and will act to prevent or halt any other such catastrophe in the future.

[Annan introduces his Srebrenica report with a quotation from Judge Riad of the International Tribunal for the Former Yugoslavia:]

> "The evidence tendered by the Prosecutor describes scenes of unimaginable savagery: thousands of men buried alive, men and women mutilated and slaughtered, children killed before their mothers' eyes, a grandfather forced to eat the liver of his own grandson. These are truly scenes from hell, written on the darkest pages of human history. . . ."

> In reviewing these events, I have in no way sought to deflect criticism directed at the United National Secretariat. . . . There is an issue of responsibility, and we in the United Nations share in that responsibility. . . . All of [the] exceptional measures that I have taken in preparing this report reflect the importance which I attach to shedding light on what Judge Riad described as the "darkest pages of human history."[45]

Simultaneously with these UN reports, President Clinton spoke to an audience of Kosovars, gaining much applause as he celebrated their liberation from attack by Serbs via NATO bombing. Then he added a caution against seeking revenge on the Serbs: "You will never forget what you suffered . . . No one can force you to forgive, but you must try." To that there was no applause.[46]

Repentant apologies, if not reconciling forgiveness, popped up in astonishing number in various world places in the 1990s, as nations seemed about to recover from the Cold War. September 11, 2001, ushered in a decided retreat from this phenomenon. It may be years before any wise combination of public repentance and forgiveness—extended to America's enemies—begins again to enter the front or back pages of our newspapers. In the meantime one can only agree with sociologist Nicholas Tavuchis that public leaders must be careful not to apologize so often that the gesture loses credibility. "The consummate collective apology is a diplomatic accomplishment of no mean order," he wrote in 1991, because leaders' constituents may not yet believe there is anything to apologize for, and the victims may find an apology too easy, cheap, and premature. If it is to be an event and not only a gesture, its practice must not be too frequent, lest its limited healing power be squandered. Indeed, apologies for great political harms will soon drown in public cynicism if unaccompanied by tangible reparations and other measures that credibly promise "never again."[47]

As upsurges of terror and genocide continue to rampage across the world of the twenty-first century, how much preventive action, including risk to American lives, will national leaders and publics be willing to undertake? What costs will we be willing to pay for protecting our world neighbors from mass deaths imposed, not by volcanos, earthquakes, and hurricanes, but by organized, fellow human hands? It is a last, most open of questions to be posed in these pages.

3. The Scope and Limit of American Responsibility for the Lives of Our World Neighbors

> Ah! As our commerce spreads, the flag of liberty will circle the globe, and the highways of the ocean–carrying trade of all mankind, be guarded by the guns of the republic . . . Fellow Americans, we are God's chosen people.
>
> —Albert Beveridge, Indiana Republican, in an address, "The March of the Flag," calling for annexation of the Philippines, September 1898

> Expansion and imperialism are a grand onslaught on democracy.
> —William Graham Sumner, later in 1898[48]

This book comes to print in months of raging worldwide debate over the degree to which Americans, our soldiers, businesses, NGOs, and national government are responsible for intervening in the lives of other peoples. Though many world conditions have changed, the debate between the Beveridge and the Sumner views is not over. In 1899 the Beveridge speech went to three hundred thousand copies and helped propel its author into the United States Senate.[49] A hundred years later, the speech had an astonishing echo in opening words of Representative Henry Hyde to a 2004 meeting of the House Committee on International Relations. Our unilateral pursuit of war in Iraq, he said, "is all to the good, for it is unambiguous proof that absolutely nothing will deter us, that the entire world arrayed against us cannot stop us."[50]

In 9/11, Americans experienced a new, unprecedented vulnerability to the harms that some other humans mean to inflict upon us. It is understandable that national political leaders should respond to this aggression with counter-aggression. Few seemed alert to William Graham Sumner's cautions about power in a democracy. As citizens of a "superpower," how shall we resolve the dilemma of expecting too much from our power to influence the world and expecting too little? With our ideals, economic strength, and military power, are Americans now able to control the rest of the world to the benefit of its interests and our own? To this end, a 2002 publication of the U.S. Department of Defense envisions American power in year 2020 under the rubric, "Full Spectrum Dominance":

> [G]iven the global nature of our interests and obligations, the United States must maintain its overseas presence and the ability to rapidly project power worldwide in order to achieve full spectrum dominance.[51]

A "good" nation like the United States, say supporters of this "vision," can build a good empire.

Whatever our diverse citizen attitudes toward America's stance in 2004 worldwide, we have to acknowledge that with power always comes responsibility which entails both scope and limits. Hyde's claim that "the entire world . . . cannot stop us" rings with historical ignorance and with no regard for the choices that all wielders of power must make. Consistency in those choices is hard to find in recent American history. Moral realists have to ask how, if military intervention in famine-wasted Somalia in 1993 was justified, was not intervention in Serb-invaded Bosnia yet more justified? And, most of all, in genocide-ravaged Rwanda? Realists have to add: Once military force acquires a cloak of justice, does the precedent make easier the disguise of unjust interests under cover of the same cloak? It is one thing to say that America had to strike back at terrorists in Afghanistan; another to ask where, in the name of just interests, American power must halt before the just interests of others; and yet another to ask: What *sacrifices* of life and wealth should Americans consider for serving the life and well-being of non-American peoples? What restrictions are we willing to put on the pursuit of our interests in service to those others? And what changes of intention are called for when our best intentions go awry?

In her passionate conclusion to her landmark study of "the age of genocide," Samantha Power summarizes the history of American inaction in response to this "problem from hell." No American government has seen fit to risk even a few American lives on behalf of halting the mass killing of Armenians, Cambodians, Kurds, Shiites, Bosnians, or Rwandans while time for a halt was still open. Rallying the nation to attack Iraq in 2003 depended most of all on government claims that weapons of mass destruction and terrorist havens there directly threatened America. Those claims gave way eventually to the humanitarian argument of liberating the Iraqi people from tyranny. If that argument is worth the lives of a thousand American soldiers, why were not a million deaths of Muslims in Bosnia and Tutsis in Rwanda worth the same risk? Power's indictment of our government's sins of omission brings this American to the shamed conclusion that across many administrations, Democratic and Republican, Washington has taught us citizens that the United States will go to war for oil but not to halt mass murder.

> American leaders have been able to persist in turning away because genocide in distant lands has not captivated senators, congressional caucuses, Washington lobbyists, elite opinion shapers, grassroots groups, or individual citizens. The battle to stop genocide has thus been repeatedly lost in the realm of domestic politics. . . . In the end, however, the inertia of the governed cannot be disentangled from the indifference of the government.[52]

The history of slavery and the defiance of Indian interests, as we have seen, abound with such mutual entanglement. "If democracy is about the right to choose one's leaders," said one South African recently, "it is also about taking responsibility for their leadership."[53] To this should be added: Governments have some responsibility for modeling and critiquing the idea of "public service." Americans like to call their leaders public servants, so power to dominate often disguises itself as power to serve. As ethicist Edward LeRoy Long, Jr., says in his 2004 book, *Facing Terrorism*, there is a radical difference between "full spectrum dominance" and a "servanthood" understanding of political power:

> One is a form of playing God; the other is an acknowledgment of being human. The temptation to take on the world and make it into the images of our own ideals, especially by the use of power, is a form of idolatry, even in morally plausible versions.[54]

Political theology is no monopoly of theologians. In exact reflection of Long's fear of idolatry of power, journalist Michael Ignatieff, a Canadian, wrote in June 2004 in the wake of Ronald Reagan's funeral:

The signal illusion from which America has to awake in Iraq and everywhere is that it serves God's providence or (for those with more secular beliefs) that it is the engine of history. . . . [T]he world does not exist to be molded to American wishes. It is good that the United States has wanted to be better than it is. It is good that the death of a president gave it a week to revive its belief in itself. But it cannot continue to bear this burden of destiny. For believing that it is Providence's chosen instrument makes the country overestimate its power; it encourages it to lie to itself about its mistakes; and it makes it harder to live with the painful truth that history does not always—or even very often—obey the magnificent but dangerous illusions of American will.[55]

It is a sober note on which to end this book, but the question presses upon Americans now as seldom before in our history: For what displays of *hubris*, in our current collective stance in the world, may the American government one day have to consider apologizing?

Power and Humility: A Conclusion

The world jury may be out on this question, but there is one aspect of the current American face in the world on which many critics external and internal are agreeing: *Supercertainty of its virtue ill becomes a superpower.* One does not have to be sure of the ultimately good or bad outcome of the Iraq War to know that arrogance and self-righteousness are unbecoming to both interpersonal and international relations. The terrorists who destroyed life and property on 9/11 were guilty of this vice, and unfortunately all religions have sometimes nourished it. Paradoxically, religion can provoke either supercertainty or modesty in human claims about right and wrong. Its "views of the Absolute" often morph into "absolute views."[56] Long quotes journalist Joe Klein of *Time* on the religious stances of the 2003 White House:

> George W. Bush's faith offers no speed bumps on the road to Baghdad; it does not give him pause or force him to reflect. It is a source of comfort and strength but not of wisdom. . . . The world might have more confidence in the judgment of this President if he weren't always bathed in the blinding glare of his own certainty.[57]

Reinhold Niebuhr was acutely conscious of this wisdom as he wrote about Soviet-American hostility in the 1950s. He could have written it about the post-9/11 reactions of the White House to the challenge of terrorism:

> The cure for a pretentious idealism, which claims to know more about the future and about other men than is given mortal man to

know, is not egotism. It is a concern for both the self and the other in which the self, whether individual or collective, preserves a "decent respect of the opinions of mankind," derived from a modest awareness of the limits of its own knowledge and power.[58]

Two very different relations between religious-moral conviction and political policy-justification are at conflict here, two different *spirits* in American devotion to our most cherished word for democracy: *freedom.* Said the American president to Congress in January 2003, "The advance of human freedom—the great achievement and the great hope of every time—now depends on us . . . We go forward with confidence, because the call of history has come to the right country."[59] Such rhetoric parallels that of the Albert Beveridges and the Josiah Stongs of American history, but it is far distant from Judge Learned Hand's definition of freedom: "The spirit of liberty is the spirit that is not too sure it is right."

In the immediacies of 2004, the right and wrong of America's current role in world affairs has to be subject to the judgment of future generations. Who knows for what contributions to the world the United States may yet be thanked, for what injustices our descendants may have to apologize? The caution of historians about writing any history of events less than twenty-five years old comes to mind here, providing a convenient exit, for the end of this book, from judgments about the uses of American power in 2004. As citizens, of course, we do not and should not claim that luxury. If the cases of national, local, and personal repentance in this book offer any precedental political wisdom, a first resource for human *metanoia* is *listening* to one's critics. The Learned Hand version of "liberty" implies freedom to learn about the "right" from the perspectives of other human beings. That is the hope inherent in constitutional freedoms of citizen protest against government power, whether long ago in the 1735 free-press case of John Peter Zenger or the 2004 case of civil rights for foreign prisoners taken in a "war" against terrorism.

How then should Americans respond to our contemporary world neighbors who think ill of us? To answer that question one needs a nuanced concept of responsibility, such as H. Richard Niebuhr crafted when he wrote,

> An agent's action is like a statement in a dialogue. Such a statement . . . is made in anticipation of reply. It looks forward as well as backward; it anticipates objections, confirmations, and corrections. It is made as part of a total conversation that leads forward and is to have meaning as a whole. Thus a political action, in this sense, is responsible not only when it is responsive to a prior deed but when it is so made that the agent anticipates the reactions to his action. . . . Responsibility lies in the agent who stays with his action, who accepts the consequences in the form of reactions and looks forward in the present deed to the continued interaction.[60]

In short, responsibility has to be learned. We learn it, if at all, first by being willing to listen. No doubt the most difficult critics to listen to are those most foreign to one's own perspectives. Thomas Jefferson's "decent respect for the opinions of mankind" will require of Americans a rigorous, patient discipline for the rest of the twenty-first century. Whether this dialogue issues in proud rejection or in contrite acceptance of the critics' points of view, future debate among Americans will have to determine. Meantime, when a former mayor of Berlin writes in 2003 that "above all we need to listen to each other," he remembers how important it was for Germans to listen to Americans in the post-1945 world. Even about the "unilateralism" to which he objects in current American foreign policy, he feels bound to remember that he is a citizen of a country that had to learn lessons of political repentance from its enemy, the United States.

> As a German I know by instinct that I have to be very careful when making judgments on German-American relations. After all, they were hostile for the first half of the past century. During those decades, America was basically right and Germany wrong. But didn't Germany learn, at least [the Western] half of our country, how to live and behave in an alliance which is based on international law? Didn't German society learn from the American way of life? . . . Germans have no moral right to lecture Americans on the dangers of unilateralism. But I believe that American democracy itself will find out those dangers through its deep-rooted checks and balances.[61]

These words come from a person who has spent years in the United States and whose hope for change in its worldwide relationships rises from close personal acquaintance with numerous Americans. Another eminent German statesman, also a former mayor of Berlin, echoes a similar mixture of admiration and alarm when he reflects on his eighty years of learning and relearning how to combine repentance and pride in the history of his country and how to shift the national ideals of Germany from domination of other countries to collaboration with them:

> America's self-reliant political and moral guidelines are based on a general American idealism which aspires to make the world a better place. Yet they appear as a kind of missionary work which in its core will not make a dialogue of civilizations around the globe easier. In the long run the world is not prepared to accept a unipolar globe.
> American patriotism and idealism are admirable. But in the long run America will not be able to go it alone. The most important tasks around the globe are not solvable by military means. . . .
> Germans believe that partnership will be needed on both sides of

the Atlantic. Neither side will find anywhere else a better fitting partner. Neither side will serve its own interests and indeed it mission without that partnership.[62]

Repentance and forgiveness are optimists among the virtues, for they oppose tragedy with hopes for healing. Symbolic and practical healing of politically enacted hurts have been celebrated in the foregoing pages, and the author is among those Americans who hope for the healing of contemporary, widespread, hostile rifts in my country's relations to the world of nations. The healing will not be easy, but we have to read accusations like the above as helps to William Sloane Coffin's "lover's quarrel" with America.

Among others who know what such quarreling is like, inside their own countries, are two knowledgeable South Africans quoted in chapter 2 of this book. Their mixtures of admiration and alarm about contemporary America parallels that of many Europeans. Against the background of their own country's historic need of help from abroad for combating the evils of the apartheid regime, one writes:

> I recall vividly the bleakness of South Africa during the 1980s. . . . It was during that time that I turned to the United States Congress for moral support and for statements of opposition from members of the House and Senate. I went to Washington on a number of occasions and was greatly encouraged by the response I received from leading congress people. This experience, coupled with my time in America during the civil rights movement, has always filled me with admiration for the United States as a leader in democracy and human rights. . . . But now, if South Africa were in crisis, I'm not sure I would turn to the U.S.A. For me and so many others around the world, this is tragic. Everywhere I travel, people look to America, not for freedom and justice and human rights, but rather for the abuse of power. America must find itself again and use its enormous resources so that it is seen to be strong, but also fair and compassionate. If it does so, its leadership will be rewarded; but if fails, the whole world will fail with it.[63]

Coming as it does from a man who experienced 9/11 a few blocks from the World Trade Center and who since has visited hundreds of political leaders on six continents, this is painful testimony. A like mixture of pain and hope came in early 2004 from the Methodist minister to whose career the district Six Museum in Cape Town is monument and memorial:

> Ever since 1966 I have traveled to the United States at least once a year. Most of those journeys were about seeking help in our struggle against apartheid in South Africa, and through it all you never failed us. The story of your nation itself was an inspiration. But it may be

our turn to challenge you now, because of the great *disconnect* between the kindness, compassion and caring of most American people, and the way American power is experienced across the
world. . . .

Perhaps there are two Americas. This week in Duke University
Chapel, we commissioned a fine group of young American students
to go out and serve the struggling people of Costa Rica, and spent
time with some remarkable ex-students working in the mountains
of Haiti. These are people who have voluntarily left their "bubble of
comfort" to care and listen and serve. They are the other America,
and there are many thousands of them. "Alienation of Empire" does
not have to be the last word on this great enterprise called the
United States. It could be reversed, if only enough good Americans
came to see that the national interest of the wealthiest, most powerful nation on earth might be better served if it translated its power
into different, more compassionate ways of relating to the rest of
our troubled planet.[64]

No one can predict the mix of justice and injustice, benefit and harm,
which a future generation of Americans may need to remember from our
relation to the rest of humanity in 2004. We must hope that the justice and
benefit will outweigh the injustice and harm, but we will *never* have an excuse
for clothing that hope in the drapery of arrogance.

Two theologians, one German and the other a German-descended American, graced the beginning of this book. Let two Christian laypersons from
Germany, in echo of those two, grace the end:

America will achieve leadership in self-restraint and critical self-
reflection. The problems ahead of us in the global village are too big
even for the strongest nation to handle alone. Gratitude and contrition make honest patriots, and such patriots are best qualified to be
responsible World Citizens.[65]

Notes

INTRODUCTION

1. William Sloane Coffin, *Credo* (Louisville: Westminster/John Knox Press, 2004), p. 84.

2. Samantha Power, *A Problem from Hell: America and the Age of Genocide* (New York: Basic Books, 2002), pp. 511–512.

3. *New York Times*, December 31, 2001, p. A10.

4. Alexis de Tocqueville, *Democracy in America*, ed. J. P. Mayer, trans. George Lawrence (Anchor Books; Garden City, N.Y.: Doubleday and Company, 1969), p. 237.

5. Ibid., p. 235.

6 Reinhold Niebuhr, *The Irony of American History* (New York: Charles Scribner's Sons, 1952), pp. 23, 24–25, 34, 128, 133, 147.

7. Ibid., p. 172.

8. Ibid., p. 137.

9. Ibid., pp. 37, 125–126.

10. The historian was Arthur Schlesinger, Jr., who wrote a letter to Niebuhr while *The Irony of American History* was still in galleys, asking him why he had so largely omitted the enduring crisis in black-white relations in contemporary America. So far as we know, Niebuhr did not change anything in the book in response to this inquiry from a friend: "One irony deserving comment somewhere perhaps [in this book] is the relationship between our democratic and equalitarian pretensions and our treatment of the Negro. This remains, as John Quincy Adams called it in 1820, 'the great and foul stain upon the North American Union,' and I think you might consider mentioning it." See Ursula Niebuhr, ed., *Remembering Reinhold Niebuhr: Letters of Reinhold and Ursula M. Niebuhr* (New York: HarperCollins, 1991), p. 371. I owe this discovery to my colleague James H. Cone of Union Theological Seminary.

11. C. Vann Woodward, "The Irony of Southern History," in *The Burden of Southern History*, 3rd ed. (Baton Rouge: Louisiana State University Press, 1993), p. 204. The essay is also found in the *Journal of Southern History* 19 (1953).

12. Woodward, "Irony," pp. 198–199.

13. Ibid., p. 188.

14. Ibid., pp. 190–191.

15. James McBride Dabbs, *Who Speaks for the South?* (New York: Funk & Wagnalls, 1964), p. 375.

16. *Fragments from Tegel*, translated from *Werke*, Band 16, "Konspiration und Haft" (Gütersloh: Christian Kaiser Verlag, 1996), p. 492. In 1939, deciding to leave America for Germany, he wrote to Reinhold Niebuhr, saying: "I have made a mistake in coming to America. I must live through this difficult period of our national history with the Christian people of Germany. I will have no right to participate in the reconstruction of Christian life in Germany after the war if I do not share the trials of this time with my people." For the sake of them, he concluded, he had to work for the defeat of his country in the upcoming war. See Eberhard Bethge, *Dietrich Bonhoeffer* (New York: Harper and Row, 1977), p. 559.

CHAPTER I

1. William Faulkner, *The Hamlet* (Vintage Books; New York: Random House, 1956), p. 86.

2. Robert Bretall, ed., *A Kierkegaard Anthology* (Princeton: Princeton University Press, 1951), p. 28.

3. So called by Professor Reinhard Rürup, founder and director of the museum *Typography of Terror*, located in the excavated remains of the central Gestapo prison (interview, April 6, 1999).

4. The Bus 100 *Denkmal* is the achievement of leading educator and former member of parliament Hanna Renate Laurien. Her career-long work in the education of teachers of young people rests on the principle: "Ask the students to find out what happened, during the Nazi time, in your city and in your school" (interview, March, 1999).

5. See Brian Ladd, *Ghosts of Berlin: Confronting German History in the Urban Landscape* (Chicago: University of Chicago Press, 1997), p. 170. This book brilliantly summarizes this "landscape of memory" from the standpoint of urban architecture and uses of public space.

6. So remarked several students in an upper-division *Gymnasium* class conversation in the spring of 1999 in the Berlin suburb of Zehlendorf, underlining their astonishment at how ignorant their peers in America seemed to be about what postwar third-generation Germans know about the Nazi era. One teacher in a discussion in Bremen remarked, "Young people say, 'We know that the Holocaust is important, but not as something endlessly repeated to shame us. That makes us clam up' " (April 1999).

7. From a lecture delivered at Princeton University in the spring of 1999; copy given to me by Blumenthal and summarized in an interview in Berlin, April 1999.

8. For example, in early 1942, Polish Catholic diplomat Jan Karski smuggled himself into the Warsaw Ghetto and into Belsec and then escaped with hundreds of

microfilmed documents, which he shared with Supreme Court Justice Felix Frankfurter, who responded, "I don't believe you. I do not mean that you are lying. I simply said that I cannot believe you." Even when the documentation appeared in print, American public response was much the same. Says Samantha Power, "The notion of getting attacked for being (rather than doing) was too discomfiting and too foreign to process readily." See Power, *A Problem from Hell: America and the Age of Genocide* (Perennial Books; New York: HarperCollins, 2002), pp. 32–37.

9. Dr. Helmut Reihlen, now of Berlin, personal communication, January 2004. Cf. below, section on "The Steglitz Mirror Wall."

10. As late as 1966, driving through Bavaria, my wife and I decided to visit the Dachau camp. With no help from road signs, we finally found it by following railroad tracks. One attendant seemed surprised and suspicious that Americans had come to visit. Few tangible reminders of the former camp were around.

11. For an analysis of this address, see my *An Ethic for Enemies: Forgiveness in Politics* (New York: Oxford University Press, 1995), pp. 108–112.

12. A. D. Moses, "The Forty-Fivers: A Generation Between Fascism and Democracy," *German Politics and Society* 17, no. 1 (Spring 1999), 117–119.

13. Among the first were the ecumenical youth conferences in Oslo in 1947 and in South India in 1952. Both saw many vigorous exchanges between German delegates and others from countries devastated by World War Two.

14. Moses, "Forty-Fivers," p. 119.

15. Quotations from the Herzog speech here are taken from the full text as published in *Frankfurter Allgemeine Zeitung*, January 28, 1999, p. 52. Translations mine. The speech was entitled "The Future of Memory."

16. Interview with Bill Moyers, Public Broadcasting System, *Facing Hate*, November 27, 1991.

17. James E. Young, *The Texture of Memory: Holocaust Memorials and Meaning* (New Haven: Yale University Press, 1993), p. 41. In 2003–2004 Young was a member of the jury charged with designing a World Trade Center memorial to the dead of 9/11/01. In comments on the design recommended by the jury, he said: "A memorial should encourage us to contemplate inwardly." *New York Times*, January 19, 2004, B4.

18. See Stefanie Endlich et al., eds., *Gedenkstätten für die Opfer des Nationalsozialismus: Eine Dokumentation*, 2 vols. (Bonn: Federal Center for Political Education, 1999). These two books run to 2,000 pages describing the memorials, their builders, and their historical context in great detail. A third volume has now been added.

19. Young, *Texture of Memory*, p. 65. Scarcely seven weeks after Hitler's assumption of power on January 30, 1933, Heinrich Himmler announced the opening of a new camp for political prisoners outside the village of Dachau. Not completed until 1938, Dachau was reputed to be the most comfortable of all the camps (a bed, library, sports, etc.). For his preaching against the Nazis, Niemoeller became Hitler's "personal prisoner" and stayed in Dachau for seven years. He said to his audience in India in 1952 that he could look out on the gallows from his cell window and "had often to pray for its victims" and had to wonder if, when he should be about to be executed, he could practice Christian forgiveness toward his executioners.

20. Ibid., pp. 71–72.

21. Spoken before SS leaders on October 4, 1943, in Posen, Poland, as massacres of Jews and others in Poland, the Ukraine, and Auschwitz were in full tilt. Mem-

bers of the SS were supposed to demonstrate three major virtues: obedience to Hitler, toughness, and refusal to profit from the property of victims.

22. See Stefanie Lutz and Thomas Lutz, *Gedenken und Lernen an Historischen Orten: Ein Wegweisen zu Gedenkstätten Für Die Opfer des Nationalsozialismus in Berlin*, 2nd ed. (Berlin: Territorial Office for Political Education, 1998), p. 75. Quotations from this invaluable guidebook I note below as Lutz.

23. For example, Siemens, AEG, Henschel, Daimler-Benz, and IG Farben (Lutz, *Gedenken und Lernen*, p. 76).

24. Ravensbruck was the Berlin-region camp for women.

25. Young, *Texture of Memory*, pp. 75–79. Only late in the war were numerous Jews brought to Buchenwald as death camps in the east began to fall to the Soviets. The Nazis housed Jews in a "Little Camp" where "they were neither protected by the [Communist] Committee nor recalled afterwards in the committee's memorials." (Young, p. 74) In their official versions of history neither Communists nor the citizens of the DDR shared any guilt for the Final Solution, an inheritance that belonged exclusively to capitalistic West Germany.

26. Young, *Texture of Memory*, p. 79, records that 130,000 Germans passed through the eleven Soviet-occupied camps, of whom 50,000 died.

27. See Paul's Second Letter to the Thessalonians, 2:7a. The phrase, with the Greek work *anomia*, has been variously translated as "mystery of iniquity" (KJV), "mystery of lawlessness" (RSV), and "the secret power of wickedness" (NEB). Equally mysterious is the "Restrainer" (2:7b) whom Paul believed was holding this "lawless one" in check.

28. Young, *Texture of Memory*, p. 74.

29. Ladd, *The Ghosts of Berlin*, p. 172.

30. Kirsten Grieshaber, "Plaques for Nazi Victims Offer a Personal Impact," *New York Times*, November 29, 2003, p. B23. Schools and citizen groups all over the country have asked Demnig to help them install such plaques in their own locales, and he has received similar requests from Amsterdam, Antwerp, Paris, Thessaloniki, and Austria. Among major German cities, only in Munich have officials balked at the idea with the claim that the plaques "could easily be ignored or vandalized."

31. One might add that the memorials have multiplied "even" in southern Germany where Nazis had some of their strongest original support. An example is the long investigation in the late 1980s and early 1990s in the city of Coburg, famous for its castle in which Luther worked on his translation of the Bible. See the 350-page study of Hubert Fromm, *Die Coburger Juden: Geschichte und Schicksal* (Coburg: Neue Presse, 1990).

32. A Mahnmal on the street bridge over the other major rail deportation site, on the north side of central Berlin, is a concatenation of a similar set of off-center strokes which incorporate a Star of David. But the new Jewish museum, designed by Daniel Liebeskind, makes the most extensive, uncanny use of this architectural motif. Slashes, not windows, pervade this structure. Virtually none of its walls, corridors, or ceilings are built at right angles. In a literal sense, the building means to be "disconcerting."

33. Much of the following account I owe to Dr. Helmut Reihlen and his wife Dr. Erika Reihlen, longtime residents of Steglitz who offered this summary report to a roundtable session of the annual meeting of the International Society of Political Psy-

chology in Berlin in July 2002. Quotations here are taken from their report, for which I am much indebted.

34. Reflecting a concept widely used in Roman Catholic social philosophy, the Berlin constitution makers affirmed the principle of "subsidiarity"—that every political decision is to be made at the lowest level of society consistent with local interests and the interest of the whole.

35. James E. Young, *At Memory's Edge: After-Images of the Holocaust in Contemporary Art and Architecture* (New Haven: Yale University Press, 2000), p. 113.

36. Endlich et al., *Gedenkstätten* p. 152.

37. Ibid. The pictographic sides of the signs, says this catalogue, are likely to "awaken nostalgic feelings," so ordinary are the privileges yanked away by the reverse sides.

38. From Von Buttlar's presentation to the July 2002 meeting of the International Society of Political Psychology. He is referring here to the discussion among German artists and philosophers about whether the Holocaust was so unspeakably evil that, out of respect, it is better not to speak of it, paint pictures of it, or write fiction about it. See Adorno's famous remark, "After Auschwitz it is impossible to write a poem." (Sadly, Von Buttlar died in the spring of 2004.)

39. Young, *At Memory's Edge*, pp. 116, 118–119.

40. Harold Alderman, "The Text of Memory," in *Philosophy and Archaic Experience: Essays in Honor of Edward G. Ballard*, ed. John Sallis (Pittsburgh: Duquesne University Press, 1982), p. 154.

41. Susan Whalen, "The Dialectic of Memory and Forgetting in Histories of Rhetoric," in *Communication Theory and Interpersonal Practice: Selected Proceedings from the Fourth International Conference on Culture and Communication*, ed. Sari Thomas, vol. 3 (Norwood, N.J.: Ablex Publishing, 1984), p. 162. Whalen begins this insightful article (p. 157) with a reference to a story by Jorge Luis Borges of a forgetful old man who suddenly acquires an "exquisite memory" of everything in his past. But "joy fades as the man slowly discovers that he is unable to discriminate between those things he longs to remember and those he longs to forget."

42. Details summarized in Endlich et al., *Gedankstätten*, Band II, pp. 218–219. Schönberner, a Christian, fourteen years old in 1945, was an early strong supporter of Wulf. In a 1999 interview he said to me that "every attempt to deal with the German past was frozen by the Cold War," as former Nazis were installed by the Allies in West Germany. Americans, in particular, found study of the 1933–1945 past "too theoretical and useless" for fighting Soviet communism. Schönberner says he owes to his family his growing post-1945 shame over the Holocaust. His father, a Protestant minister, kept him out of the Hitler Youth during the war, and two aunts hid Jews. His mission for Wannsee is "to demonstrate that all Germany was involved" in Nazi crimes. Said his friend Heinz Galinski: "You must make this memory a school for democracy. You are not guilty for the Nazis, but you are responsible for a different future. You too may be asked by your children, 'What did you do in 1999?' " (interview, March 8, 1999).

43. Aired in 2002, a subsequent HBO docudrama, *Conspiracy*, starred Shakespearean actor Kenneth Branagh as Heydrich, who comes across as an educated, sophisticated, powerful man whose velvet-glove exterior conceals the claws of a cool killer. He manipulates every bureaucrat around the table into believing that "legal"

dealing with the Jews—expulsion, sterilization, death by overwork—would not do the job. Especially shrewd is his insistence that the will of the Führer must be carried out without implicating him directly in the deed. After the war Hitler must be able to deny that he ordered it.

44. My translation. The original German: *Erinnern/Das is/Vielleicht/Die qualvol- lste Art/Des Vergessens/und vielleicht/Die freundlichste Art/Der Linderung/Dieser Qual.*

45. Jews in Berlin today remember how their Great Synagogue on Orienburger- strasse was protected from burning on November 9, 1938, by the intervention of single member of the Berlin police. A plaque near the entrance to the partly restored building (destoyed by Allied bombs) celebrates this man, and annually the synagogue observes the event in a public meeting on the spot, attended by representatives of the police.

46. Doris Fürstenberg, ed., *Steglitz im Dritten Reich* (Berlin: Druckhaus Hen- trich, 1992). The authors included teachers, school administrators, lawyers, librarians, social scientists, social workers, physicians, counselors, and one engineer. All except the engineer (b. 1916) were born after the war or just before the war. See p. 331.

47. Ibid., p. 20. The system depended on the judgments of local medical doctors. "Thereby it is remarkable how ready and willing were members of this professional group to abandon its own ethical foundations." The nadir of that abandonment was in Auschwitz. See Robert Jay Lifton, *The Nazi Doctors* (New York: Basic Books, 1986).

48. There are some positive church examples in Fürstenberg's book, such as page 177, a letter written in October 1941 by church superintendent Max Diestel to the vice president of the territorial church, pleading for pastors and congregants to protect their members with Jewish backgrounds. "They have through baptism become our brothers who through Jesus Christ want to be God's children." Whether non- Christians are also God's children, the letter does not say. "So far as we know the letter never received an answer" from the church official.

49. Ibid., p. 193.

50. Ibid., p. 227.

51. Ibid., p. 301. Prior to 1933, classes for Jewish children had been a feature of the curriculum, but the next five years saw the gradual tightening of spaces, times, teachers, and financial support for this purpose. November 10, 1938, marked the final exclusion of Jews from the realm of public education.

52. The ordinary German school rule for children is that they should not be taken to a concentration camp museum before age twelve. Scenes of horror can be boring, too, as the term "psychic numbing" suggests. Studying the outrageous context of Dr. Mengele and other Auschwitz doctors, Lifton writes of the same symptom. Studies of the Rwanda genocide of 1994, whose Hutu perpetrators acquired the name *genocidaires,* tell of a similar syndrome: the first murder is hard, the second easier, the rest easier and easier.

53. Klaus Bergmann et al., eds., *Geschichte und Geschenhen* (Stuttgart: Ernst Klett Verlag, 1997), p. 131.

54. In early 1943 a group of Berlin non-Jewish women married to Jewish hus- bands saw them arrested by the Gestapo, who, in response to the women's public demonstrations, released the husbands. In memory of this event, a Mahnmal stands now in Berlin on the Rosenstrasse.

55. Bergmann, *Geschichte und Geschenhen,* p. 133.

56. Ibid., quoted from *Ruhr-Zeitung,* Bochum, May 12, 1945.

CHAPTER 2

1. Nelson Mandela, *Long Walk to Freedom: The Autobiography of Nelson Mandela* (Abacus Books; London: Little, Brown and Company, 1994), pp. 438, 456. The first quotation is the concluding paragraph of his four-hour address to the South African Supreme Court in Pretoria, site of the "Rivonia Trial" of eleven leaders of the African National Congress for sabotage and conspiracy to overthrow the government, October 1963–June 1964. Mandela and others admitted that, beginning in 1961, the ANC had indeed begun armed resistance of the Nationalist government. He defended the strategy on moral grounds and addressed the court at this great length, knowing that he and his colleagues were about to be silenced either by execution or by severe isolation in the South African prison system. Mandela believed that the international pressures surrounding this trial pushed the government away from sentences of execution to life imprisonment. Cf. pp. 442–449.

2. Ibid., p. 456.

3. Walter Sisulu, *I Will Go Singing* (Cape Town: Robben Island Museum in Association with the Africa Fund, 1997), p. 182. In conversation with George M. Houser and Herbert Shore.

4. Interview with Dr. Joseph Roberts, pastor of the Ebenezer Baptist Church in Atlanta, July 10, 2003. This church is the one led by Martin Luther King, Sr., and in which his son was raised.

5. A mere ten dollars for Americans in 2002, who were lucky to benefit from an exchange rate much to the disadvantage of South Africa. Not many older black citizens can afford the trip nor do they need to: They know well enough what happened on Robben Island from 1961 to 1996. It is the young of all races whom teachers should persuade to go.

6. Charlene Smith, *Robben Island* (Cape Town: Struik Publishers, 1997), p. 5.

7. G. F. Gresley, in an article published in 1895, quoted by Smith, p. 5. "Few places so small and insignificant looking can boast of having played so important a part in the history of a vast multitude of people."

8. See Mandela, *Long Walk*, p. 481.

9. Albie Sachs, anti-apartheid lawyer in the 1960s, who would become a member of the Constitutional Court in the 1990s, suffered 168 days of such confinement under the Ninety Days Detention Law. He expressed the fear that sanity is impossible to preserve under such circumstances. "Man is not isolated and alone; the crowd is not his enemy. If that were in fact so, solitary confinement would not affect one so viciously . . . man is interdependent in his very depths." Albie Sachs, *The Jail Diary of Albie Sachs* (Cape Town: David Philip, 1990), p. 97.

10. Mandela, *Long Walk*, p. 463.

11. Any civilian caught without a pass was immediately, without excuse, fined sixty rand.

12. Mandela, *Long Walk*, p. 459.

13. Ibid., p. 482. Even at that, the prisoner had to pay for the glasses.

14. Ibid., p. 589.

15. In 1940 the Cape Town City Council proposed the clearance of the area, deeming it a slum. But, said the city engineer: "One must not lose sight of the fact that the District is capable of being one of the finest in the city, as it at one time was,

before being allowed to deteriorate . . . it is a healthy site and commands a magnificent outlook." The passive "being allowed" was evasive but prophetic. In the next two decades the city government would neglect systematically the physical upkeep of streets and sanitation facilities in the District, in preparation for its destruction under the national Group Areas Act of 1950.

16. In writing about modern South Africa, it is almost impossible not to refer to the old four-fold racial classifications of the system—black, colored, Asian, and white. Tragically, the racial component of a citizen's current identity carries continuing economic, political, and cultural meaning. It is not much different still in the United States.

17. As transcribed from my notes in the interview, March 2002.

18. Peggy Delport, "Signposts for retrieval: a visual framework for enabling memory of place and time," in *Recalling Community in Cape Town: Creating and Curating the District Six Museum*, eds. Ciraj Rassool and Sandra Prosalendis (Cape Town: District Six Museum, 2001), p. 33. She reports that the content of this work was influenced, on the spot, by "the verbal responses and interjections of ex-residents and passersby," a fact that accords with the insistence of the later museum designers that it be a creation of the ex-residents as well experts.

19. Correspondence with Peter J. Storey, April 27, 2002. After five years in Cape Town Storey became pastor of the Central Methodist Church in Johannesburg in 1976. He was one of the most vocal church opponents of the regime all during the 1980s. In that decade he was president of the South African Council of Churches, the leading church body of opponents and advocate of many ANC claims. In this period, Desmond Tutu and Beyers Naudé were general secretaries of the SACC. See Storey, *From the Crucible: Sermons and Addresses in a Time of Crisis* (Nashville: Abingdon Press, 2002).

20. All three quotations are from former residents as recorded in essays in *Lost Communities, Living Memories: Remembering Forced Removals in Cape Town*, ed. Sean Field (Cape Town: David Philip, 2001), pp. 62, 67, 121. See the essays " 'Ja! So was District Six! But it was a beautiful place': Oral Histories, Memory, and Identity," by Felicity Swanson and Jane Harries, and " 'I dream of our old house, you see there are things that can never go away': Memory, Restitution, and Democracy," by Sean Field.

21. As in the history of many a depressed neighborhood in the United States, District Six residents who came into middle-class incomes sometimes moved out to more affluent neighborhoods. The fact that, in spite of energetic anti-apartheid political activity in the District, leaders mounted little protest against the initial removals of black residents underscores one of the tragic "successes" of the apartheid regime: exploitation of racial animosity between groups of "nonwhites."

22. Amos Oz, "Calling a Spade a Spade," *New South African Outlook*, February 1986, as quoted by Peggy Delport, "Signposts," p. 39.

23. Swanson and Harries, " 'Ja! So was District Six!' " Field, in *Lost Communities*, p. 80.

24. In the 1966–1982 removals, city officials destroyed records of names and residences, making the memory of survivors the essential documentation of the history. This obliteration, comments Peggy Delport, was supported by "the willing amnesia of most of the white population." "Signposts," p. 36. "Official" memory often

tends to statistics and abstractions. The array of everyday items in the museum makes it a very concrete evocation of social history.

25. Delport, "Signposts," p. 79.

26. A vivid image of the abstractness and arrogance of the township projects in the 1970s and 1980s, as the government prepared the bare area that was to become Khayelitsha, is a photograph of aluminum outhouses constructed there, standing like sentinels every fifty yards on empty ground. The townships were cuts above prison camps; they had "amenities" like outhouses. But human communities cannot be so artificially and rootlessly constructed. See Vivian Bickford-Smith, "Mapping Cape Town: From Slavery to Apartheid," in Field, ed., *Lost Communities*, p. 23.

27. "Mrs. F," Field, *Lost Communities*, p. 76. "Ms. N. N." recollects how shared poverty often occasioned the sharing of surplus: "Every Friday afternoon we were sent to fetch fruit and vegetables. When we got to the market we would find the bags ready for us to take home, and not a single penny was spent. Bhut' Gosa gave us fruit. Tat'u gave us cabbage and carrots, then from Bhut' Michael we collected potatoes and onions." Interdependence pushed residents of other communities, subject to the removals, into intimate acquaintance with each other. Cedric van Reenen, former resident of another Cape Town long-settled neighborhood, Protea Village, described his memory of his neighbors in poignant terms: "We used to know each other by the sound of the footsteps in the dark. That was how close-knit the community was. When they moved us they broke the spirit." Quoted by Delport, "Signposts," p. 39.

28. So listed on the final page of Rassool and Prosalendis, *Recalling Community*.

29. As described by Caroline Hooper-Box, in *Sunday Independent* (Cape Town), December 16, 2001. This rural area is famous for cultivation of the herbs used by traditional African healers. This article reports on a conference of six hundred healers who met in Vlakplaas on this date. Said Mongane Wally Serote, a parliamentary committee chair, "People were killed here, and suffered a great deal here. If we have succeeded in putting in place a process which resulted in reconciliation and democracy, we can then put in place institutions which express this. Hence the idea of a national [Vlakplaas] centre. . . . The idea is that this place which caused so much pain must be a place of hope, and inspire us about he possibility to change evil." De Kock is currently serving a life sentence. For profound insight into his character, see the book by TRC staff psychologist Pumla Gobodo-Madikizela, *A Human Being Died That Night: A South African Story of Forgiveness* (Boston: Houghton Mifflin, 2003), recording her extensive interviews with the man who earned the nickname "Prime Evil."

30. "Children can't process this information," she says, in agreement with German educators who, for example, recommend that no child under twelve be asked to visit one of the concentration camp museums.

31. Interview with Marlene Silbert, April 8, 2002. She added, regretfully, "Since 9/11 Muslims have stopped coming to the museum."

32. Interview, March 12, 2002. His best known English-translated novel is *Ancestral Voices,* a story centered on cultural and class conflict in an extended Afrikaner rural family. Among other dimensions, the book portrays the inescapable relations between Afrikaners and surrounding Xhosa people.

33. Zakes Mda, "Africanness Still in the Making," in a paper for a conference sponsored by the Institute for Justice and Reconciliation, Cape Town, on December 4, 2001.

34. Interview, March 18, 2002. Field is director of the Centre for Popular Memory at UCT. The Centre's speciality is collection and archiving of oral history. Note that the first forced removals from District Six occurred in 1901 and that the first removals in the 1960s were of blacks, resulting in little or no protest from local colored residents. Cape Town and the Western Cape have the largest concentration of so-called colored in South Africa, and tension between them and "Africans" has long been a fact of social-political life. In the election of 1994, a majority sided with the National Party. But in April 2004 Western Cape went ANC.

35. Any attempt in 2002 to offer a comprehensive overview will speedily get out of date, so numerous are current local developments of new statuary, names, and ceremonies.

36. Subscript: "Presented to Rondebosch Ratepayers [Taxpayers] Association by Councillor Mrs. J. J. J. Bakker." No date.

37. Zekes Mda, *The Heart of Redness* (Cape Town: Oxford University Press, 2000), pp. 95–96.

38. Among the bits of justice finally accorded him in the 1990s has been the awarding of an honorary degree by Stellenbosch University, one-time academic champion of Dutch Reformed and Afrikaner political theology. Perhaps the crowning tribute to Naudé by this university and its theology department was the recent establishment of "The Beyers Naudé Institute for Justice and Social Policy." For a portrait of Naudé by a major American journalist in the early 1980s, see Joseph Lelyveld, *Move Your Shadow: South Africa Black and White* (New York: Times Books, 1985), pp. 301–314. Lelyveld, who is Jewish, heard a sermon by Naude, based on the Ahab and Naboth story in I Kings 21. Afterward he wrote: "I am neither Christian nor South African, but I thought, if I were South African, the experience of hearing that sermon could have changed my life" (p. 314). Naudé died in September 2004 at age eighty-nine.

39. The *Umkhonto we Sizwe* ("Sword of the Nation") or MK. The reluctant turn of ANC leaders to politically targeted violence came in 1960 as nonviolent appeals to the government had failed to stem the tide of tighter and tighter apartheid legislation. For their avowal of this new policy, Mandela and his colleagues were charged with conspiracy, tried and imprisoned. Into the 1980s, MK strategy called for destruction of physical objects but for no direct attack on civilians.

40. David Chidester, "Stories, Fragments and Monuments," in *Facing the Truth: South African Faith Communities and the Truth and Reconciliation Commission,* eds. James Cochrane, John de Gruchy, and Stephen Martin (Cape Town: David Philip Publishers, 1999), p. 133. Chidester is a faculty member of the Department of Religious Studies in the University of Cape Town. He heard this story from one of the MK generals present in this discussion with Tambo. Interview, April 15, 2002.

41. One meets this phenomenon repeatedly in contemporary conversation with blacks, for example, in the observation that "the British have dual citizenship. They can go back to Britain if things get tough for them or to one of the commonwealth countries like Australia or Canada. But the Boers are like us: they have nowhere to go but South Africa. We have to live together, and we have lived together for centuries."

42. Serote, as quoted in the South African Tourist Bureau publication, *Sawubona*, April 2004, p. 45.

43. Associated Press, *New York Times*, December 17, 1998, p. A35.

44. Pietermaritzburg, a major city of Kwazulu-Natal, has a privately supported

Voortrekker museum which seeks to portray both sides of the battle and subsequent diverse memories of its significance.

45. Rodney Davenport and Christopher Saunders, *South Africa: A Modern History*, 5th ed. (London: Macmillan, 2000), p. 672.

46. Three civic holidays are also specialized: May 1, Workers Day, precious to Communists the world around; August 9, Women's Day, more important to modern South Africans then for most previous generations; and September 24, Heritage Day, for English descendants who honor the founding of the British colony in 1806.

47. Personal communication, April 2002.

48. In 2002 Ms. Goniwe served on the staff of the new Institute for Justice and Reconciliation (IJR) in Cape Town, an outgrowth of the TRC directed by TRC researcher Charles Villa-Vicencio. Her work centers on helping local communities to deal with their painful past. In their appearance before the TRC in 1997, the Security Police told how they had disguised the identities of the corpses of the four men. In this hearing, the commanding officer, Colonel DuPlessis, confessed that he was "appalled to hear his own [Security] superior say, 'Killing in defence of the state is not murder.' . . . I can only ask [Ms. Goniwe] to forgive me." But Ms. Goniwe concluded that she should not offer forgiveness. "The police who killed my husband did not express understanding of my suffering. Had they displayed that, I would be obliged to consider reconciliation with them." The TRC itself also refused to recommend amnesty (interview, April 2002).

49. There is a now-famous photograph of the sister of young Hector Peterson, shot and killed in the Soweto student demonstrations of 1976. To the designers of the new Soweto museum, the image of his limp body in her arms strongly suggested Michaelangelo's *Pieta* in the Vatican. They placed the photograph at the entrance of the museum.

50. Johan Snyman, "Ways of Remembering," in *Transcending a Century of Injustice*, ed. Charles Villa-Vicencio (Cape Town: Institute for Justice and Reconciliation, 2000), p. 32.

51. Quoted in Snyman, "Ways of Remembering," p. 32.

52. Leonard Thompson quotes these statistics from historian Peter Warwick. "In fact, both sides made extensive use of black labor, and Africans as well as Afrikaners suffered from the [British] scorched earth policy." Afrikaner camp deaths, all told, came to almost 28,000, "most of them children [who] died of dysentery, measles, and other diseases. . . ." Thompson, *A History of South Africa*, 3rd ed. (New Haven: Yale University Press), p. 143.

53. Snyman, "Ways of Remembering," p. 33. Strictly parallel to this insult to history was the naming, in the Cold War era, of a United States nuclear submarine after the city of Corpus Christi. One has to wonder if many American Christians, whether or not they knew Latin, shuddered at this choice of name.

54. Ibid., p. 34. Snyman and the editors conclude his essay with three pictures: the Bloemfontein monument, the Michaelangelo Pieta, and a now-famous photograph by Sam Nzima "of the limp body of Hector Petersen, taken in Soweto in 1976." Inclusion of the latter validates Snyman's moral analysis here in a powerful way (pp. 36–37).

55. June Bam and Pippa Visser, *A New History for a New South Africa* (Cape Town: Kagiso Publishers, 1996), pp. 1, 37. Teachers are the book's intended readers. It

breaks ground in educational theory and practice that should interest history teachers worldwide. The book is one element in the South Africa History Project, sponsored by the new Department of Education in Pretoria.

56. Bam and Visser, *New History*, p. 64.

57. Ibid., pp. 6–7.

58. Ibid., pp. 34–35

59. Ibid., p. 30.

60. The final chapter of the book, "A Sample Chapter for a New History Textbook," sets out lines for study of a famous nineteenth-century incident in South African history, the Xhosa Cattle Killing, "not often taught in school." (p. 155). Readers of Mda's novel, *The Color of Redness*, will know that the incident evokes exquisite insights into traditional African culture, the incursions of European colonialism and military conquest, and resulting nineteenth-century political conflicts.

61. G. J. J. Smit, H. G. J. Lintvelt, T. A. Eksteen, and F. P. J. Smit, *History Standard Ten* (Cape Town: Maskew Miller Ltd., 1976). In their preface, the authors recommend "individual activity" for good teaching of students, and they underscore the key role of teachers, for "it is the teacher who has to interpret and revitalize the facts." Compared to the new texts, however, this advice gets only modest reinforcement in the questions and projects recommended at the end of the chapters, which are keyed to the anticipated content of the matriculation exams.

62. Ibid., Phrases to be found on pages 214, 218,221, 224, 226, 229, 235.

63. Ibid., pp. 229–230.

64. Ibid., pp. 212, 224.

65. Ibid., p. 192.

66. Ibid., p. 255. Italics in the original.

67. A quotation from the introductory "A Note to the Reader," *In Search of History: Secondary Book 1*, authored by Vivian Bickford-Smith, Jean Bottaro, Bruce Mohammed, Pippa Visser, and Nigel Worden (Cape Town: Oxford University Press, 1995) [to be designated below as *Search, Book 1*]. A second text perused here is *In Search of History: Secondary Book*, eds. Jane Rosenthal and Pippa Visser with the assistance of five other historians (Cape Town: Oxford University Press, 1996) [here to be designated as *Search, Book 2*]. And a third: *In Search of History: Standard 12*, eds. Jean Bottaro and Pippa Visser (Cape Town: Oxford, 1999) [here to be designated as *Search, Standard 12*].

68. Bickford-Smith, *Search, Book 1*, Introduction.

69. Rosenthal, *Search, Book 2*, pp. 24, 54. The latter comes after an account of the ruins of Great Zimbabwe, about which a British historian, Lord Gayre, wrote in 1972: "It is clear that the already-ruined civilization . . . could not have been the product of the Bantu then, or at an earlier period . . . unless under the lash of the taskmaster and slave owner."

70. Ibid., pp. 159–162.

71. Ibid., pp. 88, 109, 117, 130, 134, 138, 145, 187.

72. Bickford-Smith, *Search, Book 1*. The earliest (1995) of the high school texts in this Oxford series and for the same standards seven through eight, the book covers the twentieth-century and is numbered "1" while *Search, Book 2* (1996) covers the earlier periods.

73. Bickford-Smith, *Search Book 1*, p. 40.

74. Ibid., pp. 63, 118, 124, 125, 130, 136, 137, 143, 150, 160, 174.

75. The new apartheid museum in Johannesburg requires visitors to enter one of the two doors—"Whites" and "non-Whites"—and at first the two groups are not permitted to talk to each other. Various glimpses of apartheid society line hallways and rooms: film, news clips, posters, photos, biographies of ANC leaders which mention their indebtedness to Christian mission schooling, and a speech by Hendrik Verwoerd justifying apartheid as "good neighborliness." A next display chronicles the step-by-step enactment of 150 petty-apartheid laws, reminiscent of the Schoneberg memorial. The final stages of the museum present a list of people executed as protesters, a collection of hangman's nooses on a ceiling, a formidable "hippo" (the tanklike vehicle used by the police to control the townships), and an array of weapons used by both sides of the struggle. Not having visited this museum, I am indebted to Rev. David Markey, of the Methodist Board of Global Ministries, for a report on his 2002 visit. He says that the Verwoerd speech "all sounded so reasonable" and that, before the nooses and lists of people executed, visitors in his group experienced anger and tears. Staff of this museum say that, like Jennifer Wallace, local high school history teachers often bring their classes here.

76. "The [political] party meetings at Kempton Park in 1991–3 had taken place at a time when annual deaths from civil strife had actually risen from between 600 and 1,400 in the late 1980s to between 2,700 and 3,800 in the early 1990s. Mortalities from political violence in 1994 more than tripled those during the Soweto uprising of 1976–7." Davenport and Saunders, *South Africa: A Modern History*, p. 562. In 1990–1991 the annual murder rate per 100,000 population in France and Germany was four, in the USA ten, in the Netherlands fifteen, and in South Africa ninety-eight. See Leonard Thompson, *History of South Africa*, p. 267.

77. A group of American church leaders, invited to Tutu's installation as new Archbishop of the Anglican Church of Southern Africa, arranged to spend a day in Lusaka with ANC leaders on their way back to the United States.

78. See Njabulo Ndebele, "Of Lions and Rabbits: Thoughts on Democracy and Reconciliation," in *After the TRC: Reflections on Truth and Reconciliation in South Africa*, ed. Wilmot James and Linda van de Vijver (Cape Town: David Philip, 2000), p. 147. Ndebele, a poet and professor of literature, is Vice Chancellor of the University of Cape Town. He is quoting from Allister Sparks, *Tomorrow is Another Country: The Inside Story of South Africa's Negotiated Revolution* (Johannesburg: Struik Book Publishers, 1994), p. 204.

79. Lourens du Plessis, "The South African Constitution as Memory and Promise," *Stellenbosch Law Review* 11, no. 3 (2000): 385, originally given for the launching of the Institute for Justice and Reconciliation in Cape Town, May 11, 2000.

80. Johnny De Lange, "The Historical Context, Legal Origins and Philosophical Foundations of the South African Truth and Reconciliation Commission," in *Looking Back and Reaching Forward: Reflections on the Truth and Reconciliation Commission of South Africa*, eds. Charles Villa-Vicencio and Wilhelm Verwoerd (Cape Town: University of Cape Town Press, 2000), p. 21.

81. As quoted by De Lange, "Historical Context," p. 21. Italics in original.

82. *The Constitution of the Republic of South Africa, 1996* (Pretoria: The Govern-

ment Printer, 2002). The "Founding Provisions" section ends (p. 5) with mention of twenty-four languages which deserve respect in the life of the country.

83. Du Plessis, "South African Constitution," p. 386.

84. Ibid., p. 393.

85. Ibid., p. 389.

86. De Lange, "Historical Context," p. 18.

87. Ibid., p. 20.

88. In late 1998 the ANC went to court to prevent the publication of the report. President Mandela overruled his political colleagues and accepted the report from the hands of Desmond Tutu.

89. Elizabeth Kiss, "Moral Ambition Within and Beyond Political Constraints," in *Truth v. Justice: The Morality of Truth Commissions*, ed. Robert I. Rotberg and Dennis Thompson (Princeton: Princeton University Press, 2000), p. 69.

90. Cited by Kiss, "Moral Ambition," p. 85, from the records of the case, *AZAPO and Others v. President of SA and Others.*

91. Alasdair MacIntyre, *After Virtue: A Study in Moral Theory*, 2nd ed. (Notre Dame: University of Notre Dame Press, 1984), p. 222. MacIntyre (p. 163) quotes Australian philosopher John Anderson, who suggests that we should ask of a social institution not, "What end or purpose does it serve?" but rather, "Of what conflicts is it the scene?"

92. Antjie Krog, *Country of My Skull: Guilt, Sorrow, and the Limits of Forgiveness in the New South Africa* (Times Books; New York: Random House, 1998), p. 311. Krog is a poet and a journalist whose roots are Afrikaner. In its vividness her book can hardly be matched as an account of the daily procedures of the TRC.

93. Alex Boraine, *A Country Unmasked: Inside South Africa's Truth and Reconciliation Commission* (New York: Oxford Univesity Press, 2000), p. 143. Boraine, a former Methodist minister and Liberal Party leader who resigned from Parliament in the 1980s, had a major role in the deliberations that led to the TRC. President Mandela appointed him Deputy Chair of the Commission. This book will remain as one of the standard summary accounts of its work.

94. Interview, March 2003. Some among the twenty-two thousand hesitated, he says, to come forward under an identiry as "victims" rather than "soldiers in the struggle." But many of the latter finally decided that they too "had a story to tell."

95. Krog, *Country of My Skull*, p. 208.

96. James and van de Vijver, eds., *After the TRC*, p. 1, editors' introduction.

97. See Boraine, *A Country Unmasked*, pp. 258, 274–275.

98. Cornel du Toit, "Dealing with the Past," in *To Remember and to Heal: Theological and Psychological Reflections on Truth and Reconciliation*, ed. H. Russel Botman and Robin M. Petersen (Cape Town: Human and Rousseau, 1996), p. 120.

99. Boraine, *A Country Unmasked*, p. 441.

100. See Priscilla B. Hayner, *Unspeakable Truths: Confronting State Terror and Atrocity* (New York: Routledge, 2001), pp. 107–132, for a careful discussion of the importance and the cautions that ought, in law and ethics, be accorded the public naming of perpetrators by truth commissions. She believes (p. 130) that the South African TRC struck the best balance between public accusations and due process for the accused.

101. See discussion in "Contested Monuments and Memorials" section earlier in this chapter.

102. Kondlo went on to assess the power of public grief displayed in funerals, especially in the mid-1980s: "The funeral of the Cradock Four on 20 July 1985 changed the political landscape of this country forever. It was like a raging fire. ANC and SACP [South African Communist Party] flags were defiantly displayed, buses and buses full of people turned up—a state of emergency was declared [by the government]. But in a sense it was the real beginning of the end of apartheid" (Krog, pp. 57–58).

103. See Hayner, *Unspeakable Truths*, pp. 141–144.

104. Ibid., p. 139.

105. In the first months of the TRC, public viewing of its hearings via radio and television was widespread in South Africa. But two years of atrocity stories proved hard for the public to continue absorbing. The syndrome around nuclear weaponry, which Robert Lifton called "nuclear numbing," had an analogy here—TRC-numbing.

106. Boraine, *A Country Unmasked*, pp. 354–355.

107. One of the controversial rules set down for the TRC by parliament was that perpetrators had to tell the truth about their deeds but were not required to show remorse. Whether or not remorse in any form should be such a requirement remains a controversy.

108. Amos Oz, as quoted in an exhibit of the United States Holocaust Memorial, Washington, D.C.

109. Krog, *Country of My Skull*, p. 159.

110. Mamphela Ramphele, "Law, Corruption and Morality" in *After the TRC*, ed. James and van de Vijver, p. 173.

111. The inner quote was from F. W. De Klerk testifying about the Cradock Four. "If we had known what happened . . . the perpetrators would have been arrested." The "archbishop," of course, was Chairman Tutu. Krog, *Country of My Skull*, p. 136.

112. Ibid.

113. Quoted from the Final Report of the TRC by Charles Villa-Vicencio and Wilhelm Verwoerd, "Constructing a Report: Writing up the 'Truth,' " in *Truth v. Justice*, ed. Rothberg and Thompson, p. 288.

114. Boraine, *A Country Unmasked* pp. 139–140.

115. Ibid.

116. De Klerk and his staff associate David Steward continue to have bitter feelings toward Boraine, after the fashion of many southern politicians in the American civil rights era who accused white liberal supporters of Martin Luther King of being "traitors." In my April 2002 interview with De Klerk and Steward, they characterized Boraine as a "Grand Inquisitor Torquemada."

117. Boraine, *A Country Unmasked*, p. 187.

118. Boraine, interview, March 2002.

119. See below, point 5.

120. H. Russel Botman, "The Offender and the Church," in *Facing the Truth*, ed. Cochrane et al., p. 127. Botman, now a member of the faculty of theology at Stellenbosch University, was first director of the new Beyers Naudé Center for Public Justice and is now a university dean.

302 NOTES TO PAGES 115–122

121. Van Zyl Slabbert, "Truth Without Reconciliation, Reconciliation Without Truth," in *Facing the Truth*, ed. Cochrane et al., pp. 64–65.

122. Ibid. He goes on to express pessimism about the capacity of a truth commission to summon such confessional truth or to get at the truth of crimes with the rigor expected of law courts. For a contrasting view that each institution has unique capacities and limitations, cf. my essay, "Truth Commissions and Judicial Trials: Complementary or Antagonistic Servants of Public Justice?" *Journal of Law and Religion* 16 no. 1 (2001), pp. 1–33.

123. Krog, *Country of My Skull*, p. 285.

124. Richard Steigel, *Time*, April 26, 2004, p. 132.

125. As quoted by Krog, *Country of My Skull*, pp. 209–210.

126. Ibid., p. 284, quoting Ms. Lakotse, in a hearing in Ladybrand in the Transvaal.

127. Jane Lawrence, sister of Stanley Abrahams, now on the staff of the District Six Museum,speaking in summer 2002 to a visiting group of fellow Methodists headed by David Markay.

128. Boraine, *Country Unmasked*, pp. 185–186. Cf. TRC Report, Vol. 4, pp. 107–108.

129. De Lange, "The Historical Context," in *Looking Back, Reaching Forward*, ed. Villa-Vicencio and Veivoerd, pp. 18, 24.

130. De Klerk is a member of the so-called Reformed Church, a nineteenth-century breakaway body from the dominant Dutch Reformed Church. It is probably fair to say that it represents a pietistic form of Calvinism not overtly concerned with politics. See *F. W. De Klerk: The Autobiography* (London: Macmillan, 1999), p. 7.

131. Boraine, *Country Unmasked*, pp. 220, 180–181.

132. Charles Villa-Vicencio, "On Taking Responsibility," in *To Remember and to Heal*, ed. Botman and Peterson, p. 138, quoting Ellen Kuzwayo.

133. Slabbert, "Truth Without Reconciliation," in *Facing the Truth*, ed Cochrane et al., p. 71.

134. Timothy Garten Ash, *The File: A Personal History* (New York: Random House, 1997), pp. 225–226.

135. See the whole article, "Truth Without Reconciliation," in *Facing the Truth*, ed. Cochrane et al., pp. 62–72. His blunt rejection of truth about atrocity, as an important contribution to the healing of the fractured body politic, is rather puzzling in light of his confidence that "confession" (e.g. in his fantasied pair of speeches for the 1994 presidential inauguration) is the other major road to both truth and reconciliation. Coerced or not, there was enough confession in the TRC process to command some admiration from his viewpoint, one might surmise.

136. Albie Sachs, "His Name Was Henry," in *After the TRC*, ed. James and van de Vijver, p. 97.

137. Krog, *Country of My Skull*, pp. 43, 192.

138. Piet Meiring, "The *Baruti* Versus the Lawyers: The Role of Religion in the TRC process," in *Looking Backward, Reaching Forward*, ed. Villa-Vicencio and Vervend, pp. 129–130.

139. Ibid., p. 129.

140. Hayner, *Unspeakable Truths*, p. 153.

141. "Faith Communities and Apartheid," Report of the Research Institute on

Christianity in South Africa," in *Facing the Truth*, ed. Cochrane et al., p. 59, and John W. de Gruchy, *Reconciliation: Restoring Justice* (Minneapolis: Fortress Press, 2002), p. 162. The latter book is the best post-TRC theological exploration to date of the inseparable connection between personal repentance in the Christian tradition, often associated exclusively with personal sins, and social-political repentance that works toward concrete just change. De Gruchy believes that "the sacrament of penance is the sacrament of restorative justice" and that "penance . . . sends us forth to make reparation" (pp. 100–101).

142. Njabulo Ndebele, "Of Lions and Rabbits: Thoughts on Democracy and Reconciliation," in *Facing the Past*, ed. Cochrane et al., pp. 147–155 *passim*. A recent paper by Nico Koopman, a theologian at the Beyers Naudé Centre for Public Theology at the University of Stellenbosch, salutes some of the remarkable economic achievements of the new South African government: "We have brought clean water to more than 9 million people who did not have it before, electricity to more than 2 million, and telephones . . . to 1.5 million. We have integrated, at least nominally, more than 30,000 public schools . . . raised the literacy rate of fifteen-to-twenty-four-year-olds to 95 percent, and brought free health care to millions of children." In addition the government has cut budget deficits, reduced prime interest rates from 24 percent to 14 percent, and lifted trade barriers. On the other hand, he concedes, the gap between rich and poor has widened, some 41.4 percent of households remain poor, and the 65 percent youth unemployment of 1995 has not much changed. Koopman, "After Ten Years: Public Theology in Postapartheid South Africa," presented at the annual meeting of the Society Of Christian Ethics, Chicago, January 11, 2004.

143. Boraine, *A Country Unmasked*, p. 415.

144. These quotations from Niebuhr can be found in H. Richard Niebuhr, *The Meaning of Revelation* (New York: Macmillan, 1941), pp. 113–114, 118–120. I am indebted to Professor Smit for his references to this classic American work. As one of Niebuhr's students, I have long cherished this book, but without Professor Smit I would have forgotten its astonishing pertinence to the legitimation of the TRC. Niebuhr wrote that in the moment of God's self-revelation, persons of faith find themselves "remembering what we have forgotten" (p. 110). Partners in the faith serve us with the same reminding. See Smit's invaluable article, "Confession-Guilt-Truth-and-Forgiveness in the Christian Tradition," in *To Remember and to Heal*, ed. Botman and Petersen, pp. 96–101.

145. Krog, *Country of My Skull*, pp. 354–355. There is little question that whites offered the weakest support for the TRC before, during, and after its work. A survey report from the late 1990s found only 37 percent of white respondents approving of the TRC. James L. Gibson and Helen MacDonald, *Truth—Yes—Reconciliation—Maybe* (Rondebosch, Cape Town: Institute for Justice and Reconciliation, 2002).

146. Mary Burton, "Reparation, Amnesty and a National Archive," in *After the TRC*, ed. James and van de Vijver, p. 114.

CHAPTER 3

1. Jerry Adler, in the *Encyclopedia of Religion* (New York: Macmillan, 1987), as quoted by Martin Marty, *Context*, February 1, 1996, p. 6.

2. As quoted by Carny James, "Timeless and Timely, 'Roots' Returns after a Quarter Century," *New York Times*, January 18, 2002, p. E37.

3. Milan Kundera, *Ignorance*, trans. Linda Asher (London: Faber and Faber, 2002), p. 33.

4. David Blight, *Race and Reunion: The Civil War in American Memory* (Cambridge, Mass.: Harvard University Press, 2001), p. 288. In 1910 a member of the Richmond, Virginia, elite, Janet Randolph, replied to the monument proposal: "No monument to them, if you please, until we have tended to their earthly wants."

5. I Corinthians 13:11.

6. Charles Villa-Vicencio, unpublished paper, 2002. He is the former director of research for the South African TRC and now director of the Institute for Justice and Reconciliation in Cape Town.

7. Second Thessalonians 2:7.

8. In December 2002 the "Trent Lott Affair" was resolved by the Republican Party's decision to drop him as U.S. Senate majority leader, all for one nostalgic remark about the 1948 segregationist campaign of fellow Senator Strom Thurmond. It was a form of Freud's "return of the repressed," but it demonstrated that nostalgia for past racist law in the United States was no longer overtly, politically salesworthy.

9. Blight, *Race and Reunion*, p. 261. New England was the other major contender for control of the national memory.

10. Statement in the text of a 1987 videofilm, *The Courage to Change: A Story from Richmond, Virginia*, written by Robert Cochoran, twenty-year resident, and produced by the organization Hope in the Cities. When white families moved to one of the counties surrounding the central city, they lost all direct political connection to city politics because in Virginia law county and city boundaries do not overlap.

11. Quoted from the video documentary, *Healing the Heart of America*, (Richmond: Moral Rearmament and Cornerstone Communications, 1993), an account of the Unity Walk Through History.

12. As stated in the above film, *The Courage to Change*, which records various such mini-breakthroughs in the 1970s and 1980s.

13. John Hope Franklin, *From Slavery to Freedom: A History of Negro Americans* (Vintage Books; New York: Alfred A. Knopf, 1967), pp. 72–75. By 1700 a thousand slaves arrived every year, mostly at the Richmond docks. By 1756 the proportion of whites to blacks in Virginia was 173,316 to 120,156.

14. It was the first building in the colonies specifically designed as a state capitol, after plans drawn by Thomas Jefferson during his time as ambassador to France in the 1780s. His model was the ancient Roman temple in Nimes, La Maison de Carree.

15. Statement by Rev. Paige Chargois, interview June 2002. She is a parish minister long active in the organization, and helped found Hope for the Cities in 1993.

16. The Letter to the Hebrews 12:1.

17. The Virginia State Museum, since 1995, has display rooms devoted to Virginia history which include well-researched images of Indians, colonists, slaves, and the commerical development of the state. At the exit, in 2002, curators placed the plaster-cast original of the Arthur Ashe statue now on Monument Avenue.

18. In 2001 the latter changed its name internationally to "Initiatives for Change," as a result of a mission shift to social as well as personal transformation.

19. Karen Elliott Greisdorf, "The City that Dares to Talk," in the newly titled MRA publication, *For a Change* 15, No. 1 (February/March 2002), p. 4. Historian David Blight says that the capital worth of slaves in 1860 exceeded the whole of other capital assets in the entire country. (Comment in a public meeting in New York City, June 12, 2003. See his volume, *Race and Reunion*.)

20. Historians estimate that a total of half a million slaves moved through Virginia to the Deep South between 1790 and 1859. The Virginia legislature outlawed the importation of slaves in 1778, but in that act it heightened the economic value of slaves already in the country. By 1840 Richmond had moved ahead of Alexandria as a "slave depot." In 1860 there were fifteen slave-trade companies in Richmond, nineteen auctioneers, and fifteen "general and collecting agents." (Data compiled by Philip J. Schwartz of the Virginia Commonwealth University, principally from R. H. Gudmestad, "The Richmond Slave Market, 1840–1860," master's thesis, University of Richmond, 1993, and Michael Tadman, *Speculators and Slaves: Masters, Traders, and Slaves in the Old South* (Madison, Wis.: University of Wisconsin Press, 1989).

21. Letter to Robert Pleasants, in Samuel E. Morison and Henry S. Commager, *The Growth of the American Republic*, vol. 1 (New York: Oxford University Press, 1942), p. 246.

22. See introduction to this volume, p. 2.

23. Introduction to Morison and Commager, *Growth*, p. 246. See C. Vann Woodward's observations, noted in the introduction to this volume, that as late as the 1830s there were more antislavery societies in Virginia than in any other state, and that virtually all had disappeared by the 1840s.

24. Geiko Müller-Fahrenholz, "Die Erinnerung An Das Leid Und Das Nein Zum Krieg," *Publik Forum*, January 2003. Rev. Paige Chargois, Baptist pastor and Associate National Director of Hope in the Cities, recently joined a leading member of the city's UDC in an appeal to the governor of Minnesota that its state museum return its Confederate flag, captured in battle. The museum did so. In what sense African Americans might find it possible to "honor" Confederate veterans will remain a difficult question. In 2001, the Board of Chesterfield County, neighbor to Richmond, proclaimed April as "Confederate History and Heritage Month." Confrontation ensued between Gerald O. Glenn, bishop of the local New Deliverance Evangelistic Church, and Henry Kidd, Commander of the Virginia Division of the Sons of Confederate Veterans. County officials subsequently agreed to consult black leaders before they mounted another such proclamation. See (Richmond) *Times Dispatch*, August 27, 2001, and "Tear Down the Walls" in the newsletter of Hope in the Cities, *A Call to Community* (January 2002). White Southerners who want respect for the suffering of ancestors will find a readier reception of such respect if leaders like Henry Kidd could learn to exemplify the combination of empathy and morality in Ulysses S. Grant's journal entry on the day of Lee's surrender at Appomattox: "I felt sad and depressed at the downfall of a foe who had fought so long and valiantly, and had suffered so much for a cause, though that cause was, I believe, one of the worst for which a people ever fought." Quoted by James McPherson, *Battle Cry of Freedom* (New York: Ballantine Books, 1988), pp. 849–850. On southern and northern retrospective diminishment of the importance of slavery as the key cause of the war, and the rush to "reconciliation" among white Americans in the thirty years following Appomattox, see David Blight, *Race and Reunion*.

25. As the Blight book makes clear, northern and southern public commemorations of the war did not, in the late nineteenth century, acknowledge slavery as it central cause, any more than did the initial public rhetoric on either side in 1860. There was reason for the remark made by the black Union soldier played by Denzel Washington in the film *Glory* on the eve of the fatal attack on Fort Wagner: "This is not my war." In the 1876–1955 era, blacks had continuing reason to wonder if the war was about their legal freedom.

26. Quotations from Cindy Austin Brown, "The Missing Piece," *Northeast Magazine*, August 4, 2002. Motley's collection of three thousand items is to be the heart of the new museum. It includes slave auction fliers, bills of sale, runaway reward posters, and freedom papers.

27. Marie Tyler McGraw, *At the Falls: Richmond, Virginia and Its People* (Chapel Hill: The University of North Carolina Press, 1994), p. 311. While governor (1990–1994), Wilder proposed a museum of slavery for Richmond, but property and funding offers persuaded him to establish it in Fredericksburg, where it is now under construction.

28. For example: Like Charleston and New Orleans, tourism is naturally a resource for modern Richmond. In a recent colorful brochure of the Historic Richmond Foundation, "A Guide to Historic Richmond," the place of African Americans gets scarce mention beyond a picture of the Arthur Ashe monument. Among dozens of pictured landmarks is not one explicit association with slavery.

29. The summary below owes much to the Rosewood Website, which alleges the total number of items as 28,000. Partial search uncovers considerable redundancy, but this number of entries approaches the incredible.

30. This sketchy summary is based on the extensive research of five faculty members of three Florida universities, whose work was commissioned by the Florida State Legislature in the fall of 1993: *A Documented History of the Incident which Occurred at Rosewood, Florida, in January 1923*, submitted to the Board of Regents (and thence to the state legislature), December 22, 1993 (to be noted below as *A Documented History*; references are to the Website version at http://dlis.dos.state.fl.us/slib/rosewood.html). I have depended chiefly on this document because it supplied the information on which the legislature acted in 1994 to offer reparations to the surviving Rosewood black families. The fine book-length history is Michael D'Orso, *Like Judgment Day: The Ruin and Redemption of a Town Called Rosewood* (New York: G. P. Putnam's Sons, 1996). D'Orso lives and works in my native city, Norfolk, Virginia.

31. According to the research to be quoted further below, 38 lynchings took place in 1917, and 58 in 1918; and, in all, from 1918 to 1927 mobs killed 454 persons, of whom 416 were blacks. In the same period 47 blacks were murdered in Florida alone. The Tuskegee Institute records some 5000 lychings from the end of the Civil War into the 1940s. The "reign of terror" during and immediately after World War One, as the Florida document describes it, convulsed Tulsa, Omaha, East St. Louis, Chicago, "and many communities in between." In Chicago, "law and order were suspended for thirteen days in July 1919 as white mobs made foray after foray into black neighborhoods, killing and wounding 365 black residents and leaving another 1000 homeless." *A Documented History*, p. 3.

32. *A Documented History*, pp. 20–21, printout version www.tfn.net/doc/rosewood.txt, dated 1/6/03.

33. Ibid., p. 32.

34. See "A Chronology of Race Riots in America" by the relatively new Northstar Network, which begins with Cincinnati in 1829 and ends with Los Angeles in 1992. By far the greatest concentration of these forty-five murderous events (eleven) comes, in this chronology, between 1917 and 1923.

35. As quoted by Charles Flowers, "Is Singleton's Movie a Scandal or a Black 'Schindler's List?' " in *Seminole Tribune*, a publication of the Florida Seminole Tribe, March 1997, from its Website. This long article concentrates on diverse views of the 1997 movie *Rosewood*, directed by John Singleton.

36. The modest commercial success of the films *Amistad*, based on the revolt of African slaves on the ship of that name in the 1830s, and *Beloved*, based on the Toni Morrison novel, leads some African Americans (like my colleague James H. Cone) to suspect that whites want to avoid the pain of these histories.

37. E. R. Shipp, "Taking Control of Old Demons by Forcing Them into the Light," *New York Times*, March 16, 1997, section H, pp. 13 and 26. Shipp is a professor in the Columbia University School of Journalism.

38. State Representative Don Ross, "Prologue" to *Tulsa Race Riot: A Report of the Oklahoma Commission to Study the Tulsa Race Riot of 1921* (Oklahoma City: State of Oklahoma, 2001), pp. iv–v. Hereafter referred to as, *Commission Report*.

39. Much of the following account is derived from the long article of December 19, 1999, by Brent Staples of the *New York Times Magazine*, "Unearthing a Riot," as copied from the *New York Times* Archives, 2/9/00, page 2 of this ten-page transcript.

40. Ibid., transcript page 8. One should not assume that a state of true amnesia had settled over the Tulsa community. Black survivors of the riot certainly had not forgotten, nor those business men in the 1970s. A scattering of journalistic and academic essays appeared occasionally around the country, but hardly at all in Oklahoma. Memories were there, but highly segmented in both psychological and social senses.

41. The best and most recent is Alfred L. Brophy, *Reconstructing the Dreamland: The Tulsa Riot of 1921—Race, Repartions, and Reconciliation* (New York: Oxford University Press, 2002). Newspapers local and national covered the riot extensively in June, 1921. "Coverage" in the two white-owned Tulsa papers was laced with the theory of black responsibility for instigating the riot. An unpublished University of Tulsa M.A. thesis by Loren L. Gill was completed in 1946, but the next academic study, by R. Halliburton, Jr., in 1975, began with the note that, with two minor local exceptions, "[T]he Tulsa race riot was the only major American racial disturbance that has been ignored by scholars" (*The Tulsa Race War of 1921* [San Francisco: R & E Research Associates, 1975]). Halliburton's work, which unearths a plethora of documents, must have fortified Ross's early work on the history. Major historical scholarship awaited the early 1980s with the publication of *Death in a Promised Land*, by Scott Ellsworth (Foreword by John Hope Franklin; Baton Rouge: Louisiana State University Press, 1982.) The end of the 1990s saw a virtual blizzard of journalistic attention to 1921, spurred by Ross's work in the Oklahoma legislature. Two other long, detailed, somewhat less academic versions of the riot appeared in the next two years: Tim Madigan, *The Burning: Massacre, Destruction, and the Tulsa Race Riot of 1921* (New York: St. Martin's Press, 2001) and James S. Hirsch, *Riot and Remembrance: The Tulsa Race War and Its Legacy* (New York: Houghton Mifflin, 2002). Ellsworth and Brophy were

important contributors to 2001 Report of the Oklahoma commission study of the riot.

42. Randy Krehbiel, editor of *The Tulsa World*, personal communication, February 4, 2003.

43. "Unearthing a Riot," *New York Times Magazine*, December 19, 1999, Archives-internet version, p. 6: "As the morning wore on, a wall of fire worked its way across Greenwood, destroying everything in its path. The mob burst into one house after another, sometimes killing the occupants outright, often looting the house and setting it afire from within."

44. Among the indexes to how buried was the Tulsa memory, even among historians, is the 1981 high school history text by the distinguished Daniel Boorstin, Director of the Library of Congress. The text notes that twenty-five post–World War One race riots occurred in the United States and tags that in Chicago as the worst—with the death of fifteen whites and twenty-three blacks. Tulsan blacks believe that in cost of lives and property, theirs in 1921 was the worst. There is no mention of Tulsa-1921 in this book. The irony is that Boorstin was a native of Tulsa. See Daniel J. Boorstin and Brooks M. Kelley, with Ruth Frankel Boorstin, *A History of the United States* (Lexington, Mass.: Ginn and Company, 1981), p. 469.

45. Staples, "Unearthing a Riot," *New York Times Magazine*, December 19, 1999.

46. *Commission Report*, p. 12.

47. Quoted in *Commission Report*, p. 159.

48. *Tulsa World*, June 8, 1921, as quoted by Alfred L. Brophy, "Assessing State and City Culpability: The Riot and the Law," in *Commission Report*, pp. 153–173. Brophy is professor of law in the Oklahoma City University.

49. The use of initials for personal identification among African Americans (e.g., "W. D. Williams") has long been a protection against the propensity of racist white culture to call blacks by their first names, which, through initials, can remain hidden.

50. Allegations against both the mayor and the police chief—such as that they had ordered these "deputies" to kill and to burn—were never legally verified. But numerous witnesses testified that the rioters, by a large majority, were white people, and that local police had encouraged them. See Brophy, "Assessing State and City Culpability," *Commission Report*, pp. 159–168.

51. Brophy, "Assessing State and City Culpability," *Commission Report*, p. 165.

52. In the debates of 2001 in the Oklahoma legislature, some Republican members proposed to include in the Commission Report the statement that the riot had to be blamed on the Democratic Party, which dominated local Tulsa government of the time. The legislature, Republicans in the majority, voted down the proposal.

53. As quoted by Maxine Horner, State Senator from Tulsa, in her "Epilogue" to the *Commission Report*, p. 178.

54. Ibid., pp. 167–168, 173, quoting from the *Tulsa World*, June 29, 1921, under a headline: "Grand Jury Blames Negroes for Inciting Race Rioting: Whites Clearly Exonerated."

55. John Hope Franklin was born in Rentiesville, Oklahoma, an all-black village sixty-five miles southeast of Tulsa. His father left in February 1921 to found a law office in Tulsa, expecting his family soon to follow him. The riot interrupted this ex-

pectation, and the family arrived in Tulsa only in 1925. See John Hope Franklin's foreword to Ellsworth, *Death in a Promised Land*, pp. xv–xvii.

56. "The Tulsa Race Riot," *Commission Report*, p. 89.

57. *Commission Report*, p. 19.

58. Randy Krehbiel, "Recognizing a Wrong," *Tulsa World*, April 11, 2002: "The bulk of the money paid out last week came from the Unitarian-Universalist Association, which contributed $20,000."

59. Ibid., p. 20.

60. Ibid., p. 178.

61. On February 28, 1947, the troops of Chang Kai-chek, in retreat from mainland China to Taiwan, began a massacre of some twenty thousand Taiwanese civilians, most of them in the educated professional classes. Only with some installation of democratic freedoms of speech in 1988 was the restriction lifted. Then it became not only legal to talk about the event but also to plan a museum in Taipei for memorializing it. During my discussion with Taipei academics and students in 1998, a woman professor burst into tears as she remarked, "This is the first time I have ever been able to express out loud my sorrow over the death of my favorite uncle in 1947."

62. See above, p. 119.

63. Krehbiel, personal communication, February 4, 2003.

64. Senator Lott's casual salute to the segregationist stands of his retiring colleague Senator Strom Thurmond in December 2002 met with a punitive response in his Republican Party, whose majority members found themselves remembering Lincoln, the civil rights movment, and new Republican hopes for winning black votes. Apparently Lott forgot that times had changed enough to make overt admiration for a segregated society a political no-no.

65. *Commission Report*, pp. 17–18. As its first order of business, the new Oklahoma legislature of 1907 passed a comprehensive set of laws mandating the segregation of the races.

66. *General Laws of Oregon* (1843–1872), as quoted by a publication of the organization, Oregon Uniting, a principal sponsor of the revocation of this law as about to be described.

67. Personal communication, October 6, 2000.

68. Enrolled (joint) House and Senate Resolution, HR 3—INTRO and SR 3— INTRO, 1999. Success in the Senate, Rasmussen notes, was due chiefly to the efforts of State Senator Avel Gordly, the first African American to serve in that office (personal communication, October 9, 2000).

69. HR3 Floor Speech, copy from Representative Rasmussen.

70. The Buffalo Soldiers were a large troop of African Americans recruited by the Federal government for bringing "law and order" to the post–Civil War West. Ironically, one of their functions was to impose law and order on Indians.

71. Speakers were Mark Hatfield; former Chief Justice Ed Peterson; Brady Adams, President of the Senate; Lynn Snodgrass, Speaker of the House; Governor John Kitzhauber; Rose High Bear, member of the Athabascan Nation in Alaska; Susan Casio, first Hispanic member of the legislature; Peggy Nagai, lead attorney for the case which led to apologies and reparations to Japanese Americans 1975–1990; Merlie Evers Williams, widow of Medgar Evers, president of the NAACP and Oregon resident;

and Avel Gordly, first African American member of the Senate. I have taken quotations from these speeches from the videotape made of the occasion, with some liberties of condensation. A bill for the development of a multicultural public school curriculum, authored by Senator Gordly, passed the senate during this same April 19 "Acknowledgment" day.

72. Nagai was the attorney who took up the case of Minoru Yasui, imprisoned in 1942 for his refusal to obey the curfew which government imposed on all Japanese Americans prior to their deportation to western camps. The final vindication of Yasui by the U.S. Supreme Court was one of the first steps toward the 1976–1990 apology and reparation.

73. From two *Oregonian* articles by Gwenda Richards Oshiro, "Some Racial Minorities Wary of the Day of Acknowledgment" (April 21) and "State Faces Up to the Racism of Its Past" (April 23). The Bobbi Gary and Sue Shaffer remarks came before April 22, the others afterwards. Ms. Oshiro comments at the beginning of her April 23 article that the House debate on HR3 was "rancorous." The video tape of the event makes this description very questionable. In fact the several speeches of the seven opponents decried racism while quietly urging "move on." If their praise of African American heroes and their preference for moving on cloaked lingering personal racism, the cloak was subtle and not laced with apparent rancor.

74. Diane Ravitch and Chester E. Finn, Jr., *What Do Our 17-Year-Olds Know?* (New York: Harper and Row, 1987), p. 250.

75. Ibid. The sample and the report concentrated on white, black, and Hispanic groups.

76. At least 20 of the 141 questions concern history that clearly impacts current black-white relations in American society. Scores for the two groups, expressed as percentages of those who answered correctly, were as follows:

	White	Black
The Underground Railroad	90.9	69.6
The Ku Klux Klan	85.4	82.1
Harriet Tubman	84.2	92.4
The civil rights movement of 1960s	73.1	71.8
"Secession"	74.4	49.2
Brown v. Board of Education, 1954	66.4	55.5
Find the area of the Confederacy	67.6	47.6
Plessy v. Ferguson, 1896	64.9	53.6
Booker T. Washington	57.9	55.2
"Before Civil War the nation debated slavery."	53.2	43.7
The Montgomery Boycott, led by Martin Luther King, Jr.	45.6	71.9
The Missouri Compromise	43.6	40.7
"Reconstruction occurred between 1850–1900"	42.3	27.8
The Dred Scott decision	41.5	36.6
"The Emancipation Proclamation freed slaves."	36.3	43.6
The "three-fifths compromise" in the original U.S. Constitution	40.1	27.3
"The Civil War occurred between 1850–1900."	33.9	25.8
Jim Crow laws	30.6	31.8

"Abraham Lincoln was president betweeen 1860–1880."   26.0   17.5
"Reconstruction" refers to readmission of Confederate states   21.9   16.9

77. Ravitch and Finn, *17-Year-olds*, p. 35.

78. Cornel West, *Race Matters* (Boston: Beacon Press, 1993), p. 73, and David K. Shipler, *A Country of Strangers: Blacks and Whites in America* (New York: Alfred A. Knopf, 1997). West names as the major events "slavery, lynching, segregation, and second-class citizenship." As tags to vast suffering in the lives of African Americans, one might expect enough knowledge on the part of long-privileged whites to fend against easy dismissal of the weight of such pasts.

79. T. V. Smith, *The Ethics of Compromise and the Art of Containment* (Boston: Starr King Press, 1956), p. 75. Smith practiced politics as a state legislator and member of Congress. He served in official educational missions to Italy, Germany, and Japan during and after World War Two and taught philosophy at two universities—Chicago and Syracuse.

80. To speak personally: had my only acquaintance with academic history been that gleaned from my high school in the 1940s, I would never have had enough interest in history to major in it in college. And even college textbooks of that era were not half as inviting for study as those now offered to high school juniors and seniors in the 1990s.

81. The custom among many publishers of school texts is to "update" a book by the addition of new authors, new emphases, and new formats, sometimes designed to fit the standards of various state boards of education and markets. Into the economics and politics of textbook adoptions I will not enter here, but to be observed is the drastic difference between the ordinary writings of scholars in universities, who cope with relatively few political and economic pressures, over against authors of school texts to be adopted (or not) for use in thousands of public school classrooms. Numerous anonymous authors contribute to these texts over time, so that tags like "Todd-Curti" come to mean less and less about the actual authors. I have sampled these five of the ten successive editions of the Todd-Curti book and have indicated edition and page numbers in the form (1972: 65). The five are:

(1) Todd and Curti, *The Rise of the American Nation* (New York: Harcourt, Brace and Company, 1950 and 1961).
(2) 2nd edition, 1966 (New York: Harcourt, Brace and World).
(3) Todd, Curti, and five additional authors with editor Mark M. Krug, 3rd edition (New York: Harcourt Brace Jovanovich, 1972).
(4) "Heritage Edition," only Todd and Curti listed as authors (New York: Harcourt Brace Jovanovich, 1977).
(5) Todd, Curti, and two consultants, Phillip Bacon and Gloria S. Sesso, *The Triumph of the American Nation* (Orlando, Fla.: Harcourt Brace Jovanovich, 1986).

82. It may be more to the point to believe that their parents, with memories of the civil rights movement, were less tolerant of papered-over history. See p. 65 in this volume for the problem of disconnects of awareness between the movement generation and their children.

83. Frances Fitzgerald, *America Revised: History Schoolbooks in the Twentieth Century* (Boston: Little, Brown and Company, 1979), pp. 9, 84.

84. Ibid., p. 58.

85. Fitzgerald's fine analysis treats the texts along dimensions far more extensive than I have attempted here. My focus is simply on how they have expanded and improved their treatment of the African American past, especially slavery. She argues convincingly, for example, that foreign relations are strangely absent from much American history as written for schools, that statistics on the large economic inequalities and class conflict are also mostly absent, and that ever and again authors have little criticism of the international "exceptionalism" that Americans seem so serenely to celebrate.

86. Paul Boyer, *Boyer's The American Nation* (Austin, Tex.: Holt Rinehart and Winston, 2001). The publisher subtitles itself, "A Harcourt Classroom Education Company," which connects the book to the previous publisher of the 1950–1995 texts sampled here. Boyer is the Merle Curti Professor of History at the University of Wisconsin. Like almost all high school history texts, this one has multiple authors, and the multiplication here is geometric: a five-member "Editorial Review Board," seven listed "contributors," twelve "content reviewers," fifteen "educational reviewers," and nine "field test teachers"—forty-eight in all. The five-member review board is studiedly multicultural: one white woman, one white man, one Japanese-American man, one Hispanic woman, and one African American. The latter is John Hope Franklin.

87. So said in a review of the 2003 AOL–Time Warner film on the Civil War, *Gods and Generals*, in the *Charlotte Observer*. Quoted in a roundup of reviews in *New York Times*, March 9, 2003, p. WK7.

88. See Fitzgerald, *America Revised*, p. 109.

89. On page 268, with a picture of two southern writers, Edgar Allan Poe and Caroline Howard Gilman, a paragraph from the latter's *Recollections of a Southern Matron* (New York: Harper & Brothers, 1838) reads: "I must seek indulgence of general readers for mingling so much of the peculiarities of negroes with my details. Surrounded with them from infancy, they form a part of the landscape of a southern woman's life; take them away, and the picture would lose half of its reality. They watch our cradles; they are the companions of our sports; it is they who aid our bridal decorations, and they wrap us in our shrouds."

90. The text mentions *Gone with the Wind* as a cultural event of 1939 but not *Birth of a Nation*, the landmark feature film of 1915 which so distorted the story of black roles in the politics of that era that many white Americans settled on its images as all they needed to know about 1865–1890 in the South. There is no critique of the racist images in either of these films in the text, no mention, for example of the fact that *Birth* previewed in the 1915 Woodrow Wilson White House much to the praise of its presidential occupant, who had instigated new segregation rules for federal employees throughout the government.

91. Without the Tulsa riot history recovered by scholars in the 1980s and 1990s, as referenced above, the Tulsa story could hardly have received mention. Rosewood does not appear.

92. In a surge of effort to bring this 2001 book into the present, the publishers have appended a belated ten pages describing the November 2000 election and the new Bush administration of 2001.

93. In 1965, only 2.5 percent of Alabama blacks had successfully registered to vote. That particular day in March found a group of Southern Presbyterian ministers, including myself, marching out of Selma's Brown Chapel led by King, Walter Ruether, and Archbishop Iakovos of the Greek Orthodox Church. The path to the county courthouse—where another appeal for honest registration of black voters would be offered—was well lined with armed state troopers and unfriendly white residents. The most unforgettable note in the day, however, was the speech of the President that night to a joint session of Congress, to which we listened by car radio. Johnson's last words were: "We *shall* overcome." King is said to have broken out in tears when he heard this.

94. As reported by Alvin Benn and Jannell McGrew in *Montgomery Advertiser*, March 10, 2003, p. A1.

95. In his column, "A Civil Rights Pilgrimage," *Washington Times*, March 13, 2003. As quarterback for the Detroit Lions in 1957, Kemp had played in Birmingham, where his teammate John Henry Johnson was not allowed to stay in the hotel with the white players. Kemp, Secretary of Housing and Urban Development in the Reagan Administration, was one of only three Republicans in this delegation, and he lamented, "I just don't understand it. . . . Our party was the party of civil rights, and I can't imagine people not wanting to take an opportunity to see these historical sites." He vowed to help the party secure the confidence of more black voters.

96. As reported by Melanie Eversley, *Atlanta Journal-Constitution*, March 9, 2003, p. 3A. Republican Sam Brownbeck, says this article, grew up in Parker, Kans., in the mid-1960s and learned about the civil rights movement via television. The recent coming of immigrants to Kansas (especially Hispanic ones) has brought him face-to-face, he said, with "diversity issues."

97. Melanie Eversley, Cox News Service, March 9, 2003.

98. Many supporters and detractors have agreed that Freud's psychoanalysis owed its success less to his theories than to the therapy of the doctor's listening ear. Modern psychological research has offered much confirmation of this. I am indebted to Professor Paul Lehrer of the Robert Wood Johnson Medical School for bibliographic references related to the experimental evidence. Among the pertinent references are these two: James W. Pennebaker, "The Effects of Traumatic Disclosure on Physical and Mental Health," in John M. Violanti et al. eds., *Posttraumatic Stress Intervention* (Springfield, Ill.: C. C. Thomas, 2000), pp. 97–144, and Stephen J. Lepore and Joshua M. Smyth, eds., *The Writing Cure: How Expressive Writing Promotes Health and Emotional Well-Being* (Washington, D.C.: American Psychological Association, 2002).

99. Clarisse Jones, "Bringing Slavery's Long Shadow to the Light," *New York Times*, April 2, 1995, p. 43.

100. As reported by Larry Copeland, "From a Whisper to a Shout: Museums Teach Black History," *USA Today*, May 15, 2002, p. 1A.

101. Dan Carter, text of this address, furnished me by an Atlanta friend, P. G. Enniss.

102. Ibid., manuscript, pp. 9–10. Carter targets his own profession in this address for its long post-1865 tendency to caricature the role of newly freed slaves in the Reconstruction era. The targets include distinguished Northern university scholars like John Hicks, Samuel Eliot Morison, and Henry Steele Commager. Their dis-

dain for "premature" black suffrage was not written with the same drip of contempt found in some southern historians, but their more sophisticated version was substantively similar. With much chagrin for his profession, Carter quotes the 1933 book of Vanderbilt historian Frank Owsley: "For ten years after the war, the South . . . was turned over to three millions of former slaves, some of whom could still remember the taste of human flesh and the bulk of them hardly three generations removed from cannibalism." Counter to such caricatures is the masterwork of a successor of Commager at Columbia: see Eric Foner, *Reconstruction: America's Unfinished Revolution* (New York: Harper and Row, 1988).

103. Favored by the commission is a triangular plot to the immediate northwest of the Capitol.

104. Commission on a National Museum of African American History and Culture, *The Time Has Come* (Washington, D.C.: Smithsonian Institution, 2003), has a comprehensive review of this history, pp. 7–9. Congress had focused discussion of such a memorial-museum in 1919, 1929, 1968, 1969, 1980, 1986, 1988, 1989, 1991, 1992, and 1994. At various times a bill to establish the museum actually passed the House or the Senate, respectively, but failed in the other house. The count of 238 local and state museum related to the African American heritage was compiled in the work of the Commission, 2001–2003.

105. Survivors of the 180,000 blacks who fought on the Union side were denied participation in the march down Pennsylvania Avenue in the company of white veterans. Meantime Woodrow Wilson had resegregated the White House and many governmental departments.

106. Keith Bradsher, "Up From Slavery: A New Museum," *New York Times*, April 12, 1997. The two museums mentioned here resemble many others in their origins in some person's private collection—for example, that of Charles Wright, MD, in this Detroit case, who housed the collection in his home beginning in 1965 after viewing in Denmark a memorial to Danish World War Two heroes.

107. Jeffrey Gettleman, "15,000 Objects Testify to a Peculiar Institution," *New York Times*, November 30, 2002, p. A13. Petty says that so far few whites or blacks in Gulfport want to view his collection, and several schools and other institutions have refused to house it.

108. Winnie Hu, "Relics of Slavery, Up From the Deep," *New York Times*, December 24, 2001, pp. F1, F5.

109. Sandee Brawarsky, "Safe Havens on the Freedom Line," *New York Times*, January 19, 2001, p. E46. Small museums among America's current 238 outnumber the large, but each tends to have a very specific, often very local signficance. Cincinnati's National Underground Railroad Freedom Center, which opened in August 2004, is an 80,000-square-foot structure commemorating the perilous crossing of the river from Kentucky to Ohio. It will be the second largest black history museum in the country at a cost some $110 million. (Cf. Bruce Weber, "The Road to Freedom Revisited," *New York Times*, August 1, 2004, pp. TR 6–7.) Other large museums related to slavery, the achievements of African Americans, or other aspects of the history are now in place or being built in Detroit, Philadelphia, Baltimore, Fredericksburg, Chicago, Atlanta, and Memphis. The latter is built on the site of the assassination of Martin Luther King, Jr. Its display rooms trace the history of the civil rights

movement and, at the end, visitors are ushered onto the balcony of the former Lorraine Motel where King was shot. Few of these institutions, however, attempt to organize so comprehensive a portrayal of the history as do the designers of the proposed Washington museum, which like the Holocaust Museum and the now-being-completed Museum of the American Indian is to occupy some 350,000 gross square feet. See *The Time Has Come*, p. 80.

110. The documentary, *Family Reunion*, ends with pictures of the two sides of the family coming to a reunion dinner on a plantation lawn in eastern North Carolina.

111. David Firestone, "Identity Restored to 100,000 Louisiana Slaves," *New York Times*, July 30, 2000, pp. 1, 16.

112. John W. Fountain, "Finding Black History's Lost Stories," *New York Times*, December 29, 2002, p. A20.

113. See chapter 1, pp. 40–41.

114. Brent Staples, "The Perils of Growing Comfortable With Evil," *New York Times*, April 9, 2000, p. 16. Title of the exhibit was, "Without Sanctuary: Lynching Photography in America," published in book form, *Without Sanctuary: Lynching in America*, ed. James Allen et al. (Santa Fe: Twin Palms Publishers, 2000). Staples's fear of the perils was countered in a subsequent letter to the *Times* by an exhibit intern, William Rushing of Brooklyn, saying that a facilitator-led discussion visitors was open regularly to them all, "and those that I have attended have been thoughtful, honest, and constructive" ("Letters," April 1, 2000, p. A28).

115. The six were the New England states and Utah. Underlining the national scope of these crimes was an event on October 10, 2003—the unveiling of a memorial in Duluth, Minnesota to three African Americans lynched there by a mob of ten thousand in 1920. "The emotional high point came with a speech by Warren Read, a fourth-grade teacher from Kingston, Washington, who had learned while researching his family that his great-grandfather had helped lead the mob. . . . His voice choking with emotion, he apologized to the victims and their families. . . . The memorial in Duluth is part of a national journey that began in the 1990s, when scholars and museums began to pull back the covers on a shameful and horrific period" (editorial, *New York Times*, December 5, 2003, p. A38).

116. Robert Jay Lifton, *The Nazi Doctors: Medical Killing and the Psychology of Genocide* (New York: Basic Books, 1986), p. 427.

117. Statement by J. R. Design Group, Inc., on a collage of leading Harlem artistic, political, and religious leaders.

118. Article, "From the Chief," *African Heritage*, publication of the New York Public Library and the Schomberg Center, Vol. 4, No. 1, 2004, page 2. The October 4, 2003, march from Wall Street to the burial ground, in sight of the Federal Court buildings, brought thousands to the ceremonies, which included a libation ritual of "welcome" performed by Dr. Kofi Asare Opoku of Ghana. Ibid., p. 7.

119. Photograph and subscript, *New York Times*, August 5, 1995, Metro Section, p. 2. Said a member of the National House of Chiefs of Ghana, "We have come to appease our great-grandfathers and mothers who have been buried here."

120. "Slave Traders in Yale's Past Fuel Debate on Restitution," *New York Times*, August 13, 2001, p. 1. Graduate student researchers claimed that seven of Yale's nine colleges bore names of slave traders or owners.

121. Paul Zielbauer, "A Newspaper Apologizes for Slave-Era Ads," *New York Times*, July 6, 2000, p. B1. A *Courant* ad from 1810 offered a reward of five dollars for the return of a runaway slave. Connecticut abolished slavery only in 1848.

122. "How Slavery Fueled Business in the North," *New York Times*, July 24, 2000, p. A18.

123. Pam Belluck, "Brown U. To Examine Debt to Slave Trade," *New York Times*, March 13, 2004, p. A10.

124. Eric Foner, "Slavery's Fellow Travelers," *New York Times*, July 13, 2000, p. A29.

125. The original promise of "forty acres" came from General William Sherman to recently liberated slaves in the border states of 1864. Apparently reconstuctionist Congressman Thadeus Stevens added the "mule." By agreement with House leadership Conyers has kept the number "40" for his annual reintroduction of the bill.

126. From Conyers's "major issues" Web page dated March 31, 2003, which omits the implicit verb "acknowledged" (JohnConyers@mail.house.gov. and www .house.gov/conyers/).

127. In 1991 sociologist Nicholas Tavuchis, of the University of Manitoba published, *Mea Culpa: A Sociology of Apology and Reconciliation* (Stanford, Calif.: Stanford University Press), virtually the first systematic sociological analysis of the subject. In the late 1990s, in a personal communication, Tavuchis remarked that he was tempted to think, with Aesop's rooster, that his book had brought up the sun of apology that shone through an unprecedented range of political rhetoric throughout the 1990s. See also my *An Ethic for Enemies: Forgiveness in Politics* (New York: Oxford University Press, 1995), pp. 220–224.

128. Randall Robinson, *The Debt: What America Owes to Blacks* (New York: Penguin Books, 2000), pp. 3, 6–7.

129. Apparently the fourth hijacked plane, which crashed due to passenger initiative in Pennsylvania, was headed for either the Capitol or the White House.

130. Above, pp. 137–138.

131. Robinson, *Debt*, p. 243.

132. Quoted from the essay by J. A. Passmore, "John Anderson and Twentieth-Century Philosophy," introductory essay in *Studies in Empirical Philosophy* by John Anderson (Sydney: Angus and Robertson, 1962). See MacIntyre, *After Virtue: A Study in Moral Theory*, 2nd ed. (Notre Dame, Ind.: University of Notre Dame Press, 1984), p. 163.

133. Roger Wilkins, *Jefferson's Pillow: The Founding Fathers and the Dilemma of Black Patriotism* (Boston: Beacon Press, 2001), p. 146.

134. Robinson, *The Debt*, pp. 228, 231.

135. Ibid., pp. 75–80.

136. Robinson ends his book with a letter, from Jourdon Anderson, a former slave, to his previous owner in Tennessee. Dated August 7, 1865, the letter recounts, with scarcely concealed irony and anger, the worth of thirty-two years of labor on his own and his wife's part, given his current wages in Ohio of $25 per month. Including the $2 per month being paid now to his wife, the total came to $11,680. Calculations of average wage differences between white and black workers in the years 1876–1970 would yield a meaningful analogous measure (Robinson, *The Debt*, pp. 240–241).

137. Bonn Information Office in a publication of 1988. See my *An Ethic for Enemies*, p. 89.

138. So wrote Robert Lifton in an awareness that humans can wrest meanings from a vast spectrum of actions ranging from the cruel to the benign. "Auschwitz makes all too clear the principle that the human psyche can create meaning out of anything," for example a lynching. The matter to explore here is the possibility of politically and morally constructive meanings shareable across the racial divides of American society. One illustration of this would be an agreement that the Civil War really was about slavery in all of its moral, political, and economic ramifications. See Lifton, *The Nazi Doctors*, p. 459, and the recent book by Chris Hedges, *War Is a Force that Gives Us Meaning* (New York: Public Affairs, 2002).

139. The reparations movement for Japanese Americans, which climaxed in a series of U.S. government actions from 1976 through 1990, is a virtual model of what Conyers is calling for: a presidential apology (1976), a congressionally authorized investigatory commission (1980–1982), and authorization of a $50,000,000 educational fund (1988) plus symbolic individual reparations ($20,000) to survivors of the World War camps (paid in 1990).

140. As discussed by de Greiff in a lecture, "The Role of Reparations in Transitions to Democracy," The Carnegie Council on Ethics and International Affairs, May 6, 2004.

141. So observed by Miles in "Blacks vs. Browns," *The Atlantic*, October 1992; See p. 72 and my *An Ethic for Enemies*, pp. 213–214.

142. This incredible opinion I met, to my astonishment, in 1973 among some mostly Kikuyu Protestant ministers in Kenya.

143. Robinson, *The Debt*, p. 232.

144. Wilkins, *Jefferson's Pillow*, p. 115.

145. Ibid., p. 117.

146. Ibid., pp. 121–122.

147. Ibid., p. 120.

148. A story told to me by James M. Dabbs, summer 1958.

149. Romans 12:12.

150. Cf. Shaila K. Dewan, "Civil Rights Battlegrounds Enter World of Tourism," *New York Times*, August 10, 2004, pp. A1, A19. The Greensboro museum is scheduled to open in 2005. The pamphlet, *The Rich Heritage of African Americans in North Carolina*, is distributed at tourist highway welcome centers. It begins with historical summaries by John Hope Franklin and state archivist Jeffrey J. Crow (Raleigh: North Carolina Division of Tourism, Film, and Sports Development, 2004, www.visitnc.com).

151. Sally Bernamzohn, as quoted by Marjory Garrison, "The Greensboro Massacre," New York University, at journalweb.journalism.myu.edu n.d. (circa October 2003). The Greensboro Commission was instigated by former Mayor (1993–1999) Carolyn Allen and Presbyterian minister Zeb Holler, with the active outside support of Archbishop Desmond Tutu, a thirty-member National Advisory Committee, and the International Center for Transitional Justice. The latter, as noted in Chapter Two, is an outgrowth of the South African TRC and was headed until 2004 by the TRC Deputy Chair, Dr. Alex Boraine. For information about the work of the Greensboro commission into 2005, go to belovedcommunitycenter.org or write to P.O. Box 875, Greensboro, NC 27402.

152. James Baldwin, *The Price of the Ticket* (New York: St. Martin's Press, 1985), p. xix.

CHAPTER 4

1. Helen C. Rountree, *Pocahontas's People: The Powhatan Indians of Virginia Through Four Centuries* (Norman, Okla.: University of Oklahoma Press, 1990), p. 153.

2. Inscription beside his figure in the Jamestown Settlement Museum, 2003.

3. As quoted by Paula Mitchell Marks, *In a Barren Land: American Indian Dispossession and Survival* (New York: William Morrow and Company, 1998), p. 59.

4. Glenn Collins and David W. Dunlap, "Unveiling of Memorial Reveals a Wealth of New Details," *New York Times*, January 15, 2004, p. B4.

5. Descendants of ethnic groups in American history should have the right to choose their own names. When Native Americans do so today, they are likely to identify themselves with the specific nations of their origins—Pamunkey, Lakota, Navaho. Anthropologists like Rountree now use "Indian" as a comprehensive category without racist intent. One might use "European" in the same sense.

6. Frequent in the 1930s were Saturday movie "chapters" of ongoing stories of cowboys, replete with Indians. "Western" novels and movies were mostly off-limits in my household, but as children we all knew how to play "cowboys and indians."

7. James W. Loewen, *Lies My Teacher Told Me: Everything Your American History Textbook Got Wrong* (New York: Simon and Schuster, 1996), p. 99.

8. All 104 were men.

9. Rountree believes that this tribe was exterminated between 1608 and 1610 by Powhatan "before the Jamestown colonists could interview them" (Rountree, p. 23). On the corner of our house lot, however, there was a marker noting that on this ground there was encamped, 1861–1862, companies of Confederate soldiers, prior to the capture of Norfolk by the Federals.

10. In a 1997 seminar around my book *An Ethic for Enemies: Forgiveness in Politics* (New York: Oxford University Press, 1995), a Union Seminary student commented, "This would have been a better book if it had treated the case of Native Americans in addition to African Americans." He was right, and the present chapter is an attempt at remedying this omission.

11. Only in connection with the writing of this book did I learn that "Appomattox" was the name of one of the Powhatan nations pushed west by the English invasion. Every Southerner knows that this was the locus of Lee's surrender to Grant in 1865. Few of us know where the name came from.

12. Evan T. Pritchard, *Native New Yorkers: The Legacy of the Algonquin People of New York* (San Francisco: Council Oak Books, 2002), p. 134. Unfortunately, this book has a very low reputation among careful historians, who accuse Pritchard of granting various of his fantasies the status of documentable fact.

13. Among other prejudices and historical inaccuracies enclosed in our language is the term "settler" versus "original inhabitants." Like many other Indian nations, the Powhatans were farmers as well as hunters. They had as profound an attachment to *place* as would any future Anglo-Virginian.

14. This is the ironic comment of the settler in the film *Jamestown: The Begin-*

ning whose fictitious commentary combines tribute to both the English and the Indians with candor about their cultural and power conflicts.

15. In what comes closest to a display of historical fact, offensive to some and accurate to others, the English-culture room says that the Irish and the Indians, in English minds, were equally "salvage" (*sic*).

16. Rountree, *Pocahontas's People*, p. 72, note 57, from Smith's *Generall Historie of Virginia*.

17. Rountree, *Pocahontas's People*, pp. 87–89.

18. Ibid, pp. 89–91. This astonishing book is the fruit of decades of Rountree's diligent field interviews as an anthropologist and records study as a historian. Her data and summary conclusions neither idealize nor derogate Indian responses to the English invaders—making it clear, for example, that Powhatan's own far-reaching domination of neighbors cost many a war death, and, in the case of the Chesapeakes in 1610, the obliteration of a whole settlement. This fact has particular meaning for me because the suburban quarter-acre on which I grew up as adolescent in Norfolk was probably once occupied by the Chesapeakes (Rountree, p. 21). On the whole, she observes, both "the English and the Indians of that time were both apt to be arrogant and touchy . . . sixteenth-century Europeans were quick to give advice to 'barbarians,' by whose standards such advice was probbly insufferably rude and aggressive" (p. 23).

19. As early as the 1646 treaty the word "inhabitant" was officially reserved to the English.

20. The former remark is that of Daniel B. Murphy, designer of the New Tredegar National Civil War Center in Richmond, described above in chapter 3. The latter words came at the end of an address by the Honorable H. E. Wolfgang Ischinger, German ambasssador to the United States, to a meeting of the Richmond chapter of the American Council on Germany on August 23, 2002 (American Council on Germany, *Occasional Paper #11*. 2002, p. 6).

21. In his fine recent book, *The Earth Shall Weep: A History of Native America* (New York: Grove Press, 1998), James Wilson critiques these opposites as follows: "The awkward truth is that the Algonquian world was neither a depraved nightmare nor an idyll. Like any society, it was an irreducible mixture of conflict, harmony, brutality, nobility, hardship, and joy. As the Virginia colonist William Strachey reported apparently with some surprise: Among Native Americans, as 'amongst Christians,' some were 'great people . . . some very little . . . , some speaking likewise, more articulate and plaine, and some more inward and hollow . . . , some curteous and more civill, others cruell and bloudy' " (p. 56).

22. No historian has produced a textbook which records the facts more resolutely than Howard Zinn in *A People's History of the United States: 1492–Present* (New York: HarperCollins, 2003). He has severe criticisms of mainline historians who do scant justice to the bloody history of European treatment of Native Americans, but early in the book (page 7) he salutes Samuel Eliot Morison for his brief, accurate comment on his hero, Christopher Columbus: "The cruel policy initiated by Columbus and pursued by his successors resulted in complete genocide." The latter word was not invented until the 1940s by Raphael Lemkin, but the reality, in the fate of Native Americans, was there long before. See Samantha Power, *A Problem from Hell: America and the Age of Genocide* (New York: Basic Books, 2002), pp. 17–30.

23. Wilson, *Earth Shall Weep*, pp. 56–57.

24. Shirley W. Dunn, *The Mohicans and Their Land, 1609–1730* (Fleishmanns, N.Y.: Purple Mountain Press, 1994), p. 130, quoting Wolley, *A Two Years Journal in New York*, p. 26.

25. That was what the Indians called it, but Columbus promptly named it San Salvador and as promptly "took possession of it for their Catholic majesties of Castile and Leon" (*Encyclopedia Britannica*, 11th ed. [1910], Vol. 6, p. 743).

26. The distinction between "settlers" and "natives" is old in the lexicon of imperialism. The Powatan and many other Indian nations were throughly "settled" on their traditional lands, and though their agricultural practices may have seemed "primitive" to those English manor-workers, those very practices accounted for the first-winter survival of many of the starving immigrants of Jamestown and Plymouth. Seventeeth-century Dutch coming to South Africa had similar attitudes toward land: The sparse population made it seem virtually "uninhabited," empty, and ready for the taking by people who knew how to farm it. Early British colonists of Australia looked on it with similar presuppositions.

27. As quoted by Marks, *In a Barren Land*, p. 215.

28. Rountree, *Pocahontas's People*, p. 80.

29. Ibid., p. 88.

30. Ibid., pp. 100–101.

31. Ibid., pp. 93, 113.

32. Ibid., pp. 142, 167.

33. Ibid., pp. 200, 239. As an anthropolgist, she says toward the end of the book, she has often argued with her Virginia Indian friends but has "failed in my attempts to tell them that their outlook is dated" (p. 276). This issue should be an important catalyst of discussion about the limits of multicultural ethical relativity in relation to the changing mythology of contemporary cultures. Myths of blood have damaged countless human beings in the twentieth century, and the abolishing of this measure of racial identity in Virginia's 1975 law was a real gain for opponents of racism. In Virginia, after 1975, says Rountree, "people could be whatever they claimed to be; however, in practice they could be tribal Indians only if the tribe admitted them as members" (p. 249). In the early centuries the tribes often adopted outsiders, including whites, and thus set a liberal example which most English refused to copy. Political and cultural measures of rights to membership are clearly a gain for justice over against myths of blood. In his editorial on this issue, Brent Staples comments that "the tribes fought black membership from the very beginning, but federal courts have upheld the treaties" which after 1866 mandated equal membership rights for blacks enslaved by Indians. He quotes John Hope Franklin, whose Oklahoma family had black and Indian members: "It is perfectly absurd to talk about dividing Indians and blacks. Any Indians who speak in exclusionary terms do not represent the historic interests or the historic relationships of Indians and blacks." Brent Staples, "When Racial Discrimination Is Not Just Black and White," *New York Times*, September 12, 2003, p. A30.

34. Time-Life Books, eds., *The Algonquians of the East Coast* (Alexandria, Va: Time-Life Books, 1995), p. 146, a volume in a colorful, well-researched series, *The American Indians*. The publishers reported in 2003 that "the series has been discontinued due to lack of interest."

35. Rountree, *Pocahontas's People*, p. 156.

36. Quoted by the Native American Rights Fund of Boulder, Colorado, 2003, www.narf.org.

37. Robert Moss, "A Lost Tribe and a Reborn Tradition in Columbia County," in *Columbia Yuletide* (Winter 1988), p. 17. Moss, a writer living in Chatham, has been a professor of ancient history in the Australian National University, a journalist, and a novelist. For his novels he learned the Mohawk language.

38. Dominic C. Lizzi, "Mohicans Once Prospered Here," reprinted from the *Independent* (Chatham N.Y.), November 17, 1996, in *Columbia County History and Heritage* (Columbia County Historical Society), 1, no. 3 (Winter 2003), pp. 6–7.

39. Time-Life, *The Algonquians*, pp. 79–80.

40. My authority for these spellings and translations is Stephen Comer, the one surviving lineal descendant of the Mohicans living in this region. Comer is currently a doctoral student in Mohican Studies in the anthropology department of the New York State University at Albany. I am indebted to him for these data and his review of this section of chapter 4. He prefers the translation "People of the Waters that are Never Still," or "Everflowing Waters," but believes that the extended name actually came into general use with the work of the Mohican John Quinney in the nineteenth century. On Quinney, see pp. 257–258 below.

41. See chapter 2, pp. 81–82.

42. Among them: Taghkanic, Copake, Schodack, Schagticoke, Bash Bish, Housatonic.

43. Ironically enough, a scenic turnoff on the northern end of the Taconic Parkway (a Mohican-derived name) has a state marker, overlooking the Hudson Valley, which details the Dutch and English settlement of the county without ever mentioning the original Mohican inhabitants.

44. Kenneth Mynter, "First Indians Roamed Columbia County as Early as 5,000 B.C.," *The Paper* (Hillsdale, N.Y.: The Journal Register), May 1986.

45. From the superscription of "An Indian Calendar for Columbia County," at the end of Lizzi "Mohicans Once Prospered."

46. Cooper published the novel in 1826. His home in Westchester County and his schooling in Albany and New Haven must have made him aware of some of this history. But his references to the Mohicans were based on his knowledge of the Mohegans of Connecticut (not the same tribe as the Mohicans of the Hudson Valley) and the Delaware in eastern Pennsylvania, so that one learns little from his famous novel about the people who met Henry Hudson.

47. Shirley W. Dunn, *The Mohicans and Their Land*, p. 130. With her companion volume, *The Mohican World, 1680–1750* (Fleishmanns, N.Y.: Purple Mountain Press, 2000), she does for the Mohicans what Helen Rountree has done for the Powhatans.

48. Personal correspondence, March 19, 2004. Comer, who lives just north of Columbia County, is active in national Mohican affairs. I am indebted to him for conversations about this history.

49. Ibid.

50. Jim Eyre, "The Selling of the Mohican Lands," *Columbia County History and Heritage* (Winter 2003), p. 7.

51. Time-Life, *Algonquians of the East Coast*, p. 76.

52. Eyre, "Selling," p. 7, goes on to record a conflict thirteen years later over ownership of a southern portion of this huge tract.

53. Kenneth Mynter, "War Drums Throbbed Hatred of Dutch Families in 1664," *The Paper* (Hillsdale, N.Y.: The Journal Register), July, 1986.

54. Much the same applies to the most famous of Indian land "sales": the 1624 Lenape Indians' acceptance of $24 in trinkets from the Dutch for the latter's rights to Manhattan Island. The story is now much encrusted with myth and humor. "At the time . . . the sale of land had no meaning in Algonquian culture. The Lenapes probably regarded the payment as a considertaion that was due them for tolerating the presence of the visitors and allowing them to make use of the land for a while." His Dutch sponsors had advised Peter Minuit to abstain from "force or threats" against the local inhabitants and to "give them something, to let us live amongst them" (Time-Life, *The Algonquians*, p. 78).

55. Robert Moss, "A Lost Tribe and a Reborn Tradition," *Columbia Yuletide* (Winter 1988), p. 15.

56. Massachusetts claimed territory to the Hudson River, but federal courts settled on the modern state line with New York in 1790.

57. John J. McCusker, Economic History Services, www.eh.net/hmit/ppowerbp/ (March 2004). Pure capitalist thinking might specify this sort of comparison as an example of a long-range profitable investment. The point to underline is that the worth of land to owners in some distant future and the very idea of land as an "investment" must have totally escaped the nets of the Indian cultural imagination. One could install in the Western imagination the idea that all future values resulting from a purchase should be shared with the original "owners" as original "stockholders." But that would require a radical change in concepts of ownership at the foundations of Western economic systems.

58. County records of these transactions are astonishingly detailed and complete. The earliest long catalogue of purchases was compiled in 1878 by Franklin Ellis, *History of Columbia County, New York*. This and other documents have been studiously summarized in the two authoritative volumes by Dunn, *The Mohicans and Their Land* and *The Mohican World*.

59. Kenneth Mynter, "Their Land Gone, Less Than 100 Indians Were in Columbia Co. By 1770," *The Paper* (Hillsdale, N.Y.: The Journal Register), July–August 1986

60. Kenneth Mynter, "Native Americans of the Mid and Upper Hudson Valley," *The Paper* (Hillsdale, N.Y.: The Journal Register), August–September 1986, p. 13.

61. According to Richard Powell, Director of the Institute of Native Americans Studies at Columbia-Greene College in Hudson, N.Y., as quoted by Bruce Allen, "Native American Institute Draws Interest, Many ideas," *Independent*, November 27, 1996.

62. Lizzi, "Mohicans Once Prospered," p. 7.

63. Modern demographers are divided in their estimates of the number of pre-1492 inhabitants of the Americas. On the moderate end, David E. Stannard estimated the two-continent total as 75,000,000 to 100,000,000, "with approximately 8,000,000 to 12,000,000 north of Mexico." Others demographers go higher, but almost all are sure that the once-accepted total of 1,000,000 for pre-1492 continental United States was drastically low. The horror in Stannard's exhaustive study is his conclusion that by 1900 only *one-third of 1 percent* of the original numbers of Indians

survived in United States territory. At least 98 percent of Indians died of causes that accompanied the European invasion. Stannard names the four-hundred-year event "the worst human holocaust the world has ever witnessed." See Stannard, *American Holocaust: Columbus and the Conquest of the New World* (New York: Oxford University Press, 1992), pp. 11, 146, 267–268.

64. Reflecting the new Indian activism of the early 1970s, *Soldier Blue* (1970) retells the story of the Sand Lake Massacre of 1864, in which seven hundred Colorado volunteers, under Colonel John M. Chivington, murdered old men, women, and children in a Cheyenne and Arapaho camp. The deaths were variously calculated as between seventy and two hundred. *Little Big Man* (1971) portrays General George A. Custer and the Battle of Little Big Horn from the Lakota and Cheyenne point of view. According to Theodore S. Jojola, this movie "established a milestone in Hollywood cinema in its human portrayal of the Lakota people, and featured . . . one of the finest performances by a native actor—Chief Dan George as Chief Old Lodge Skins." He sees the 1990 *Dances with Wolves* as "a remarkable clone of *Little Big Man*" and as the film that "ushered forth a wave of Indian New Age films and created a need for the film industry to employ native actors." "Movies," in *Encyclopedia of North American Indians*, ed. Frederick E. Hoxie (New York: Houghton Mifflin, 1996), pp. 404–405 (hereafter referenced as ENAI).

65. Robert Warrior, Professor of Indian Studies, the University of Oklahoma. He recommends *New from Indian Country*, a paper published in Hayward, Wisconsin, with a countrywide focus that is not controlled by a tribal government. Personal correspondence, November 18, 2003.

66. Joseph V. Montville, "Reconciliation as Realpolitik: Facing the Burdens of History in Political Conflict Resolution," unpublished essay furnished me by the author. Among other contributions to the transformation of severe international conflicts, Montville invented the concept "Track Two" for efforts at conflict resolution apart from the official channels of diplomacy. See Montville, "Justice and the Burdens of History," in *Reconciliation, Justice, and Coexistence: Theory and Practice*, ed. Mohammed Abu-Nimer (Lanham, Md.: Lexington Books, 2001), pp. 115–128.

67. The year the transcontinental railroad was completed.

68. Geiko Müller-Fahrenholz, in a lecture at the Lay Academy in Bad Boll, Germany, May 1999. He adds, "Pride and patriotism are in my opinion too often linked to what I call the 'winner syndrome' " (personal communication, April 27, 1999).

69. "How the West Was Lost" is the title of a series of some fifteen videotapes about a diversity of American Indian nations, developed by Time-Life Books in the 1990s. The series is an excellent example of contemporary attempts of historians, educators, and filmmakers to teach history from an Indian point of view.

70. Howard Zinn, *A People's History of the United States*, p. 10. He goes on to concede, with Joseph Montville, that victims and oppressors, over time, are apt to trade roles. "[T]he victims, themselves desperate and tainted with the culture that oppresses them, turn on other victims."

71. Frances Fitzgerald, *America Revised: History Schoolbooks in the Twentieth Century* (Boston: Little, Brown and Company, 1979), pp. 49, 90–92.

72. Ibid., pp. 94–96.

73. As in chapter 3, these summaries are based upon my study of six of the nine editions of the Todd-Curti series from 1961 to 2000: 1961, 1966, 1972, 1977, 1986,

and 2001. For titles and publishers, see chapter 3, note 81. The 2001 edition is virtually a new book. The previous editions build cumulatively on each other as new authors, some anonymous, join in the writing. The 2001 edition lists forty-nine authors.

74. I have yet to discover a competent survey of the uses and apparent impacts of these school texts. Holt, Rinehart and Winston is the current inheritor of the Todd-Curti series, but my attempts to get its leaders to share with me research on the reception of their 2001 edition by teachers and students have come to naught, even after five or six phone inquiries and three letters. The politics and economics of the textbook business apparently make for huge barriers to scholars who want to assess the real "bottom line" of education through books: How do the books affect the minds and views of students? Perhaps some answer to this question comes when publishers run classroom tests of books they plan to publish. The data may exist, but HRW has failed to offer any to me after several inquiries.

75. See chapter 3, p. 166.

76. Sequoya invented a written Cherokee language, published the first Indian newspaper, and is remembered as a pioneer of Indian literacy. Winnemucca was a Paiute woman who, in the late 1870s, toured the country offering vigorous public lectures protesting the forced removal of the Paiutes from their Yakima Reservation in the State of Washington. Her appeal to President Rutherford Hayes in 1880 resulted in his reversal of the removal order, "but the BIA's agents did not carry out the president's order" (2001:440). The 1986 set of forty-three profiles included sixteen women, twenty-four men, nine African Amercans, three Jews, and two groups—Vietnam veterans and Holocaust survivors.

77. Richard Salvucci, "The Mexican War," 2001: 326. In 1947 President Harry S Truman, on an official visit to Mexico City, laid a wreath on the Chapultepec monument. The gesture created a sensation. Said a local cab driver, "To think that the most powerful man in the world would come and apologize." Truman commented, "Brave men don't belong to any one country. I respect bravery wherever I see it." David McCullough, *Truman* (New York: Simon and Schuster, 1992), pp. 542–543. See my treatment of this incident in *An Ethic for Enemies: Forgiveness in Politics*, p. 221.

78. Unlike the sidebar by Salvucci, referred to in the previous note, not all of the sidebars in this 2001 text are credited to named authors. Does naming authors help to flag controversial ideas?

79. Among the unprecedented additions to the 2001 text (over all previous) is a complete copy of the Declaration of Independence, wherein Jefferson accuses the British Crown of "exciting" Indian war against the colonists and accuses the Indians of practicing as a "rule of warfare . . . an undistinguished destruction of all ages, sexes, and conditions" (2001: 122). Jefferson, not Andrew Jackson, was the first U.S. president to suggest that Indians should be exiled westward for separation from Americans.

80. Marks, *In a Barren Land*, p. 345.

81. Suzan Shown Harjo, "Arts," in ENAI, p. 52.

82. Ward Churchill, "Radicals and Redicalism, 1900 to the Present," in ENAI, p. 528.

83. Marks, *In a Barren Land*, p. 103. The quotation is from Brad Agnew, *Fort Gibson: Terminal on the Trail of Tears* (Norman, Okla.: University of Oklahoma Press, 1980), p. 4.

84. Marks, *In a Barren Land*, p. 158.

85. Paul Chaat Smith and Robert Allen Warrior, *Like a Hurricane: The Indian Movement from Alcatraz to Wounded Knee* (New York: The New Press, 1996), p. 123. Smith, a Cheyenne, and Warrior, an Osage, have written here the fairest and most comprehensive current account of the new Indian activism of these years.

86. Steve Schlarb, ed., "Oglala Lakota Sioux: Russell Means, Eagle Man, laws, issues" ed. Steve Schlarb, Part 2, "History & Leaders of the Oglala Lakota Sioux," www.lakotamall.com/oglalasiouxtribe/, pp. 2–3 (last accessed August 2003). Among the measures most important to the Lakota was their claim to the Black Hills. In 1980, the U.S. Supreme Court mandated compensation of some millions of dollars to the Lakota for the United States taking their home country. But the Lakotas refused. "[They] want the Black Hills returned" (p. 3).

87. This quotation concludes Dee Brown's *Bury My Heart at Wounded Knee* (1970; reprint, New York: Bantam Books, 1972, p. 419). Neihardt's *Black Elk Speaks* went through many editions and offered one of the earliest Indian voices to reach the American reading public. As of 1972 Dee Brown's book had gone through fifteen printings.

88. Not quite the last if one counts "Wounded Knee Two" of 1973 with its two Indian deaths. But for Indians and others alike, Wounded Knee 1890 had the feel of finality in the Indians Wars.

89. "These are the same Indians who mercilessly shot down the gallant Custer and 300 of the Seventh Calvary [*sic*] on that memorable day of June 25, 1876 . . . and it is safe to say the Sioux will receive no quarter from this famous regiment should an opportunity occur to wreak our vengeance for the blood taken at the battle of the Little Big Horn." That prophecy, comments Paul M. Robertson of Oglala Lakota College in "Wounded Knee Massacre, 1890" "reflected the vengeful mood, and the racism, of much of the country" (ENAI, p. 697). Seventh Cavalry deaths in 1876 were actually 215.

90. Words of Edmund Fuller, in a 1971 book review in the *Wall Street Journal* and quoted on the inside cover page of the Bantam 1972 edition.

91. Brown, *Bury My Heart*, pp. 413, 417.

92. Robertson, "Wounded Knee Massacre, 1890," ENAI, p. 697.

93. Ibid.

94. So quoted in the Lakota Website Canpe Opi [Wounded Knee], www.woptura .com, 8/20/03, in a series of quotations of Senate debate and resolution between 1990 and 1995. The current burden of claim in the Lakota campaign is that Congress rescind the eighteen Medals of Honor.

95. Smith and Warrior, *Like a Hurricane*, pp. 113, 117, 119.

96. See Churchill, "Radicals and Radicalism," ENAI, pp. 528–529.

97. Ibid. A third defendant, Leonard Peltier, was soon after tried, found guilty, and sentenced to double life imprisonment. His case is still the object of an international protest.

98. Smith and Warrior, *Like a Hurricane*, p. 269.

99. Website of the Oglala Sioux, August 21, 2003, recording a Council meeting of January 22, 1998, www.lakotamall.com/oglalasiouxtribe/.

100. "American Indian Movement," ENAI, p. 23.

101. Smith and Warrior, *Like a Hurricane*, p. 277.

102. Marks, *A Barren Land*, p. 332.

103. "Alcatraz, Occupation of," ENAI, p. 14.

104. See "The Long Trail to Apology," editorial, *New York Times*, June 28, 2004, p. A18.

105. T. V. Smith, *The Ethics of Compromise and the Art of Containment* (Boston: Starr King Press, 1956), p. 45.

106. For a helpful, thoughtful summary, see Marks, *A Barren Land*, pp. 350–380.

107. Todd-Curti 1986, p. 957.

108. Oglala Lakota Sioux Website, "History and Leaders," part 2, p. 2 www .lakotamall.com/oglalasiouxtr.

109. *USA Today*, October 2, 2003, p. 4A. The theme of this article is the explosion of Indian contributions to congressional election campaigns, which climbed from $1.75 million in 1990 to $6.8 million in 2002.

110. So termed by columnist William Safire, who points to inequity in the fact that 3 percent of the Indian population takes in 44 percent of current gambling revenue, while states with "half our 1.8 million Indians account for less than 3 percent of the take." As in a *Time* cover story the same week ("Wheel of Fortune," December 16, 2002, pp. 44–58), Safire also complains of the large role of foreign billionaires like Lim Goh Tong in making loans to tribes, at high interest rates, for casino construction. This complaint omits the traditional Protestant moral objection to gambling (Safire, "Tribes of Gamblers," *New York Times*, December 12, 2002, p. A39).

111. The Oneida casino near Syracuse attracts more than 4 million patrons a year, most from New York State, who spend $230 million. Profits are estimated at $70 million, says Eleanor Randolph in her article, "New York's Native American Casinos Contributes, but Not to Tax Rolls" (*New York Times*, October 18, 2003, p. A12). As Oneida have bought land in the town of Oneida, removing it from the tax rolls, town income has declined from $700,000 to $139,000. On the other hand, as of May 2004, the Cayugas have compromised on taxes, agreeing to pay $15 million a year to Sullivan County for fire, police, school, and other services as part of their plan to build a casino just south of the Catskill park. The Mohawks and the Stockbridge Munsees expect to make similar deals in the same area. Charles V. Bagli, "Cayuga Tribe Moves Closer to a Casino In the Catskills," *New York Times*, May 4, 2004, p. B5.

112. Randolph, "New York's Native American Casinos," p. A12.

113. So quoted by Joel Brinkley, "American Indians Say Documents Show Government Has Cheated Them Out of Billions," *New York Times*, January 7, 2003, p. A17. Robert Warrior, of the University of Oklahoma, says that this is the most important current example of justice delayed in the relation of the Indian nations to the U.S. government, but it "has gone pretty much unnoticed by most Americans and ignored in most media outlets. . . . As an Individual Indian Moneys account holder, I know what it is like to be held hostage to the ongoing injustice of this trust being held in bad faith. I despair, though, of the United States's coming to a point of making even gestures towards public justice in a way that New Zealand has or even Canada" (personal communication, November 18, 2003).

114. Francis Prucha, quoted by Marks, *In a Barren Land*, p. 379.

115. National Public Radio, *Weekend Edition*, "Profile: Cayuga Indians' Court Battle over New York Land," March 24, 2002, Lynn Neary host and Jon Miller reporting (eLibrary, www.elibrary.com/, August 8, 2003, p. 1).

116. Ibid., interview, p. 2.

117. Bob Herbert, "In America, 200 Years Later," *New York Times*, November 26, 2001 (New York Times Premium Archive), pp. 1–2.

118. Ibid., p. 2.

119. United Citizens for Equality, www.upstate-citizens.org, "Get the Facts on UCE," August 26, 2003, p. 1.

120. NPR interview (eLibrary, www.elibrary.com/), 8/8/2003, pp. 1–3.

121. Ibid.

122. Ibid.

123. The complete text of the speech is available in the small Indian Museum attached to the John Sergeant Mission House in modern Stockbridge, Massachusetts. The making of such a text available to visitors is itself a cause for contemporary celebration.

124. Cheyenne Council President John Wooden, in the mid-1950s. See Marks, *In a Barren Land*, p. 309.

125. James Dao, "Drums and Bells Open Indian Museum," *New York Times*, September 22, 2004, p. A14.

CHAPTER 5

1. Quoted at *A.Word.A.Day.com*, 6/19/2003, by *The Christian Century*, August 23, 2003, p. 7.

2. Reinhold Niebuhr, *The Irony of American History* (New York: Charles Scribner's Sons, 1952), p. 139.

3. Albert Camus, *Resistance, Rebellion, and Death* (London: Hamilton, 1961), p. 5. I owe reference to this quotation to Johannes Degenaar, professor of political philosophy in the University of Stellenbosch, South Africa, and his essay "Philosophical Roots of Nationalism," in *Church and Nationalism in South Africa*, ed. Theo Sundermeier (Johannesburg: Ravan Press, 1975).

4. Elazar Barkan, Introduction to *The Guilt of Nations: Restitution and Negotiating Historical Injustices* (New York: W. W. Norton, 2000), p. xviii. Barkan believes that the ubiquity of *local* negotiations, slowly but persistently, constitutes grassroots growth of an international moral consensus concerning gross collective crimes.

5. There is irony in the fact that the word "amok" comes from Southeast Asia. *Webster's* third definition is "a murderous frenzy that occurs chiefly among Malays."

6. *Newshour with Jim Lehrer*, May 11, 2004. In the early 1990s I asked the German minister of defense, Volker Ruhe, if all NATO forces had such rules. He answered, "No, it was we Germans who needed those rules." Some Americans in the discussion were prompt to disagree. Americans can be glad that on this issue our military has caught up with the Germans.

7. Quotations taken from the official program of the event, March 6, 1998, provided by the Pentagon. Andreotta subsequently died in combat. His name is on the Wall. In April 2004 Thompson was inducted into the Army Aviation Hall of Fame in ceremonies in Nashville. It meant more to him than the Pentagon award, he said, "because they were my peers" (*Newshour* interview, 5/11/2004).

8. So quoted by his wife, Dr. Elise Boulding, in a conference at the College of the Holy Cross, Worchester, Mass., October 2001.

9. Rev. Fred Anderson, to a congregational study group in the spring of 2003. He observed and participated in so much unjust killing in Vietnam that he lost confidence in the just war theory and is sure that Christians should never take unambiguous comfort in that theory for support of any war.

10. Not that many American military or political leaders have voiced much criticism in the past fifty years about the strategy of city-bombing that escalated in the final months of World War Two. Invented by the Germans early in the war, developed by the British and the Americans as the war in Europe went on, and brought to a climax in the atomic bombing of Hiroshima and Nagasaki, the strategy has often been justified as the only way to bring that war to an end. Debate over this issue flared up in 1995 concerning how Hiroshima was to be remembered publicly at the Smithsonian Institution in Washington. That debate would have been sobered on both sides if each had conceded that, by 1945, discrimination of military and civilian targets had been routinely abandoned. More Japanese civilians perished from "conventional," mostly incendiary, bombs than from the two atomic bombs, for example, in the March 10–11 fire bombing of Tokyo. For two accounts, see Robert Jay Lifton and Greg Mitchell, *Hiroshima in America: Fifty Years of Denial* (New York: Avon Books, 1995), chapter 3, pp. 245–297, and John Dower, *War Without Mercy: Race and Power in the Pacific War* (New York: Pantheon Books, 1987), pp. 300–301.

11. Quoted by James W. Loewen, *Lies My Teacher Told Me: Everything Your American History Textbook Got Wrong* (Touchstone Books; New York: Simon and Schuster, 1996), p. 126, from Gordon Craig, "History as a Humanistic Discipline," in *Historical Literacy*, edited by Paul Gagnon (New York: Macmillan, 1989), p. 134. Craig goes on to observe that to teach history from the standpoint of the options actors faced would be to make history teaching more vivid, human, and memorable for students.

12. As quoted by Walter Davis, *Shattered Dream: America's Search for Its Soul* (Valley Forge, Pa.: Trinity Press International, 1994), p. 106. Davis based this book on interviews with some two hundred veterans in California VA hospitals.

13. See introduction, to this volume p. 10.

14. Rowan Williams, *Writing in the Dust: After September 11* (Grand Rapids, Mich.: Williams B. Eerdmans, 2002), p. 60.

15. Donald W. Shriver, *An Ethic for Enemies: Forgiveness in Politics* (New York: Oxford University Press, 1995), p. 111.

16. As quoted in "Tattletales for an Open Society," *The Nation*, an article posted online January 10, 2002 (www.thenation.com/doc.mhtml?i=20020121& tattle20020110). Dr. Simonwitz is one of the 117 academics quoted in this compilation, all of whom are protesting the proposal of Ms. Lynn Chaney, former head of the National Endowment for the Humanities, to the American Council of Trustees and Alumni (ACTA) that it start compiling a list of academics who are disloyal to the country in a time of crisis. All of the 117 are voluntarily asking to be included in any such list.

17. William Sloane Coffin, *Credo* (Louisville: Westminster/John Knox Press, 2004), p. 53.

18. Belinda Cooper in a review of Peter Balakian, *The Burning Tigris: The Armenian Genocide and America's Response* (New York: HarperCollins, 2003), in *New York Times Book Review*, October 19, 2003, p. 35. About this same time, the Turkish sociologist Taner Akcam became "the first Turkish specialist to use the word 'genocide' "

about the Armenians of 1915. Now a university teacher in Minneapolis, he says that he "began to confront his own country's past" while observing how Germans were doing so. So far, several Turkish universities, "fearing government harassment," have refused to hire him. Belinda Cooper, "Turks Breach Wall of Silence on Armenians," *New York Times*, March 6, 2004.

19. In interviews done for the making of the 2003 film *The Fog of War*, Robert McNamara uses the figure 3.4 million for the dead of the Vietnam War. No one knows the exact figure, but this one is the highest that any public figure has advanced. Others have said "between one and two million." Stephen Holden, "Revisiting McNamara and the War He Headed," *New York Times*, October 11, 2003, p. B9.

20. In July 1950, as inexperienced American troops were attempting to stop the advance of the North Korean army, a group of Korean civilians sought protection under this bridge. Thinking that many of them were North Korean infiltrators, Americans opened fire. In the late 1990s, South Korean scholars and officials presented data on this tragedy to the Pentagon, which, after its own belated investigation, responded with the indefinite conclusion that in the confusions of those early weeks of the war, no blame could be clearly assigned. In 2003, as this is written, a film on the incident is underway at the direction of a Korean director captured by North Korea in the 1980s and forced to make films for that government. The experience left him with little admiration for that society.

21. From interviews in July 2003, I know that elderly contemporary residents of the former East Germany have bitter memories of the systematic looting and raping that Soviet troops undertook in the final months of the war, quite under the direction and approval of their officers.

22. See Jeffrey Gettleman, "For Iraqis in Harm's Way, $5000 and 'I'm Sorry,' " *New York Times*, March 17, 2004, pp. A1, A9. The payments come under the U.S. Foreign Claims Act for compensation to civilians in noncombat situations. So far, payments are unaccompanied by "a formal apology or claim of responsibility." Upon accepting $6000 in compensation for the death of his wife and three children, Said Abbas Ahmed commented bitterly: "This war of yours cost billions. Are we not worth more than a few thousand" (p. A9)?

23. Jack Kelly, *Pittsburgh Post-Gazette*, February 16, 2003, from the newspaper's Website of October 18, 2003. The official Pentagon tally of American combat deaths was 148, of noncombat deaths 145. In 1993 Daponte concluded that 56,000 Iraqi soldiers died and 3,500 civilians, meaning that the rest of deaths came from "adverse health effects" and subsequent slaughter of Kurds and Shiites by Saddam Hussein's army. A National Defense University study puts the soldier deaths between 20,000 and 25,000 and the civilian, 1,000 to 3,000, close to the Iraqi government's claim of 2,278 civilian deaths.

24. Yvonne Klein, letter to editor, *New York Times*, November 15, 2003, p. A12. Ms. Klein is Canadian.

25. Luc Sante, "Tourist and Torturers," *New York Times*, May 11, 2004, p. A 23. He teaches creative writing and photography at Bard College.

26. Howard Zinn quotes Samuel Eliot Morison of Harvard, who celebrates the contribution of the Columbus voyages to world history but who concedes that "the cruel policy initiated by Columbus and pursued by his successors resulted in complete genocide" (Zinn, *A People's History of the United States: 1492–Present* [New York:

HarperCollins, 2003], p. 7). Zinn insists that the details of this genocide need to enter American history texts, for example, how, "in two years, through murder, mutilation, or suicide, half of the 250,000 Indians on Haiti were dead" (p. 5).

27. In Clyde Haberman, "As Opposed to Numbness, Pain Is Good," *New York Times,* October 21, 2003, p. B1. The therapist was Dr. Lauren Howard.

28. Claudia Rosett, "Letter From America," *Wall Street Journal,* January 17, 2002.

29. Thus, the remark of two Russian Orthodox laymen to me in Odessa, October 1984.

30. Terms used by the writer of the Pauline Epistle to the Ephesians, 2: 17 (RSV).

31. In his "Address to the Electors of Bristol." I shall never forget the 1964 campaign speech by a North Carolina congressman in Raleigh, N.C., in which he reminded his rural audience that "in order to get my colleagues in Congress to vote for our agricultural interests, I have to support their urban interests."

32. John Donne, *Devotions upon Emergent Occasions* (1634), "Meditation XVII," in *The Oxford Dictionary of Quotations,* 4th ed. (Oxford: Oxford University Press, 1992), p. 253.

33. See Ronald C. White, Jr., *Lincoln's Greatest Speech: The Second Inaugural* (New York: Simon & Schuster, 2002), p. 189, quoting from the negative editorial response to the address by *The New York Times* of March 6, 1865: "He makes no boasts of what he has done, or promises of what he will do. He does not reexpound the principles of the war; does not redeclare the worth of the Union; does not reproclaim that absolute submission of the Constitution is the only peace."

34. Quoted by Forrest Church, *The American Creed: A Spiritual and Patriotic Primer* (New York: St. Martin's Press, 2002), p. 55, from the volume *Lincoln's Greatest Speeches,* p. 197.

35. Quoted by Martin E. Marty, "Motley Crew," M.E.M.O. *The Christian Century,* August 9, 2003, p. 39.

36. David McCullough, *Truman* (New York: Simon & Schuster, 1992), pp. 542–543.

37. See Marty, "Motley Crew."

38. Modern Americans can easily forget that the Revolution gained the support of only about a third of the population of the thirteen colonies, while a third opposed it and a third waited to see which side would win.

39. My first and only encounter with this memory among Nova Scotians was a visit to Halifax in 1978. They express some resentment that Americans tend to forget how the Patriots forced hundreds of Tories into exile in Canada.

40. Howard Zinn notes that ten to fifteen million slaves had been transported alive from Africa to the West by 1800 and that deaths before and during transport brought the total to fifty million (Zinn, *People's History,* p. 29).

41. As described by Paul A. Wee, head of the Luther Center in Wittenberg, Germany, in a paper, "Reflections on Terror and Justification," April 2002.

42. "World War Two," *Encyclopedia Britannica,* Vol. 19, p. 1011. This range of uncertainty about the total underscores the degree to which many twentieth-century wars have so buried, mutilated, and otherwise hidden human bodies that the deaths sink irretrievably into anonymity. Capital cities need to add an "Unknown Civilian" grave to that of their "Unknown Soldier."

43. "War and Never Having to Say You're Sorry," *New York Times*, December 14, 2003, Arts and Leisure Section, p. 33. "Whether regarding the Vietnam War, America's cold war assassinations or our misguided former alliance with Saddam Hussein, American officials keep their eyes fixed on the future."

44. Power, *A Problem From Hell: America and the Age of Genocide* (New York: Basic Books, 2002), p. 386, quoting the article by James Bennet, "Clinton Declares U.S., with World, Failed Rwandans," *New York Times*, March 26, 1998, pp. A6, A12. A few months after his Africa visit, Clinton delivered "an 'unplanned' semiapology" for American slavery, "a half measure that satisfied many supporters and only moderately angered conservatives," says Elazar Barkan (*The Guilt of Nations*, p. 287).

45. Kofi Annan, *Statement on Receiving the Report of the Independent Inquiry into the Actions of the United Nations During the 1994 Genocide in Rwanda*, December 16, 1999, pp. 1–2, and *Report of the Secretary-General pursuant to General Assembly resolution 53/35. The fall of Srebrenica*, November 15, 1999, pp. 6–7. At the beginning of the Rwanda report he calls attention to the 1948 UN enactment of the Convention Against Genocide, "under which States accepted an obligation to 'prevent and punish' this most heinous of crimes."

46. National Public Radio News, November 23, 1999.

47. Nichoas Tavuchis, *Mea Culpa: A Sociology of Apology and Reconciliation* (Stanford, Calif.: Stanford University Press, 1991), p. 100. For further appropriation of Tavuchis's pioneering book and on the relation of political apology to political forgiveness, see my *An Ethic for Enemies*, pp. 220–224.

48. Beveridge in *The Library of Oratory*, ed. Chauncey M. Depew (New York: Globe Publishing Co., 1902), pp. 448–449. Sumner in *War, and Other Essays*, ed. A. G. Keller (New Haven: Yale University Press, 1911), pp. 325–326, 334, as reproduced in *Retrieving the American Past*, compiled by the history faculty of Elon University (Needham, Mass.: Pearson Custom Publishing, 1999), pp. 98, 101.

49. See Church, *The American Creed*, pp. 73–77. Theological ground for Beveridge's imperialism had been prepared by Josiah Strong, leading liberal nineteenth-century Congregational theologian. Strong did not always distinguish between the world mission of the Christian church and the mission of the United States. "Protestant Christianity and American democracy were exported in the same package" (Church, p. 74). Beveridge could have written Strong's proclamation: "We are the chosen people. We cannot afford to wait. The plans of God will not wait. Those plans seem to have brought us to one of the closing stages in the world's career, in which we can no longer *drift* with safety to our destiny" (Josiah Strong, *Our Country: Its Possible Future and Its Present Crisis* [Baker and Taylor, 1875], p. 218).

50. House Committee on International Relations hearing, March 30, 2004, as recorded by the East Asia Policy Education Project Website, www.fcnl.org. Hyde went on to say that North Korea should see U.S. determination in the Iraq War as a warning to its own aspiration to power.

51. *Joint Vision 2020*, U.S. Department of Defense, www.dtic.mil/jointvision, (Fall, 2002).

52. Samantha Power, *A Problem from Hell*, p. 509.

53. Charles Villa-Vicencio, personal correspondence, February 2004.

54. Edward LeRoy Long, Jr., *Facing Terrorism: Responding as Christians* (Louisville: Westminster/John Knox Press, 2004), p. 111.

55. Ignatieff, "9.27.04," *New York Times Magazine,* June 27, 2004, p. 16.

56. A distinction often made by the late H. Richard Niebuhr.

57. Quoted by Long, *Facing Terrorism,* p. 91, from Joe Klein, "The Blinding Glare of His Certainty," *Time,* February 23, 2003, p. 19.

58. Reinhold Niebuhr, *The Irony of American History,* p. 148.

59. State of the Union Address, January 2003.

60. H. Richard Niebuhr, *The Responsible Self: An Essay in Christian Moral Philosophy* (New York: Harper and Row, 1963), p. 64.

61. Dietrich Stobbe, governing mayor of Berlin, 1977–1981, Social Democratic member of the Bundestag, 1983–1990, business executive in the 1990s, in personal correspondence, December 2003.

62. Former Bundespräsident Richard von Weizsäcker, personal correspondence, December 2003.

63. Dr. Alex, Boraine, personal correspondence, February 2004.

64. Rev. Peter J. Storey, now professor at Duke University Divinity School, personal correspondence, March 2004.

65. Drs. Helmut and Erika Reihlen, personal correspondence, December 2003.

Bibliography

Abu-Nimer, Mohammed, ed. *Reconciliation, Justice, and Coexistence: Theory and Practice*. Lanham, Md.: Lexington Books, 2001.

Ash, Timothy Garton. *The File: A Personal History*. New York: Random House, 1997.

Bam, June, and Pippa Visser. *A New History for a New South Africa*. Cape Town: Kagiso Publishers, 1996.

Barkan, Elazar. *The Guilt of Nations: Restitution and Negotiating Historical Injustices*. New York: W. W. Norton, 2000.

Bergmann, Klaus, et al., eds. *Geschichte und Geschenhen*. Stuttgart: Ernst Klett Verlag, 1997.

Bethge, Eberhard. *Dietrich Bonhoeffer*. New York: Harper and Row, 1977.

Bickford-Smith, Vivian, et al., eds. *In Search of History: Secondary Book 1*. Cape Town: Oxford University Press, 1995.

Blight, David. *Race and Reunion: The Civil War in American Memory*. Cambridge, Mass.: Harvard University Press, 2001.

Bonhoeffer, Dietrich. *Fragments from Tegel*. Translated from *Werke*, Volume 16, "Konspiration und Haft." Gütersloh: Christian Kaiser Verlag, 1996.

Boraine, Alex. *A Country Unmasked: Inside South Africa's Truth and Reconciliation Commission*. New York: Oxford University Press, 2000.

Botman, H. Russel, and Robin M. Petersen, eds. *To Remember and to Heal: Theological and Psychological Reflections on Truth and Reconciliation*. Cape Town: Human & Rousseau, 1996.

Bottaro, Jean, and Pippa Visser, *In Search of History: Standard 12*. Cape Town: Oxford University Press, 1999.

Boyer, Paul. *The American Nation*. Austin: Holt, Rinehart and Winston, 2001.

Bretall, Robert, ed. *A Kierkegaard Anthology*. Princeton: Princeton University Press, 1951.

Brophy, Alfred L. *Reconstructing the Dreamland: The Tulsa Riot of 1921–Race, Reparations, and Reconciliation.* New York: Oxford University Press, 2002.

Brown, Dee. *Bury My Heart at Wounded Knee.* New York: Holt, Rinehart and Winston, 1970.

Camus, Albert. *Resistance, Rebellion, and Death.* London: Hamilton, 1961.

Chapman, Audrey R., and Bernard Spong, eds., *Religion and Reconciliation in South Africa: Voices of Religious Leaders.* Philadelphia, Pa.: Templeton Foundation Press, 2003.

Church, Forrest. *The American Creed: A Spiritual and Patriotic Primer.* New York: St. Martin's Press, 2002.

Cochrane, James, John de Gruchy, and Stephen Martin, eds. *Facing the Truth: South African Faith Communities and the Truth and Reconciliation Commission.* Cape Town: David Philip, 1999.

Coffin, William Sloane. *Credo.* Louisville: Westminster/John Knox Press, 2004.

Daalder, Ivo H., and James M. Lindsay. *America Unbound: The Bush Revolution in Foreign Policy.* Washington, D.C.: Brookings Institution Press, 2003.

Dabbs, James McBride. *Who Speaks for the South?* New York: Funk & Wagnalls, 1964.

Davenport, Rodney, and Christopher Saunders. *South Africa: A Modern History.* 5th ed. London: Macmillan, 2000.

Davis, Walter. *Shattered Dream: America's Search for Its Soul.* Valley Forge, Pa.: Trinity Press International, 1994.

De Gruchy, John W. *Reconciliation: Restoring Justice.* Minneapolis, Minn.: Fortress Press, 2002.

De Klerk, F. W. *F. W. De Klerk: The Autobiography.* London: Macmillan, 1999.

De Tocqueville, Alexis. *Democracy in America.* Ed. J. P. Mayeer and trans. George Lawrence. Anchor Books. Garden City, N.Y.: Doubleday and Company, 1969.

D'Orso, Michael. *Like Judgment Day: The Ruin and Redemption of a Town Called Rosewood.* New York: G. P. Putnam's Sons, 1996.

Dower, John. *War Without Mercy: Race and Power in the Pacific War.* New York: Pantheon Books, 1987.

Dunn, Shirley W. *The Mohican World, 1680–1750.* Fleishmanns, N.Y.: Purple Mountain Press, 2000.

Dunn, Shirley W. *The Mohicans and Their Land, 1609–1730.* Fleishmanns, N.Y.: Purple Mountain Press, 1994.

Du Plessis, Lourens. "The South African Constitution as Memory and Promise." *Stellenbosch Law Review* 11, no. 3 (2000).

Ellsworth, Scott. *Death in a Promised Land: The Tulsa Race Riot of 1921.* Baton Rouge: Louisiana State University Press, 1982.

Elon College Faculty, compilers, *Retrieving the American Past: A Customized U.S. History Reader.* Needham Heights, Mass.: Pearson Custom Publishing, 1999.

Endlich, Stefanie, et al., eds., *Gedenkstätten für die Opfer des Nationalsozilismus: Eine Dokumentation.* 2 vols. Bonn: Bundeszentrale für politische Bildung, 1999.

Faulkner, William. *The Hamlet.* Vintage Books. New York: Random House, 1956.

Field, Sean, ed. *Lost Communities, Living Memories: Remembering Forced Removals in Cape Town.* Cape Town: David Philip, 2001.

Fitzgerald, Frances. *America Revised: History Schoolbooks in the Twentieth Century.* Boston: Little, Brown and Company, 1979.

Foner, Eric. *Reconstruction: America's Unfinished Revolution.* New York: Harper and Row, 1988.

Franklin, John Hope. *From Slavery to Freedom: A History of Negro Americans.* Vintage Books. New York: Alfred A. Knopf, 1967.

Fürstenberg, Doris, ed. *Steglitz im Dritten Reich.* Berlin: Druckhaus Hentrich, 1992.

Gobodo-Madikizela, Pumla. *A Human Being Died That Night: A South African Story of Forgiveness.* Boston: Houghton Mifflin, 2003.

Gudmestad, R. H. "The Richmond Slave Market, 1940–1860." Master's thesis, University of Richmond, 1993.

Halliburton, R., Jr. *The Tulsa Race War of 1921.* San Francisco: R & E Research Associates, 1975.

Hayner, Priscilla B. *Unspeakable Truths: Confronting State Terror and Atrocity.* New York: Routledge, 2001.

Hedges, Chris. *War Is a Force that Gives Us Meaning.* New York: Public Affairs, 2002.

Hirsch, James S. *Riot and Remembrance: The Tulsa Race War and Its Legacy.* New York: Houghton Mifflin, 2002.

Hoxie, Frederick E., ed. *Encyclopedia of North American Indians.* New York: Houghton Mifflin, 1996.

James, Wilmot, and Linda van de Vijver, eds. *After the TRC: Reflections on Truth and Reconciliation in South Africa.* Cape Town: David Philip, 2000.

Koshy, Ninan. *The War on Terror: Reordering the World.* Hong Kong: Daga Press, 2002.

Krog, Antjie, *Country of My Skull: Guilt, Sorrow, and the Limits of Forgiveness in the New South Africa.* Times Books. New York: Random House, 1998.

Kundera, Milan. *Ignorance.* Trans. Linda Asher. London: Faber and Faber, 2002.

Ladd, Brian. *Ghosts of Berlin: Confronting German History in the Urban Landscape.* Chicago: University of Chicago Press, 1997.

Lelyveld, Joseph. *Move Your Shadow: South Africa Black and White.* New York: Times Books, 1985.

LePore, Stephen J., and Joshua M. Smyth, eds. *The Writing Cure: How Expressive Writing Promotes Health and Emotional Well-Being.* Washington, D.C.: American Psychological Association, 2002.

Lifton, Robert Jay. *The Nazi Doctors: Medical Killing and the Psychology of Genocide.* New York: Basic Books, 1986.

Lifton, Robert Jay, and Greg Mitchell. *Hiroshima in America: Fifty Years of Denial.* New York: Putnam Books, 1995.

Loewen, James W. *Lies Across America: What Our Historic Sites Get Wrong.* New York: The New Press, 1999.

Loewen, James W. *Lies My Teacher Told Me: Everything Your American History Textbook Got Wrong.* Touchstone Books. New York: Simon and Schuster, 1996.

Long, Edward LeRoy, Jr. *Facing Terrorism: Responding as Christians.* Louisville: Westminster/John Knox Press, 2004.

Lutz, Stefanie, and Thomas Lutz. *Gedenken und Lernen An Historische Orten: ein Weg-*

weisen zu Gedenkstätten Für DieOpfer des Nationalsozialismus in Berlin. 2nd ed. Berlin: Territorial Office for Political Education, 1998.

MacIntyre, Alasdair. *After Virtue: A Study in Moral Theory.* 2nd ed. Notre Dame: University of Notre Dame Press, 1984.

Madigan, Tim. *The Burning: Massacre, Destruction, and the Tulsa Race Riot of 1921.* New York: St. Martin's Press, 2001.

Mandela, Nelson. *Long Walk to Freedom: The Autobiography of Nelson Mandela.* Abacus Books. London: Little, Brown and Company, 1994.

Marks, Paula Mitchell. *In a Barren Land: American Indian Dispossession and Survival.* New York: William Morrow and Company, 1998.

McCullough, David. *Truman.* New York: Simon and Schuster, 1992.

McGraw, Marie Tyler. *At the Falls: Richmond, Virginia and Its People.* Chapel Hill: University of North Carolina Press, 1994.

McPherson, James. *Battle Cry of Freedom.* New York: Ballantine Books, 1988.

Mda, Zakes. *The Heart of Redness.* Cape Town: Oxford University Press, 2000.

Morison, Samuel E., and Henry S. Commager. *The Growth of the American Republic.* Vol. 1. New York: Oxford University Press, 1942.

Müller-Fahrenholz, Geiko. *In göttlicher Mission: Politik im Namen des Herrn–Warum George W. Bush die Welt erlösen will.* Munich: Knaur Taschenbuch, 2003.

Müller-Fahrenholz, Geiko. "Die Erinnerung An Das Leid Und Das Nein Zum Krieg," *Public Forum.* January 2003.

Niebuhr, H. Richard. *The Meaning of Revelation.* New York: Macmillan, 1941.

Niebuhr, H. Richard. *The Responsible Self: An Essay in Christian Moral Philosophy.* New York: Harper and Row, 1963.

Niebuhr, Reinhold. *The Irony of American History.* New York: Charles Scribner's Sons, 1952.

Niebuhr, Ursula, ed. *Remembering Reinhold Niebuhr: Letters of Reinhold and Ursula M. Niebuhr.* New York: HarperCollins, 1991.

Nye, Joseph S. *The Paradox of American Power: Why the World's Only Superpower Can't Go It Alone.* New York: Oxford University Press, 2002.

Power, Samantha. *A Problem from Hell: America and the Age of Genocide.* New York: Basic Books, 2002.

Pritchard, Evan T. *Native New Yorkers: The Legacy of the Algonquin People of New York.* San Francisco: Council Oak Books, 2002.

Rassool, Ciraj, and Sandra Prosalendis. *Recalling Community in Cape Town: Creating and Curating the District Six Museum.* Cape Town: District Six Museum, 2001.

Ravitch, Diane, and Chester E. Finn, Jr. *What Do Our 17-Year-Olds Know? A Report on the First National Assessment of History and Literature.* New York: Harper and Row, 1987.

Robinson, Randall. *The Debt: What America Owes to Blacks.* Penguin Books. New York: Dutton, 2000.

Rosenthal, Jane, and Pippa Visser. *In Search of History: Book 2.* Cape Town: Oxford University Press, 1996.

Rotberg, Robert I., and Dennis Thompson, eds. *Truth v. Justice: The Morality of Truth Commissions.* Princeton: Princeton University Press, 2000.

Rountree, Helen C. *Pocahontas's People: The Powhatan Indians of Virginia through Four Centuries.* Norman, Okla.: University of Oklahoma Press, 1990.

Sachs, Albie. *The Jail Diary of Albie Sachs*. Cape Town: David Philip, 1990.

Sallis, John, ed. *Philosophy and Archaic Experience: Essays in Honor of Edward G. Ballard*. Pittsburgh: Duquesne Press, 1982.

Shipler, David K. *A Country of Strangers: Blacks and Whites in America*. New York: Alfred A. Knopf, 1997.

Shriver, Donald W. *An Ethic for Enemies: Forgiveness in Politics*. New York: Oxford University Press, 1995.

Sisulu, Walter. *I Will Go Singing*. Cape Town: Robben Island Museum in Association with Africa Fund, 1997.

Smit, G. J. J., et al., eds. *History Standard Ten*. Cape Town: Maskew Miller Ltd., 1976.

Smith, Charlene. *Robben Island*. Cape Town: Struik Publishers, 1997.

Smith, Paul Chaat, and Robert Allen Warrior. *Like a Hurricane: The Indian Movement from Alcatraz to Wounded Knee*. New York: The New Press, 1996.

Smith, T. V. *The Ethics of Compromise and the Art of Containment*. Boston: Starr King Press, 1956.

Soros, George. *The Bubble of American Supremacy*. New York: Public Affairs, 2004.

Sparks, Allister. *Tomorrow Is Another Country: The Inside Story of South Africa's Negotiated Revolution*. Johannesburg: Struik Book Publishers, 1994.

Stannard, David. *American Holocaust: Columbus and the Conquest of the New World*. New York: Oxford University Press, 1992.

Steyn, Melissa. *"Whitness Just Isn't What It Used to Be": White Identity in a Changing South Africa*. Albany: State University of New York, 2001.

Storey, Peter J. *From the Crucible: Sermons and Addresses in a Time of Crisis*. Nashville: Abingdon Press, 2002.

Sundermeier, Theo. *Church and Nationalism in South Africa*. Johannesburg: Ravan Press, 1975.

Tadman, Michael. *Speculators and Slaves: Masters, Traders, and Slaves in the Old South*. Madison: University of Wisconsin Press, 1989.

Tavuchis, Nicholas. *Mea Culpa: A Sociology of Apology and Reconciliation*. Stanford, Calif.: Stanford University Press, 1991.

Thomas, Sari, ed. *Communication Theory and Interpersonal Practice: Selected Proceedings from the Fourth International Conference on Culture and Communication*. 3 vols. Norwood, N.J.: Ablex Publishing, 1984.

Thompson, Leonard. *A History of South Africa*. 3rd ed. New Haven: Yale University Press, 2001.

Time-Life Books, eds. *The Algonquins of the East Coast*. Alexandria, Va.: Time-Life Books, 1995.

Todd, Paul, and Merle Curti. *The Rise of the American Nation*. New York: Harcourt Brace and Company, 1950 and 1961.

Todd, Paul, Merle Curti, et al. *The Triumph of the American Nation*. Orlando, Fla.: Harcourt Brace Jovanovich, 1986.

Tutu, Desmond. *No Future Without Forgiveness*. New York: Doubleday, 1999.

United States Department of Defense. *Joint Vision 2020*. Washington, D.C., 2002.

Van Heerden, Etienne. *Ancestral Voices*. Trans. Malcolm Hacksley. Cape Town: Penguin Books, 2000.

Villa-Vicencio, Charles, ed. *Transcending a Century of Injustice*. Cape Town: Institute for Justice and Reconciliation, 2000.

Villa-Vicencio, Charles, and Tyrone Savage. *Rwanda and South Africa in Dialogue: Addressing the Legacies of Genocide and a Crime Against Humanity.* Cape Town: Institute for Justice and Reconciliation, 2001.

Villa-Vicencio, Charles, and Wilhelm Verwoerd, eds. *Looking Backward and Reaching Forward: Reflections on the Truth and Reconciliation Commission of South Africa.* Cape Town: University of Cape Town Press, 2000.

Violanti, John M., et al., eds. *Posttraumatic Stress Intervention.* Springfield, Ill.: C. C. Thomas. 2000.

West, Cornel. *Race Matters.* Boston: Beacon Press, 1993.

White, Ronald C., Jr. *Lincoln's Greatest Speech: The Second Inaugural.* New York: Simon and Schuster, 2002.

Wilkins, Roger. *Jefferson's Pillow: The Founding Fathers and the Dilemma of Black Patriotism.* Boston: Beacon Press, 2001.

Williams, Rowan. *Writing in the Dust: After September 11.* Grand Rapids, Mich.: William B. Eerdmans, 2002.

Wilson, James. *The Earth Shall Weep: A History of Native America.* New York: Grove Press, 1998.

Woodward, C. Vann. *The Burden of Southern History.* 3rd ed. Baton Rouge: Louisiana State University Press, 1993.

Young, James E. *At Memory's Edge: After-Images of the Holocaust in Contemporary Art and Architecture.* New Haven: Yale University Press, 2000.

Young, James E. *The Texture of Memory: Holocaust Memorials and Meaning.* New Haven: Yale University Press, 1993.

Zinn, Howard. *A People's History of the United States: 1492–Present.* New York: HarperCollins, 2003.

COMMISSION REPORTS

Commission on a National Museum of African American History and Culture. *The Time Has Come.* Washington, D.C.: Smithsonian Institution, 2003.

Jones, Maxine, et al. *A Documented History of the Incident which Occurred at Rosewood, Florida, in January 1923.* Tallahassee: State of Florida, 1993.

Oklahoma State Legislature. *Tulsa Race Riot: A Report of the Oklahoma Commission to Study the Tulsa Race Riot of 1921.* Oklahoma City: State of Oklahoma, 2001.

Villa-Vicencio, Charles, and Susan de Villers, eds. *Truth and Reconciliation Commission of South Africa Report.* 5 vols. Cape Town: CTP Book Printers (Pty) Ltd., 1998.

Index